WOUNDED LIONS

SPORT AND SOCIETY

Series Editors
Randy Roberts
Aram Goudsouzian
Founding Editors
Benjamin G. Rader
Randy Roberts

A list of books in the series appears at the end of this book.

Wounded Lions

Joe Paterno, Jerry Sandusky,
and the Crises in Penn State Athletics

RONALD A. SMITH

UNIVERSITY OF ILLINOIS PRESS

URBANA, CHICAGO, AND SPRINGFIELD

1 2 3 4 5 C P 5 4 3 2 1
∞ This book is printed on acid-free paper.

Library of Congress Cataloging-in-Publication Data
Names: Smith, Ronald A. (Ronald Austin), 1936–
Title: Wounded lions : Joe Paterno, Jerry Sandusky, and the crises in
    Penn State athletics / Ronald A. Smith.
Description: Urbana : University of Illinois Press, [2016] | Series: Sport
    and society | Includes bibliographical references and index.
Identifiers: LCCN 2015029793 | ISBN 9780252040016 (hardcover : alk.
    paper) | ISBN 9780252081491 (pbk. : alk. paper) |
    ISBN 9780252098215 (e-book)
Subjects: LCSH: Pennsylvania State University—Sports. | Pennsylvania
    State University—Football. | Paterno, Joe, 1926–2012. | Sandusky,
    Jerry. | Pennsylvania State University—Sports—Administration.
    | College sports—Corrupt practices—Pennsylvania—University
    Park.
Classification: LCC GV691.P4 S65 2016 | DDC 796.04309748/53—dc23
    LC record available at http://lccn.loc.gov/2015029793

To Karl G. Stoedefalke,

who, more than anyone else, influenced me to pursue a career in sport history at the time I was completing my master's degree in history at the University of Wisconsin

CONTENTS

Acknowledgments   ix

Sifting and Winnowing   xi

Prologue   xiii

1 Life in Happy Valley: The Name and the Paterno Impact   1

2 Penn State Presidents: Cheerleading the Teams to Victory   12

3 A Joe Paterno–Jerry Sandusky Connection:
  A Look at Penn State Football Coaches and Assistant Coaches   24

4 Alumni and Taking Control of Penn State Athletics   35

5 Hugo Bezdek's Saga—Alumni, Trustees, and Presidents   43

6 The Great Experiment That Failed: Alumnus
  Casey Jones, President Hetzel, and Coach Bob Higgins   53

7 The Ernie McCoy–Rip Engle Era and the Beginning
  of the Grand Experiment in College Football   64

8 The Joe Paterno, Steve Garban, John Oswald Coup d'État   75

9 President Bryce Jordan and Penn State's Entry into the Big Ten   89

10 The Image of Joe Paterno's Grand Experiment   100

11 Shaping Reality: Saving Joe Paterno's Legacy   112

12 Insularity, The Second Mile, and Sandusky's
   On-Campus Incidents   127

13 Rene Portland and the Culture of Athletic Silence   140

14 The Board of Trustees, Insularity, and Athletic Administration   150

15 Paterno, Spanier, Schultz, Curley, and the Penn State
   Pandora's Box   161

16 From the Grand Jury to Beyond the NCAA
   Consent Decree   173

Timeline   185

Notes   199

Index   249

Photographs follow page 126

ACKNOWLEDGMENTS

I have been fortunate to be associated with Penn State University since the late 1960s, when I took a position in sport history with its top-rated Physical Education Department. After my retirement in 1996, it has remained the highest rated Kinesiology Department in the nation, if not the world. I have seen the Penn State Library become one of the premier libraries in America, and that includes its superior Archives, where a century and a half of materials relating to Penn State and its athletics have been preserved. Following the Jerry Sandusky Scandal revelation, I spent the better part of two years in the Penn State Archives with its staff of first-rate individuals bringing its expertise, service, and boxes upon boxes of material to "my" table to be examined. For the number of archivists who have helped me in my pursuit of Penn State athletic history, I salute you, including the head of Archives, Jackie Esposito.

I would also like to thank the many undergraduates and graduate students in my classes who produced some notable term papers and several masters and doctoral dissertations—a number of them cited in this volume specifically looking at how Penn State has administered athletics over a century and a half. A good number of the term papers have been preserved in the Penn State Archives.

I have been fortunate to have conducted research in more than eighty university libraries and other archives with material that has contributed to six volumes dealing with athletics in higher education. This book includes data from university and conference archives including Alabama, Cornell, Eastern Collegiate Athletic Conference, Georgia Tech, Harvard, Kentucky, NCAA Headquarters, Nebraska, North Carolina, Notre Dame, Penn State, Tennessee, and Wisconsin. The preponderance of material has come from the Penn State University Archives.

During the writing, I have had a number of individuals read and comment on parts of the manuscript. I am indebted to those who made comments for the betterment of the volume. Of the more than fifty individuals who were involved in the process, I want to specially thank Bob Downs, Jackie Esposito, Mary Gage, Betz Hanley, Drew Hyman, Nadine Kofman, Scott Kretchmar, Dan Nathan, Joan Nessler, Paul Silvis, and Dave Zang. Specifically, I greatly appreciated three individuals who read and critiqued the entire manuscript—Jim Anderson, Evan Pugh Professor at Penn State; Michael Bezilla, author of a history of Penn State; and John Swisher, Professor Emeritus of Education at Penn State. I salute one of the University of Illinois Press readers of the manuscript, Joseph Crawley, former history professor and president of the University of Nevada, Reno, president of the National Collegiate Athletic Association, and author of a history of the NCAA. No one, however, spent more time reading and critiquing the manuscript than my wife of over a half-century, Susan Catherine Bard McFarland Fernald Smith.

I had the pleasure in early 2015 of presenting a multi-session course offered through the Penn State–connected Osher Lifelong Learning Institute (OLLI). I chose six topics based on my research for this book that I felt would be interesting to an audience in Happy Valley. The five dozen participants raised important questions and offered a variety of comments from admirers of Joe Paterno and the athletic program at Penn State to those who questioned the place of athletics in higher education and the negative role of the National Collegiate Athletic Association. It also included several lawyers who spoke out more about the Sandusky Scandal than any of the seven lawyers on the Penn State Board of Trustees who have questioned little. And there were critics, including long-time admirers of the Penn State women's basketball team, wondering why I even brought up its deposed coach, Rene Portland, in context with her sexual-orientation policies and the athletic administration isolating her legally challenged actions in violation of university, state, and federal law. I acknowledge all of the participants for helping me rethink several issues that are discussed in this book. I recognize that what I have said in these pages will certainly not be the last in the volatile situation surrounding the Jerry Sandusky Scandal at Penn State.

Lastly, I want to acknowledge several individuals associated with the University of Illinois Press. Bill Regier, longtime head of the Press, has attended many conferences of the best history of sport society, the North American Society for Sport History. His presence at NASSH meetings and persuading a number of the best sport historians to publish with the UIP has been instrumental in maintaining the leading series of books on the history of sport. Specifically working on my manuscript, I was most fortunate to have a copy editor with four decades of experience, Geof Garvey, who had a keen eye for any inconsistencies. It was a pleasure working with a true professional.

SIFTING AND WINNOWING

Early in the summer of 1960 after teaching two years of high school history, I drove to Madison, Wisconsin, home of the University of Wisconsin, carrying with me my transcript from Northwestern University, where I had recently graduated. I came to ask for admittance into master's degree program in the Department of History. The prominent University of Wisconsin History Department was located just inside the Bascom Hall, the administrative home of that fine institution. As I walked up Bascom Hill, I noticed an old plaque on the wall. It read:

> Whatever may be the limitations which trammel inquiry elsewhere, we believe that the great state University of Wisconsin should ever encourage that continual and fearless sifting and winnowing by which alone the truth can be found.

"Sifting and winnowing," in an effort to approach the truth, stuck in my mind. Every time I approached Bascom Hall, I would glance at that plaque, close to the statue honoring Abraham Lincoln, who was stationed militarily in Wisconsin prior to his entrance into the political life of the nation. Later, I found out why the plaque with the words of the 1894 Governing Board was placed in such a prominent place. It was to honor what a university should stand for: free inquiry and expression in an effort to find the truth.

When controversial issues present themselves, the search for truth should prevail. Such was the case of the University of Wisconsin Professor of Economics, Richard T. Ely, who discussed and wrote about socialism at the end of the nineteenth century. Because of his political writing, a government employee called for his firing. However, the Board of Regents at the University of Wisconsin backed Ely, stating "the investigator should be absolutely free to follow the indications of truth wherever they may lead." Ely was allowed to sift and winnow, remaining true to academic freedom.

With all the controversy surrounding how Penn State University dealt with the Jerry Sandusky Scandal, I have had the freedom to sift and winnow through the records in an attempt to approximate the truth. I have spent several years searching through 140 years of records in an endeavor to find out how athletics has been administered at Penn State and why it may have contributed to Penn State's administrative approach to the scandal.

"Is this opening of Pandora's box?" asked Penn State's senior vice president for Business and Finance Gary Schultz when informed of the first allegation that Jerry Sandusky had sexually molested a young boy from Sandusky's Second Mile foundation. Several thousand years before, when Pandora, the first woman in Greek mythology, opened a vessel given to her by the god Zeus, all the evils in the world were unleashed. Unlike Joe Paterno, who knew some ancient Greek and Roman writings as a literature major at an Ivy League institution, Schultz may not have known the mythological origin of Pandora's box. He was trained in industrial engineering with two degrees from Penn State shortly after Paterno became head football coach. As the administrator in 1998 overseeing Penn State athletics, was Schultz aware of a mythic woman releasing the evils of the world several millennia before—evils such as disease, poverty, revenge, corruption, and child abuse? He almost surely did not know what the opening of Pandora's box would unleash upon Penn State and its athletic program.

Did the leaders of Penn State athletics, Schultz, President Graham Spanier, Athletic Director Tim Curley, and Coach Joe Paterno hope to keep the lid of the media vessel tightly closed? Were they more interested in treating this not as an assault on a young boy but as a public relations crisis that needed to be managed? Those questions caused me to almost immediately search for clues about the history of Penn State athletics to see whether the way Penn State athletics had been administered historically could have contributed to the worst scandal in the school's long history and, according to some, the worst scandal in collegiate athletic history. Was there a Penn State Pandora's box hidden away in the serenity of Happy Valley, out of sight of those living in the central mountains of Pennsylvania—a box that was opened only when a furtive event from 1998 came to light a decade later? The insulation of athletics in a business office of the university and, as it turns out, the separation of athletics from any effective academic function within the university, would help to keep Pandora's box festering but closed. Penn State officials had no idea how something they were deeply involved in would end. Isolating concerns about sexual criminality presaged a foreboding result in Happy Valley—an Unhappy Valley, from which wounded lions would emerge.

CHAPTER 1

Life in Happy Valley

The Name and the Paterno Impact

"Be not too hasty to trust or to admire the teachers of morality; they discourse like angels, but they live like men."
—Samuel Johnson (1759)

"The winds of fate can turn you around, run you aground, sink you, and sometimes you can't do a thing about it."
—Joe Paterno (2000)

In small-town America with a big-time football team, life can be different from life for other folks across the nation. When I interviewed for a position in sport history at Penn State in early April 1968, I came away with an idealized view of Happy Valley. Spring had arrived, the flowers were out as was the sun, it was warm, and my interviews went well. I called back to my wife in Wisconsin, where the snow had only recently melted away. She was about to have our second child, and I told her how great it would be to move here. It seemed idyllic, and that even included being picked up at the isolated airport up in the mountains at Black Moshannon, twenty long miles from State College. I was told that airport workers regularly drove the deer off the runway with a jeep, and from there a long, winding road finally led to civilization, something less than an hour away. I began my short stay in State College, hopeful that if I were offered and accepted the position, I wouldn't have to fly often on Allegheny Airlines.

The low mountains of Appalachia hid much of the near poverty that was only a few miles away from the university. State College, the epicenter of Happy Valley, was and is essentially an appendage to Penn State University. Located in the center of the state in Centre County, Mount Nittany overlooks the university in fertile Nittany Valley. The area appeared to have had no poverty, or it was hidden from the well-traveled routes into the town of about 30,000. It was a little oasis of green. It appeared lush and prosperous, a contrast to the surrounding Appalachia that was verdant but much poorer. On my interview visit, I was paraded past Beaver Stadium, the less than impressive 40-some thousand capacity home of the Nittany Lions, that had only recently had its steel stands removed from near the center of the university and erected again on the bare eastern edge of campus. There, parking was available and cows were abundant. It was home to a young and outspoken coach who had a modestly impressive 13 and 7 record in his first two years at the helm. During my short visit to State College, I was housed on the outskirts of town, with a single stoplight on its major street, in one of its few motels, a Holiday Inn. From there I was transported daily from South Atherton Street to the university located on the appropriately named College Avenue. Along College Avenue, from its earliest existence at the founding of the mid-nineteenth-century Farmers' High School (Penn State), was the business district, devoted to serving the university, and close by were a number of single-family houses and fraternities.

I was impressed that the Physical Education Department had its own library, likely the result of the influence of John Lawther, basketball coach at Penn State for thirteen years beginning in the midst of the Great Depression. Lawther had degrees in psychology, wrote a book, *Psychology of Coaching*, and had earned the respect of Penn State academics after he resigned his coaching responsibilities in 1949 to become a demanding professor and associate dean of the college that also housed athletics. The small library in the college, the John Lawther Reading Room, indicated to me that the Penn State Physical Education Department took academics seriously, something that was not always the case in other universities, where it might be the dumping ground for mediocre students with athletic skills.

Well before the naming of Joe Paterno's Grand Experiment of promoting academics and athletics, Penn State was already doing so under Lawther as associate dean and Ernie McCoy as athletic director and dean of the College of Physical Education and Athletics. McCoy, a transplant from the University of Michigan, wanted successful athletics and a strong academic department, and he gave the academic responsibility to Lawther. It was Lawther's duty to hire individuals across the country who might bring distinction to the Physical Education Department. Thus he hired professors known internationally for research in sport and physical activity, such as Elsworth Buskirk, a physiology researcher at the National Institutes of Health, sport psychologist Dorothy Harris, and Richard Nelson, a biomechanics expert. Penn State's Physical Education Department would become Number One nationally, long before Joe Paterno's Nittany Lion football team gained that status.

Still, Happy Valley became best known for its football team, not its nationally prominent Physical Education Department or, for that matter, its nationally recognized Penn State ice cream. Joe Paterno, for his coaching performance, was given the title of full professor in my department, as had been done for the previous head coach, Rip Engle, and a title often conferred upon coaches across America. This was done to foster security within the university, not for academic reasons, for in Paterno's case he lacked academic degrees and would never teach an academic class or attend more than one faculty meeting in my tenure with the department. Nevertheless, he would become the image of Happy Valley within a half decade of becoming head coach. Football, for a half century before Paterno came to central Pennsylvania, had become the dominating sport at Penn State in the late nineteenth and early twentieth centuries. Penn State had produced highly ranked teams and eight undefeated seasons well before Joe Paterno was born and had sent a team to the Rose Bowl game more than seven decades before Paterno and the Nittany Lions arrived there for the second time. Happy Valley was happy and contented at times with its football team well before Paterno. Still, what Paterno did for the community was unusual and gave a different meaning to the term Happy Valley.

Joe Paterno, like no one before, gave a face to those in the community who liked to believe Happy Valley was different in positive ways from other communities. Many believed that Paterno epitomized what was good about living in State College and the surrounding area. He was, to many, Penn State, and Penn State was the organization upon which the community was built. There appeared to be a naïve belief that Happy Valley, this insular and idyllic place in the geographic center of Pennsylvania, was different from the rest of America and that Joe Paterno made much of the difference.

There is an often-noted concept of American exceptionalism; that America has a special destiny as a shining "city upon a hill," as Puritan Massachusetts Governor John Winthrop put it in 1630 just before landing in America.[1] In a similar way, those who lived in Happy Valley believed that their community was special—exceptional—and that Penn State athletics was the beacon upon the hill on which Penn State was built. Specifically, many believed that not only was Penn State football exceptional, but it was nearly as pure as the valley in which it was born. Steve Nicklas, a Penn State fan and financial adviser in Florida, summed up the picture of Penn State football and its place in Happy Valley: "I grew up worshipping Penn State football," he said, "the program possessed everything—sanctity, simplicity, purity." He went on to say, "There was the sanctity of the place they played in, nicknamed 'Happy Valley.' It always seemed sunny there on fall afternoons. There was simplicity," Nicklas said, "of the uniforms with no names and a coach with black-rimmed glasses who looked like your grandfather." Then too, he believed, "there was purity of a program in which the players graduated and no one got into trouble. But like a lot of things in life," Nicklas came to believe, "something that appeared so perfect and virtuous as a kid turns out to be a mirage."[2] Nevertheless, the expression "Happy Valley" may have been repeated far more after the Jerry Sandusky affair than before. As an iconic image, it was important to so many people that the symbolic name was repeated as if it remained as pure as before or, possibly, as if the region would return to being a happy place.

Where the term "Happy Valley" came from originally is not known, but it was used as early as the mid-eighteenth century in England. Samuel Johnson, the English literary giant, wrote the fable *Rasselas, Prince of Abyssinia,* when the British were fighting the French and their Indian allies in colonial America. Prince Rasselas wanted to leave the enclave in Abyssinia and escape to "a spacious valley in the kingdom" called Happy Valley. This valley, surrounded by mountains and covered with trees, had the collected "blessings of nature" with all "evils extracted and excluded." Even with all the tranquility and "all the delights and superflui-ties" of Happy Valley, the young prince persisted in wanting to see the rest of the world and in leaving Abyssinia "by the first opportunity." The man who helped Rasselas escape from his velvet prison warned Rasselas about the outside world. The wise man told Rasselas: "Be not too hasty to trust or to admire the teachers of morality; they discourse like angels, but they live like men."[3] It was sage advice for those in the real world then and two and a half centuries later.

A major difference between Centre County's Happy Valley and that of Ras-selas is that those in central Pennsylvania were never in a locked-in community, except by its inaccessibility. There were no iron gates in Centre County, yet, like Abyssinia, it was isolated, was generally peaceful, and provided an abundance of life's best. Joe Paterno, when he came in 1950, wanted to leave at first because it was so dissimilar from his city life and home in Brooklyn, New York. But, unlike Rasselas, he stayed and reaped success.

The name Happy Valley was invented for Nittany Valley in Pennsylvania, per-haps in imitation of Samuel Johnson's region in Abyssinia, but when is not known for sure. Even before the term was created, people talked about this region of central Pennsylvania as something extraordinary. The term Happy Valley was not used in 1912, for example, when a "Tribute to Penn State College" was sent out to Penn State alumni. The writer, George M. Graham, described the attributes that anticipated the name Happy Valley:

> Penn State is essentially American. It is located in the kind of a section that might have produced Abraham Lincoln. Situated way up in the mountains, far from the cities, the tang of this primal is in the air. The stuff of which a pioneer is made vibrates at every turn.
>
> Up here among the mountains in the fluff, biting air, in the panorama of stretching fields and forests, in woodlands, where the hunter can still give battle to the bear, life takes a very real and earnest hue and this communicates itself to all those who are fortunate enough to come there to study.[4]

Is it any wonder that the studious athletes in this paradise more than a century ago were in the process of completing two undefeated seasons in football and graduating at a high rate?

A decade later, a new president, Ralph Dorn Hetzel, came to Penn State, arriv-ing from the New Hampshire College of Agriculture and Mechanic Arts. Hetzel almost wrote the magical words when he wrote to a friend that "State College is a beautiful place . . . making us happy and contented." He said that this "delightful place" is "on a high plateau, surrounded by hospitable mountain ranges, and we have a complete monopoly of community interest. The little town of about thirty-five hundred," Hetzel wrote, "has been built up around the College. We have not yet seen the country at its best but even during these winter months we find it most attractive."[5] President Hetzel, though never a defender of big-time athletics, was a believer in Happy Valley, where big-time athletics bloomed once more after his post–World War II death.

Fred Lewis Pattee, who was hired by President George Atherton in 1894 as a professor of English and rhetoric, could very well have been the individual to name Happy Valley, but there is no evidence that he did so. Pattee was a poet, novelist, and literary critic, writing into his eighties. He remained at Penn State until Hetzel became president and then departed to retire, but he continued to teach at Rollins College in Florida. Pattee, who wrote the words to the Penn State alma mater in 1901,[6] is the individual many claim as the first professor of an American literature as distinct from English literature. Two of his books might have called the region Happy Valley: *The House of Black Ring: A Romance of the Seven Mountains* and his autobiography published posthumously, *Penn State Yankee*. In *House of Black Ring*, Pattee wrote about life a few miles south of Happy Valley, noting that in Centre County, "all rules on how to live fail."[7]

In his autobiography, Pattee wrote of his first views of central Pennsylvania. Coming up through the Seven Mountains from the south in spring 1894, scenes were "dramatic with glimpses of wild valleys, rock-filled like the tailings of mines, varied by dashing trout streams, and all of it bowered in laurel and rhododendron in full bloom. To me," Pattee wrote, probably feeling somewhat nostalgic for his native New England farmland, "it was a new world, arousing all that was romantic with me." When Pattee first viewed the scene from the five-story Old Main building on campus, he saw "the vale of Mount Nittany with its scattered farms with cultivated fields like different-colored patches on a garment, with the two visible ranges of the Seven Mountains . . . with the smoke-hued Alleghenies dominating the whole west."[8] It surely looked like a valley of happiness to Pattee who, with a full-time position as professor, could now pay off the remainder of his huge student loans from his time at Dartmouth.

Pattee, a political conservative like Joe Paterno, referred to the Depression president Franklin D. Roosevelt and his Democrat administration as the "damned dimmercrats."[9] Ironically, President Roosevelt's Public Works Administration (PWA), working through the Pennsylvania General State Authority, built a library, along with a number of other Penn State buildings, in the late 1930s. The library was named Pattee Library after his death, and a half-century later a new Paterno Library was attached to it. During the Great Depression, Pattee hinted at why someone might call the region Happy Valley. "State College," he told his former Dartmouth College classmate who was teaching at Penn State at the time, "is known far and wide as the one town in America not hit by the Depression."[10]

There may be some truth to Pattee's observation, for a federal government agency designed to put the Depression's masses of unemployed to work—the Works Progress Administration (WPA)—turned down State College's request to build an airport west of town near the village of Pine Grove Mills. Why? Because WPA officials determined that there were not enough unemployed men in the area to work on the project.[11]

If the Depression was not felt as strongly in Happy Valley as in other parts of the state or the nation, there was a great depression in Penn State football that Professor Pattee noted. When the stock market crashed in fall 1929, the banning of athletic scholarships at Penn State was already two-year-old news.[12] (Giving money for athletic performance and a chance for an education had begun at Penn State in 1900 when its board of trustees sanctioned grants to athletes, making Penn State the first institution of higher education in America to officially give out athletic scholarships.) The removal of athletic scholarships resulted in inferior teams, putting the football team in a depressed state. Pattee, only recently having departed Happy Valley, wrote sarcastically that the Penn State football schedule should not include any team "harder than Kiski [Prep School], Slippery Rock, and Susquehanna U."[13] This was not far from actuality, as the Penn State football schedule in the not so happy valley of the Depression included games against smaller colleges such as Dickinson, Lebanon Valley, Muhlenberg, and Sewanee.

So it was likely that the moniker "Happy Valley," invented, apparently, during the Depression, had almost nothing to do with Penn State football, but rather to the happier state of the economy in and around State College in comparison with less fortunate neighbors in Pennsylvania and across the nation. Attempting to trace the origins of the designation "Happy Valley," State College's Nadine Kofman reported that a Penn State professor, who was coach of the debate team and eventual associate dean of the College of Liberal Arts, may have come up with the phrase while he was a speech instructor. By the 1950s, Harold "Pat" O'Brien was often referring to Happy Valley. So, too, did Katey Lehman, a writer for the *Centre Daily Times*, starting in 1954. It is certainly possible that the noted Pittsburgh Pirates and Steelers announcer Bob Prince used the term Happy Valley while announcing Penn State football games in the early and mid-1950s.[14] In the early 1960s, Lehman wrote, "'The mountain is better seen when viewed from the plain.' I don't know who said that but it applies to those of us who live here in 'happy valley' and sometimes take it for granted."[15]

Even the president of Penn State, Eric Walker, used the term following Rip Engle's 9–1 regular football season in 1962 and on the way to the Gator Bowl in Florida. Writing to Engle, Walker congratulated the coach for his season and stated, "things are pleasant and tranquil, footballwise, in happy valley." Walker, kidding the coach, noted a deficiency: "It is that 'one' in your 9–1 record. Just think how nice it would have been to be 10–0. We at Penn State should strive for perfection Rip, and not be satisfied with anything less. Ninety percent," Walker emphasized in jest, "is not good enough."[16] By 1970, after Rip Engle's last mediocre seasons and while Joe Paterno was adding new life to the football program, the radio voice for Penn State football, Fran Fisher, began using "Happy Valley" in his broadcasts. Though Fisher did not coin the term, he and especially national telecasts of Penn State football popularized the words.[17] With the promotion of an institution or an area that sport broadcasting can accomplish, it is not surprising that when State College achieved the federal government's Standard Metropolitan Statistical Area status after the census of 1980, the *New York Times*, in a feature article, would wax eloquently about the area:

> Many of the increasing numbers of people who can live anywhere prefer the un-hurried life of a college town, and even traveling salesmen of cities and suburbs have been settling in what they call "the happy valley" where rolling farmlands and villages are surrounded by forest-covered Appalachian ridges.[18]

By then, television's greatest football announcer in many people's minds, Keith Jackson, was reaching the entire nation with his homespun phrases, such as calling defensive linemen "big uglies down in the trenches" or noting that the defensive end has "laid a few licks on folks."[19] Jackson could, on a sunny autumn day, also look out from his ABC broadcast booth and see, about a mile away, the dominating landmark of Mount Nittany overlooking Happy Valley. That only happened with any regularity after Joe Paterno took over as coach, winning more than 80 percent of his games for a decade after his first year.

How did this small valley enclave in the middle of Pennsylvania, overlooked by Mount Nittany and bordered by Tussey Mountain and the Bald Eagle Ridge, come to think of itself as something different and special? How did Joe Paterno become the face of the community? How did an up-and-coming big-time football team, led by a bright, energetic, and cocky coach at what outsiders called a "cow college," help bring national prominence to the area that many insiders considered an idyllic place to live, work, and bring up children? When Paterno arrived in 1950, just out of an Ivy League college, Penn State had only the year before renewed the policy of giving athletic scholarships, half of which went to football players.[20]

Without scholarships—from the late 1920s until after World War II—Penn State had had a minor football program, playing the likes of Bucknell, Colgate, and Waynesburg with modest success and always losing to the University of Pittsburgh until Pitt stopped paying its players in the late 1930s.[21] There were only two coaches between the firing of Hugo Bezdek in 1930, for consistently losing to Pitt, and the hiring of Rip Engle, who brought Joe Paterno with him from Brown University in 1950. They were Bob Higgins, who won two-thirds of his games over nineteen years, often against minor opponents, and Joe Bedenk, the baseball coach who took over for one year and had a 5-4 record. With the advent of athletic scholarships after World War II and the coaching talents of Rip Engle, greater recognition began to come to Penn State and, along with it, a happier valley. For sixteen years Engle was a winner, never having a losing season, but it was not until Paterno turned out undefeated teams early in his career that the term Happy Valley began to commonly be used in connection with Penn State and its athletic success. But behind the aura of winning and the godlike image of Joe Paterno in mythological Happy Valley, danger lurked. Only weeks before the Number-One ranked Paterno team lost the national championship game to Bear Bryant's Alabama on New Year's Day 1979, a local critic of Penn State football, John Swinton, made a prescient remark about the Penn State football program: "No one dares to think that becoming Number One," Swinton warned, "might hinge on some as yet undisclosed Faustian bargain."[22] Or for that matter an opening of Pandora's box.

No one has explained the dangers of creating a mythical place as well as has Dave Zang, an academic who has studied sport and its place in the culture. Zang grew up in the State College area, where his father for a number of years owned the Mount Nittany Inn, only a few miles east of the geographical icon of the region and on the same mountain, Nittany Mountain. Happy Valley, wrote Zang before the Scandal exploded, is America's Brigadoon, a place hidden away, unaffected by time and remote from reality. Happy Valley is not only physically inaccessible from the rest of civilization, but it is here that the Grand Experiment of Joe Paterno could be carried out in isolation, if not in secrecy.[23] The Happy Valley isolation carried a danger known to few, if any; certainly not to Joe Paterno.

The traditional Paterno could speak about the virtue of playing successful football while gaining an education at the state's land-grant institution. Thus, the virtuous football program at Penn State could be compared highly favorably with the rest of college football. Joe Paterno, whom Zang described as "old school," loved loyalty as well as simplicity; the football uniforms chosen by Paterno were as plain as a nun's habit and probably would not have included numbers except that they were required by NCAA football rules. There would be no spiking the ball in the end zone after a successful score, no unnecessary celebrations when tackles were made—unless as coach he were carried off the field after winning a national championship game, when it appeared acceptable to lift one's arm in celebration. He even held off on the construction of expensive luxury suites at the stadium and its special nearly 400-seat midfield box for the president's guests, until it was considered absolutely necessary for financial and prestige reasons by university administrators and athletic officials.[24]

Fans at Penn State, Zang believed, drew "their sense of community from the shared belief that Happy Valley is not only a mythic place, but a singularly righteous one as well."[25] All this was made possible by the enormous success Paterno had after his first two seasons. He had two undefeated seasons in his third and fourth years as coach. He earlier had turned down a coaching position at Yale, an Ivy League treasure and the winningest Division I, big-time football school in history. He turned down several offers to coach in the National Football League, including a million-dollar offer from the New England Patriots after the 1972 season. At the time, a future president of the Penn State Board of Trustees and a local entrepreneur, Mimi Barash Coppersmith, began the "Joe Don't Go Pro" campaign.[26] The success of the "Joe Don't Go Pro" crusade may have been the road to canonization for those who believed in the Happy Valley mystical church led by its secular pope, Joe Paterno. Indeed, a man of the cloth, the Reverend Elton Richards Jr. of Reading, Pennsylvania, soon followed the Paterno campaign by organizing a Joe Paterno Day and giving Paterno a congratulatory trip to Italy and the Vatican.[27]

Possibly topping being honorary patron saint of Happy Valley was being asked to give the spring 1973 Penn State Commencement Address after rejecting the New England Patriots' offer. Here the newly canonized Paterno could put a dig into President Richard Nixon and his administration's Watergate Scandal, in which forty-eight individuals were eventually found guilty of various crimes. Nixon, under siege in 1973 and a year away from resigning in disgrace, had only four years earlier honored the victor of the Texas–Arkansas game with a national championship plaque; at the time, Penn State had just completed two undefeated seasons, a fact dismissed by Nixon's action. At his address, Paterno made a comment that soon became prominent in Happy Valley and elsewhere: "How could the president know so little about Watergate in 1973 and so much about college football in 1969?" In that speech, however, was a little-remembered comment about doing the right thing with integrity when faced with difficult choices: "We shall act, and we shall act with good intention," Paterno told the thousands at the stadium graduation ceremony. "Hopefully, we will often be right, but at times, we will be wrong. When we are, let us admit it and immediately try to right the situation." He certainly was not farsighted enough about what might happen to him more than a generation later when, in 1973, he said to the new graduates and a much wider audience: "Don't underestimate the world—it can corrupt quickly and completely."[28]

At the time, it seemed that Paterno was at or near his zenith of power when he gave his commencement address, but he had not yet coached the Nittany Lions to a national championship. This would occur a decade later when, after the 1982 season, his team defeated the University of Georgia and its great running back, Herschel Walker. Carried off the field as winning vicar for Happy Valley, Paterno had won his coveted national championship, denied first by President Nixon and a few years later in a 1979 loss to Alabama. In the latter contest, he had been, Paterno said, outcoached by Paul "Bear" Bryant, the most celebrated coach since Notre Dame's Knute Rockne in the 1920s. "When I stood toe to toe with Bear Bryant," Paterno told writer Bernard Asbell, "he outcoached me."[29] With that devastating loss, Happy Valley nearly lost its godlike leader, for if Joe Paterno is to be believed, he "almost quit. I went home, said I was going to resign," and then, returning to his roots, he walked around Brooklyn for three days.[30] Psychologically wounded for several years if not for a lifetime, Paterno reconsidered; to a number of people, Happy Valley was saved from an early exit by its exalted leader. With the passage of more than three decades and another 286 victories, his unceremonious firing by the Board of Trustees placed a dark cloud over the initial national championship and several hundred additional victories. Three years after the disastrous 1979 defeat by Bryant's Alabama, however, Paterno finally achieved his desire for a national title.

Four years after the 27–23 victory over Georgia in the Orange Bowl, Penn State again played for the national championship, this time against the University of Miami in the Fiesta Bowl. In the highest-rated televised collegiate football game ever, the "good guys" from Happy Valley defeated the "bad guys" from Miami, Florida, who were dressed in combat fatigues and combat boots before the game. If there was any time that people across America were pulling for the righteous Joe Paterno and virtuous Penn State football team to defeat any team, it was on January 2, 1987, when the Nittany Lions rose to the occasion and pulled off a stunning 14–10 upset victory by intercepting Heisman Trophy winner Vinny Testaverde five times, the last by an import from Canada, Pete Giftopoulos. The winning defense operated under a game plan devised by defensive coordinator Jerry Sandusky. After intensive film study, the decision was made to jam the Miami pass receivers at the line of scrimmage and wallop them into submission when they touched Testaverde's passes. The Miami receivers' arms "got about eight inches shorter," according to Penn State's defensive back Duffy Cobbs.[31] Paterno's arms got at least that much longer as his delirious team carried him off the field. That was the last time Paterno would experience a national championship, and his reputation and power in Happy Valley was never higher.

No one openly criticized Paterno for teaming up with the Penn State financial controller, Steve Garban, and President John Oswald a few years earlier to take football and the entire athletic department out of an academic unit and placing it in a business-financial office of the university.[32] Few saw or cared that removing any effective academic oversight from an academic unit and isolating athletics from some watchful eye of the faculty might in any way jeopardize what many saw as the culmination of the Grand Experiment. Athletes who graduated at a high percentage under a coach who emphasized academics as well as winning helped make the idyllic Happy Valley what it was. Saint Joe Paterno, as he was affectionately known, could do little wrong. He, probably more than anyone else at Penn State, had helped to transform a "cow college" in central Pennsylvania into a major university. In the 1990s, when an instructor of marketing in the Business School asked his students "Why don't many people call Penn State a 'cow college' today?" the most common answer was, according to instructor Andrew Bergstein, "Penn State football and Joe Paterno."[33] Paterno's impact was considered so significant that soon this eastern university would join some of the world's elite institutions of higher education—all midwestern universities—by becoming a member of the Big Ten Conference.

By the twenty-first century the term "Happy Valley" was so ingrained in central Pennsylvania that businesses as varied as "Happy Valley Farms," "Happy Valley Vineyard and Winery," "Happy Valley Green Homes and Gardens Tour," "Happy Valley Mobile Massage Therapy," "Happy Valley Mini Golf," "Happy Valley Plumbing," "Happy Valley Cloud Cam," and another dozen businesses were striving to prosper in a valley by that name. Many of them ascribed to one of Joe Paterno's many quotes, that "true success occurs if your values and your integrity have prevailed."[34]

Then, the other side of coin, an ugly side, appeared, for as Paterno has said, "The winds of fate can turn you around, run you aground, sink you, and sometimes you can't do a thing about it."[35] Shortly after the 2012 Jerry Sandusky trial, one Nittany Lion from birth, Jerry Fisher, a well-known local radio personality, contributor to Sandusky's Second Mile, and Happy Valley promoter, stated, "When an unspeakable act tears down something you've believed in, the sting reaches deep and leaves scars that won't quickly fade."[36] For David Zang, it was as true for those in Happy Valley as with people everywhere. There is a strong desire, Zang reasoned, to "tap into our need for artificial, virtual, and even nonexistent communities."[37]

Was Happy Valley for real? Not according to one interested but distant observer of the scandal hitting central Pennsylvania after November 4, 2011. "Happy Valley," she said, "is a Fairy Tale,"[38] and like many fairy tales, it has its dark side. Mary Gage, a playwright living in State College who has previously written about animals as a metaphor for the human race, adopted a mixed but mostly dark view of Happy Valley after the scandal. Gage, whose residence is not far from the Paterno family home, wrote this wistful letter to the local newspaper a fortnight after the Sandusky scandal broke: "I find myself envying my dog. She bounds happily through Sunset Park every day, knowing nothing about football, or ruined lives or disillusionment. She scampers," stated Gage, "past Joe Paterno's house, nosing the fallen leaves. For her, nothing has changed and life in State College is as wonderful as it ever was."[39]

CHAPTER 2

Penn State Presidents

Cheerleading the Teams to Victory

"A prince . . . cannot observe all those things for which men are
esteemed, being often forced, in order to maintain the state, to act
contrary to fidelity, friendship, humanity, and religion."
—Niccolò Machiavelli (1515)

At Penn State, "It was an uneven contest between the quest for intercollegiate
success and the desire to maintain institutional integrity."[1] Wise beyond his age,
a Penn State alum and 1990s graduate student, Scott Etter, typed the comment
as he concluded writing his dissertation about the early Penn State administration of athletics. If the two collided, success on the playing field won out, Etter
believed, over academic concerns. Nowhere was this clearer at Penn State than
with the historical role of the presidents in the conduct of men's intercollegiate
athletics. This set of priorities was not, however, unique to Penn State. College
presidents in the United States, as far back as the nineteenth century, have seldom
held institutional integrity above the welfare of athletic teams, especially football
and later basketball. Those presidents who have, have often been "burned." As
an example, the University of North Carolina's President Frank Graham in the
mid-1930s attempted to do away with preferential financial aid to athletes on
the basis of athletic ability at North Carolina and in the Southern Conference
to which North Carolina belonged. He ran into unstoppable opposition from
coaches, athletic administrators, and especially alumni in his quest. On the subject
of the organized criticism from alumni groups, President Graham confided to a
presidential colleague at Yale: "This is the hottest wire that I ever got my hands
on."[2] And it probably was. He was burned and lost the battle but surprisingly
saved his job.

A generation before, the president of the University of Alabama, James Abercrombie, had ruled a player ineligible because of academic failure, and Alabama
lost a football game. Abercrombie was on the hot seat. "I do not consider the mere
winning of athletic games," stated Abercrombie in 1909, "to be the chief objective
of an institution of learning." This did not sit well with the Alabama Board of
Trustees, and Abercrombie soon resigned, a victim of trying to esteem academic

integrity over victories. Abercrombie was no "cheerleader" for victories "on the gridiron," and he was soon gone.[3] Most college presidents, however, for more than a century, have been cautious to do anything but defer to athletics. Penn State leaders have, in like manner, often deferred to athletics from the nineteenth century well into the twenty-first.

From President George Atherton in the late nineteenth century to Presidents Graham Spanier and Rodney Erickson in the twenty-first century, Penn State presidents have often acceded to those who supported athletics above other aspects of higher education.[4] This is not illogical; for it can be argued that intercollegiate athletics, while not generally considered educational in themselves, have done much good for higher education since 1852 when the first intercollegiate contest was held between Harvard and Yale. University presidents have seen the benefit of successful athletics at least from the time of President Andrew D. White of Cornell University, when Cornell's 1875 crew won the prestigious collegiate Lake Saratoga Regatta. When President White heard of the victory over Harvard and Yale, he had the university chimes rung and canons fired and wrote in his diary, "Everybody is ecstatic here." He soon had the university absorb the $1,100 debt of the crew and said that this one event did more to publicize Cornell than if the governing board had spent $100,000 advertising.[5] Paradoxically and without foresight, President White, two years later, strongly opposed Cornell playing the new game of football against Michigan by telegraphing Michigan, "I will not permit thirty men to travel four hundred miles merely to agitate a bag of wind."[6] White was a cheerleader, but he had his limits.

Other presidents, such as Penn State's Graham Spanier at the dawn of the twenty-first century, knew the value of successful athletics. University administrators since nearly the beginning of higher education in America have known the importance of publicity, and after the Civil War of the 1860s, nothing gave more publicity than winning college athletics in the key sports. Institutions of higher education in America have been fiercely independent, with historically almost no regular federal government support, and often, in the case of private schools, independent of state support. Institutions were constantly competing for financial resources and student enrollment for their own survival first and foremost and then growth and prestige. Nearly all colleges and universities would promote athletics as their most visible activity.[7] Presidents were not about to jeopardize the publicity that athletics could bring to their institutions, nor were they anxious to jeopardize their own position in the academic pecking order.

Graham Spanier was one of those; for as chancellor at the University of Nebraska, he hired an outsider as athletic director, Bill Byrne of the University of Oregon, to replace iconic former football coach Bob Devaney when he retired as athletic director. Many who backed the successful Nebraska football team wanted an insider from the football operations, Al Papik, to take the post. Both the Nebraska Beef Club and the Touchdown Club, as with the Nittany Lion Club backing Penn State sports, tried to get Spanier fired for his "traitorous" action. To appoint an outside athletic director to replace former football coach and Athletic Director Bob Devaney was nearly sacrilegious. To defend himself at that time, Spanier said the search for an athletic director was not "contrived and abused," and told supporters of the university: "You won't find a chancellor around as supportive of intercollegiate athletics as I am."[8] When he arrived at Penn State in 1995, one of the first meetings he held was not with academics but with those in intercollegiate athletics. He emphasized that he would be a backer of Penn State athletics, and for sixteen years he was.[9] Although Spanier believed he would be the president when Joe Paterno retired, the largest scandal in Penn State's history interrupted the process. Both the cheerleading Graham Spanier and Joe Paterno, possibly the most dominant individual in the history of Penn State, were exited from their positions on the same day.

Cheerleading in athletics was not new with the presidency of Graham Spanier. Nearly all Penn State presidents took on that role shortly after students first organized and directed intercollegiate competitions in the 1870s and 1880s. The first cheerleading president for athletics appears to be the dominant and longest-serving president in Penn State's history, George Washington Atherton, who presided for nearly a quarter century beginning in 1882. Atherton came to Penn State from Rutgers University, where he might have seen the first collegiate football game in America, between Rutgers and Princeton. Atherton, a Civil War veteran and Yale graduate, had just taken a chaired position in Political Economy and Constitutional Law at Rutgers in fall 1869, when Princeton journeyed by train to New Brunswick for a football game, soccer-style, generally considered the initial intercollegiate football contest.[10]

Atherton arrived as president of Penn State the year after Penn State's first football game against Bucknell in 1881. With President Atherton came his wife and several children, including his nine-year-old son, Charlie, who loved both football and baseball. Charlie was so skillful that he eventually became a star running back on the football team and later played baseball for a short time in the major leagues. The new president had plenty of reasons to improve the athletic facilities and supervision when his son, at age 14, became a freshman in 1888. President Atherton had to give permission for his young son to play football two years later as a junior in college.[11] Charlie Atherton competed in football his last two years as an undergraduate and for the next three years after graduation, though he took only a couple classes as a graduate student.[12] Eligibility rules were loose in the 1890s.

In the years that Charlie Atherton played football and baseball at Penn State, his father was involved in improving the athletic situation in a way not dissimilar to that of other colleges and universities in the United States. The student-run Athletic Association was formed and given an office in Penn State's main building, Old Main, and Atherton was involved with the Board of Trustees in giving needed help to the Athletic Association. An armory was constructed for its activities and sport events, with the basement given over to a gymnasium. A trainer-coach, specifically for the football team, was hired by Atherton and the trustees and would be paid from a $1 assessment of each Penn State student. According to the student newspaper, "the reputation of P.S.C. as a college will be greatly increased by her having a good reputation in the Athletic Field."[13] Soon a new field was constructed with a 15' track surrounding the football and baseball field and included a 500-seat covered grandstand. The football team was given meals and lodging at a special quarters, and spring practice was conducted under the new trainer-coach. The football team was even given a six-day leave of absence to play football games in Virginia; Washington, D.C.; and Maryland.[14]

While Atherton was promoting the building of facilities for athletics and hiring a "physical" instructor who could train and coach the teams, he was drawn into at least one questionable activity involving the academic integrity of athletics and specifically football. Penn State was undefeated well into November 1894 when it embarked on a three-game "western" trip to meet Washington and Jefferson, Oberlin, and the Pittsburgh Athletic Club in a period of five days. The student-run Foot Ball Committee wrote a letter asking permission for a stalwart tackle on the football team but a failing student, James A. Dunsmore, to participate during the trip. The Foot Ball Committee asked whether Atherton would overrule the faculty prohibition of his playing so that the team could continue to win and promote Penn State on its three-game trip. Dunsmore was a sophomore who, in three of his courses, was under the 65 average needed for athletic participation. The previous year Professor George Hoskins, the trainer-coach, who had anthropometric measures of the entire freshman class, showed that Dunsmore was the strongest member of the freshman class.[15] Just days before the important three-game series, the Foot Ball Committee argued that unless Atherton gave permission, "we will be very much crippled by the loss of . . . J. A. Dunsmore." At the bottom of the letter to Atherton was written Atherton's reply: "granted."[16] Dunsmore played; Penn State won all three games, and the team remained undefeated for the first significant undefeated football season in Penn State's history.[17] Academic integrity had lost out to athletic expediency.

The precedent for presidents overruling faculty on academic eligibility of athletes had been set. The involvement of faculty in Penn State's athletics was never strong, though in the mid-1870s the faculty had removed from the college the best-known baseball player in its history, John Montgomery "Monte" Ward, for allegedly stealing chickens in Puddintown, just east of the campus.[18] Ward, a good student, left Penn State, joined a professional baseball team, pitched the second perfect game in major league history, went to Law School at Columbia, and formed the first professional sport union. The faculty, however, for the most part, was reduced to symbolic influence throughout the twentieth century. Academic integrity, which the faculty should have been most concerned with, was abridged, especially in the Paterno era, when a number of "presidential admits" were routinely granted for football players. Presidential admits were granted to athletes who could not meet regular academic admissions entrance requirements but could be admitted by the president because those players were important to the success of the football team. Two years before Penn State won its first national championship, more than one-third of the Penn State recruits, an unusually high number for Joe Paterno and Penn State, were offered presidential admits.[19]

Though there is no evidence of presidential admits in the Atherton era, later in his lengthy presidency he was involved in several activities beneficial to the growth of Penn State athletics, all more or less in keeping with the growth of athletics in U.S. colleges. In order to attract and keep athletes in college, alumni, students, and others at major universities were offering financial aid to athletes. This was clearly evident nationally in the 1880s when Penn State was only beginning to compete in football. For example, the captain of the Princeton team, Knowlton "Snake" Ames, attempted to recruit Highland Stickney to play for the Tigers. "As to your coming down here, I will tell you plainly," Ames wrote to Stickney, "I will do all I can for you in every way, if you really wish to come. I can get your board, tuition, etc., free."[20] Stickney, however, went to Harvard. Penn State soon got into the act of paying players to attend.

Penn State was the first college in America to have its Board of Trustees offer athletic scholarships. In 1899, Penn State lost six of its last seven games, including blowouts by Yale, 42–0, and the University of Pennsylvania, 47–0. Almost immediately, J. Price Jackson, an electrical engineering professor and chair of the Alumni Advisory Committee of the Athletic Association (composed of alumni, professors, and some seniors, which advised the student-run Athletic Association), contacted President Atherton for help with the football team. The Alumni Advisory Committee, wrote Jackson, "have come to the point where we find it absolutely necessary to call upon you for the sum of money which you so generously agreed to advance for student aid." Within six months, Atherton met with other members of the Executive Committee of the Board of Trustees and approved athletic scholarships, ten for 1901 and increased to twenty-five by 1905.[21] Payment of players contributed to a number of winning teams, including five that were undefeated in the next two decades.

At the same time that athletics scholarship became available, William "Pop" Golden was hired as physical director and to "act as 'coach' for the training of the several athletic teams." Golden's beginning salary was $1,400 a year, and in less than two years his salary was raised to $1,800, paid principally by a gymnasium and Athletic Association fee that had been raised to $10 per student, $4 of which went to the Athletic Association.[22] Golden, a popular physical director and coach, continued at Penn State until 1912, when he resigned, but not until well after he influenced the building of a "jock" house to accommodate and feed athletes.

Once President Atherton and the Board of Trustees had decided to give athletic scholarships, most athletes were housed in Old Main, the principal building that accommodated students, provided some classrooms, and was the administrative center for Penn State. Atherton proposed the construction of a building to house a number of athletes on campus near the athletic track. It could be paid for by surplus income from the gymnasium fee and the rental of a number of rooms in Old Main supported by the athletic scholarships. In less than a year, a three-story building was constructed with dorm rooms, dining room and kitchen, locker room with toilets and showers, and a trophy room.[23] It was called the Track House and later was replaced by Varsity Hall. Though the Track House would never compare to Schwab Auditorium, the 1903 gift to Penn State from the president of U.S. Steel, Charles M. Schwab, it was still a handsome edifice.[24]

President Atherton had been a major influence in the promotion of athletics at Penn State in addition to making the college something more than an agriculture institution by building a large engineering school. Future presidents continued the tradition of fostering men's athletics. Following the acting presidency of ex-governor James Beaver after Atherton's death, Edwin Sparks was chosen to lead Penn State. Sparks had been head of the Penn State Preparatory Department in the 1890s until he departed for the University of Chicago to work on a doctorate in history. He then joined the Chicago faculty until he was called back to Penn State in 1908. When Sparks had been on the Penn State faculty, he had been involved in athletics, officiated at track meets and offered a silver cup for the baseball batter with the best average. Upon becoming president, Sparks wrote, "Athletics are a necessary and important part of every well governed American college."[25] Nevertheless, while at the University of Chicago, only three years before and during the 1905 national football crisis over brutality and ethics, he took a negative stand against athletics. Chicago at the time was, along with the University of Michigan, the major big-time athletic school in the Midwest. Sparks commented, "I do not favor athletics as now indulged in at colleges."[26]

Like most presidents before and after, when Sparks accepted the top administrative position, he became a cheerleader for the institution he ran, just as Atherton had done before him. New Beaver Field, on the northwest part of campus, was constructed in 1909 to replace the first permanent athletic field, soon called Old Beaver Field, just east of Old Main. Sparks continued praising athletics through the coaching years of Dick Harlow, who was not only a winner but, as Sparks said, does "nothing that shall injure the name of Penn State." Sparks even offered a prize for the best football song composed by a Penn Stater.[27] Later, because coach Harlow went off to World War I, Sparks hired a product of the University of Chicago, Hugo Bezdek, and saw the early glory years of Bezdek before he was relieved of his head coaching position at the end of the 1920s.

Still, Sparks was hesitant to allow the Penn State alumni, who were gaining athletic power over the Nittany Lions, to win at all costs. He persuaded the Athletic

Association to pass a freshman ineligibility rule, as some other big-time institutions were doing in the early twentieth century. Likewise, he favored the resolution passed by the Penn State faculty senate in 1908 that the "Faculty Committee on Athletics shall have jurisdiction over all athletic contests" shortly after the alumni had taken control, including the financing of athletics the year before.[28] Edwin Sparks retired from the presidency because of ill health, just before the Athletic Association voted to give successful coach Hugo Bezdek a dramatic pay increase to $10,000 per year for seven years in fall 1920. It is questionable whether Sparks could have restricted the payment even if he had desired to do so, though he had given his consent to hire Bezdek fulltime two years before for $4,500, a high salary at Penn State for any professor.[29] For most presidents, as with Sparks, it was more expedient to go along with most things athletic, or to turn a blind eye, than to question anything, such as a coach's salary. Thus, most presidents, including Sparks, continued to serve the institution as good cheerleaders.

In the early 1920s, President John Thomas came to Penn State from Middlebury College in Vermont, where he had been a very successful fundraiser, quadrupling its income in his dozen years there. John Thomas envisioned Penn State becoming a real university similar to those that had grown up in the midwestern Big Ten conference—such as Michigan, Wisconsin, and Illinois—instead of being an isolated college in the middle of Pennsylvania. Thomas looked forward to the creation of professional schools and a thriving graduate program at Penn State. In this he was eventually disappointed. When he arrived, however, he almost immediately began an Emergency Building Fund, to include a campus hospital, a home economics building, a student union building, men's and women's dormitories, and for athletics a large recreation building and a replacement of the original Track House.[30] From the first, President Thomas felt that a college must pay well to attract a high-quality coach. "If we compete in intercollegiate athletics we must have a coach," noted Thomas, "if we have a coach we must have a good one; to get a good one, we must pay the price."[31] Within a year of Thomas becoming president, Hugo Bezdek's salary surpassed that of Thomas and was far more than double any full professor's salary.[32]

Thomas was solidly in back of the athletic program, especially football, giving a rousing, cheerleading speech on "Why I Believe in Football" in support of the Emergency Building Fund:

> I believe in football because it fixes in every student the spirit of fight and the will to win. It is all a mistake to say that the men on the bleachers get no benefit. They receive incalculable benefit in the spirit that surges through them in the support of the team. . . . I believe in football because it fuses the college into a unity. . . . In the game the soul of the college is awakened anew, and he is no man at all into whose heart the thrills of the contest do not send currents of devotion and loyalty. . . . I believe in football—especially football led by big-

hearted men, hard, clean, strictly by the rules, and with every ounce in the fight to the last whistle.[33]

Penn State and President Thomas believed that in Hugo Bezdek it had the person to build upon the athletic program that was already in place. Penn State had two undefeated seasons soon after Bezdek took over, and like Joe Paterno early in his career, it had a 30-game undefeated streak. Thomas called Bezdek "the greatest coach and athletic director in the United States."[34] Thomas went along with increasing the number of athletic scholarships to 75, unrivaled as the greatest number of official scholarships in the nation.[35] Bezdek even took a Penn State team to the Rose Bowl in 1923. After returning from Pasadena, California, he turned over to the John Thomas Emergency Building Fund more than $20,000 of the $35,000 the team received from the contest.[36] That money, however, was specifically directed to the building of a new athletic dorm, Varsity Hall, to replace the Track House built two decades before. New Varsity Hall was completed a short time before John Thomas resigned as a result of a conflict with Governor Gifford Pinchot over the lack of support and funding for Penn State from the state government.[37]

For the next two decades, Penn State lacked a presidential cheerleader for its athletics, and the results showed it. Ralph Dorn Hetzel was president of the University of New Hampshire when he was chosen to lead Penn State, and his salary was raised to $15,000, just above that of the 10-year contract football coach and athletic director Bezdek had in place.[38] Hetzel took the leadership just as Penn State and its alumni were raising questions about how athletics should be governed and how much emphasis should be placed on producing winners. He agreed with an internal study by alumni that Penn State should end its policy of granting athletic scholarships, thus beginning what became known as the "Great Experiment"—attempting to win without athletic scholarships. This policy, led by President Hetzel, was in keeping with the famous Carnegie Foundation for the Advancement of Teaching study, begun in 1926. The Carnegie Report on American college athletics strongly opposed the commercialism and professionalism found in college athletics across the United States and specifically criticized Penn State for its payments to seventy-five athletic scholarship recipients.[39]

A decade after taking over the helm at Penn State, Hetzel could have picked an alumnus with strong athletic credentials to become the dean of the new School of Physical Education and Athletics, thus promoting big-time athletics once again. He chose not to. Hetzel felt the need to explain his choice of Carl Schott, a Ph.D., from Columbia University rather than an insider with winning athletics foremost in mind. Hetzel stood his ground against opposition.[40] He later said, "Institutions that continue over a long period of time having constantly winning teams build up a situation that makes it difficult for them to maintain academic standards that ought to prevail." For his entire two-decade tenure at Penn State, Hetzel maintained that "institutions are educational and the education program should be the one to dominate the situation."[41] Hetzel may never have known, as will be shown later, that Penn State alumni were increasingly providing athletes financial backing through the 1930s and into the 1940s, allowing football coach Bob Higgins enough resources to win more than 60 percent of his games for nineteen years, a record close to that of Joe Paterno in his forty-six years.[42] President Hetzel appeared satisfied with the direction of Penn State athletics and its football team, agreeing with the "fundamental soundness and merit of the plan initiated" in the late 1920s when athletic scholarships were eliminated.[43]

With Hetzel's death in 1947 from a cerebral hemorrhage, changes in the football program were rapid, once again bringing Penn State into the big time, though some could argue that the university had never abandoned it. After all, Penn State still played such institutions as Michigan State, Pittsburgh, Syracuse, and West Virginia since the Depression and overall had won more than they lost against those schools.[44] The president of the Board of Trustees, James Milholland from Pittsburgh, was the interim president of Penn State for more than two years. Milholland was well versed in Penn State athletics, for he had been president of the Alumni Association when Penn State, with backing of the alumni, eliminated athletic scholarships in 1927.[45] He was on the Board of Trustees for sixteen years before he was chosen as acting president. In less than a year, the trustees sanctioned athletic scholarships once again, in line with the new Sanity Code of the National Collegiate Athletic Association, that nationally for the first time allowed athletic scholarships but under strict guidelines. The board offered thirty tuition scholarships and fifteen more for the following year. Within a decade the original number had risen more than eightfold.[46]

Though Milholland wanted to become the permanent president, the Board of Trustees thought otherwise and chose Milton Eisenhower, the younger brother of Dwight D. Eisenhower, heroic general of the victory over Hitler in Germany a few years before. Milton Eisenhower, arriving from the presidency of Kansas State University, was more sympathetic to big-time athletics than was Hetzel, though he believed that amateur sport lost something with subsidies. Nevertheless, he said, "if there is to be subsidization, it must be in the open."[47] He was one of the many Penn State presidents who were cheerleaders for the value of college sports. "I am the biggest athletic supporter you ever saw," he exaggerated in his report to the alumni, "and am proud of the sound athletic policies we have here." Eisenhower stated that athletes at Penn State "must make normal progress toward their degree," and if not, "they are ineligible for athletics." He commended the coaching staff as "wonderful coaches. . . . I couldn't find any of the coaches I would want to change."[48] The young and energetic Joe Paterno was one of them, as the Rip Engle era in Penn State football began.

President Eisenhower was part of a major change when Dean and Athletic Director Carl Schott retired and Michigan's Ernie McCoy replaced him in 1952.

From 1908, when the position of graduate manager of athletics was created, until the Ernie McCoy era the alumni had a significant role in running Penn State athletics.[49] From the early 1900s until midcentury, the alumni-controlled graduate manager scheduled games and was the financial manager of athletics. This was the situation even though, from 1930 on, the head of the School of Physical Education and Athletics, Hugo Bezdek and later Carl Schott, were officially in charge of the program. When Ernie McCoy became dean of the School of Physical Education and Athletics and athletic director, he persuaded the Board of Trustees to make the graduate manager an assistant athletic director, moving the graduate manager's office from Old Main to Recreation Building so that Dean McCoy would have stricter control over the new assistant athletic director.[50] Dean McCoy, the trustees stated, "shall have full authority in the program of athletics."[51] President Eisenhower let the squeaky clean new dean and athletic director run the athletic show at Penn State, and Ernie McCoy did so for almost two decades.

An insider, Eric Walker was elected president when Milton Eisenhower left Penn State in 1956 for the nation's capital to be adviser to his brother Dwight, but he soon assumed the presidency of Johns Hopkins University. Walker was possibly the greatest cheerleader for Penn State athletics since George Atherton's tenure in the late 1800s—even cheering and leading Penn State's development of women's athletics.[52] Walker, born in England, came to Penn State from Harvard University along with his torpedo research project of the Harvard Underwater Sound Laboratory. Funded by the federal military, it was eventually named the Applied Research Laboratory.[53] Although research consumed much of Walker's life, he was also a sportsman and enjoyed fishing, tennis, squash, and golf, and, earlier in life, played basketball and ran track. If Walker's story can be believed, he was advised by a noted scientist, Vannevar Bush, early in his career as president that there were three ways to build a great university. Bush, like Walker an electrical engineer, told Walker you could create greatness by building a football team as Michigan State had done, by building buildings as the University of Illinois had achieved, or by building a faculty on the example of Stanford. Walker replied, "I'm going to do all three!" At the conclusion of his tenure as president, he told a friend, "I tried to do all three and I do think that our football team is great, the buildings are quite in evidence, and no one has to argue about our faculty. . . . We don't have to bow our heads to any of the Big Ten or to the Ivy League."[54]

Walker had a prescient statement about athletics in a speech to a Penn State audience as his career came to an end. He warned future presidents that they must pay attention to intercollegiate athletics by attending events other than just football, such as "wrestling, gymnastics, and track," and being the "guardian of the university's reputation for respecting the rules and doing things right." To Walker, "if the university cheats it is the president's fault. He can't hide behind 'I had no idea.'" Walker believed that the president needed a "special relationship with whoever runs intercollegiate athletics." He told those who listened to his lengthy talk, "I was lucky in that respect. I inherited a fine Dean of the College of Physical Education [Ernie McCoy], a fine coach [Rip Engle], and a set of rules and regulations."[55] Walker agreed with Rip Engle, who wanted "no football players who had not been admitted by the University admissions officer as regular students."[56] In the years that followed, there were few incidents of cheating in athletics. Only when the Sandusky Scandal broke in 2011 was a president questioned about hiding behind the assertion "I had no idea" about negative situations in athletics.

Between the presidencies of Eric Walker and Graham Spanier, all three presidents, John Oswald, Bryce Jordan, and Joab Thomas, were cheerleaders for athletics. Unlike President Hetzel, Presidents Oswald, Jordan, and Thomas promoted athletics in major ways during the ascendency of Joe Paterno as one of the country's greatest coaches.[57] Each came from another big-time institution, Oswald from the University of Kentucky and the University of California, Jordan from the University of Texas, and Thomas from the University of Alabama. All three did what was discussed with Ernie McCoy and Eric Walker during his presidency—that is, the desirability of allocating a percentage of athletes "to be admitted to the University specifically by the President of the University."[58]

After Walker, a major change in administration was accepted by each president to admit athletes who could not meet entrance requirements. This, as much as any action, gave Penn State a greater opportunity to rise to the top in football. Probably every other institution playing big-time football and basketball—and certain other sports—regularly allowed athletes into the university who could not meet university admission standards. Records show that Penn State did so to a limited extent, beginning with President Oswald in the 1970s. When Joe Paterno became athletic director in 1980, one of his first actions was to submit the names of nine football players who could not meet academic standards to President Oswald for a presidential admission.[59] There is no indication that this request or any other was ever turned down by a Penn State president.

The 1980 presidential admits were a turning point for the quest to be Number One, for as Joe Paterno said at about the same time he sent the list of nine to President Oswald, "OK, in the eyes of a lot of people we have to win a national championship or else Joe Paterno and the Grand Experiment are both failures."[60] Two years later, four of the nine individuals so recruited played substantial roles on the team, and one starred in the victory over the University of Georgia in the Sugar Bowl national championship game. Although Penn State athletes have had a stellar record for graduation, and the football team in particular ranks high among all big-time institutions, only one of those nine football presidential admits, Nicholas Haden, graduated from Penn State.[61] A statement made by the famed political philosopher, Niccolò Machiavelli, in The Prince, could be athletically applied to some college presidents and coaches. "A prince, " stated Machiavelli in the early 1500s CE, "cannot observe all those things which men are esteemed, being often forced, in order to maintain the state, to act contrary to fidelity, friendship, humanity, and religion."[62]

There is some truth to the statement of the long-time former executive director of the National Collegiate Athletic Association, Walter Byers: "Presidents glory in all the good things about college athletics and blame others for the bad," wrote Byers after his retirement. "They are more responsible than anybody else for the current hypocritical tone of college athletics." Among other charges against college presidents, Byers noted, were the number of "special admits," what Penn State called "presidential admits."[63]

The policy continued into the twenty-first century, though President Bryce Jordan wrote a paper in the early 1990s well after he retired, stating that "No academic corners should be cut in admitting an athlete to a college."[64] Bryce Jordan, like other presidents, had been under tremendous pressure to cheerlead their institutions and allow into college students with inferior academic preparation and superior athletic skills. Jordan knew from a federal study that less than 2 percent of all students are presidential admits, but that more than 20 percent of football and basketball players are special admits, and for African American athletes the percentages were much higher than that.[65] So President Jordan, who almost singlehandedly brought Penn State into the academically and athletically superior Big Ten in 1990, cut academic corners for Penn State athletes while publicly opposing the idea. Joe Paterno editorialized in his piece in the *Wall Street Journal* thus: "Some schools will bring in athletes just to have a good team."[66] That statement by Paterno is one of his paradoxes—a human condition experienced throughout history. It certainly was diametrically opposed to his promise to President John Oswald in the early 1970s that "We will never sacrifice sound academic principles for athletic success."[67]

Presidents as well as coaches have been caught in the paradox, or possibly hypocrisy, of big-time intercollegiate athletics at Penn State and elsewhere. Nevertheless, Penn State was recognized as having one of the cleanest big-time programs in the United States, and the Grand Experiment, while flawed, had much truth in it relative to maintaining academic integrity while striving for excellence on the playing field.

CHAPTER 3

A Joe Paterno–Jerry Sandusky Connection

A Look at Penn State Football Coaches

and Assistant Coaches

"True success occurs if your values and your integrity have prevailed."
—Joe Paterno (2000)

By the time Penn State and its coach Joe Paterno won its first national champion-ship in football after the 1982 season, Penn State previously had twelve undefeated seasons dating back a century. But the national championships for Penn State in 1982 and 1986 cemented the legacy of Joe Paterno above all former coaches and extended it far beyond Happy Valley in central Pennsylvania. It might have done the same for Jerry Sandusky, the most visible of Paterno's assistants. The vast majority of Paterno's assistant coaches did not wander far from Beaver Stadium, which had been moved to the outskirts of campus by 1960 and was expanded from forty-six thousand to eighty-five thousand seats in a couple of decades. Most seemed satisfied in staying with a winner, and that included Jerry Sandusky. Not only was Sandusky credited with helping Penn State win championships, but the defensive specialist became a local icon back in 1977 when he created The Second Mile to help at-risk young people. Sandusky was what Joe Paterno never became, a fun-loving, effervescent, and outgoing character—with what appeared to be a social conscience for the community. Yet Sandusky yearned for something more than being a nineteen-year assistant coach with a do-good demeanor; he wanted a head coaching position, if not at Penn State after about two decades on the staff—longer than the time Paterno had waited in the 1960s—then somewhere else. An opportunity soon arose.

An opening at Temple University existed after Owl coach Bruce Arians's firing in 1988, when he won less than a third of his games over six years. Joe Paterno tried to make Arians's misfortune into an opportunity for Sandusky. His unexpected, lavish letter of recommendation was not to get rid of Sandusky as some might claim, but to praise Sandusky for his fine example of life and of coaching. Far beyond the ac-claim for any other assistant coach looking for a head coaching position, Paterno praised Sandusky in a letter to the Philadelphia athletic director, Charles Theokas:

Of all the coaches I have had or been around, I have no doubts that Jerry Sandusky is the best head-coaching prospect. I am not suggesting to you he might do the job. I am telling you he will do the job at Temple, and furthermore, A, He is as fine a tactician and teacher of this game that I have ever known. He is a strong motivator, a tireless worker, and he has a *marvelous character with an impeccable lifestyle*. B. He knows how to get people to do things. He is a wonderful organizer and he has put together a program here called The Second Mile, which started from nothing. Jerry was able to get many of the business people in this town involved in it and they have become very active in his efforts on behalf of unfortunate, young boys. Some of the people on his Board have large-size egos and Jerry has been able to get them to work together enthusiastically and constructively, and they have really done a marvelous job. Jerry's Second Mile work is moving out throughout the State, and he has an operation in the City of Philadelphia.

Paterno concluded his high praise for Jerry Sandusky, stating that he had

the ability to put together the program, the ability to motivate people, the ability to sell the program, the role model he is, his ability to identify with the needs of young people, and above all, his *commitment to human beings*. . . . I would *very much like to keep Jerry Sandusky at Penn State*. Very few people at this institution have committed more to it. Since I have made a commitment to stay here several more years, I do not think it is fair for me to ask him to serve as an assistant. He is too good for that.[1]

After composing the first draft of his letter to the Temple athletic director, he crossed out what he must have meant as a joke. Paterno wrote that Sandusky "might be almost as good as I am."[2] Jerry Sandusky might have been as good as Joe Paterno, but he turned down the position because, among other reasons, the facilities at Temple were substandard and would stifle his attempt to turn out a winner.[3] Jerry Berndt, a one-time coach of the year in the Ivy League, was offered the position. Sandusky stayed with Paterno and with his locally organized Second Mile, dedicated to the betterment of young boys.[4]

If the common belief was that Joe Paterno and Jerry Sandusky disliked each other—as a number of writers have concluded—this letter of recommendation tends to belie that belief.[5] That the two clashed at times is well documented, but that Sandusky's coaching success most likely contributed importantly to two national championships is generally acknowledged. Paterno calling his top assistant a "marvelous character with impeccable lifestyle" with a "commitment to human beings" went beyond that of his letters for other assistants looking for head coaching positions.[6] It is not likely that Paterno would have written these statements if he detested Sandusky and merely wanted to get rid of him.

That Jerry Sandusky never became a head coach reflects a good deal about the history of assistant coaches at Penn State dating back to the nineteenth century. From the beginning of football in 1881 (with a victory over the school soon to be renamed Bucknell University) to the present, there have been only a handful of assistant coaches and only one head coach, Dick Harlow of the World War I era, who moved on from Penn State to successful head coaching positions at other institutions of higher learning. Few of Joe Paterno's assistants during his forty-six years of leading the Nittany Lions went on to head coaching positions, and none, including George Welsh and Greg Schiano, will likely be remembered very far into the twenty-first century.[7] Most stayed on the Paterno staff, turning out winning teams consistently year after year, concluding with an incredible 409 victories under Paterno, the winningest coach in big-time college football.

Coaches, one might be surprised to learn, whether head coaches or assistants, were not always the dominant factor in college football teams such as the Nittany Lions. There was no coach for Penn State's first undefeated team in 1881 when its only game resulted in a 9–0 win over the University at Lewisburg, renamed a few years later after its chief benefactor, William Bucknell. There was apparently no captain either, something that nearly every other college had when other colleges started playing rugby football in the 1870s. The Penn State leader in 1881 may have been George Chadman, later becoming a lawyer, who, according to the umpire of the game, James G. White, "was one of the star performers."[8] Umpire White, who eventually received a Ph.D. from Cornell, and Irvin P. McCreary, the referee, were in Penn State's class of 1882. It may seem illogical that two members of the senior class of the visiting team were the two officials. Penn State players, however, unlike the Lewisburg players, had purchased the latest rules for rugby football and were knowledgeable about the most recent rules.[9]

The rules booklet used by Penn State was clear—"a touch down is when a player, putting his hand upon the ball on the ground in touch or in goal, stops it so that it remains dead or fairly so." "Goals," in contrast, were not touch downs but the means of scoring, and "a goal may be obtained by any kind of kick except a punt," meaning a drop kick or place kick following a touch down or from the field of play (a field goal). Clearly it was rugby, the only football game played by the major colleges, such as Harvard, Yale, Princeton, or Pennsylvania, that included a rugby scrummage, not a scrimmage, determining the principal means of advancing the ball.[10] "A scrummage takes place," the rules read, "when the holder of the ball, being in the field of play, puts it down on the ground in front of him, and all who have closed round on their respective sides endeavor to push their opponents back, and by kicking the ball, to drive it in the direction of the opposite goal line."[11] Harvard University, which introduced the game of rugby to other U.S. institutions of higher education before it was transformed into American football, was in its eighth year of playing football when Penn State beat Lewisburg (Bucknell) in its first intercollegiate football game.[12]

How could the Penn State team even travel to Lewisburg in 1881, a distance of more than sixty miles? It was common knowledge, even when Jerry Sandusky joined Joe Paterno's football staff in 1969, that Penn State was "equally inaccessible from all directions." It would take all day to travel to Lewisburg by horse-drawn coaches in 1881. The eleven football players, without any financial or organizational help from older adults and with no coaches, found a way to make the contest happen. The game referee, James White, told part of the story, a couple generations later: "The team had no paid coach, no training table and none of the present day elaborate preparations," he said, "but only such practice on the front campus as could be easily managed by ordinary practice games between such teams or partial teams as could be mustered from day to day."[13] Fortunately, a rail line, scheduled to be built between Lewisburg, to the east of State College, and Tyrone, to the west, had tunneled westward through the low mountain near Coburn four years before, allowing a connection between Spring Mills and Lewisburg. The team, without any substitutes, and three other students, including officials James White and Irvin McCreary, took two horse-drawn rigs to Spring Mills, about twenty miles away, on a Friday afternoon, left the rigs at a livery, and hopped on the train. They then journeyed the remaining forty miles to Lewisburg, where they were "royally entertained" by the Lewisburg men as they awaited the Saturday, November 12, game.[14]

Penn State's first football game was held on a "muddy field in a drizzling rain and but little short of sleet," according to one participant. The Nittany Lions dressed in togs fashioned by a local tailor, "old Billy Hoover of Shingletown Gap," not by a deal from Nike from the more recent Joe Paterno era, in which the coach gained considerable wealth from the iconic international sportswear corporation for dressing his team in Nike blue and white. Dressed in matching uniforms in 1881, the Penn Staters overwhelmed the home team, 9–0, though no vivid descriptions of the game have been uncovered. As each kicked goal counted one point, the visitors must have produced nine goals (extra points) after touch downs or a combination of goals from the field (field goals) and "extra points"—a decisive victory.[15] Touchdowns counted for nothing, but they allowed a try at goal.

Because Penn State had no paid or unpaid coach, and certainly no assistant coaches, and there was no supportive athletic department as would be created in the near future, football depended completely on student interest. There was much more interest in baseball than in football after 1881, and after the initial game, football was dropped for the next half-decade. Interest in football grew nationally by the mid-1880s, when rugby was transformed into American football. It again arose at Penn State when a football team was organized in fall 1887. The students had formed an athletic association in 1887 and had supported three sports, baseball, tennis, and track and field until football arrived the second time.[16]

By 1887, Penn State players had chosen a team captain to run the team. The logical choice was freshman George Linsz, who had played football at the Episcopal Academy in Philadelphia—and the freshman owned the only football on campus. Because most of the less than 200 students lived in the five-story Old Main, the principal building on campus, it was natural for Linsz and another Philadelphian,

Charlie Hildebrand, to suggest playing some American football games, similar to those played at the time on the campus of the University of Pennsylvania, one of the college football's Big Four, along with Harvard, Yale, and Princeton. The two Philadelphians organized contests on the lawn just outside Old Main, readying the team that would eventually issue a challenge for the first contest in a half-dozen years. They evidently got in shape doing two activities, running and scrimmaging. The team members agreed to run in the early morning and scrimmage in the afternoon. According to *The Free Lance,* in its first year as the Penn State newspaper, "members of the Foot Ball team take a six-mile run every morning before breakfast, and they come in and devour a leg of mutton."[17] Conditioning by running was the hard work; the fun of scrimmaging followed class recitations. Three games were scheduled, but only two were played, home-and-home contests with the recently renamed Bucknell. The third game, scheduled with Dickinson College, was cancelled when the Dickinson men refused to pay Penn State a $40 guarantee for traveling expenses to Carlisle.[18]

The Penn Staters first traveled to Lewisburg, this time easier than it had been six years earlier. In 1885 the rail from Lewisburg to Spring Mills had been extended westward and around Mount Nittany to Lemont, and on to Bellefonte, ten miles northeast of Lemont. Now there was a rail station in the village of Lemont, two miles from Penn State, a short buggy ride for the team before the 60-mile train ride to Lewisburg.[19] The team was outfitted with Canton flannel pants and pink and black jersey colors, chosen by the student body. Unlike the previous trip to Lewisburg in 1881, the players asked an upper-class prelaw student, Clarence G. Cleaver, to be an advisory coach for the team.[20] In contrast to later, twentieth-century coaches, including Joe Paterno, the advisory coach had little of the dictatorial power exhibited by the power coach of big-time football. The advisory coach might advise, but the captain had the real power. This was true of most coaches and advisory coaches in other colleges at the time. If there was a coach, the captain or the team selected him, and the team or the captain got rid of him if they disapproved of his actions.

If advisory coach Cleaver had much influence, it is not clear. Penn State won 54–0 in Lewisburg in early November and won the return game at Penn State 24–0. The large scores were in part due to new rules in which a touchdown (by the modern definition) counted 2 points, the goal after a touchdown was 4 points, a goal from the field was 5 points, and a safety (being held down behind one's own goal) was 1 point, the four ways of scoring points.[21] Penn State now had its second undefeated team, winning a total of three games since 1881, all victories over Bucknell. There was not the hint of a scandal under student control, but that could easily change as winning became more important.

Penn State had some indifferent football teams for the next few years while the teams remained under the leadership of the student captain. The student-run Athletic Association provided financial and moral support for sports they deemed important, and the captain, not the coach, ran the team. President George Atherton, often considered the most important president in Penn State's history, provided office space in Old Main for the student-run Athletic Association, becoming what most presidents have been since then, cheerleaders for athletics.[22] Nevertheless there were no coaches until after the president, Board of Trustees, and faculty became involved.

President George Washington Atherton came to Penn State in 1882 from another land-grant institution, Rutgers, where, as a political scientist, he had studied the early years of the land-grant Morrill Act passed two decades before that provided valuable financial support for Penn State. Atherton wanted Penn State to advance by opening up the institution to future growth to surpass the agricultural emphasis it maintained since its beginnings a generation before as the Farmers' High School. He specifically wanted to expand the engineering offerings to meet the needs of an industrial nation. With the election of nearby Bellefonte's James A. Beaver (of Penn State's Beaver Stadium fame) as governor in 1886, greater funding and buildings came to Penn State from the state, including a botany building, a chemistry and physics building, an engineering building, and an armory. It is significant that enrollment at Penn State grew from only forty students in 1882, Atherton's first year, to 143 a decade later. Ninety-one of the 143 students were in the engineering program, and this trend continued into the twentieth century.[23]

Helping to save the teetering college in the 1880s, President Atherton became more involved in Penn State's football team and athletics in general. He was the first cheerleading president of many who were to lead Penn State. Before the armory was constructed in 1890, Atherton and the Board of Trustees agreed with the students that the basement of the armory could be used as a gymnasium, adding to a greater physical presence and contributing to the growth of intercollegiate athletics.[24] Most of the administrative help occurred after Penn State suffered its most dynamic loss in its football history, a 106–0 drubbing by Lehigh University, competing with a depleted team that played three games in four days in November 1889.[25] Soon the student newspaper, *The Free Lance*, called for a competent instructor for the gymnasium and for the team sports. In addition, a new football field was created (soon called Beaver Field) with baseball grounds enclosed by a quarter-mile running track and located just east of Old Main.[26]

The student-run Athletic Association petitioned the Board of Trustees for an "athletic instructor," because "our foot-ball men have never been properly trained." The association asked for a $1 per student gymnasium fee to pay for the instructor, who would increase "the reputation of P.S.C. as a college."[27] By fall 1891, President Atherton and the Board of Trustees authorized "a trainer for the foot-ball team," not to exceed eighty dollars per month, with the possibility of full-time employment. Besides looking for a trainer-coach, the football team also was given meals (a training table) and lodging at special quarters that fall. George W. Hoskins, a native Philadelphian, was chosen football trainer.

Hoskins had been involved in a variety of sports, including wrestling and track and field, but he also played football, baseball, and lacrosse. Prior to coming to Penn State, he had been trainer "coach" of the University of Vermont football team. Soon after arriving at Penn State, he was involved in the first spring practice for the football team.[28] Penn State was joining the big-time schools in not only hiring an individual to help turn out more winners but in holding spring practice like the big-time Ivy League schools. Hoskins did not run the team, however; at this point the captain still did. Nevertheless, Hoskins not only gave advice, but also was awarded three varsity letters for the 1892–94 seasons, participating with the team and beginning each offensive play as the team's center.[29] In his four years at Penn State, Hoskins helped give stability to Penn State athletics, notably track and baseball, including a composite record of 17 wins, 4 losses, and 4 ties by the time he left before the 1896 football season.[30] No one who followed would stay half the length of Joe Paterno, including the next physical director, Dr. Silvanus Newton, who was hired immediately after Hoskins's departure.

Unlike Hoskins, who lacked a significant academic pedigree, Silvanus Newton was a prep school graduate who earned his Ivy League–like education at Williams College in Massachusetts before going on to receive his medical degree from the University of Pennsylvania. Newton had even helped coach the football team at Trinity College (Duke) in North Carolina and at the University of Pennsylvania. Whether Newton could be considered the Penn State football coach is questionable. He was likely involved in some way during the first season of 1896 but was evidently dismissed during the next season by the captain, Max Curtin, who asked the former star player and son of the president, Charlie Atherton, to act as coach. Curtin also worked with an assistant coach, Henry Dowler, who had been a five-year veteran on the team before graduating in 1894.[31] Dowler is possibly the first Penn State assistant coach, possibly unpaid, and like Jerry Sandusky seven decades later, had been a lineman before returning to Penn State to coach. In his last year at Penn State, Newton played little or no role in training or coaching the team. He missed the two weeks of preseason practice at Hecla Park, fifteen miles east of Penn State, and the student newspaper, the *Free Lance*, reported that "The defects of the eleven are plainly due to what cannot truly be called poor coaching, but rather practically no coaching."[32] After three years of little coaching and little backing from the students, Newton left Penn State. The football record during those years was 12 wins and 14 losses.

Hiring no one as physical director for a year and a half, the Board of Trustees at the turn of the century eventually employed as physical director William N. "Pop" Golden, who arrived at Penn State to both take on the physical care of the entire student body and train and coach several athletic teams. His arrival coincided with the Board of Trustees decision to start giving athletic scholarships, a commitment by the trustees to turning out successful teams, especially in football.[33] Previously, Golden was trained in physical education and gave instruction particularly at several Young Men's Christian Associations (YMCAs). He had also been trainer for the Purdue University football team while working at the Lafayette, Indiana, YMCA, prior to coming to Penn State.

Golden came to Penn State for a yearly salary of $1,400, paid for by a mandatory $10 student gymnasium fee after a unanimous vote of the student body to subsidize athletics.[34] After leading the physical education program, coaching, and heading the intercollegiate athletic program for several years, Golden's salary was more than doubled so that it reached that of full professors, such as Henry Armsby, the director of Penn State's Agriculture Experimental Station and first dean of the School of Agriculture.[35] "Pop" Golden was successful in recruiting athletes to Penn State, a task made somewhat easier by the original ten athletic scholarships that the Board of Trustees provided in 1900 and, a few years later, by a recruiting budget that the Athletic Association provided. An early athletic scholarship recipient was William "Mother" Dunn, the initial Penn State first-string Walter Camp all-American, receiving the scholarship in 1902, retroactively to the previous fall because of "his extreme need of assistance."[36]

"Pop" Golden also led the campaign to raise money to build Penn State's first athletic dorm, the Track House, named because it was built near the outdoor track. The Track House provided room and board for the football team and a few other athletes after 1903. That year, when Golden had been appointed the first athletic director at Penn State, a fine athletic dorm was constructed just south of the track oval and paid for principally by surplus income from the gymnasium fee and income from room and board of the athletic scholarships.[37] It is not known who supervised the athletes in the Track House, but it is possible that an assistant coach directed the athletic dorm, as was the case with Joe Paterno in the early 1950s, when he was in charge of the Penn State athletic dorm in part of McKee Hall.[38] The three-story Track House for athletes included dorm rooms, a kitchen and dining room, a locker room with showers, an office, and a trophy room.[39] The Track House was constructed, ironically from an educational standpoint, before Andrew Carnegie agreed to build the first permanent library for the institution.[40]

"Pop" Golden arrived on campus at the turn of the century and has often been considered the head football coach. That may be an oversimplification, as a doctoral student once wrote: "Crediting Golden with being the football coach is a charitable usage of the term."[41] Scott Etter's dissertation well points out that Golden had some influence, but so did the captain, the historical decision maker for the football team. Golden's role included involvement with the important student-run Athletic Association and its Board of Directors, composed of three elected students. In addition, there was an Alumni Advisory Committee of the Athletic Association formed of alumni and persons drawn from the faculty or members of the senior class. The Advisory Committee advised the student team manager in financial matters and in the scheduling of games. The Athletic Association Constitution and By-Laws prescribed that the captain and the coach, with guidance of the Board of Directors, would select the team and place men in specific positions. Thus, Penn State's football, unlike baseball and track, which had prescribed coaches, was run by a conglomeration of captain, trainer-coach, alumni, students, and faculty.[42]

This may not have left much room for assistant coaches. Yet Ed Wood, an end on the 1899 team, assisted Penn State football in 1900. Having a coach from the previous year's team was common among most colleges at the turn of the century. In fact, many head coaches, as at Harvard and Yale, were generally the star players of the year before. Previous graduates at Penn State and elsewhere would come back for a short period to give advice, such as Carlton "Brute" Randolph, the 1899 captain and the first Walter Camp all-American (third string) from Penn State. Randolph "paid a visit" to the football team, according to *The Free Lance*, "to give the boys the benefit of his football experience." Wood, however, may have been the principal coach, and when he was absent, Golden filled in as a "good substitute," according to the student newspaper. Several years later, the captain of the 1900 and 1901 team, Henry Scholl, returned to assist in the coaching when the two Cornell graduates, Dan Reed for one year and Tom Fennell for five years, were considered the head coaches though often they were not present for the entire football season. "Pop" Golden continued to assist even after he had become athletic director.[43] Whether Golden should be considered the head coach is therefore difficult to answer. In any event, other coaches assisted Golden, some of whom were considered head coaches.

When Bill Hollenback, a local from Philipsburg who had starred at the University of Pennsylvania in 1908, was given the reins of football in 1909, he had one significant assistant, Henry Cooke "Irish" McIlveen, in 1911. McIlveen was given the title head coach because he was a Penn State graduate and Hollenback was not. Nevertheless, "Advisory Coach" Hollenback was the actual leader. Hollenback could be considered the most successful of the coaches between 1892 and his time, with a record of 28 wins, only 9 losses, and 3 ties—more than two-thirds victories—and three undefeated teams in his five years.[44] This compares favorably with Paterno's record, if not in longevity, for Paterno also won about two of every three games: 409 wins, 136 losses, and 3 ties, including five undefeated seasons in forty-six years.[45] Unlike Bill Hollenback, who had few assistant coaches, Paterno had eight assistants when he began as head coach in 1966 (Earl Bruce, Joe McMullen, Jim O'Hora, Frank Patrick, Bob Phillips, Dan Radakovich, George Welsh, and J. T. White). Hollenback apparently had only two assistants, "Irish" McIlveen and E. H. "Bull" McCleary, who was a 1909 Penn State graduate.

It was not easy for the student-run Athletic Association to finance assistant coaches because gate receipts generated less income than did the assessed student fees, which went principally to pay for the physical director-coach in the early years. For example, in 1908, coach Tom Fennell's salary for head coaching was $1,500 and the cost of the football training table was more than $1,000. The one big income day for the football team was the game in Pittsburgh against the University of Pittsburgh. That one game brought in a little more than $3,000 after the cost of sending the band to Pittsburgh was deducted. Athletic Association income provided for little financial support to any assistant coaches who might be hired. Income was so constrained that the Alumni Advisory Committee of the Athletic Association asked the students to drop basketball for two years, something the students refused to do.[46] Even as late as the mid-1920s, the student fee approximated the income generated by football gate receipts.[47] By then, there were at least four assistant coaches. None, however, would have the stature of assistant coach Jerry Sandusky in the 1980s.

There might be one exception—Dick Harlow. A star on the 1910 and undefeated 1911 teams, Harlow was invited to be an assistant coach the next fall under Bill Hollenback and, as it turns out, one of the greatest teams in Penn State's history, as the Nittany Lions defeated Cornell University, the University of Pennsylvania, Ohio State University, and the University of Pittsburgh. He assisted for the next two years, and when Hollenback departed, Harlow would move up to take charge. To supplement his assistant coaching salary, the Board of Trustees appointed Harlow the chief marshal of the dormitories at $12 per month, but with the important addition of providing a free room. The next year, the Board of Trustees appointed him a teaching fellow in zoology at $600 for the year.[48] Harlow, in this respect, was much like a young assistant coach at the University of Notre Dame who taught chemistry part-time to supplement his meager coaching salary.[49] Knute Rockne was hired by Jesse Harper in 1914 at $1,500, and like Dick Harlow, would become head coach after assisting for a few years.[50] Though Rockne became the icon of all football coaches, Harlow would also make a mark in the coaching profession, first at Penn State, then moving on to Colgate and Harvard, retiring in 1948.

An eventual Hall of Fame coach, Harlow decided to volunteer as a lieutenant in the infantry after the United States entered World War I. He had just received a three-year contract from the Athletic Association, but, because of strange circumstances, he was never honored as head coach when he returned. Penn State, needing a coach for its 1918 season, hired a recognized coach, Hugo Bezdek, a star under Amos Alonzo Stagg at the University of Chicago, who had coached successfully at both the University of Arkansas and the University of Oregon and at the time was baseball manager of the Pittsburgh Pirates. After World War I, Bezdek was kept on as coach and head of the physical education program at Penn State. When Harlow returned, there was no place for the previous head coach, and so he was offered the position of assistant coach under Bezdek. Penn State honored the salary of his contract of $2,100 and gave him an assistant professorship in physical education.[51] The likelihood of this chain of events working out satisfactorily was slim, though Harlow remained for three more years under Bezdek's leadership. Evidently Harlow did not feel comfortable working under

the autocratic rule of Hugo Bezdek and left after the 1921 season, generally turning out winners as head coach at Colgate, Western Maryland (where he coached
a future Penn State coach, Rip Engle), and Harvard until after World War II.

Except for Dick Harlow, no assistant coach for the first half-century of Penn
State football moved on to a significant position in the coaching ranks. This trend
continued, with a few exceptions through the Hugo Bezdek years of the 1920,
the Bob Higgins tenure in the Depression and the 1940s, the Rip Engle period of
the 1950s and 1960s, and the Joe Paterno era of almost a half-century. Paterno,
himself, was the major exception to the rule that Penn State assistant coaches did
not become highly successful head coaches. Jerry Sandusky might have become
another exception had he decided to take any of the positions offered to him,
and had he not succumbed to the temptation of violating young boys. Despite
Joe Paterno's words about his valued assistant coach in 1988 that Jerry Sandusky
had an "impeccable lifestyle" and a "commitment to human beings," this assistant
coach failed to meet one of Paterno's stated standards. "True success occurs,"
Paterno once emphasized, "if your values and your integrity have prevailed."[52]
No other assistant coach in Penn State's history had failed so completely in things
more valued than wins and losses.

CHAPTER 4

Alumni and Taking Control of Penn State Athletics

"Speak of the Moderns without contempt, and of the Ancients without
idolatry; judge them all by their merits; but not by their ages."
—Earl of Chesterfield (1748)

"For the Glory," begins the Penn State Alma Mater, words composed in 1901 by
Fred Lewis Pattee, professor of literature, whose name is immortalized on the
Penn State library building alongside its addition, immortalized in its own right
as the Paterno Library. A century plus a dozen years after the Alma Mater was
christened, Eileen Morgan and Ray Blehar, graduates of Penn State in the late
twentieth and early twenty-first centuries, quoted these three words to conclude
a diatribe against the Penn State Board of Trustees. The two members of the
alumni, in a page-long newspaper denunciation, blasted the trustees for not taking responsibility for the failures surrounding the Jerry Sandusky Scandal that
exploded in November 2011.[1] The two probably did not know that General James
Beaver, for whom the Penn State football stadium is named, was president of
the Board of Trustees when the song premiered at an Alumni Dinner at the 1901
Commencement. Beaver immediately called the song "the official song of Penn
State," although President Atherton questioned the song being named the Alma
Mater without his sanction.[2] The two Penn State alumni, along with many other
Penn State alumni, stated their view that if Penn State had a culture problem, "it
is not with the football program but with the members of the Board of Trustees."
Furthermore, they emphasized their opinion that Joe Paterno was not part of a
cover-up and that the Board of Trustees "should apologize for its unwarranted
firing of Paterno."[3] The alumni were on fire and possibly hotter than the results
of a football bonfire a century before that exploded when gasoline was poured
on the huge woodpile following a moral victory, a tie game with undefeated
Harvard in 1914.[4]

Alumni, who were once in control of Penn State athletics, may no longer
run athletics, but they have a great deal of influence affecting how Penn State
and athletics are conducted. Well into the twenty-first century, members of the
Penn State alumni are the largest dues-paying college alumni organization in the
world: the Penn State Alumni Association. The association is tied directly into

the athletic program, and especially football, more than it is into any other aspect of the institution. That has not changed since the first Penn State alumni chapter was formed in Pittsburgh in 1898 or the original issue of the Penn State *Alumni Quarterly* was produced more than a century ago. For example, the first alumni publication, the *Alumni Quarterly*, devoted about 40 percent of its pages to Penn State athletics in the October 1912 issue. On the same month a century later, the *Penn Stater*, the successor to that *Alumni Quarterly* and later the *Alumni News*, devoted more than 50 percent of the September–October issue to athletics. The unusually high percentage was a result of commentary on the Jerry Sandusky scandal.[5] The volume of athletic news going out to the Penn State alumni has been unrivaled by any other topic, and football has always dominated.

If the Penn State alumni had voted on the "firing" of Joe Paterno or the dismantling of the Joe Paterno statue next to Beaver Stadium, they almost surely would have voted no. These were two of the major reasons that the alumni voted to dispatch all alumni members of the Board of Trustees up for election in the years after the 2011 Sandusky Scandal and to elect others who were opposed to the treatment of coach Paterno.[6] The history of the alumni influence on Penn State athletics is not new, nor is it more controversial in the second decade of the twenty-first century than at any time in the previous one hundred or more years.

Organizing alumni was not unique to Penn State in the nineteenth century; it may have been little Williams College in Western Massachusetts that created the first alumni society in 1821, a half-century before Penn State did. At Williams, it was created, among other reasons, "to advance the reputation of our Alma Mater."[7] So it was with most alumni and their institutions of higher education, and so it was at Penn State. American athletics, once begun in 1852, were soon to be the central focus of alumni in the support of their colleges. Yale alumni contributions, for example, helped build a boathouse in the year before the Civil War and only eight years after the first intercollegiate contest, a boating contest between Yale and Harvard.[8] Alumni nearly everywhere came to support men's athletic teams they favored, generally football, baseball, crew, and track and field in the late 1800s. A critic of the alumni was Harvard's history professor Albert B. Hart. "If, as many alumni seem to suppose, the main function of Harvard University is to beat Yale at football and rowing," Hart complained in the early twentieth century, "then the university is in a bad way."[9]

As the alumni across America gave money, they came to take charge of athletics from the students, often in the form of graduate managers of athletics and the construction of athletic facilities. Generally this happened after two "D" events hit the student-run intercollegiate athletic programs—defeat and debts. Alumni were often embarrassed by defeats, just as Penn State alumni from Pittsburgh "fired" a once highly successful football coach in the 1920s, Hugo Bezdek, who could not defeat Pittsburgh. Alumni were also asked to pick up the deficits caused by student athletic leaders who spent more than they took in for the athletic contests, and this occurred at Penn State in the early 1900s.[10]

Probably no alumni group ever gave more financially in the early years of college athletics than the Harvard class of 1879, who for their twenty-fifth anniversary gave the Harvard Athletic Committee the enormous sum of $100,000 to build America its first steel-reinforced stadium.[11] One of the few leading college presidents ever to not cheerlead college football, President Charles Eliot of Harvard, made sure that all those interested knew that Harvard University did not contribute a cent to its stadium construction, believing that it was astonishing for a class gift to be given to build a stadium at an academic institution.[12] Even Eliot, the best-known and most powerful president of any college or university in America in those days, could not prevent the alumni from building a monument in honor of football. The classical 1903 structure, with Greek columns, was later named a National Historic Landmark along with the football stadiums used principally by colleges, the Yale Bowl and the Rose Bowl.

Penn State's colossal Beaver Stadium never reached the status of a National Historic Landmark, but the alumni followed where the major institutions of higher education led in athletics.[13] An alumni association was born, and athletics were eventually taken over by the alumni. But not at first. The Penn State Alumni Association was established in an Old Main chemistry lecture room in 1870. It was a kind of homecoming celebration, at which a professor of chemistry, A. A. Breneman, class of 1866, was elected president and John I. Thompson, class of 1862, son of a founder of the university, Moses Thompson, was elected secretary-treasurer.[14] Penn State had no intercollegiate sports to support at the time. By the mid-1870s, when baseball was played, and in the early 1880s, with football's first game, alumni soon became interested in the activities that would bring prestige to Penn State. The students organized the Athletic Association in the late 1880s to raise funds and support athletics, but the students soon asked the alumni to give greater financial support as was occurring in other eastern colleges.

Just before Penn State's first major undefeated season in 1894, the students of the Athletic Association voted to create a committee of five alumni, to be named the Alumni Advisory Committee of the Athletic Association, whom the students would elect "to devise ways and means for raising funds for the development of several branches of athletics." These funds would be controlled by the Advisory Committee.[15] For the next decade, with students running the Athletic Association, the alumni were greatly involved in making recommendations to the students, especially after the student managers of the various sports spent money beyond their ability to pay. An alumnus and faculty member became treasurer of the student Athletic Association as a direct result of student treasurer William Cochran "losing" more than $100 of athletic money in his possession and being "held responsible for all the money." As a result, the dean of the School of Natural Science, George "Swampy" Pond, class of 1892, was made treasurer.[16] The alumni agreed to try to keep the teams out of debt if the Penn State students would agree to pay up all past debts. Students then voted to give their remaining school damage deposits to the association to pay off their indebtedness.[17]

The alumni went farther in support of successful athletics with the leadership of one of them, Professor of Electrical Engineering J. Price Jackson, chair of the alumni committee. Jackson sent President Atherton a dire call for help for the football team after the unsuccessful football season of 1899. Jackson wrote that the Advisory Committee had

> come to the point where we find it absolutely necessary to call upon you for the sum of money which you so generously agreed to advance for student [athletic] aid. I, personally, and I am sure the remainder to the Committee, feel that this action is a very hard one to take. We are, however, due to the unsuccessful football season, in such a position that it will be only possible by the most earnest endeavor to put ourselves on a solid financial basis.[18]

This was the alumni stimulus for the first athletic scholarships authorized by a board of trustees in American colleges; ten by 1900, sixteen by 1902, and twenty-five by 1905—and seventy-five by the 1920s.[19]

Soon after the initiation of athletic scholarships, the position of graduate manager of athletics was created at Penn State. It came on Thanksgiving night of 1907 after Penn State lost to Pittsburgh 6–0 before a large crowd of 11,000 in the Steel City. A group of alumni formed the Association of Penn State Managers and Captains from past Penn State athletic teams and decided to meet with student leaders to move beyond only an alumni treasurer. They wanted all athletics to be controlled by a manager who was an alumnus. The position of graduate manager was the closest approximation of an athletic director; the position existed at the English universities of Oxford and Cambridge and later some eastern U.S. colleges created the position in the 1880s and 1890s.[20] At Penn State in 1907, the alumni soon met with the students of the Athletic Association, convincing the students that it was in their best interests to have alumni control of the generation-old student-controlled athletics.[21] The students agreed, and the *State Collegian* editorialized, "In many colleges the alumni have practically full charge of athletic affairs."[22] True at Penn State even though William "Pop" Golden at the time was both physical director of the entire student body and was soon made athletic director. When Golden was hired in 1900, the Board of Trustees dictated that "as far as possible," Golden should "act as 'coach' for the training of the several athletic teams."[23] Nevertheless, the graduate manager wielded much of the athletic power until after World War I and to a great extent until after World War II.

When Golden was on the faculty as athletic director, George Meek, class of 1890, the graduate manager, had more power than the athletic director had. (When Golden resigned in 1912, the position of athletic director was terminated.[24]) Meek had not been an athlete, but he was student manager of three teams, football, baseball, and tennis, before he graduated. He was also recognized by the students as editor of the student newspaper, *Free Lance,* and was the first editor of *La Vie,* the student yearbook. Meek, likely, also was the individual who influenced the choice of the first football colors, cerise (pink) and black, prior to the change to navy blue and white.[25] He was on the first Alumni Advisory Committee of the Athletic Association after he graduated. He had a strong Penn State pedigree, and rather than a salary, Meek was paid 10 percent of receipts of all games away from home—receipts were generally based on expense money, "guarantees," offered by the home team.[26] It was not a highly paid position, but Meek essentially ruled athletics. This was true despite the Faculty Senate passing a resolution that the "Faculty Committee on Athletics shall have jurisdiction over all athletic contests, and all arrangement for athletic contests."[27] Like later faculty committees dealing with athletics, they generally acted as rubber stamps for what athletics and the athletic managers were interested in doing. With well over half of the Penn State's faculty being Penn State graduates, generally no major conflicts occurred with faculty, who might have questioned a strong athletic program. A faculty member who had graduated from Dartmouth concluded that he had never known a college "where athletics were more highly favored and encouraged, particularly by the faculty."[28] Even if the faculty had differed, Penn State's faculty never had a great deal of control over Penn State athletics, reflecting the situation at most institutions of higher education throughout the twentieth century and into the twenty-first.

George Meek moved quickly in an attempt to bring the athletic indebtedness under control. "The trouble appears to have been," Meek explained, that "in the past, there was no one who knew exactly what bills had been contracted, and, a consequence, the Association was living beyond its income. There seems to have been a general disposition to go ahead without thought of how the bills were to be paid."[29] Meek had to persuade student managers of each sport to have stricter accounting of expenses. These included responsibility for equipment, which was often misplaced; training table expenses that athletes were expected to pay; and the cost of the sport of basketball, which was running a deficit. In fact, the Alumni Advisory Committee recommended dropping basketball in 1910, arguing that the sport "is always a losing venture and its deficits must be made up by other departments."[30] The student-run athletic association vetoed the alumni suggestion, and basketball continued.

The alumni and the Alumni Advisory Committee were not solely interested in winning teams at Penn State. After George Meek resigned as graduate manager and Pearl "P. E." Thomas was elected to that position in 1909, the Alumni Advisory Committee raised the question "What can Penn State do for the 90% of non-varsity athlete students?" The committee wanted the Department of Physical Education, created by the Board of Trustees in 1908, to "bring out something more than a few teams of highly trained athletes." The alumni group, thinking only of males and not of the few women at Penn State, suggested that "the college graduate of today needs more than mental strength; he must have a healthy and sturdy body . . . and must know how to keep that body in proper condition."[31]

After "Pop" Golden resigned as physical director in 1912, the Alumni Advisory Committee asked the Board of Trustees for a "more up to date system of physical education" for all students, something the Board of Trustees soon acted upon.[32] Within a year, the Board of Trustees appointed two trustees and the president of Penn State, Edwin Sparks, to a committee to "frame a complete system of physical education."

Thus was born a comprehensive plan not only for intercollegiate athletics but also physical activities for all students. It included medical examinations, corrective activities, hygiene instruction, recreational sports, and intramurals along with west campus recreation fields.[33] Along with it was a new athletic eligibility code advocated by both students and alumni, including a one-year residency prior to participation for all transfer students, no graduate school participation, and only four years of athletic participation. A freshman ineligibility rule, advocated by the Alumni Advisory Committee, and three years of athletic eligibility were soon added.[34] Combining academics with physical activity and athletics was a kind of "grand experiment" first advocated by the alumni. Alumni at Penn State may have been different from many alumni groups across America, for athletics at Penn State, while important and the most visible part of physical activity, was to be combined with the physical well-being of the entire college. The Grand Experiment of Joe Paterno dealt only with his football program and a proper education for his players; the alumni of the 1910s at Penn State, in contrast, were promoting mental and physical benefits for the entire student body as well as a big-time athletics program under a graduate manager. With a graduate manager, Penn State had undefeated football teams in 1909, 1911, and 1912, and was undefeated in 1914 until the bonfire explosion celebrating a 13–13 tie against undefeated Harvard severely injured the football captain, Yeggs Tobin, and Penn State's winning spiraled downward. The years between 1908, when the position of graduate manager was created, and World War I, during which even a Women's Athletic Association without alumni support was created, were the high point of graduate control of Penn State athletics.

Much of the change in the emphasis on big-time sports as well as sports for all students came under the leadership of Ray Smith, graduate manager from 1911 to 1918. Like P. E. Thomas before him, Smith was a graduate, class of 1905 (in electrical engineering), and after graduating was on the Alumni Advisory Committee of the Athletic Association. To promote and recruit athletes for Penn State, Smith was involved in creating a letterman's club at a Penn State–Pitt football game in 1913. It was called the Varsity Club. He became treasurer of the organization while Dick Harlow, an assistant football coach and later head coach, was chosen president.[35] Smith remained graduate manager until after the U.S. entry into World War I. He then rose from graduate manager of athletics to comptroller of Penn State. It was a progression similar to that of Steve Garban, who, after his football career as captain of the team while Joe Paterno was an assistant coach, moved from athletic administration to university business administration in the early 1970s in part "because of his experience in and knowledge of athletics."[36]

With Ray Smith and the alumni in control of athletics, Penn State gave Dick Harlow a two-year football contract after his initial one-year agreement.[37] Unfortunately, Penn State, under Harlow, lost to Pittsburgh, 20–0, 31–0, and 28–6, in the three years from 1915 to 1917. After the first year of his two-year contract, the Alumni Advisory Committee decided Penn State needed a more open offense and brought in an outsider from Western Reserve in Cleveland, Zen Scott, to be "field coach" while Harlow would be the "resident coach." This was a situation waiting to become a territorial conflict.[38] Losing to Pittsburgh brought down the wrath of many Penn State alumni from the Steel City. Just after the Thanksgiving Day game against Pittsburgh that year, Harlow, with one year left on his contract, was fed up with the coaching of Scott and told the Athletic Committee that if the committee did not get rid of Scott, then he would quit. Harlow's threat bore fruit after the third straight loss to Pitt. When the season concluded, the Athletic Association offered Harlow a one-year contract, which he rejected.[39] During negotiations, he demanded a multiyear contract despite the embarrassing losses to Pittsburgh and its legendary national champion coach Glenn "Pop" Warner. Nevertheless, the head of the Alumni Advisory Committee of the Athletic Association, Pittsburgh industrialist C. W. Heppenstall, and graduate manager Smith agreed to give Harlow a three-year contract.[40] Zen Scott was gone after his brief tenure at Penn State. Ironically, Scott soon took the head coaching position at the University of Alabama, coaching for four years with a 29-9-3 record, a team that Joe Paterno a half-century and more later could never defeat while a more famous Alabaman, Bear Bryant, was coach.[41]

To complicate the situation, Dick Harlow never became head coach under his new contract because he volunteered to join the war effort as an officer in the U.S. Army. He did not enlist in the army until just before the 1918 football season, when he asked to be released from his contract, but said that he would return to Penn State. Harlow volunteered at almost the exact time that Levi Lamb, a name that would resonate in Happy Valley and with Penn State alumni, was killed in the Second Battle of the Marne in Picardie, France. Lamb was a former football substitute playing with Harlow on the undefeated Penn State team in 1911 and then started on the undefeated team the next year when Harlow was an assistant coach. Lamb went into the service soon after graduating, and he, along with another star player and teammate, James "Red" Bebout, was killed in action.[42] Harlow joined the military late and became a trainer of soldiers and coach of the Virginia Polytechnic Institute (Virginia Tech) undefeated football team in the final days before the Armistice.[43]

Levi Lamb, a well-liked Penn Stater, kept his fellow graduates informed of his situation in the trench warfare while he devoured the *Alumni Quarterly* sent to him on the front. "One never knows how to appreciate such things until they are isolated as we are. When in the front lines," he wrote Ray Smith, graduate manager of athletics and editor of the *Alumni Quarterly*, "one can scarcely be more isolated." Writing from a trench about twenty feet below ground level, he said that it was "thoroughly infested with rats. . . . The men have great sport sitting on their bunks and trying to bayonet one." In appreciation of Penn State alumni, he wrote, "So far I have not seen a State man, but have seen men who have, and right on the spot I began to like them."[44] Weeks later he was dead, but not forgotten. The Levi Lamb Grant-in-Aid Fund was founded in 1952, merging with the Penn State Scholarship Fund for aiding athletes.[45]

As soon as the war was over, Dick Harlow returned to Penn State, but as an assistant coach rather than head coach. When Harlow had left, Penn State's Alumni Advisory Committee had quickly made a search for not only a new head football coach but also for a person who could take charge of a full program of physical education and athletics. The recommendation to the Board of Trustees was an individual who had trained at the University of Chicago under tenured professor and coach Amos Alonzo Stagg. Hugo Bezdek had starred at fullback for Stagg's great teams in the early 1900s and had played baseball as well. Bezdek had successfully coached at the University of Arkansas and the University of Oregon before becoming manager of the faltering Pittsburgh Pirates in major league baseball from 1917 to 1919. One week after hiring Bezdek at $4,500 as an associate professor, Athletic General Manager Ray Smith was elevated to become comptroller at Penn State, a position he would fill for about two decades.[46] His assistant, Neil Fleming, class of 1914, was chosen to fill his place, and he continued in that position through the successes and failures of Hugo Bezdek in the 1920s and until after World War II. Fleming witnessed the greatness and making of an icon of coach Hugo Bezdek and his unraveling as football defeats to Pittsburgh mounted when Penn State alumni living in Pittsburgh successfully fought to remove him.[47]

Penn State alumni then and nearly a century later could help dictate athletic policy, whether it was to remove a past athletic icon or to help restore iconic stature of a vilified one in the controversial 2012 Louis Freeh report following the Sandusky Scandal. Was the Englishman, the Earl of Chesterfield, correct when he stated, "Speak of the Moderns without contempt, and of the Ancients without idolatry; judge them all by their merits; but not by their ages"?[48] We can see the similarities in the iconic images of both Hugo Bezdek with a record 30 games without a defeat in the early 1920s and that of Joe Paterno with a similar record a half-century later. Alumni then and more recently have had their impact upon winning idols when periods of darkness descended.

CHAPTER 5

Hugo Bezdek's Saga—Alumni, Trustees, and Presidents

"Penn State College . . . illustrates absolute alumni control."
—Carnegie Foundation for the Advancement of Teaching, *American College Athletics* (1929)

One can argue that the two most significant football coaches in Penn State's history have been Joe Paterno and Hugo Bezdek. The two had a number of similarities. Both were outsiders from private universities; Bezdek from the University of Chicago and Paterno from Brown University. Each was a star on his collegiate team, Bezdek as a pile-driving fullback with the famous Amos Alonzo Stagg teams at Chicago in the early 1900s and Paterno as a brainy quarterback under a future Penn State coach, Rip Engle, at Brown in the late 1940s. Both in their early coaching careers had stretches of being undefeated for thirty or more games and with that gained power and prestige as outstanding coaches of their time. Both were very opinionated and often hard to endure. Both could make demands upon Penn State, with threats of leaving Penn State early in their careers. Both had very dark periods ending their careers as coaches. Yet both left legacies that would last for generations, while only Joe Paterno is likely to be remembered. Hugo Bezdek, as important as he was, resonated little among the alumni or the general public before, during, or after the Joe Paterno era. Bezdek was mostly forgotten even though he was more successful earlier in his career at Penn State than was Paterno.

While the war in Europe raged in the summer of 1918, and after Dick Harlow had left coaching football for the military, the Alumni Advisory Committee of the Athletic Association recommended to the Board of Trustees that it hire Hugo Bezdek to be director of Physical Education and to coordinate all intercollegiate sports. Born in Prague, Czechoslovakia, he and his parents emigrated to the tough south side of Chicago, where he engaged in professional boxing and attended the University of Chicago in the early 1900s, playing fullback for Amos Alonzo Stagg's dominating teams. One of those teams ended Michigan's and coach Fielding H. Yost's undefeated streak of fifty-six games. Upon graduation, he began coaching, assisting Stagg for one year at Chicago, and then serving as a successful head coach at the University of Arkansas and the University of Oregon. At Oregon, his unbeaten Ducks went to the Rose Bowl and defeated the University of Pennsylvania 14–0. During World War I, he coached the Mare Island Marines, located north of San Francisco, to another Rose Bowl victory, this time over the Fort Lewis Army team from the state of Washington.[1]

Achieving star-quality coaching status at a younger age than did Joe Paterno, Bezdek was asked in the midst of the summer of 1917 to manage the lowly Pittsburgh Pirates, a major league baseball team he had scouted for since 1909. He took a last-place team to fourth place in a year. At the same time that Bezdek was achieving some success in Pittsburgh, Dick Harlow stepped out of coaching to enter the First World War. Bezdek was available. He was offered the position at Penn State and was allowed, at the same time, to continue his three-year contract to manage the Pirates. As soon as the wartime baseball season was over, he moved to State College to coach a war-debilitated team, which a number of team members had left to volunteer for military service. All Penn State games during September and October were canceled, and the team won one of four in November. Bezdek was not off to a strong start, but when the war concluded in November, a group of war veterans returned, including Lieutenant Dick Harlow, now as assistant coach.[2]

Bezdek did not come cheaply, but the Alumni Association was willing to pay dearly for someone who, though not the most beloved, might be able to defeat Pittsburgh. His associate professor contract for 1918 as coach and director of Physical Education was $4,500, $1,200 coming from Penn State and the rest paid by the Alumni Association. Harlow was retained at a salary of $2,100, and the new graduate manager, Neil Fleming, class of 1914, was at $1,800.[3] Winning, however, would greatly raise the value of Hugo Bezdek to Penn State and its athletic program.

In Bezdek's second season, after an early loss to Dartmouth, Penn State's team went thirty games without a defeat, even after some player conflicts with Bezdek arose from his harsh and negative treatment of players. According to one assistant coach, Dutch Herman, when Bezdek first met with the 1919 players, which included many war veterans, his approach or manner did not sit well with some of the athletes. Bezdek arrived after managing the Pirates that fall with a well-planned reception on Beaver Field. The band was there along with many students. "He came running on the field in a Pirate uniform with his cap on backwards," according to Herman. "Run 'em up and down there," Bezdek yelled to the assistant coaches and the team members. "After one trip up and down the field, Bez just hollered out one word: 'Lousy!'" Herman continued: "There wasn't a sound from the players until Dick Rauch, an interior lineman, gave a great loud honking sound. Bez never found out who had made the reply. But Bez had established his character, he had shown everyone who was boss and that he was going to be a tough boss." Herman recalled, "many of the players always hated him. His entrance hadn't endeared him to many."[4] Or as another former player recalled, "Bez was generally heartless—a rough merciless person on the field."[5]

Like Joe Paterno, who many players called the "Rat" for his high-pitched and penetrating negative voice and facial features behind his horn-rimmed dark glasses, Hugo Bezdek was disliked by many of his players during his dozen years as coach. Yet, like Paterno, he won early in his career, and there were fears that, like Paterno a half-century later, he might move on to another position. During his 7–1 season in 1919, he was given a significant three-year contract at $7,500 per year, when the average salary of a Penn State professor was about $2,000.[6] Bezdek's salary might be compared favorably to the $5,000 salary paid to Harvard's successful coach in 1920, Robert Fisher, and Princeton's long-time coach, Bill Roper, who received $6,500 a few years later.[7] Higher attendance at football games and a raise in the student athletic fee by 50 percent to a hefty $15 per year helped pay for the high coaching salary and expanded sport facilities for all students.[8] By the next year, Bezdek received a seven-year contract at $10,000 with the Athletic Association paying the increase.

By 1921, with a 30-game undefeated streak and a new Penn State president, the Bezdek ante was raised to $14,000 and a bonus of $2,000, more than President John Thomas was being paid. It was significantly more than the president of the most prestigious university in America was making; Harvard's president, A. Lawrence Lowell, was paid $2,000 less at that time.[9] The following year, Bezdek was given a 10-year contract at $14,000, tripling his salary in four years.[10] The new athletic cheerleading president Thomas wrote an article titled "Why I Believe in Football" and called Bezdek "the greatest coach and athletic director in the United States" and "a great 'stabilizer' of student morale and student morals on the campus."[11] President Thomas was the first Penn State president to attempt to make the institution into a true university such as Illinois, Michigan, and Wisconsin with professional schools and graduate programs and an emphasis on research—and at the same time competing in big-time athletics.[12] Thomas, however, was successful only in promoting big-time intercollegiate sport while Penn State remained a college without university status until after World War II. Thomas knew that Penn State must pay dearly for a top-quality coach. "If we compete in intercollegiate athletics," he told a newspaper reporter, "we must have a coach; if we have a coach we must have a good one; to get a good one, we must pay the price."[13] The value of Bezdek as coach had risen after Bezdek was offered a rumored $20,000-per-year, three-year contract to manage the Philadelphia Phillies baseball team in the National League. He also had an offer to return to coach at the University of Oregon, and the University of Minnesota courted him. Campaigns to keep Bezdek arose, and the Women's Student Government Association at Penn State proclaimed "We want you," something similar to the "Joe Don't Go Pro" campaign, an attempt to keep Joe Paterno at Penn State in the early 1970s.[14]

Hugo Bezdek was a hero to many, not only for winning football games, but also for expanding the sport facilities and opportunities at Penn State. Shortly after Bezdek arrived at Penn State, *Outing Magazine* carried a lengthy article titled "Everybody Playing at Penn State." This was a program of mass athletics, something stimulated by the U.S. entry into World War I. With the advocacy of Bezdek, a hundred-acre playing field on the west campus was used to accommodate more than two thousand students at one time. It included a nine-hole golf course, twelve football fields, forty tennis courts, ten basketball courts, six volleyball courts, two hockey rinks, and a half-mile cinder track. Competitive leagues, for men, were organized in football, baseball, basketball, track, volleyball, tennis, boxing, wrestling, and pushball contests, culminating in what he called a Hippodrome Field Day nine days before the armistice concluded the war.[15] This, along with his winning record, endeared him with the alumni. Penn State, by the end of the decade, with Bezdek's leadership, had constructed an indoor arena seating five thousand, the Recreation Building; built a new "jock" house called Varsity Hall (today's Irvin Hall) to replace the old Track House; expanded Beaver Field to twenty thousand seats that including a new grandstand; built a new baseball field; created a Willie Park–designed golf course; constructed a number of intramural fields; got the faculty and administration to rearrange schedules to allow for daily afternoon mass athletics at 4:30; increased the number of athletic scholarships to seventy-five, and helped purchase new uniforms for the Penn State band.[16] He even, unsuccessfully, advocated that Penn State be part of an Eastern Conference to include all the future Ivy League institutions, plus Pittsburgh and Syracuse, but, like Joe Paterno two generations later, was a failure in his promotion of a conference in the East for football and all sports.[17]

All of that, but Bezdek, with his unpleasant personality, lost continuously to the University of Pittsburgh, leading to his downfall. For Bezdek's first four years, his record was 23 wins and only 5 losses and only 1 loss in the previous three years. He even beat Pitt once and tied the Steel City team three times. From 1922 through 1929, he had 42 wins and 27 losses, but eight of those losses were successive ones to Pitt, scoring only 26 points to 191 for the University of Pittsburgh. How embarrassing to the Penn State alumni living in and around Pittsburgh. Was it any wonder that the call for Bezdek's head came from Penn State's first alumni club, the Alumni Association of Pittsburgh?

The decline of success occurred the same year Dick Harlow decided to leave Penn State and once again become a head coach. Most athletes who played for him before he entered the army in 1918 apparently loved Harlow. When he returned as an assistant coach, there was some conflict between him and coach Bezdek. Glenn Killinger, the all-American quarterback in Bezdek's early years, noted that he "was always a Bezdek man & against Harlow & the western [Pittsburgh] alumni."[18] Hinkey Haines, who played at the same time as Killinger and later played baseball with the New York Yankees and football with the New York Giants, called Bezdek "a hard, harsh, unsympathetic man," who would shout out his important position with an "'I am the Czar.'"[19] Bezdek was generally either loved or hated by those who played for him, not unusual for most coaches, including Joe Paterno; there seemed to be no middle ground. Though Harlow coached with Bezdek for a couple years, he decided to take an offer from Colgate.

When Harlow departed to coach the Hamilton, New York, football team after the 1921 season, Bezdek might have been relieved, for it appeared that Harlow was much more popular with the players than Bezdek was as head coach. This was observed when there was a mass meeting of students to say goodbye to Harlow. There, the students presented Harlow with a watch, an action that "made Bez mad," according to Joe Bedenk, who played with both Glenn Killinger and Hinkey Haines on the great Bezdek teams of the early 1920s and who would coach both baseball and football at Penn State into the Rip Engle era in the 1950s.[20] What disturbed Bezdek even more were the six disgruntled players who transferred, all following Harlow to his new position, as when several players followed coach James Franklin after he left Vanderbilt University for Penn State in 2014.[21] Harlow had a fine 24–9–3 record at Colgate before leaving for Western Maryland, where he coached a future Penn State coach, Rip Engle. At Western Maryland with big-time football then, he produced great teams and was 61–12–7 before taking the head coaching position at Harvard 1935 and coaching the Crimson until after World War II, while also serving as a professor and curator of the Harvard Museum of Comparative Zoology for a quarter-century.[22] With the talented Harlow gone, Bezdek continued with modest success, except he never again beat Pitt.

The six players leaving Penn State for Colgate in 1922 may have been the beginning of an eventual failure to satisfy the Penn State alumni who controlled athletics even as Bezdek was also athletic director. Nevertheless, after the fall 1922 season and a 6–3–1 record, Penn State was invited to the 1923 Rose Bowl in Pasadena, California. They were invited not for their just completed season but because Bezdek had been so successful in the previous years. In June, well before the 1922 season, the Alumni Advisory Committee of the Athletic Association authorized acceptance of the expected Carnival of Roses Committee invitation to the next Rose Bowl. Yet, as late as October, there was no formal invitation, and in early December, the Alumni Advisory Committee was discussing a possible postseason game with Vanderbilt, and a game with West Virginia University was held in reserve.[23] Finally, an official Rose Bowl invitation was extended to play the University of Southern California (USC). Though Penn State lost to USC, a major benefit of playing at the Rose Bowl was the nearly $22,000 net receipts paid to the Athletic Association. The money was quickly given to President Thomas's Emergency Building Fund, begun in 1921 in an attempt to raise $2 million. The Rose Bowl money was earmarked for an athletic dorm and facility, eventually completed in 1924 as Varsity Hall.[24]

Rumblings about the coaching abilities of Hugo Bezdek and his inability to beat Pitt came by the mid-20s. Bezdek's ten-year contract, however, written in 1922, probably the longest in the nation, gave him considerable security. To get rid of

Bezdek and have to pay off years of a salary higher than the college president's would be a stiff load for the Athletic Association to carry financially. Three years after his long-term contract and a fourth straight loss to Pittsburgh, the Penn State Alumni Club of Pittsburgh appointed a Committee on College Relations, a euphemism for looking at how losing to Pittsburgh might affect Penn State College. The committee reported to the Penn State Alumni Association by spring 1926. The influential Pittsburgh group of Penn State alumni called for the elimination of the Alumni Advisory Committee and the creation of a new Athletic Council, without Hugo Bezdek on it, to take control of athletics.[25]

When Bezdek heard of the alumni recommendations, he wrote to the president of Harvard University, A. Lawrence Lowell, about the role of athletics in higher education. "Do you think," Bezdek wrote, "that it is advisable to have the control and dictation of athletic policies in the hands of the Alumni?" If not, he wanted a suggestion from Lowell on who should have control. Lowell quickly replied that Harvard had just begun "an experiment of putting the control of athletics into the hands of an athletic director" not appointed by the alumni as Harvard had traditionally done with a graduate manager, but one "appointed by the University authorities."[26] Thus, Harvard was going through similar questions about who controlled athletics in institutions of higher education. This complicated question existed through the years at Penn State, and the control of athletics was a major question at the time that Joe Paterno was removed as coach shortly after the Jerry Sandusky Scandal broke in 2011.

The Penn State alumni, however, were nearly supreme in control of athletics in the mid-1920s, and they agreed that action must be taken. The Alumni Association appointed a new committee headed by John Beaver White, class of 1894, to make recommendations for the improvement of athletics at Penn State. The Beaver White Committee surveyed alumni, faculty, and some students, and presented a report in early 1927. The influential Beaver White Committee made several recommendations to the Alumni Association that eventually changed the way athletics would be administered and affected the tenure of Hugo Bezdek as football coach. First, the committee recommended a new Board of Athletic Control to replace the Alumni Advisory Committee of the Athletic Association. The board would have more alumni representatives than representatives from other university interests, but it would also have representatives from students, faculty, and the Board of Trustees. Second, the head of the Physical Education Department (Bezdek) would not be allowed to coach, and the department would be separated from the athletic program. Third, and surprisingly, athletic scholarships would be eliminated.[27]

The reason the committee wanted to separate the Physical Education Department from coaching was rather obvious. The committee wanted to eliminate Hugo Bezdek, with his long-term contract, from continuing to coach. It would allow him to remain, if he wished, as head of the Physical Education program. To further isolate athletics from physical education, the Board of Athletic Control would not have to deal with the physical education program and other sport programs for the students. Thus the supervision of men's intercollegiate athletics, the Board of Athletic Control desired, would be separate from the supervision of other physical activity programs.

The motivation to recommend elimination of athletic scholarships was more complicated but logical from some points of view. Nationally, there was a great deal of bad publicity about college athletics in the 1920s because of its growing crass commercialism and professionalism. This criticism was especially aimed at athletes who were aided financially by alumni or the university to participate primarily in football. The stadium building, especially after World War I, added to the professional and commercial aspect of college sport that had already manifested itself before the war with giant stadiums at Harvard, Yale, and Princeton.[28] The controlling faculty representatives of the National Collegiate Athletic Association, formed after a 1905 crisis in football, called for an investigation of professionalism and commercialism in college sport two decades later in an effort to keep football amateur.[29] In less than a half-year after it was announced in 1926 that the Carnegie Foundation for the Advancement of Teaching would make a thorough study of college athletics, Penn State alumni, who largely controlled athletics, began their own internal study.[30] A significant number of Penn State alumni believed that the scholarship athletes at Penn State were not only discouraging nonscholarship students from participating in competitive athletics but that athletic scholarships showed poor sportsmanship by being contrary to the spirit of amateurism.[31] When a Penn State alumnus from Philadelphia asked "if it might not be impractical at present to eliminate athletic scholarships owing to the practices followed at other colleges and universities?" John Beaver White responded, "The sentiment is growing everywhere against athletic scholarships." However untrue that might have been, White pointed to the Carnegie Foundation research favoring true amateurism and indicated that Penn State would gain status by eliminating athletic scholarships.[32] It is surprising that, when the Penn State alumni were asked to vote on the proposition at meetings in Pittsburgh, Philadelphia, Wilkes-Barre, Harrisburg, and State College, more than three-fourths of the alumni voted to eliminate athletic scholarships.[33] The *Penn State Alumni Newsletter* editorialized, "Maybe we can develop better teams by spending on additional coaches some of the money spent today on scholarships."[34] As history would show, maybe not.

The Beaver White Committee and alumni involvement resulted in a new Board of Athletic Control banning athletic scholarships beginning in 1928. "The Great Experiment" commenced—winning without athletic scholarships and obtaining athletes from the general student body. The coaching career for Hugo Bezdek was doomed. He could no longer recruit a sufficient number of quality athletes to satisfy the controlling alumni, especially those in Pittsburgh, who experienced only one Penn State victory over Pittsburgh in fourteen tries. With the University of Pittsburgh paying its players in the 1920s up to $100 a month and with no scholarships at Penn State, the odds were strongly stacked against the Nittany Lions no matter who coached.[35]

The beginning of Penn State's athletic reform by doing away with scholarships came just as a new president, Ralph Dorn Hetzel, came on the scene. Hetzel opposed big-time college athletics, and he pointed that out early in his tenure as president. "I have seen many colleges suffer grievously at the hands of a football team," Hetzel told students at a 1927 mass meeting, "which was on the right side of the score but on the wrong side of wholesome college ideals."[36] Another 26–0 shutout by Pittsburgh in 1928 may not have concerned President Hetzel a great deal, but the Pittsburgh contingent of Penn State alumni was highly dissatisfied. After that loss, both the president and secretary of the Penn State alumni club in Pittsburgh addressed the Penn State Board of Trustees complaining that most athletic teams at Penn State were maintaining high standards while football was not. "We earnestly believe that there should be a change in the present foot-ball coaching system," the trustees were told.[37]

The Board of Trustees quickly formed a committee of three, Jesse B. Warriner, William L. Affelder, and Furman H. Gyger—the Warriner Committee—to study the athletic situation and give recommendations to the entire Board of Trustees. The Warriner Committee soon got plenty of advice from Charles Heppenstall, a wealthy and influential alumnus from the Pittsburgh area. Using language that sounded similar to that employed by those who protested the findings of the Louis Freeh Report of 2012, claiming that Penn State's culture was dominated by football, Heppenstall stated,

> We are not of the opinion that football is the paramount issue in the life of Penn State, but we believe . . . it is the most popular sport with the public, with the Alumni and with the Student Body and Faculty. The status of the college football team works for healthy and unhealthy publicity. It is a means of engendering college spirit in the undergraduate and in keeping alive in the graduate the spirit which was planted with him during his college life, and from a material standpoint it is absolutely the financial support of all other athletic activity at the College.[38]

Heppenstall told the Warriner group that only the football administration needed to be changed. "Winning against the best teams is decreasing," Heppenstall stated, "Gate receipts are decreasing, leading to a deficit in the treasury of the Athletic Association." Athletic finances, even before the Depression of the 1930s, were looking bleak, as each of previous three years there had been a deficit.[39] Heppenstall then pointed out that poor football teams affect "the Penn State spirit" and that it has "gradually and is now definitely broken among the Alumni and among the Student Body." What to do? Heppenstall went right to the point: Bezdek's "usefulness to Penn State as a head football coach is at an end."[40]

The Warriner Committee, armed with the Beaver White Committee Report of 1927 and strong opinions such as Heppenstall's, went to work to determine what recommendations should be made about football coaching and administration of the physical education program while keeping Penn State "free from every taint of professionalism" with the elimination of "athletic scholarships."[41] Although Heppenstall, a major financial contributor to Penn State athletics, wanted athletics and physical education to be separated, the Warriner Committee believed that the two should remain together. This was a major question that was to reappear a half-century later when Joe Paterno became athletic director. President Hetzel wanted athletics to remain in physical education, but he raised the question with chairman Warriner: "Is athletics to be separate, completely divorced from physical education," Hetzel asked, "or shall the Director of Physical Education not be coach but athletics be part of physical education?" Hetzel stated he "would go along unqualifiedly," with athletics and physical education remaining together, but if separate, Hetzel would "raise a question."[42] Warriner, in concert with Hetzel and in opposition to Heppenstall and the Pittsburgh alumni, quickly replied: "PE and Athletics one—Head coach no head of PE."[43]

But what about the new Board of Athletic Control? Was it to really control athletics as the old Alumni Advisory Committee of the Athletic Association had for the previous two decades when it hired coaches, constructed facilities, and scheduled games? Although Hetzel wanted an academic unit to have control, many members of the Board of Athletic Control wanted to continue past practices.[44] After a half-year of discussion, the Board of Athletic Control and President Hetzel agreed to present a resolution to the Board of Trustees for action. The result: The Director of Physical Education would not coach but would administer athletics and control the budget; intercollegiate athletics would be part of a new School of Physical Education and Athletics; and the Board of Athletic Control would only be advisory.[45] If the official policy was for the Board of Athletic Control to be advisory, there is strong evidence that for the period until after World War II, the Board of Athletic Control continued to negotiate coaching contracts, made schedules, approved budgets, and chose the graduate manager.[46]

The trustees approved a major change in the creation of a new School of Physical Education and Athletics to replace the Department of Physical Education. The trustees essentially fired Hugo Bezdek from his coaching position and promoted him to become the director of the new school, a position equivalent to the deanship of the other schools of the College. Penn State would pick up $8,000 of Bezdek's salary from the last two years of his ten-year contract, and the Athletic Association would contribute the other $6,000 of his very high early Depression salary.[47] The Penn State alumni from Pittsburgh appeared pleased as the alumni club president wrote to President Hetzel of the "enthusiastic approval of the Board's actions." Apparently the ouster of Hugo Bezdek as coach overrode the desire to separate athletics from physical education. Athletics in an academic

unit continued for the next half-century until in 1980 Joe Paterno, business officer
Steve Garban, and President John Oswald, as will be seen, pulled athletics out of
the academic unit and isolated athletics within the business office of Penn State.
But, for the foreseeable future, athletics would technically be operating out of
the new School of Physical Education and Athletics, and the dominant football
program would be operating as the "Great Experiment" without athletic scholarships under a new coach, Bob Higgins.

CHAPTER 6

The Great Experiment That Failed

Alumnus Casey Jones, President Hetzel,

and Coach Bob Higgins

"Hitherto, athletics has absorbed the college; it is time for the college to
absorb athletics."
—Henry S. Pritchett (1926)

There were two prominent "Experiments" in Penn State's athletic history, the Great
Experiment and the Grand Experiment. They should not be confused. The best
known is the Grand Experiment articulated by Joe Paterno shortly after becoming
head coach of football in 1966. In short, it was an effort in big-time football to
produce winning teams while players were integrated into Penn State and received
a sound college education. The other, the Great Experiment, was an attempt in
the 1930s and 1940s to remain in big-time football with winning teams but not
recruiting athletes with the lure of athletic scholarships. Although there remain
doubters about the success of the Grand Experiment, especially in the aftermath
of the Jerry Sandusky Scandal, there is little evidence that the Great Experiment
in big-time athletics was anything but a dismal failure, however well intentioned
as being educationally sound and embracing the ideals of amateur sport.

The origin of Penn State's Great Experiment can be traced at least as far back
as the creation of the Carnegie Foundation for the Advancement of Teaching investigation into big-time college athletics, meaning principally football. That was
in 1926, the year Joe Paterno was born. The Carnegie Foundation was under the
presidency of Henry S. Pritchett, former president of the Massachusetts Institute
of Technology and an educational elitist who opposed allowing nonintellectual
activities to garner the interests of college students. The Carnegie Foundation
had earlier done a major study of medical education in America, and its study
was influential in reforming how future doctors were trained. Pritchett and the
foundation believed that an investigation of college athletics would lead to another
successful reform of what they considered was a broken system of amateurism
infested with professionalism and crass commercialism.

Pritchett "knew" the solutions to the problems of big-time sports before the study was conducted.[1] Before the investigation by the Carnegie Foundation, Pritchett stated, "The paid coach, the professional organization of the college athletics, the demoralization of students by participation in the use of extravagant sums of money, constitute a reproach of American colleges and to those who govern them."[2] Just as the study was underway, Pritchett proclaimed, "Hitherto, athletics has absorbed the college; it is time for the college to absorb athletics."[3] Later, the foundation president wrote in the preface to the Carnegie Report, "A system of recruiting and subsidizing has grown up [that is] demoralizing and corrupt, alike for the boy who takes the money and for the agent who arranges it, and for the whole group of college and secondary school boys who know about it."[4] The Carnegie Report is still quoted by athletic reformers well into the twenty-first century, but it had a major influence on only a few colleges across America. One was Penn State.

Only months after the Carnegie Foundation began its research of more than 100 colleges and universities in North America, including Penn State College, the Beaver White Committee began its Alumni Association investigation of the system of athletics at Penn State. The Beaver White group knew full well that the Carnegie Foundation was in strong opposition to athletic scholarships and that Penn State probably had the most college-sponsored athletic scholarships in the nation.[5] Believing that Penn State could gain prominence by being in the forefront of a sweeping athletic reform movement to maintain amateurism, the Beaver White Committee recommended eliminating athletic scholarships. The recommendations, along with a method of getting rid of Hugo Bezdek, were soon discussed among students, faculty, members of the Board of Athletic Control, the president, and the Alumni Association. Each group, including the new president Ralph Dorn Hetzel, bought into the drastic move to eliminate athletic scholarships. With the elimination of the payment of athletes to attend Penn State beginning in 1928, and the purging of Hugo Bezdek as coach, many Penn Staters believed a successful era would begin under new coach Bob Higgins, a former Penn State all-American and assistant coach under Bezdek. The Great Experiment began.

Higgins was the first two-time all-American lineman at Penn State in the 1910s and came on board as an assistant coach under Bezdek in 1928, just as Bezdek was under heavy pressure from the alumni. The Athletic Association hired Higgins, who had earlier coached at West Virginia Wesleyan and St. Louis University, as an assistant professor and football coach for a nice salary of $4,300, more than the salary of most professors. It was raised it to $4,700 the next year. With evidently little formal discussion, Higgins was hired as head coach for $6,000 when Bezdek was "fired" as football coach and "promoted" to become director of the new School of Physical Education and Athletics.[6] Higgins knew that he was undermanned to be playing big-time schools such as Notre Dame, Pittsburgh, and Syracuse as Penn State was doing during the last years under Bezdek, so the scheduling with these teams was reduced. More schools, such as Bucknell, Dickinson, Gettysburg, Johns Hopkins, Lafayette, Lebanon Valley, Lehigh, Marshall, Muhlenberg, New York University, Niagara, and Villanova, became prominent in the annual schedule. Yet in Higgins's first four years as coach, Penn State won only 10 while losing 20 times.

One of the most devastating losses that had a great impact upon later success under Higgins was a 1931 opening loss to Waynesburg College, a small sectarian institution southwest of Pittsburgh. Waynesburg's athletic claim to fame is that it was the team that played Fordham University in the first televised football game in 1939, a game telecast by NBC at Triboro Stadium in New York City.[7] But eight years before, Waynesburg beat Penn State 7–0 in the opening game at Penn State. At that game was Ben C. "Casey" Jones. He was a Penn State classmate of Bob Higgins, the two friends having been best man in each other's weddings. Jones, a former letter winner in football, track, and lacrosse, was devastated by the loss to the little Presbyterian College with a men's and women's student body of just over 200.[8] At the time, Jones decided to try to help his classmate and friend, Higgins, by recruiting players in the Pittsburgh area and helping to subsidize their expenses at Penn State. Casey Jones recalled that he "sat in great disgust and watched Rab Curry of little Waynesburg College pin our ears back."[9] Rab Curry's touchdown run was the winning score in 1931, and Waynesburg again beat Penn State the next year, to be one of the few teams to have remained unbeaten against Penn State. Humiliated by the experience, for the next two decades Casey Jones became the most important benefactor of Penn State football, culminating with the undefeated Cotton Bowl season of 1947.

Casey Jones was another of the Penn State's Pittsburgh Alumni Club who bled blue and white, but he more than anyone else was the key to recruiting athletes from Western Pennsylvania during Higgins's nineteen-year tenure as coach. Jones had played on the football team prior to World War I and eventually became the most prominent person in helping the Nittany Lions recruit athletes. He was a World War I veteran, having been a pilot and serving with the great flying ace Captain Eddie Rickenbacker. He returned to graduate in engineering, like so many Penn State students, and took a long-time position with West Penn Power Company in Pittsburgh. Jones got on the Executive Board of the Alumni Council and eventually was elected to the Board of Trustees for eighteen years, until the Joe Paterno era, where he was the trustee member of the Athletic Advisory Board.[10]

As a Penn Stater from Pittsburgh, Jones still had difficulty recruiting the very best athletes who were being paid high monthly wages by the Pitt athletic program to play for the Panthers. The great Pitt coach, John Bain "Jock" Sutherland, followed the legendary Glenn "Pop" Warner when Warner left for Stanford in the mid-1920s. Sutherland continued the tradition of winning set by Warner. Pitt players were paid monthly up to $100 but averaged about $65 a month in the early years of the Depression, a handsome wage. This allowed a number of team members to get married, with the team gaining the nickname the "married man's team." According to Jones, "Pitt recruited the first 10 of my picks and I had to take what was left for Penn State."[11] With Pitt's clearly superior athletes, Higgins lost the first eight games to Pitt before finally winning a game in the last year of the Depression. This occurred shortly after Pitt dropped athletic scholarships, and Sutherland resigned because, as he said, "the University could no longer supply the necessary assistance or support to the boys."[12] Penn State won 10–0 that year and began a half-century of never having a losing season until finally Joe Paterno's team, after two national championships, had a five-win, six-loss season in 1988.

The recruiting and financial aid that Casey Jones brought to Penn State football more than likely allowed Bob Higgins to win nearly two-thirds of his games over nineteen years, 1930–1948, though they were often against second-rank teams. Jones was not alone in his efforts, for there were alumni recruiting in eastern Pennsylvania, but he was by far the most active.[13] He established a scholarship fund for alumni contributions, which came heavily from Penn State alumni in the Pittsburgh area. Jones came up with another major fundraiser, a car raffle, generally with its drawing on the night of the Pittsburgh game. With the money raised, Jones would confer with coach Higgins who, according to Jones, "made the decisions as to what to recruit, backs, linemen, etc., and I produced what talent I could line up, and paid the bills."[14] The aid generally went for tuition, books, and incidental fees with the athletes working for their board and room. Jones also collaborated with fraternities, who provided many athletes with jobs. Other jobs were obtained in the dormitories and in restaurants and other businesses in State College. During the summers, Jones helped find work for athletes, a number working for his West Penn Power Company, where Jones was a staff engineer.[15]

Casey Jones also worked to get housing for the recruited athletes. During World War II, a Penn State Forestry fraternity closed and was rented by the Athletic Association for housing football players. After the war, however, housing was extremely difficult to find in State College. A large stone fraternity house came up for sale, and Casey Jones was the high bidder for what became the athletes' house for a couple of years. It was called the Gray Stone Manor, housing a number of those who went to the first bowl game since Hugo Bezdek's team took a trip to the Rose Bowl in 1923. The Gray Stone Manor, Jones said, "damn near bankrupted both me and the [scholarship] fund" because of the expenses of coal, electricity, and other utilities.[16] An assistant coach, Earle Edwards, who nearly became head coach when Higgins retired, was put in charge of the $42,000 Gray Stone Manor, but it was soon sold back to the original fraternity for $60,000.[17] Jones and the alumni got out of the athletic housing business and did so at a profit. As housing of students on campus eased up after the flood of veterans returning to Penn State slowed, an athletic dorm became available, and the youthful Joe Paterno became an athletic dorm counselor in the early 1950s, a position he opposed after his tour of duty in the position.

The importance of the alumnus Casey Jones to the administrative history of Penn State athletics should not be underestimated. The likelihood of Penn State going to its first bowl game since the 1923 Rose Bowl was slight without the efforts of Jones. After the 1947 undefeated season, Penn State was invited to the Cotton Bowl to play undefeated Southern Methodist University (SMU) with its great back, Doak Walker. That was the game sometimes named the "Chocolate Bowl" because two Penn State African Americans, Dennis Hoggard and Wally Triplett, were the first blacks to desegregate the Dallas, Texas, Cotton Bowl. The starting team, in the 13–13 tie with SMU, was composed of a majority of players recruited by Jones. Looking back over his career of helping Penn State football succeed, Jones said that the happiest moment in his Penn State saga was at the beginning of the 1947 undefeated season. The first game was against Washington State University, a 27–4 victory in the Hershey Stadium, and a proud Casey Jones recalled that seven of the team's "starting lineup were my men."[18] Jones, if he had been present in a later period, would have been called recruiting coordinator, an important position in big-time football.

While Jones was recruiting, the president during most of Higgins's career was proclaiming the Great Experiment's success playing winning football without athletic scholarships. Ralph Dorn Hetzel was one of the few Penn State presidents who was not an outgoing cheerleader for a big-time program. He likely was neither naïve about Casey Jones and other alumni recruiters nor blind to what was going on in athletics during the Higgins era. More likely he feared antagonizing the alumni if he outwardly condemned those who were professionalizing athletes as most big-time universities were doing at the time. Hetzel's background would not indicate any naïveté about athletics. Hetzel played high school football on his Merrill, Wisconsin, football team in the late 1800s and was on the freshman football team at the University of Wisconsin and captain of the Wisconsin freshman rowing team early in the twentieth century. He gave up athletics after his freshman year to earn his way through college as a newspaper correspondent. While at Wisconsin he was a member of the Athletic Committee of the Badger Board, at a time when famous historian of the frontier Frederick Jackson Turner was attempting to ban football at Wisconsin and in the Big Ten.[19]

Hetzel, with his law degree from Wisconsin, would not have been unsophisticated about athletics and the possibility of banning football after the 1905 national football crisis. More likely, Hetzel would have come to dislike the commercialized and professionalized football that was taking place across America and at the institutions at which he was professing, Oregon State College, and presiding, New Hampshire College of Agriculture and Mechanics Arts (University of New Hampshire). In the year before accepting the presidency at Penn State, Hetzel unexcitedly told a newspaper reporter that he "was interested in athletics. Most colleges and universities are." He said, however, that coaches at New Hampshire, unlike a number of professional college coaches, were recognized members of the faculty "just as intimately a part of the institution as any other."[20] When he arrived at Penn State, there was turmoil over the coaching of Hugo Bezdek and the question of eliminating athletic scholarships. He told his first fall mass meeting of students at Penn State: "I have seen many colleges suffer grievously at the hands of a football team which was on the right side of the score but on the wrong side of wholesome college ideals."[21] Hetzel carried that theme through his two-decade tenure as president of Penn State.

Almost as soon as Hetzel arrived at Penn State, he was embroiled in the athletic administration and coaching controversy led by the alumni living in and around Pittsburgh. He let the athletic leaders know that he wanted athletics to be integrated into an academic unit, not separate and run completely by the Board of Athletic Control. Having athletics as part of the Physical Education Department, Hetzel said, "I would go along unqualifiedly." If separate, he would "raise a question."[22] Hetzel was successful in his desire for athletics to be part of an educational unit in opposition to those who favored the control by the separate Board of Athletic Control run principally by alumni. For fifty years, athletics remained part of an educational component of Penn State—until President Oswald, pressured by Joe Paterno and Steve Garban, removed it and placed it in a business unit of the university in 1980.[23]

By the early 1930s, President Hetzel discussed various programs at Penn State and stated to the alumni that he was "a little embarrassed" that he felt it necessary "to offer special comment upon the subject of athletics." He understood that some believed that if Penn State did not win its football games, it would be in the "educational scrap heap." Penn State was not winning, but Hetzel remained steadfast in the position that the Penn State program should not be "subsidizing . . . students because of athletic ability." And, Hetzel said, the coaching "salaries shall be commensurate with the compensation of other members of the staff."[24] In other words, Hetzel wanted Penn State to continue with controls over the commercialism and professionalism of football and to place an emphasis on education.

After hiring Penn State's first sports information director, Ridge Riley, in 1934, to promote football first and foremost, Hetzel told alumni at a major dinner of the "fundamental soundness and merit of the plan initiated some five years ago" in which the program with "no athletic scholarships" was a success.[25] Many did not agree, and the alumni were once again agitated because Penn State was not discovering enough good athletes within its own student body and was losing every year to Pittsburgh. It also appeared that Hugo Bezdek, running the School of Physical Education and Athletics, was having no more success than he had as coach at the end of the 1920s. Bezdek may have made a political gaff shortly after returning from a National Collegiate Athletic Association meeting in early

1935. The *Penn State Collegian* headlined Bezdek's suggestion to once again offer athletic scholarships through gifts made by the alumni, fraternities, individuals, or even possibly Penn State College as it had done from 1900 to 1927. Bezdek believed his plan would meet the new Code of Ethics of the NCAA on recruitment and payment of players. He recommended structuring the aid like Rhodes Scholarships given to college graduates to attend Oxford University. That is, the scholarships would be based upon three criteria—mental ability, athletic prowess, and character—with three faculty members sitting as judges of the scholarship recipients.[26] Again offering athletic scholarships did not sit well with President Hetzel, who opposed any creeping professionalization of athletics at Penn State.

Once again, as in the late 1920s, the Penn State Alumni Association was not satisfied with the new School of Physical Education and Athletics or with its head Hugo Bezdek. As a result, the Executive Board of the Alumni Association appointed a Special Athletic Committee in June 1935 to study the deteriorating athletic problem—losing in football. The committee, headed by Eugene Gramley, would do a thorough study of the athletic situation, interviewing coaches, former coaches, college officials, athletes, and student and alumni leaders, as the Beaver White Committee had done for the alumni in the 1920s.[27] Its findings were presented one year later, but by then the situation had worsened for Hugo Bezdek as Penn State lost in football to Bucknell (the Orange Bowl victor that year), Pennsylvania, Syracuse, and Pittsburgh and won over Lehigh, Lebanon Valley, Western Maryland, and Villanova. It was probably easier to blame Bezdek, because his rough personality was ready-made for criticism, rather than coach Higgins, who was held dear by many people.

In the meantime, the student newspaper, the *Collegian,* editorialized for subsidization through a training table for the football players. The Board of Athletic Control maintained that a training table did "not constitute subsidization," but on a vote to recommend a three-meal-a-day training table for the football team "effective as soon as possible" the motion lost in a 5–5 tie with one abstention. Finally, with President Hetzel's approval, a training table for lunch and dinner was provided during the football season on practice and game days only.[28] Penn State was officially moving slowly back toward official subsidization, even if it was only paying for feeding football players.

As the Special Athletic Committee of the alumni was conducting its year-long investigation, President Hetzel was continually agitated over the athletic situation. During 1936, he met numerous times and separately with Hugo Bezdek, the Board of Athletic Control, the Faculty Senate Committee on Athletics, the Board of Trustees' Committee on Athletics, and the Alumni Special Athletic Committee.[29] He even spoke out, in obfuscating terms worthy of any head of the U.S. Federal Reserve, to the alumni shortly after a meeting with the Board of Athletic Control. At a Pittsburgh Testimonial Dinner, he spoke highly of progress at Penn State but not about the new School of Physical Education and Athletics, which he said had not "reached that period of maturity which makes it possible for us to judge it fairly and finally." The school, he said, "shows distressing signs of temperament [and we] find ourselves irritated and in despair at its conduct." While indicating that the school "is inherently sound . . . [and] affords us much joy and satisfaction," there are "times when we are tempted to pitch it out of the window." He concluded that if it becomes clear that change is necessary, "changes will be made."[30] Reading between the lines of Hetzel's rhetoric, it was a clear warning that Hugo Bezdek and the new school were in trouble, especially Director Bezdek. Hetzel soon wrote with more honesty about the athletic situation to his son in London, England, that the "present fever has been caused by alumni irritants," such as the group he had just spoken to in Pittsburgh.[31]

By then, there were two groups intently looking at Penn State athletics. First, the Alumni Association's Special Athletic Committee had nearly completed its thorough study, and the Board of Trustees Executive Committee had already formed its own Trustee Special Committee on Athletics in early 1936 and would have its recommendations completed by that fall. The alumni committee presented its findings to the Board of Trustees Special Committee in June after intensive interviews and concluded the School of Physical Education and Athletics "needs new leadership." Six years after the alumni attained what it wanted by the "firing" of coach Hugo Bezdek up to the position of director of the School of Physical Education and Athletics, the former Penn Staters wanted him out entirely. In a few months, that would occur.

The Eugene Gramley Special Athletic Committee of the alumni had a number of other recommendations, most of which soon became policy. "We do not at the present time," the committee reported, "favor college subsidy of athletes." This reflected the NCAA code of recruiting and subsidizing athletics that opposed all institutional athletic subsidies and no indirect subsidies by alumni, with scholarships given only through the institution.[32] The Gramley Committee wanted to finance a training table, however, for both varsity and freshman teams, find jobs for athletes, and have the alumni clubs and others provide financing for worthy athletes "similar to that done by most other colleges," such as the University of Pittsburgh. The committee also recommended changing the name of the Board of Athletic Control, dominated by alumni, to be retitled the Athletic Advisory Board, allowing Penn State to control athletics instead of the alumni, as was the intent in 1930. With these somewhat mixed messages, the committee recognized the restraints on the success of Penn State football by calling for scheduling of competition "between teams with reasonably equal opportunities to win," presumably not against the dominating Pittsburghs and Notre Dames of big-time football.[33]

The Trustee Special Committee on Athletics used the Gramley Committee report as it delivered its policy statement to the Board of Trustees in fall 1936. The Trustee Committee was not a lightweight committee, in that Vance McCormick chaired it. McCormick was a star in several fields, including athletics and politics. He had graduated from Yale, where he participated in football as its quarterback and captain, gaining all-American status in the 1890s. He was elected mayor of Harrisburg, Pennsylvania, in 1902 and was national chairman of the Democratic Party in 1916; at President Woodrow Wilson's request, he attended the Paris Peace Conference after World War I. Not only was McCormick a longtime member of the Yale Corporation, he was on the Penn State Executive Committee for thirty-four years beginning in 1912.[34] Along with J. H. M. Andrews, J. T. Harris, and Boyd A. Musser, the Trustee Special Committee also included James Milholland and George H. Deike. Milholland, who had been president of the Penn State Alumni Association, helped revise athletic policy while on the Beaver White Committee in the 1920s and would eventually become president of the Board of Trustees and interregnum president of Penn State upon the death of Ralph Hetzel.[35] George Deike was the founder of the Cadet Band that became the Penn State Blue Band and was a friend of H. D. "Joe" Mason, who invented the Nittany Lion symbol of Penn State. Deike was a millionaire safety mining engineer who later headed the search committee that chose Milton Eisenhower after Hetzel's sudden death in 1947.[36]

First, the Trustee Special Committee recommended choosing a new dean of the School of Physical Education and Athletics to replace Director Hugo Bezdek. According to Bezdek, President Hetzel met with him and relayed the message of the Board of Trustees: "Either I get rid of you or they get rid of me." Bezdek resigned after receiving a one-year sabbatical.[37] To administer athletics, the committee suggested a troika consisting of Elwood C. Davis of the Department of Physical Education, Neil Fleming, the graduate manager of athletics, and Professor F. L. Bentley, an agriculture professor and chair of the Faculty Senate Committee on Athletics.

The trustees accepted the recommendations, and a new dean was eventually chosen to replace Director Bezdek. This time, the new Athletic Advisory Board replacing the Board of Athletic Control had little influence on the hiring of the head of physical education and athletics. To ease this situation, President Hetzel held a special meeting with the Athletic Advisory Board in spring 1937 to announce that an outsider had been chosen, though alumni names had been proposed. Dr. Carl Schott would be the new dean of the School of Physical Education and Athletics.[38] The Athletic Advisory Board would rather have chosen a known insider for the position. For powerful individuals in athletics to desire an alumnus to be appointed to positions such as the dean of the School of Physical Education and Athletics or athletic director is not unusual. More than a half-century later, the chancellor of the University of Nebraska and future president of Penn State, Graham Spanier, was condemned by backers of Nebraska football for choosing an outsider to be athletic director, Bill Byrne of the University of Oregon. Both the financially important and influential Husker Beef Club and Nebraska Touchdown

Club championed the recommendation of Athletic Director Bob Devaney and football coach Tom Osborne. The two Nebraska icons wanted an inside football man, Al Papik, to be chosen.[39] Perhaps President Spanier had learned a lesson at Nebraska when athletic interests wanted Spanier fired for his choice of an outsider. More than a decade later as president of Penn State, Spanier and three others went to Coach Joe Paterno's home in 2004 asking for Penn State's hero, Joe Paterno, to step aside as coach. Spanier was rebuffed and apparently went no further with his desire to remove the coach. The irony is that in another seven years, and hours after Spanier was removed as president of the university, Joe Paterno was out as football coach.

In the parallel incident three-quarters of a century earlier, President Hetzel continued in office and only Hugo Bezdek was gone. Dean Carl Schott, with a doctorate from Columbia, soon headed the School of Physical Education and Athletics while Bob Higgins continued as football coach for the next dozen years. In that time, he was successful in winning 75 percent of his games with a 72-24-8 record, including an undefeated Cotton Bowl team in 1947. As for President Hetzel, he was a rather hot commodity to lead institutions more prestigious than the isolated college in the middle of Pennsylvania as two Big Ten institutions, Wisconsin and Ohio State, made inquiries into Hetzel's availability. After going through a tough time with the Pittsburgh alumni and the question of Hugo Bezdek's administration, Hetzel wrote to a Wisconsin insider that Penn State has the "most congenial governing board, a loyal faculty and student body, and with strong alumni and public support is I think most unusual."[40] More significant to Hetzel and to Penn State was Hetzel's revelation that "significant developments" were occurring at Penn State. "There seems to be a promise that the maintenance appropriation to the College will be considerably increased," he told a friend at Wisconsin, "and that we may receive in the neighborhood of six millions of dollars for buildings."[41] And that was in the midst of the Great Depression.

Hetzel showed his ability to gain money from the new Pennsylvania General State Authority, a way to finance state building construction, through money supplied by the federal Public Works Administration of the Franklin Roosevelt Administration New Deal. The money came through grants and bond issues to nearly double the number of Penn State buildings and move closer to university status. Of most significance was the construction of a new library, which eventually was named Pattee Library after the long-time professor of English and rhetoric at Penn State. The dedication in 1938 and completion of ten major buildings in two years included several science, engineering, and agriculture buildings and a new wing for Liberal Arts as well as the new library.[42] Hetzel was given much credit for building Penn State's structures, and all along, in contrast with a number of other institutions, he did not come under strong alumni pressure for a lack of a winning football team playing other big-time universities.

Just before the U.S. entry into World War II, Hetzel still believed that Penn State had a deemphasized football program that had "kept athletics in a true perspective" and had "solved our problem with our School of Physical Education and Athletics."[43] He told an Associated Press writer, "Institutions that continue over a long period of time having constantly winning teams build up a situation that makes it difficult for them to maintain academic standards that ought to prevail."[44] In other words, he still believed Penn State football's Great Experiment was a success, competing successfully without athletic scholarships and with control principally in an academic unit. While Hetzel seemed to make sense educationally, he was out of favor with much of society in the 1940s, as he would also have been in 1900 or a century later. The Great Experiment continued through World War II, but not as President Hetzel believed. Alumni, such as Casey Jones in Pennsylvania's west and Jim Gilligan of Dunmore in the east, were recruiting players and offering financial help, the training table had returned, jobs were procured for football players, off-campus housing was used to entice athletes from across the state, and a Quarterback Club was organized to help fund the football program.[45]

After the military victories over Germany and Japan, Penn State was ready once again to enter the big time in college sport. The return of war veterans and the Cotton Bowl season set the stage at the end of Bob Higgins's long tenure as football coach. According to Ridge Riley, head of the Alumni Association and the individual who started the popular "Football Letter" to alumni in 1938, Higgins under President Hetzel "was frustrated continuously by an administrative 'purity' policy not of his own doing."[46] Possibly the trigger for a change in policy occurred with the sudden death of President Hetzel in October 1947. He likely went to his grave believing that the Great Experiment had worked. Outwardly, it appeared to be true, but underneath the Great Experiment was a football program that was increasingly successful because the professionalism and commercialism of football was providing the athletes needed to turn out winning teams. The improving record by the football team would be continued under the leadership of Brown University's Rip Engle, who returned to coach in his home state.

The Ernie McCoy–Rip Engle Era and the Beginning of the Grand Experiment in College Football

"We will have no dealings under the table."
—President Milton Eisenhower (1950)

"Put academic requirements above the ability to play football."
—President Eric Walker (1971)

By the conclusion of World War II, the Great Experiment of the 1930s was a failure, and the Grand Experiment was soon to follow. The Great Experiment failed under President Ralph Dorn Hetzel because underground subsidization by alumnus Casey Jones and others was undermining the concept of amateur sport espoused by the long-time president. But a new era began shortly after Hetzel's death after the war when veterans and veteran players inundated the campus to overflowing. Most veterans would not give a damn about pure amateurism after serving as professional soldiers, sailors, and marines and fighting and winning a war on the European and Asian fronts. The refusal to pay schooling costs for veterans and others to participate in athletics no longer seemed important to most students and alumni, nor would competent coaches likely come to Penn State unless there was aid to athletes so they could compete with other major schools. Soon a new athletic administration and an outside coach would arrive in the person of Dean and Athletic Director Ernie McCoy from a major Big Ten school and Coach Rip Engle from an Ivy League institution. Those two, along with an academic and retired basketball coach, John Lawther, would launch what Joe Paterno would eventually name the Grand Experiment.

In order for the Grand Experiment to come into existence, a change in the administration of Penn State was needed, and athletic scholarships had to be reinstated after being dropped in 1927. With President Hetzel's death, one obstacle to the renewal of aid to athletes was removed. The other obstacle was the dean of the School of Physical Education and Athletics, Carl Schott. He was in his position for a decade as a caretaker of those in physical education, but, despite his title, he was under restraints in the direction taken in athletics. Though athletics had been put under the control of an academic unit since the creation of the school in 1930, it was really the alumni who had major financial control, working though the graduate manager, Neil Fleming, since World War I. Fleming's office was in the administration building, Old Main, not in Recreation Building and removed from the office of the dean. Dean Schott pointed out the problem of isolating athletics from his academic office in his latter years at Penn State. "When I first came to Penn State," Schott informed new president Milton Eisenhower in 1952, "I became aware that The Pennsylvania State College had a program of recruitment. In many of its phases, I felt that it was not seriously out of line because athletes came in on the same basis as other students, and where aid was given, only enough was provided to supplement the athlete's financial needs. This plan worked out very satisfactorily for a time."[1] Thus Schott was reasonably satisfied with the situation when alumni such as Casey Jones would provide some aid to athletes, though Schott wanted it quite limited. To this, Jones would later respond, "Carl Schott was a washout as a helping hand." As an alumnus who wanted a return to athletic glory, Jones wrote disparagingly about Dean Schott, probably more than was justified, calling Schott's position relative to athletics as "the Do Little Office."[2]

Schott was looking at athletics as part of an education and pointed out as much to Eisenhower. "The competition for athletes," Schott noted, "became more keen and, as a result, if Penn State was to get an athlete, more and more would have to be provided." This, according to Schott "involved not only financial inducements, but, often compromising entrance requirements."[3] What Schott wanted to do was to bring recruiting and financial aid under the dean of the School of Physical Education and Athletics and rein in alumni control. The problem of control had existed throughout Hetzel's presidency, when Schott unsuccessfully had attempted to place the Athletic Advisory Board and its graduate manager of athletics under the dean.[4] Schott even spoke before the National Collegiate Athletic Association (NCAA) proposing that college football must do something "to justify its retention as an integral part of our system of higher education" to prove that it is "an amateur rather than a professional sport."[5]

So Schott must have been disappointed when the Athletic Advisory Board in 1947 recommended creating twenty-five athletic scholarships in addition to the free lodging at Casey Jones's Gray Stone Manor and a free training table of three meals a day during the season, preseason, and spring practice.[6] At the time, none of these activities was in conformity with two organizations to which Penn State belonged. The first was the Eastern College Athletic Conference (ECAC), originally formed in the 1930s to assign game officials for its many schools and then to create eligibility standards in eastern U.S. institutions.[7] The other was the NCAA, which had set guidelines early in its history and began legislating recruiting and subsidization standards in 1948. Penn State athletics, with recruiting and subsidization being financed outside the regular channels of the college, was in violation of both ECAC and NCAA standards. Corralling financial grants to athletes, the Penn State Board of Trustees in 1948 passed legislation creating one hundred athletic scholarships to be awarded by the Faculty Senate Committee of Scholarships. When implemented the following year, football received nearly half the scholarships, and the others were spread among baseball, basketball, boxing, gymnastics, track and cross-country, and wrestling.[8] Soon the Levi Lamb Grant-in-Aid Fund was created in 1952 to provide room, board, and tuition, bringing together fundraising efforts for Penn State athletics. (Levi Lamb was the three-sport athlete at Penn State who was killed in trench warfare action toward the end of World War I.)[9]

The new Penn State system of bringing in athletes came just at the time coach Bob Higgins was retiring, Joe Bedenk was taking over for one year, and Rip Engle was about to be hired as head coach. Assistant coach Joe Bedenk was chosen to be coach in 1949 by the Athletic Advisory Board, a board composed of alumni, trustees, and faculty. Several on the board wanted to hire an outsider, after Bob Higgins's sudden announcement that he was retiring, but it was felt there was not enough time to do an outside search and be ready for the fall season. Two assistant coaches came to the fore: Joe Bedenk, who was also the baseball coach, and Earle Edwards, the known choice of outgoing Bob Higgins. Ironically, almost exactly a half-century later, Joe Paterno believed he could control who his successor would be when he told Jerry Sandusky that he would not be the next football coach because he was spending too much time with The Second Mile program for troubled children. Higgins was mistaken about his influence, however, as Joe Paterno might have been had he retired at age 70. Board member J. C. "Hap" Frank, an alumnus, wanted an outsider and got several on the board to vote for Joe Bedenk as an interim coach for one year. Because Edwards had been assured by retiring coach Higgins that he would almost certainly be the next coach, Edwards, from nearby Huntingdon, was devastated by the decision and resigned.[10] Edwards eventually was offered the head coaching position at North Carolina State, where he won five Atlantic Coach Conference championships. When Edwards was not chosen and Bedenk's one-year contract ended, the door was open in 1950 for an outsider.

Two years after Milton Eisenhower assumed the presidency stating, "We will have no dealings under the table,"[11] Charles "Rip" Engle of Brown University was chosen unanimously by the Athletic Advisory Board to head a clean football program. Engle had been recommended to the Athletic Advisory Board by Penn State's former football coach Dick Harlow, who had coached Engle at Western Maryland.[12] With the hiring of Engle, there was a proviso that he be "empowered to name two assistants" to join the coaching staff already at Penn State.[13] After having two of Engle's experienced assistant coaches turn down his offer to bring them on the staff at Penn State, Engle turned to a recent Brown University quarterback, who could help change the Penn State offense from its traditional single wing to a wing-T formation. Joe Paterno was an untried 23-year-old who had helped Engle at that year's Brown University spring practice. Paterno's salary as an instructor and assistant coach was similar to that of a beginning Penn State assistant professor at $3,600.[14] Engle had a modest 28-20-4 record in his six years at the Ivy League school, but he had a fine 15-3 record his last two years while Paterno was quarterbacking the team and his younger brother George Paterno was the running back. During World War II, Engle had turned down the head coaching position at his alma mater, Western Maryland College, and in the two years before taking the Penn State position, he rejected offers from Yale University and the University of Wisconsin. Harvard had rejected Engle for Lloyd Jordan a month before Engle accepted the offer from Happy Valley.[15]

Nevertheless, the new coach was a rather hot commodity, probably not in the same class as Paul "Bear" Bryant, who coached Kentucky to its first Southeastern Conference championship that same year, but Engle had received considerable interest from big-time universities. It was surprising that Engle brought with him an unknown assistant, Joe Paterno, who had indicated his strong desire to coach after his football and basketball career at Brown. That is, if one believes a publicity questionnaire at Brown during his senior year, when Paterno wrote he wanted to pursue a coaching career and not noting any desire to pursue a law degree.[16] It may be true that going to law school was on Paterno's agenda as he reported consistently through the years, and a law degree certainly was a possibility for the intelligent and bookish athlete from Brown. The law degree possibility may also have been a way to please his father, who had achieved a law degree the hard way, at night school. The desire to be a coach was uppermost in his mind as he agreed to give coaching a try at the isolated institution in Appalachia away from what Paterno considered civilization at the time. Rip Engle came with his young protégé to join Penn State coaches Joe Bedenk (who remained as an assistant), Earl Bruce, Al Michaels, Jim O'Hora, Frank Patrick, and Sever Toretti, holdovers from the Bedenk and Higgins coaching regimes.

In two years, a major administrative change occurred within the School of Physical Education and Athletics that placed coach Engle under a new dean and athletic director, Ernie McCoy. Along with the school's assistant academic dean, John Lawther, McCoy and Engle created the climate for the Grand Experiment. Whereas Dean Carl Schott headed the school in which athletics was embedded by order of the Board of Trustees, it was Dean Ernie McCoy who truly brought athletics within an academic arm of Penn State and away from the alumni. In Schott's last year, 1952, he outlined much of what McCoy accomplished by asking that athletic recruiting and scholarship arrangements be brought under Penn State control as well as overseeing scholastic eligibility, athletic employment, and housing and food service. Whereas Schott attempted to remove alumni control through the Athletic Association and its graduate manager and place it under the dean, it was McCoy, whose $12,000 salary signified his importance, who executed it.[17]

The by-laws of the Penn State Athletic Association were a major problem in the locus of athletic control, inside or outside an academic unit. The by-laws of the Athletic Association had not been revised since the mid-1930s and continued into the early years of the McCoy era. The 1937 by-laws stated that the dean of the School of Physical Education and Athletics "shall advise and counsel" with the Athletic Advisory Board rather than having advice offered by the alumni-dominated group. In other words, an advisory board often set policy rather than giving advice. Second, the by-laws stated all "coaches shall be chosen" by the Athletic Advisory Board. It was difficult for a dean to control athletics under those directives. Schott did not achieve his desires, and McCoy decided to correct the situation. But change was slow under the six years of the Eisenhower administration. The president noted, just before McCoy became dean, "the sound athletic policies we have here" and the "wonderful situation that Dean Schott has left for the new dean."[18] Those who followed in positions of power did not think that athletic control with a strong alumni influence was either wonderful or educationally sound.

The president who was elected after Eisenhower's resignation, Eric Walker, may have been right when he said President Eisenhower "did not know what was going on" in athletics.[19] Walker appears to have believed that athletics being controlled outside an academic unit or outside the institution, as in many other universities, often led to corruption and cover-ups. Walker came along just as the nation was experiencing what may have been the most corrupt period in American intercollegiate athletics history in the post–World War 1940s and early 1950s, manifested with numerous scandals. These included the national basketball point-shaving scandal at many schools, including that of coach Adolph Rupp's team at the University of Kentucky, and the cheating dishonor at the West Point Military Academy and expulsion of nearly the entire football team. The scandals also included the presidential cover-up of illegal recruitment and payment of athletes at William and Mary College, the "slush fund" cover-up by the president of the University of Tennessee of famous coach and athletic director Robert Neyland, and the multiple violations of recruiting and scholarship regulations of the NCAA.[20] Although a major scandal at Penn State did not occur, pressure was increasing to eliminate the isolation of athletics under alumni influence and the new graduate manager, Ike Gilbert, and return management to the institution under a stronger form of academic control.[21]

President Walker was determined to build a greater university by emphasizing the three efforts told to him by his friend Vannevar Bush, dean of the Massachusetts Institute of Technology—hiring a strong faculty, constructing buildings, and having a winning football team. There is little question that Penn State began hiring the faculty who would give the institution national status—research professors—in his years as president, 1956–70. Even the provincial Department of Physical Education asked for a research professor in 1958 after the Penn State Faculty Senate's Committee on Research Policy admonished the department for lack of research.[22] Relative to buildings on campus, Penn State was in a construction frenzy under Walker's presidency, nearly as great as at the end of the 1930s when federal Public Works Administration poured millions into the General State Authority and helped to nearly double the number of campus buildings.[23] To meet Bush's triad of suggestions for achieving greatness, the athletic program, especially football, compiled a winning record under coach Engle and then Joe Paterno.

Eric Walker summed up the situation at Penn State during his years in command. He gave a rather lengthy accounting of Penn State athletics in the 1950s and 1960s that appears quite accurate:

> A formal grant-in-aid system was established, giving the best players free tuition, and room and board, as long as they met the standard academic requirements. This formal approved system was to replace a sort of helter skelter arrangement that had existed in the past, with alumni running car raffles to find some extra cash for the players and the company holding the food concessions at the stadium being required to return a percentage of the profits to the student athletes. It was further decided that we would do it right, do it cleanly, and to put academic requirements above the ability to play football. No special dormitories, no special classes, and no under-the-table handouts. All of these arrangements had the approval of the board of trustees, the tacit approval of the faculty and certainly the approval of the football coach [Rip Engle] as shown when he came into my office and said that he wanted no football players who had not been admitted by the University admissions officer as regular students, and he wanted none of his coaches making appeals to the faculty to go easy on the grades. "Eric," he said, "I am tired of taking in a freshman who is a good football player, spending a whole year teaching him how to play the Penn State way, and then having him flunk out. After all, being smart helps a man be a good football player, and that's the kind I want." I firmly believe that this philosophy and its continuation under Joe Paterno has given us football teams [of] which we can be proud.[24]

Much credit must go to Ernie McCoy and John Lawther for creating the climate for, if not the name, the Grand Experiment. McCoy came from the University of Michigan, where he was basketball coach and assistant athletic director. At Michigan, where McCoy was an honors student, the athletic program was controlled by the athletic administration, not the alumni, and athletic aid was institutionally controlled and aboveboard. When McCoy arrived at Penn State, the members of the coaching staff were members of the faculty and most taught in the expanded basic instruction program in physical education. It was McCoy, working with the associate dean in the School of Physical Education and Athletics, John Lawther, who began hiring research professors and building up the academic side of the School of Physical Education and Athletics to complement the national stature of the athletic program in such men's sports as football, gymnastics, wrestling, track and field, and—for a brief period—basketball. It was also during the McCoy era that women's intercollegiate sports were formed and quickly became national leaders in both administration and national championships.

To achieve a national athletic reputation with sound academics under an academic dean, later promoted as the Grand Experiment by Joe Paterno, the School of Physical Education would need to be academically more respectable. Male coaches who had academic rank and tenure with few academic credentials could not dominate it. President Walker, during the 1950s, decided to have a special outside assessment of the entire Penn State institution. The resulting report indicated that Penn State was strongest in technical and scientific fields such as engineering, mineral industries, chemistry, physics, and agriculture while it was weakest in liberal arts, nontechnical areas such as home economics, and particularly weak in education and physical education. The report even brought up the notion that Penn State had "certain disadvantages in its 'cow college' heritage, its isolated location, its lack of certain professional schools usually associated with a great university."[25] Academically, it was not a pretty picture for Dean Ernie McCoy or the academic associate dean for resident instruction, John Lawther, probably the only academic in the School of Physical Education with the writing of a book to his credit.

What to do? Dean McCoy, who had earlier won a Big Ten Conference Medal for scholarship and athletics at Michigan and completed an advanced degree from Columbia University, was not satisfied with the record in either athletics or academics. Both needed greater stature in his mind. Similarly, John Lawther, who had achieved a 150-93 record (61.7 percent) as basketball coach from 1936 to 1949, retired from coaching to devote his time to leading the academic program in the school. Lawther's workload was almost unbelievable in his last semester as basketball coach. He was involved as an adviser with committee work and taught two 400-level courses and one 200-level course while serving on several thesis committees and acting as chairman of another.[26] Lawther had graduated from Westminster College in Pennsylvania, completed a master's degree from Columbia University, and had additional academic work at the University of Pittsburgh, New York University, and the University of Chicago. He had even headed the Department of Psychology while coaching in the mid-1930s at Westminster. With the team of McCoy and Lawther, Penn State's School of Physical Education and Athletics began its move to national status academically just as Rip Engle was moving Penn State once more to greater national prominence in football.

The School of Physical Education and Athletics produced a policy statement in 1958, the year Penn State became a member of the nationally prestigious Association of American Universities.[27] Under Dean McCoy, the policy read, "A high percentage of new personnel must be qualified . . . for admission to the graduate faculty. Competition for personnel of this caliber demands that we must offer an attractive atmosphere for scholarly growth and attainment."[28] The Executive Committee of the school recognized that it was weak in the important area of physiology as well as other faculty positions and budget.[29] To accomplish both academic excellence and winning primarily in big-time football would require a difficult administrative balancing act. It was accomplished in the period from the 1950s to 1980, at which time athletics was removed from an academic unit and placed in a business unit.

The team of McCoy and Lawther made the first major move to greater academic and research respectability in 1963 when they hired Elsworth Buskirk, with a Ph.D. in physiology from the University of Minnesota. Buskirk was the first of a number of faculty members hired in the 1960s and 1970s, many of whom came to the School of Physical Education with degrees in specific academic disciplines outside physical education, such as physiology, anatomy, engineering, psychology, history, and philosophy. Buskirk, a research physiologist hired out of the National Institute of Health, gave academic status to the school. For research, he almost immediately created a Human Performance Laboratory (later Noll Laboratory) in the abandoned team room complex under the bleachers of the football stadium, after the stadium was moved from central campus to the periphery of campus in 1959.[30] In the next decade after the creation of Buskirk's research position, faculty were added in exercise physiology, biomechanics, sport psychology, motor learning and neuromuscular performance, and sport history. Only one coach, Tom Tait, a Ph.D. in physiology who coached men's and women's volleyball in the 1970s, made the crossover of being highly involved in both academics and athletics.

Tait became part of physical education and athletics that reflected the status of a high-quality academic and athletic program that was integrated into the same academic unit, and in that respect Penn State stood out among all institutions with big-time athletics. Early on, members of the coaching staff attended the same faculty meetings that noncoaches attended. For instance, of the ten faculty meetings in 1953, Ernie McCoy, John Lawther, and Marie Haidt, the head of women's physical education, attended every meeting. Frank Patrick and Jim O'Hora, assistant football coaches, made nearly all the faculty meetings, while Rip Engle and Joe Paterno made half of them. Harold "Ike" Gilbert, the graduate manager of athletics, and Ed Czekaj, the athletic assistant business manager, also attended, though seldom.[31] The coaches were integrated with other physical education faculty. It was a unique program developed under Ernie McCoy and John Lawther. The physical education (kinesiology) program came to be ranked Number One in the nation by the 1970s and continued in that position well into the twenty-first century, and the football team achieved that status in the 1980s, with several men's and women's teams achieving national championships earlier than football.

Athletics within an academic unit was not easy to administer, but Dean McCoy was eventually able to make it prosper in the Rip Engle football era and beyond. First, McCoy needed to bring the financing, scheduling, and hiring aspect of football under his control. That meant he needed to diminish the power of the alumni, the position of graduate manager of athletics, and the Athletic Advisory Board, which had previously hired Rip Engle. A generation before, the Board of Trustees had changed the name of the Board of Athletic Control, set up in 1930, to the Athletic Advisory Board in 1936, but most of the power had remained with the Advisory Board, which was not under the control of the head of the School of Physical Education and Athletics. Since the Athletic Advisory Board and its graduate manager dominated control of the money, it had most of the power. Once Penn State again sanctioned athletic scholarships and set up the Levi Lamb fund under Penn State control, it basically undermined the power of individuals such as alumnus Casey Jones to handle payment of athlete's expenses even though Jones was the Board of Trustees appointee on the Athletic Advisory Board in the 1950s and 1960s.[32] Thus a major source of financing came under institutional control.

Almost as soon as Ernie McCoy took over the deanship, the Board of Trustees reaffirmed the dean's authority over athletics, including the position of graduate manager. Within less than a year, the graduate manager of athletics, "Ike" Gilbert, who succeeded long-time Neil Fleming in 1947, was retitled assistant director of athletics, and his office was removed from his Old Main administrative building and brought to Recreation Building under Dean McCoy. The graduate manager move had been recommended by Dean Schott a half-decade before. Dean McCoy, though, took charge and began scheduling future football games, arranging a greater variety of intersectional games, such as Illinois, Nebraska, Purdue, Ohio State, Texas Christian, and Wisconsin, bringing Penn State football to a more visible national stage.[33]

Dean McCoy was determined to eliminate any influence of the Athletic Advisory Board, created in 1936 to give advice rather than control of athletics principally by the alumni. The Athletic Advisory Board did more than advise, such as hiring the football coach, and McCoy believed that the institution, rather than an entity dominated by alumni, should control athletics. McCoy was much like Joe Paterno, who later would often say about the alumni, "we want your money but we don't want your two cents worth." It was not all that easy to do away with an organization that had traditionally influenced the direction taken by athletics, an organization that had been created by the Board of Trustees. All the same, McCoy worked to have it eliminated, beginning soon after he became dean and athletic director. When the Executive Committee of the Board of Trustees voted to give McCoy "full authority in the program of athletics" the year after he arrived at Penn State, McCoy generally ignored the Athletic Advisory Board, answering only to the president.[34] He could do so because President Eric Walker supported McCoy in the belief that the longstanding Athletic Association, formed in the 1880s, and the Athletic Advisory Board of the 1930s had outlived their usefulness.[35] Finally, in 1965, the Board of Trustees discontinued the Athletic Advisory Board.[36]

The Board of Trustees made an important statement about athletics and an academic unit of Penn State when it wrote the following shortly before Joe Paterno became head coach:

> The minutes of the past four decades frequently include statements which tend to reinforce the idea of an intercollegiate athletic program which is a part of the *total offerings of an academic unit* rather than an independent entity subject to varying influences of alumni boards, business influences and the like.

The Trustees further stated that

> Intercollegiate athletics must not be developed to the detriment of the *academic and recreational offerings* of the College.[37]

This would remain policy until 1980 when President John Oswald at the urging of Joe Paterno and Steve Garban withdrew athletics from an academic unit. Athletics were then placed in a business unit, rejecting the Board of Trustees policy of 1965. As will be seen, President Oswald never went to the Board of Trustees to change trustee policy, and that may have contributed to the isolation of athletics from academic restraints.

As Dean Ernie McCoy was bringing athletics completely under an academic unit, the question of the admission of athletes to Penn State arose. Obviously if an institution wants to have national-caliber teams, the university will tend to allow some superior athletes but mediocre students into the schools—a procedure at Penn State called "presidential admits." The policy at Penn State under Dean McCoy is not clear, though there seem to have been fewer, if any, presidential admits during the McCoy-Engle-Lawther era than in the Joe Paterno era. Providing for special athletic admissions was not a new phenomenon nationally. They existed in the nineteenth century when the power schools in football were Yale, Princeton, and Harvard, just as they were present at institutions and conferences such as the Southeastern Conference (SEC) at the time Rip Engle was coaching at Penn State. The commissioner of the SEC, Bernie Moore, reported that in his conference "very few of the institutions made inquiry about an athlete's grades" upon entry into the universities.[38] This was the situation at a dominating SEC school, Tennessee, at about the same time. Coach Robert Neyland, the greatest name in southern football in the 1930s and into the early 1950s, asked to keep eligibility requirements low so that Tennessee could obtain quality football players. Since the state of Tennessee permitted students to graduate from high school without any mathematics credits, he thought it was unreasonable that "the University of Tennessee should require two units of math in order to enter."[39] In other words, if they were good athletes, let them in and forget about entrance requirements.

Ignoring academic standards did not appear to be the situation at Penn State throughout most of its history and in the Engle coaching regime. There were those who felt that faculty might restrict the athletic program and who still wanted alumni influence to bring winners to old State. One wrote Dean McCoy that alumni should "serve as a watchdog for the boys as well as a watchdog over the University Senate Committee on Athletics to see to it that the faculty don't install unrealistic rules concerning athletics." This alumnus opposed the idea that the Penn State Faculty Senate Committee on Athletics, as the committee claimed, should "have jurisdiction over all intercollegiate athletic contests."[40]

Both Coach Engle and Dean McCoy raised questions about Penn State academic standards for athletes. Rip Engle was concerned that he might be limited in recruiting some of the best athletes to come to Penn State by what he considered overly high academic standards. Though he did not request an easing of academic standards for athletics upon accepting the position, Engle eventually questioned "the extremely high academic admissions and eligibility requirements."[41] Engle complained to Dean McCoy that less than 25 percent of the outstanding high school athletes were acceptable to the Penn State admissions office. He said "fine schools throughout our nation have made this adjustment after the facts became apparent on the football field."[42] Even Dean McCoy once told the Athletic Advisory Board "we should have to gamble occasionally on a low-standing athlete who showed promise of keeping up with college standards."[43]

President Eric Walker's observation, though, appears to have merit that "no football players who had not been admitted by the University admissions officer as regular students" were allowed into Penn State. President Walker made a case for the Grand Experiment, without naming it, when he stated Penn State would "do it right, do it cleanly, and to put academic requirements above the ability to play football." Walker called for "no special dormitories, no special classes, and [no] under-the-table handouts" and with no "coaches making appeals to the faculty to go easy on the grades."[44] Despite questioning some of Penn State's academic standards, there is good reason to believe that the foundation for the Grand Experiment was in existence before it was named, and it was established under athletic leadership during the Ernie McCoy–Rip Engle era.

CHAPTER 8

The Joe Paterno, Steve Garban, John Oswald Coup d'État

"One mountain cannot accommodate two tigers."
—Chinese proverb (antiquity)

"Power confuses itself with virtue and tends also to take itself for omnipotence."
—J. William Fulbright (1966)

Two years before Joe Paterno's team won Penn State's first national football championship, a half-century tradition of athletic control under an academic dean was quietly buried. This covert and academically disturbing coup d'état of athletic control significantly isolated Penn State athletics away from any watchful eye of academic control. The power grab, more than any other single action, placed athletics in an insular division of Penn State, a financial, not an academic, arm of the university. The fact that the president of Penn State, John Oswald, made the decision without going to the Board of Trustees, logically the policymaker in the university, represented a major change from the actions of the Board of Trustees in 1930.[1] At that time the trustees placed athletics within a new School of Physical Education and Athletics. The removal and isolation of athletics from academics may very well have contributed to questionable if not illegal actions taken by individuals at Penn State in the Sandusky Scandal. One should ponder the significance of two of the major figures in Penn State's involvement in the Sandusky Scandal, Joe Paterno (head coach) and Steve Garban (president of the Board of Trustees), who were central figures in the 1980 athletic power coup.

Five decades before Joe Paterno secured the athletic director's position, another football coach, Hugo Bezdek, was dismissed, some called it fired, from the head coaching position at Penn State and made director of a new School of Physical Education and Athletics. The position was created in part to provide an accommodation for one of the highest paid football coaches in America, for Bezdek still had a few years to go on his 10-year coaching contract.[2] President Ralph Dorn Hetzel, who did not like big-time commercial and professional athletics in institutions of higher learning, was able to satisfy alumni who wanted to get rid of

Hugo Bezdek as coach. Hetzel, at the same time that he appeased the alumni by relieving Bezdek from coaching, would also recommend to the Board of Trustees the creation of a new school. Structurally it was similar to a School of Education or School of Engineering, but it was created principally to remove alumni control over athletics by placing athletics within an academic unit.

Athletic control by the Penn State Board of Trustees in one of Penn State College's schools continued from the 1930s until well after World War II. Nevertheless, alumni exercised a great deal of control during those years through the Alumni Association, first under the Board of Athletic Control and later the Alumni Advisory Committee of the Athletic Association. There were discussions about academic control throughout those years, including the period before the 1930 Board of Trustees decision. When the Penn State alumni met in the late 1920s to discuss the athletic problems, 91 percent of the alumni across the state voted to separate athletics from, not integrate athletics with, physical education—in part to get Hugo Bezdek out as coach.[3] Throughout all this, President Hetzel prevailed in his effort to keep athletics in an academic unit. It remained there when Dean Ernie McCoy took over as athletic director in the early 1950s.

At that time, the Board of Trustees again emphasized that athletics were to continue "within the structure of an academic unit and subject to the authority of an academic administrator."[4] Joe Paterno was then a seven-year assistant coach and probably did not know that the trustees had taken such an action, and 27 years later, when he was often considered the most powerful individual at Penn State, he paid no attention to it, for he was in pursuit of a national championship.

By the 1960s, with Dean McCoy still in charge of athletics, a special committee of the Board of Trustees stated, "intercollegiate athletics must not be developed to the detriment of the academic and recreational offerings of the College."[5] It was this policy of the trustees that went awry in 1980. Then, as Joe Paterno was made athletic director, Steve Garban eyed his own involvement in athletics, and President John Oswald, who was earlier essentially fired as president of the University of Kentucky by the influence of a power coach, changed policy without trustee approval.

The tradition at Penn State through most of the twentieth century was for profitmaking football to subsidize athletic and recreational facilities for the entire student body. The most expensive student facility was the Recreation Building in the 1920s with a significant amount of the total construction cost coming from football revenue.[6] Only a few years earlier, athletics paid for the construction of the Willie Park Jr. (famous golf course designer) golf course on the west side of campus. Intramural fields also were constructed out of intercollegiate athletic funds. After World War II, other athletic and recreational facilities were financed by football income, including an ice rink, bowling alleys, and outdoor and indoor tennis courts. A new academic Sports Research Institute in the College of Health and Physical Education could boast in 1969 about the athletic department and its "many hundreds of thousands of dollars from excess receipts to build recreational facilities."[7] This occurred specifically under Dean Ernie McCoy's leadership and was continued under his successor, Robert Scannell. There was grumbling from some in athletics that athletic money should remain with athletics and not used to build an outdoor swimming pool or help intramurals.

One method of preventing athletic money from going to build facilities for the entire student body was to separate athletics from the then College of Health and Physical Education, the expanded version of the School of Physical Education and Athletics. When outside experts in 1963 were brought in to evaluate the College that included athletics, the team, led by Professor Ben Massey of the University of Maryland, recommended a "more complete separation of the academic and athletic functions" of the school.[8] Massey's view was a reflection of a separation similar to the separation in many other institutions of higher education between athletics and physical education. Massey, who would soon join the Penn State faculty as a leader in exercise physiology and as an associate dean, was quietly opposed to big-time athletics. In Massey's mind it was logical to separate athletics from physical education, because he believed athletics smothered physical education and physical educators, even though coaches at Penn State were part of both units.[9]

When members of the Executive Committee of the College of Health and Physical Education met to discuss the Massey Report, they fervently opposed the recommendations. "Staff members expressed strong opinions in support of our present College administrative set-up," the minutes reported. The Executive Committee was composed of coaches and noncoaches and both men and women. Everyone, even the present and past coaches John Lawther (basketball), Ray Conger (track), Elmer Gross (basketball), Jim O'Hora (football), and Nick Thiel (lacrosse), was opposed to the recommendations "whereby our academic division would be completely divorced from athletics." The Executive Committee agreed unanimously that the "present scheme is superior to alternatives." The committee stated, "The direct relationship that now exists between our academic program and athletics enables us to exert a measure of influence on the latter to the extent that they continue to contribute to our major program." The College leaders went on to say, "Both programs would suffer if this influence were to be lost through complete administrative separation of the two agencies."[10] The policy of athletics within an academic unit continued from Dean McCoy's tenure well into Robert Scannell's deanship of the 1970s. It was Joe Paterno's demand of President Oswald that caused a change in policy. Paterno would accept the position of athletic director only if athletics were removed from the academic unit, where he was a full professor, and became independent in the business office of the university.[11]

The change in athletic directors from Ed Czekaj to Joe Paterno came at time of difficulty in Penn State athletics, for the 1970s were a period of great economic inflation, coming on the heels of the Vietnam War and civil-rights strife. The rapid increase in the cost of equipment, travel, athletic scholarships, and coaching salaries and the growth of women's athletics and the demands of equality under Title IX of the Education Amendments of 1972 added to the financial difficulties athletics was having at Penn State. It is no wonder Joe Paterno might have resented any athletic money going to nonfootball facilities and other sports at this period. With some justification, Paterno wanted an indoor football practice facility, artificial turf on his practice field, a high-quality football weight-training facility, a lighted stadium, a better football office facility, and a sports museum.[12] All this took money that, he believed, should no longer be used for other facilities not related to football or for the entire student body.

Paterno's desires for football money going to football principally in quest of a national championship came in conflict with the long tradition at Penn State of using athletic money not only for varsity athletics but for facilities that could be used by all Penn State students, men and women. In the year of the athletic coup, Ralph Zilly, vice president for business, told the Board of Trustees, "The University has long been a believer in the philosophy of using athletic contest receipts to improve athletic facilities, not just for competitive varsity athletics, but to serve the entire campus population." These facilities, Zilly said, would include intramural playfields, swimming pools, tennis courts, and an ice rink.[13] Yet these nonfootball facilities were eating into athletic money at the same time that the inflation of the 1970s was causing financial difficulties for football and other varsity sports.

Coaching salaries were adding to financial concerns. About a quarter of the $2 million expended by football at the end of the 1970s went to coaches' salaries, more than the cost of running the entire women's athletic program.[14] Paterno's salary began at $20,000 when he became head coach. By 1973, after three undefeated teams, it had jumped to $33,000. Four years later, with his first chance to compete for a national title against Alabama, it stood at $55,000. There was, though, additional Paterno compensation for a television program worth $15,000, football camps in which the hundreds of campers contributed $10 each to Paterno's income, and a $25,000 bonus often achieved for participation in one of the major bowl games each year. There was even a clause in his eight-page contract that a cash bonus "may be awarded to him from time to time by the University acting through its President."[15] With these additions, Paterno was earning more than $100,000 a year, not including his pay from numerous speeches and attendance at other events. Paterno was doing well financially even as the athletic program, under the control of an academic dean, was in some trouble.

Paradoxically, Joe Paterno's Grand Experiment of accomplishments on the field and in the classroom had been operating rather successfully for a long period within an educational unit. Some people believed that this was one of the principal reasons why the athletic program at Penn State became known for its academic integrity. With some academic oversight over athletics, which in other universities with little supervision were often breaking rules, there may be some justification for believing the brilliant Supreme Court justice Louis Brandeis's admonition that "sunlight is said to be the best of disinfectants."[16] In any event, no major athletic scandals occurred at Penn State during the five decades that athletics operated under a deanship. By contrast, a number of national athletic programs, principally separated from their institutions or not associated with an academic unit, were involved in academic scandals. A few examples in the 1950s and 1960s were Boston College, the University of California at Los Angeles (UCLA), City College of New York, Long Island University, the University of Kentucky (which was given the first death penalty for basketball violations under Coach Adolph Rupp), the University of San Francisco, West Point Military Academy, and the College of William and Mary. In the following three decades, Arizona State, Auburn, Colorado, Miami of Florida, Minnesota, Southern Methodist, Oklahoma, Texas A&M, Washington, and Southern Methodist (SMU) and a number of others had their own scandals.[17] The case of Southern Methodist may have been the most notable, for the National Collegiate Athletic Association (NCAA) gave its football program the NCAA's second "death penalty" after multiple-year major violations of NCAA rules. SMU officials provided illegal signing bonuses for recruits, new automobiles for players, and other blatant payments to athletes. It involved not only the football coaches but the athletic director, the president, and the former governor of Texas and member of the SMU Board of Trustees, Bill Clements.[18]

Then, in 1980, President Oswald altered the locus of control, without Board of Trustee approval, by appointing Joe Paterno athletic director. As Robert Scannell noted soon after becoming dean in 1970, "structurally and philosophically" Penn State does not "have the separation of athletics." Scannell was proud of a college structure different from any other big-time school. At Penn State there coexisted a physical education department ranked Number One nationally and a football team with several undefeated seasons. "We have a college," Scannell boasted, "the same as a college of liberal arts [where] intercollegiate athletics is a department of that college."[19]

In the mid-1970s, Maurice Goddard, one of the trustees, questioning Penn State's withdrawal from the Eastern Collegiate Athletic Conference, wanted to know who made athletic policy. Goddard, secretary of the Pennsylvania Department of Forests and Water, requested of President Oswald a report for the Board of Trustees on policymaking in athletics. The request went to Dean Scannell of the College of Health and Physical Education. He sent an assistant, Glenn "Nick" Thiel, to report to the board. Thiel, who had been in the Physical Education Department since the 1930s, reported that Penn State athletics were "totally a part of one of the academic colleges of the University." Thiel told the trustees that Penn State was "well ahead of all" other universities in a 1974 NCAA survey with the number of sports it sponsored, 25, and 23 club sports.[20] Being "totally a part" of an academic college continued only for another five years. Ridge Riley, executive secretary of the Alumni Association, could brag as follows:

> Not one cent of the tax-payers' money goes into our athletic program—build-ings, stadium, grants-in-aid, athletic fields, indoor and outdoor tennis courts, ice rink, 36 holes of golf, astro-turf practice field, all other intercollege sports (including the women's—God bless them)—all paid for by football. We have been successful athletically because of good athletic management, good coach-ing, good recruiting, and superb alumni support. This hasn't been a sudden development—it has been going on for 25 years.[21]

The fact that football was paying for most of the physical activities and facilities on campus was a major problem for the most successful football coach in the nation, Joe Paterno, and possibly for the financial stability of the athletic program.

Following in Dean McCoy's footsteps, Bob Scannell continued to use athletic money for various projects as he continued to build the academic program in his college just as Joe Paterno was continuing to build his football program. The old Chinese proverb, "one mountain cannot accommodate two tigers; one country cannot tolerate two kings,"[22] seemed applicable to an impending clash of egos between Joe Paterno and Bob Scannell as well as a conflict over priorities. The faculty representative to the NCAA, John Coyle, summed up the situation and a growing conflict between Scannell and Paterno: "Paterno felt that any surpluses should be put directly back into athletics in case of shortfalls," Coyle, a business professor of logistics, commented some years later. "Scannell lived year-by-year and he would move monies around," stated Coyle. "If there was a shortfall in one area, he would patch it up by moving monies in from another area."[23] Often that area from which money was moved was athletics, because it was the most flush. One example occurred in 1977 as the end of the fiscal year was nearing. In a memo that he evidently did not send, Scannell intended to notify a budget officer of a projected shortfall when he wrote: "After moving costs normally handled in instructional budgets to athletic budgets . . . we will come out short. . . . We must reach an agreement," Scannell wrote, "between you, Mr. Patterson, Mr. Garban, and myself concerning the manner in which we will 'play off' this situation against year-end lapse funds."[24]

One physical education researcher confirmed the academic benefit of money exchanged between athletics and physical education: "Several professors were able to purchase new lab equipment," the researcher reported, "with [football] money. That's how our labs gained national reputations."[25] Helping the quality physical education faculty to succeed with financial resources may have been what Dean Scannell was referring to when he informed a university-appointed committee conducting a review of his office in 1978. He wrote, "I see the overall role of an administrator in a College today as being one of making it possible for a faculty of excellence to excel." He underscored this by telling the committee examining his office that the college had "assembled a grouping of talent that is difficult to equal in any college or division of this type in the nation."[26] Athletic money had been significant in this academic development.

Joe Paterno probably did not know about some of these financial transactions, but he did know about specific expenditures of "his" football money. In the fall that followed the New Year's crushing defeat by Alabama for the national championship in 1979, Paterno was still extremely testy to be around. "I let my anger turn against the staff and against the team," Paterno said.[27] He also turned his venom toward the dean of his college, Bob Scannell. Only a couple weeks after Paterno questionably took the great Matt Millen's captaincy away from him for not completing a lengthy preseason run and after two starters had flunked out of school, Paterno lashed out about what was happening to "our football money." Clearly intended for Scannell's eyes, Paterno told the student newspaper,

> If football can go out and build all the tennis courts we have, all of the intramural football fields, finance 36 holes of golf, pay for that outdoor swimming pool—-all for the benefit of students, they wouldn't have any of those recreational facilities if football hadn't made the money—I think every once in a while we can say we have to keep upgrading our intercollegiate [football] facilities.[28]

Paterno was building up to his real dispute with Scannell. It had to do with athletic money going to build a temporary ice hockey rink for a club sport and some recreational use. "To be very honest," Paterno vented his spleen, "I really resented even the way Dean Scannell handled [the hockey situation], the fact that we spent the kind of money [nearly $100,000] we did for a temporary hockey rink." It was Scannell, according to Paterno, who "comes in and changes the emphasis on intercollegiate athletics and wants to start taking away things from us." Foretelling the athletic directorship and increase in power that would come to him in about three months, he told the reporter, "that would not have been the way I would have done it."[29]

The fall of 1979 was the culmination of activity that had been going on at the university and in the college since the mid-1970s, and the result was a major change in the administration of athletics at Penn State. Much of it centered on the power that Joe Paterno had accrued as he turned out winner after winner in the football program. An ad hoc committee on varsity athletics of the College of Health and Physical education met for more than a year trying to determine how to both rank the 31 sports and cut costs and expand income. The committee of seven coaches and one teacher-researcher who served as chair favored the present broad-based athletic program that the college supported, but it suggested that there was a need to reexamine the administrative structure of the Athletic Department.[30] There was no suggestion that athletics should be removed from an academic unit and placed in a business unit. The committee recommended numerous ways of cutting costs, such as reducing the number of road trips and overnight stays and cutting training table costs, but they stated that cutting the number of sports should be done only as a "last resort." The group also suggested revenue-raising actions, such as taking control of the summer sport camps, expanding sport-related auxiliary enterprises, sponsoring nonathletic events in Recreation Building and Beaver Stadium, and financially exploiting the Blue–White spring football game.[31] The report may have given some impetus to reorganizing the athletic department at the end of the 1970s.

This internal document of the college, however, did not have nearly the effect of a review of Dean Scannell's office emanating from the university administration in 1978. The review likely received encouragement from the office of the vice president for business and finance, Robert Patterson, and his assistant, Steve Garban, who had an athletic background. As a former captain of the football team while Paterno was an assistant coach, Garban was in a strategic position to gain a great deal of control over athletics. That possibility is something he likely looked forward to since Ed Czekaj, not Garban, had been chosen athletic director when he was an administrator in the athletic department in the 1960s. According to Patterson, Garban was "my main link to athletics."[32] Both Patterson and Garban certainly knew of Bob Scannell's interchange of academic and athletic money in his position as dean and of Joe Paterno's dislike for athletic money being used for other purposes.

Coming from the university administrative offices in Old Main was a call for a review of the dean of what was then titled the College of Health, Physical Education and Recreation. It was just a routine review, the administration could claim, something that was to be done for all academic deans and academic vice presidents. Dean Scannell's review, however, was the first. This one was specific—to look at the administration of the athletic program and see if Dean Scannell was spending too much time on athletics at the expense of the academic side of the college. The Dean Scannell Review Committee was created, which looked like a balanced representation of the college and outside sources. The chair was an associate dean in the College of Agriculture, Howard Thoele. The three members from the College of Health, Physical Education and Recreation were Walter Bahr, a soccer coach of some reputation and a participant on the 1950 World Cup team that beat the great British team; Patricia Farrell, a professor of Recreation and Parks with a knowledgeable history of Penn State as well as a resident of State College from birth; and professor Ronald Smith, with research interests in the history of intercollegiate athletics and a strong background as an athlete at Northwestern University in baseball and basketball. There were two outsiders other than chairman Thoele. Ben Niebel, professor of industrial engineering, had a solid interest in sports, especially wrestling and tennis. The other, and placed strategically, was Steve Garban, controller and assistant to the senior vice president for finance and operations, a former football captain who had been hired originally at Penn State in the athletic department as ticket manager.

The makeup of the committee is important historically because one member, Steve Garban, had vested interests in the outcome of the committee findings. If the committee would come to the conclusion that the dean's involvement with athletics within his college was dominating the academic interests, it could be argued that athletics should be withdrawn from that unit to strengthen the academic arm. Where would athletics be logically placed in that case? Because the financing of athletics and football dominated much of the most visible activity on campus, it would logically be placed in a business or financial arm of the university. Thus, athletics would come under the wing of the most knowledgeable individual in Finance and Operations, Steve Garban, as the right-hand man of Senior Vice President Bob Patterson.

Dean Thoele led a thorough study of the college, the athletic program, and the place of Dean Scannell in its operation that began with a seven-page letter by Dean Scannell on his views of the operation of the college and athletics. All the major individuals relative to athletics were interviewed, including the athletic director, the assistant and associated athletic directors, the associate dean of the college, the head football coach, and the dean himself. A survey was taken of the entire faculty and staff of the college, including all those on the Commonwealth of Pennsylvania campuses. One common answer, especially of those questioned and surveyed at the University Park campus, was that Scannell spent too much time dealing with athletics, some felt up to 80 or 90 percent of his time, and Scannell himself said it was more than 50 percent.[33] There was a sense that Athletic Director Ed Czekaj spent most of his time in public relations and that Dean Scannell was making most of the athletic decisions.

When the report was completed, several things stood out that would have significance almost immediately and implications for the future. First, even though the report stated that Dean Scannell was "an outstanding administrator," too much of the dean's time was dedicated to athletics. Second, there needed to be a budget and staffing reorganization of the athletic department. Third, and significant for what actually happened, athletics should remain an integral part of the college. The report made a strong statement for the Penn State academic-athletic model rather than the business-financial model, favored by Steve Garban and used by most big-time institutions of higher education:

> The Committee, after many hours of discussion, recommends that the *integration of Intercollegiate Athletics and Academics be retained.* Penn State has a unique marriage that works, and the union provides a great deal of prestige to the faculty, coaches, and athletes as well as to the research and instructional components where many of the same personnel function.[34]

The only person who argued against the statement was Steve Garban, who believed that Penn State should have control of athletics in a business office. This could be argued effectively, as Garban did, because that was where athletics were controlled in most of the big-time institutions.[35] It also could have been argued that Steve Garban, former staff member in the athletic department, really wanted to control athletics at Penn State. Yet control of Penn State's athletics was unique in the nation. The other members of the committee recognized that Penn State probably had the cleanest program in big-time athletics in part because it was in an academic unit of the university, not hidden away and isolated from the faculty in a financial office under a former football player without academic credentials.

Between May 1979 when President Oswald received the report and December of that year, Oswald came up with what he rationalized was a sound resolution to athletic administration. His solution was influenced by two individuals in the business office, Steve Garban and Bob Patterson, and by one coach, Joe Paterno. Because the Athletic Department needed different leadership, Oswald would replace Athletic Director Ed Czekaj as part of the reorganization recognized by the Dean Scannell Review Committee. John Oswald, Bob Patterson, Joe Paterno, and Bob Scannell held a meeting on November 18, 1979. They decided to replace Czekaj, hoping that he would voluntarily accept an associate athletic director position, but if he would not do that or take another position such as an executive position with the new national College Football Association, he would be fired.[36] Czekaj reluctantly accepted a fabricated position as a special assistant to the senior vice president for finance and operations, Robert Patterson, and Joe Paterno was asked to take the athletic director position.

Then, to the complete surprise of Bob Scannell until the fait accompli, Oswald severed the athletic connection to the College of Health, Physical Education and Recreation after being influenced to do so by Bob Patterson, Steve Garban, and especially Joe Paterno. Oswald would place athletics under Bob Patterson, but more important, under the controller, Steve Garban. Significantly, John Oswald had been president of the University of Kentucky the previous decade. At that time, he had been forced out as president by the greatest name in basketball coaching in America, Adolph Rupp.[37] The iconic Rupp never had a black on his team, even though the university had been desegregated for much more than a decade. The split between Rupp and President Oswald came over this issue. Rupp said he was called into President Oswald's office and told by the president "I'm going to demand that you get some colored boys" on the team.[38] No one was going to tell Adolph Rupp what he would do with his team, which dominated basketball in the United States for a generation. He had the power to do what he wanted to do. After all, there is at present a statue of Adolph Rupp on the Kentucky campus and not one of John Oswald (though an obscure building is named for him). Oswald lost the battle and lost his position. At Penn State, President Oswald did not want another encounter with a powerful coach similar to Rupp, and Paterno was the best-known individual on the Penn State campus and in Pennsylvania. Even if President Oswald had some misgivings about taking athletics out of an academic unit, he was likely willing to do it to prevent a greater conflict with Paterno.

Only a few years before, a seemingly small incident in May 1972 occurred to show Oswald that he should be afraid of Coach Paterno's power, and Paterno certainly did not fear Oswald. At a Nittany Lion Club meeting, both the president and Paterno spoke, with Oswald addressing the supporters of athletics first. President Oswald bragged about his involvement in an athletic agreement between Penn State and the other three members of the Big Four, Pittsburgh, Syracuse, and West Virginia University. After Oswald's talk, Joe Paterno spoke and highly criticized Oswald's agreement with the Big Four, indicating that Penn State should not be comparing itself to an institution like West Virginia but should have higher national aspirations. Oswald took it as a slam on his integrity as president. At the conclusion of the event, Oswald, Paterno, and the head of Penn State Gifts and Endowments, Charlie Lupton, were in the men's restroom before heading home. Lupton, who later reported the exchange, was astonished when the two sparred. President Oswald told Paterno that "if you ever again do something in public like you did this evening, you'll be gone." Immediately Paterno shot back with a likely truism, "John, you'll be gone before I am."[39]

Soon Paterno, rather than apologizing, wrote to Oswald stating that he should not be shocked by his statement "in an academic community which believes in the right of honest disagreement." He told Oswald that "you should not think it a personal matter if I publicly disagree with the wisdom of such an agreement."[40] Oswald, a Phi Beta Kappa scholar and football captain at DePauw University with a doctoral degree from Berkeley, and a World War II PT boat captain like John F. Kennedy, was placed in a defensive position by a literature major from Brown University. It was as if he remembered what power coach Adolph Rupp did to him at Kentucky only a few years before by demanding of the coach that he integrate his basketball team. In 1972, after several undefeated seasons and a number of possibilities of coaching elsewhere, Paterno knew that he had both the alumni and the Board of Trustees in his pocket. And he did. It is not likely that Paterno ever feared any Penn State president, nor thought that anyone could fire him—until on November 9, 2011, in the wake of the Sandusky Scandal, the Board of Trustees, not a president, did just that.

Paterno, in the 1970s, knew he could make demands upon President Oswald. At the end of 1979, before Joe Paterno would become athletic director, he listed his requirements for accepting the athletic directorship from President Oswald. Paterno wrote a three-page letter to Oswald noting that after "discussions with you and talks with other Penn State people in your confidence," and "with certain conditions," he would accept the athletic directorship. But there was a major condition, for he would not accept the position "if the present athletic department structure is maintained and if athletics is completely responsible to the Dean of the College of Health, Physical Education and Recreation." To Paterno, the dean, Bob Scannell, could not effectively "do justice to his primary academic responsibilities" and "manage an intercollegiate program with thirty-one sports and an operating budget in excess of eight million dollars." Paterno told Oswald that the "Athletic Director should deal directly with your administration, preferably with the Senior Vice-President for Finance because of the tremendous future financial problems inherent in athletics." Paterno insisted that "budgeting, finances, contractual arrangements, and personnel matters" be severed from the dean's control, in other words, make a clean cut with the previous control of the Athletic Department. Paterno stated specifically that only the athletic director should have "sole responsibility" of intercollegiate athletic facilities, something that Dean Scannell had been directly involved with previously and which Paterno strongly opposed.[41] Paterno was in a strong position to exact his demands even if Oswald might have questioned any of them. Oswald, hypocritically, responded favorably to the demands of Paterno, rather than confirm his belief that athletics within an academic unit was a good policy. Only a few years before, Oswald had stated, "More than any University I've known the intercollegiate athletic program is an integral part of the overall education program."[42] Either Oswald was a liar or he feared the power of Joe Paterno—or both.

When President Oswald accepted Paterno's demands, without going to the Board of Trustees for this important decision, a new athletic regime came into being. The president abrogated the half-century-old Board of Trustees policy of retaining athletics within an academic unit, and Joe Paterno was then in control. Could J. William Fulbright's comments about power be applied to John Oswald, Joe Paterno, and Penn State athletics? In 1966, during the early years of the Vietnam War, Senator Fulbright stated: "Power confuses itself with virtue and tends also to take itself for omnipotence."[43] What Penn State received when Oswald appointed the new athletic director, according to Joe Paterno, was "enlightened leadership," which Paterno believed he would provide as athletic director. This seemed to be a case of Paterno believing he had the answer to athletic questions or, as he once said to writer Bernard Asbell, "I was too sure of myself to listen to others."[44] A sportswriter for the *Philadelphia Inquirer* quoted Paterno in a similar way as saying "I thought I was right all the time."[45] Or as was stated by Jim Tarman, a friend of Paterno who replaced him as athletic director in 1982, "once he thinks he's right and you're wrong, he doesn't waver."[46] Then, too, Paterno agreed that he wanted control over everything affecting his program. "Something in me," Paterno stated in his autobiography, "demands control of detail from top to bottom."[47] With the athletic directorships, he was now in control. Upon winning his coveted national championship two years later, Paterno this time stated of President Oswald, "We would not be No. 1 in athletics if it had not been for his cooperation."[48] The two national championships in the half-dozen years after Oswald's decision to take athletics out of an academic unit confirms to some that it was the right decision. In the 14 years before the coup, however, Paterno won 82 percent of his games while dropping to 75 percent in the following 14 years, and the criminal and academic problems that beset the program in the 1980s and 1990s took luster off the championship achievements.

Dean Robert Scannell, at the time of the coup, was kept in the dark about the major change in the locus of athletic control. Though Scannell was in on a number of the discussions with Penn State administrators about the need for reorganizing the Athletic Department, including bringing in a new athletic director, he had no knowledge that he and the college would be divested of the half-century connection with the athletic program. On the first day of classes in the spring 1980 school term, Scannell walked into a faculty meeting, flushed in the face, just after being told by President Oswald that he was no longer dean over the athletic program. Scannell said quietly to one faculty member, "They've done it to us, the College has lost control of athletics."[49] Scannell did not protest at that time, for he was protecting his academic-administrative career, and he may have felt that challenging the decision could further jeopardize the status of the college.[50] He later told a researcher, however, that taking athletics out of an academic college had destroyed "an operation that had become a national model." A dozen years after Paterno had become athletic director, Scannell summed up his view of the situation:

> Look at what's happened since. The College no longer exists. Athletics is now strictly a business operation. Coaches are no longer faculty. . . . I felt we had it right. Our program was a national example. It was more than just Paterno. Our women's programs were big and very successful. Tying athletics and academics together was the key. Breaking athletics loose wasn't the way to go.[51]

Scannell's opinion was echoed by others, including the associate dean in the college, Karl Stoedefalke. For him, the "symbiotic relationship" among "coaches and faculty went out the window." He said, "You used to sit in the same room with coaches like Jerry Sandusky and Dick Anderson. After the realignment," Stoedefalke remarked, "coaches lost out on classroom experiences and the faculty no longer felt a part of intercollegiate athletics."[52] A major part of the tradition was lost forever as the academic arm to athletics was severed. If it was hypocritical for President Oswald to make his decision without Board of Trustee input, one could recall the words of François de La Rochefoucauld 300 years before: "Hypocrisy is the homage vice pays to virtue."[53]

It is not surprising that Bob Scannell was soon elevated above his deanship by being promoted to vice president of the commonwealth campus system only months after the athletic coup. It was a position that Scannell had eyed prior to the athletic coup, but the loss of athletic control may have triggered greater interest.[54] From an outward appearance, this symbolically was a move not dissimilar to the case of Hugo Bezdek a half-century before, being "promoted" to head a new School of Physical Education and Athletics, while being removed as head football coach. Nor did it appear significantly different from the 1968 firing of the basketball coach, John Egli, who was then given a large raise as he was made athletic director of the Penn State Commonwealth System.[55] Penn State had a tradition of cover-up firings by elevating the individual to a new and sometimes more highly paid position as had been done when John Bach was released as head basketball coach in 1978, given a title and placed in a hidden-away office off the running track in Recreation Building until he found another position coaching in the National Basketball Association.

Soon after athletics was removed from its academic setting, the College of Health, Physical Education and Recreation was joined with the College of Human Development to become the College of Health and Human Development. Athletics became isolated in a financial arm of the university and isolated in new buildings devoted entirely to athletics. Athletics, nevertheless, remained far purer than most big-time programs and had no major violations, though a number of minor ones, of NCAA rules well into the twenty-first century. The tradition of honesty that was promoted beginning with Dean Ernie McCoy continued after Joe Paterno's short, two-year tenure as athletic director and when Jim Tarman and then Tim Curley, two Paterno choices, led the program.

The outward image of football and the other varsity sports was clean if not spotless as athletics became more insular as a business, not part of an educational, operation. Athletics at Penn State, like those in many other big-time institutions, could be run as its own fiefdom, sequestered from the academic mission of the university and dominated in a financial office by a former football captain and later president of the Board of Trustees, Steve Garban. This could work effectively, and did so generally, as most of those in leadership roles were honorable individuals. When, however, there were charges of malfeasance by individuals associated with athletics in the Jerry Sandusky Scandal, the structure of the university allowed those charges to be hidden to preserve the reputation of individuals and, more important, the reputation of football as the driving force in the athletic program. Unfortunately, Penn State would have to deal with the charges of insularity when a scandal enveloped athletics and the entire university. For a short period, the coach was still Joe Paterno, the financial office was headed by the successor to Steve Garban, who was then president of the Board of Trustees, and the athletic director, Tim Curley, another former Penn State football player and an individual principally selected by the football coach. One could wonder how much the athletic coup three decades before had contributed to the worst crisis in Penn State's history.

CHAPTER 9

President Bryce Jordan and Penn State's Entry into the Big Ten

"Not being heard is no reason for silence."
—Victor Hugo (1862)

The new tradition of Penn State presidents changing policy without Board of Trustees involvement, as in the 1980 athletic control coup d'état, continued one decade later as Penn State made a dramatic move into the prestigious Big Ten Conference. Previous Penn State presidents had not ignored the Board of Trustees in the creation of a new academic school to house athletics in 1930, and the trustees were directly involved in creating athletic scholarships (1900), eliminating them (1927), and creating scholarships again (1948). To the contrary, both President Oswald and President Bryce Jordan avoided the Board of Trustees in two major athletic-changing athletic policies in 1980 and 1990. President Oswald's course of action, withdrawing athletics from an academic unit, had a negative impact on the academic integrity of the athletic program. In contrast, President Jordan's decision to join the Big Ten was likely more important in raising Penn State academically than anything positive done for athletics. Whereas Joe Paterno's move into the athletic director's position contributed to isolating athletics from academics, Paterno's iconic image was significant in convincing skeptics in the Big Ten to bring Penn State into a league with a number of superior educational institutions and raise the status of Penn State. Although the legacy of John Oswald will likely be lost to history, Bryce Jordan's foresight in bringing Penn State into the Big Ten (without trustee involvement) will likely be one of the more significant accomplishments in the history of Penn State.

Until joining the Big Ten, Penn State football had almost always been played independent of a conference, except for a short period in the 1890s.[1] In the early 1920s when Hugo Bezdek was involved in a 30-game undefeated streak, he suggested to the Penn State alumni in Western Pennsylvania that an eastern conference should be created in football. Bezdek's proposed conference would consist of all of the future Ivy League teams along with Pittsburgh and Syracuse. At the time, he hoped Harvard, Yale, and Princeton would "drop the purple saga of athletic aristocracy" in creating the conference.[2] Obviously speaking like that would not

endear Bezdek to any of the elite eastern schools, but Bezdek was not an endear-
ing person. Nothing came of Bezdek's suggestion. In the 1930s and 1940s with
no athletic scholarships and Penn State playing mostly second- and third-rank
institutions, there was no major discussion of a former big-time school joining
the Lebanon Valleys and Dickinsons of the athletic world.

Not until well after World War II, when Penn State became one of the athletic
scholarship schools again, was there a movement to join a conference. There
were attempts by Joe Paterno and others at Penn State to join an all-sports eastern conference. Before those efforts came about, however, and before Paterno
became head coach, there was an agreement, if not a conference, among Pittsburgh, Syracuse, West Virginia, and Penn State to raise eligibility standards and
entrance requirements to level the playing field among those four competing
schools.[3] When an extension on the ten-year agreement was being discussed
in 1972, among other concerns, the "Big 4" would eliminate the practice of "red
shirting" athletes (keeping football players out of competition for a year so that
they could add physical maturity for later competition).[4] Joe Paterno was opposed
to both red shirting and freshman eligibility, but he did not like the extension.
(He had opposed freshman eligibility and the National Collegiate Athletic Association [NCAA] decision to allow freshman to participate in varsity football
and basketball in 1972.[5])

Paterno opposed President Oswald's acceptance of the Big 4 agreement because,
among other reasons, he said that having Western Pennsylvania's Pittsburgh in
the group of four would put pressure to include an eastern Pennsylvania school,
Temple. "If Temple and Pitt are in it," Paterno believed, "Penn State without a big
city press will be greatly hurt as 'poor cousins.'" He could see Pitt and Temple and
two professional teams in the cities of Pittsburgh and Philadelphia dominating
football and leaving Penn State with diminishing crowds. Paterno told President
Oswald that, like George Washington, we should steer "clear of permanent alliances."[6] For once, Paterno's wishes were not acceded to, but soon afterward the
extension became moot when Pitt withdrew from the Big 4 at about the same
time it hired Johnny Majors as coach in 1973.[7] Majors wanted to offer more than
the agreed 25 freshman football scholarships and also wanted to redshirt athletes.
When he got his way, Majors recruited Tony Dorsett and a number of other
athletes and in three years won a national championship a half a decade before
Paterno won his first. Paterno might then have wished for a stronger commitment
to the Big 4 agreement from Pitt, not to eliminate it.

Paterno was really concerned at the time with being included with regional
"outlaw" schools such as Pitt, West Virginia, and Syracuse. Paterno asked the
new dean, Bob Scannell, "Why should Penn State be involved in an agreement
wherein there is no trust and in fact the athletic departments of all four schools
have in practice agreed to disregard the rules of the agreement whenever it is
convenient?" Besides, Paterno did not want to be associated exclusively with the

other three members of the Big 4, because "our future is in the national picture and not in the regional image I believe our 'agreement' now presents." He told Scannell, "Our national prestige and image is not, I hope, enhanced by West Virginia."[8] Having won more than 80 percent of his games, Paterno was looking for a greater national presence.

The drive by Joe Paterno for national exposures also applied to Penn State's membership in the Eastern College Athletic Conference (ECAC). The ECAC was a very large group of institutions in the East organized originally in the 1930s to bring about common rules and better officiating of contests. For the Nittany Lions, football was little involved with the ECAC in scheduling of contests, but the image of Penn State was affected by the national contempt for eastern sports, especially football, as being inferior. The ECAC also had rules on television and bowl game contributions to the organization from football contests. Penn State was concerned in the early 1970s that of the 214 colleges in the ECAC, Penn State's ECAC contribution was 16 percent of the ECAC's entire budget.[9] Although what Penn State considered the inequitable financial arrangements of the ECAC to tax television income from the richest schools to the benefit of the smaller institutions, the major argument concerned the image question. Scotty Whitelaw, ECAC commissioner, argued against Penn State's withdrawal. "I am not sure that there would be favorable effect upon Penn State's future image," Whitelaw wrote to President Oswald, "resulting from your withdrawal from the ECAC and your consequential isolation from involvement with the 'Eastern image.'"[10] The Penn State Athletic Department was not impressed with Whitelaw's reasoning, nor was the Board of Trustees, which was involved in this conference decision, and Penn State withdrew from the ECAC in 1974.[11]

As television money was in many ways driving college football in the 1970s and the early 1980s, a group of disaffected big-time football institutions of the NCAA, including Penn State, decided to organize the College Football Association (CFA) to gain a larger share of television revenue. The CFA was in opposition to the NCAA television policy that was disbursing its television revenues among all NCAA members, not just the big-time schools. All of the members of the CFA, conceptualized in 1975, were members of big-time conferences, with the exception of two major independents, Notre Dame and Penn State. The Big Ten and the PAC-8 conference remained outside the CFA, evidently satisfied that their share of television money and the highly profitable Rose Bowl could be divided up among conference teams. Conferences such as the Southeastern Conference (with teams such as Alabama and Georgia), however, and the Big Eight (with the likes of Texas and Oklahoma) did not appreciate the distribution of television money by the NCAA, with too much being spent on smaller colleges and programs other than football.[12] Smaller and less successful colleges wanted a "share the wealth" program for the distribution of football revenues coming into the NCAA. The NCAA had a policy of limiting the number of times an institution could have a national or regional telecast, spreading telecasting among a number of lesser programs. This antagonized the best of the big-time schools such as Notre Dame, Georgia, Oklahoma, and Penn State.

Upon the scene came the share-the-wealth, Robin Hood president of California State University, Long Beach, Stephen Horn. When President Horn went before the NCAA convention in 1974 with a plan to distribute big-time football revenue from football to all divisions of the NCAA, the big-time schools revolted, including Joe Paterno's Penn State. Horn's proposal to cut costs of football during the inflation caused by the Vietnam War included cutting the number of football scholarships drastically and helping out the small institutions by dividing up television revenues among them. The vitriol created by Horn's Robin Hood proposition stimulated the football powers of seven conferences and independents Notre Dame and Penn State in 1975, out of which the CFA was born. Only the Big Ten and the PAC-8 (soon to be PAC-10) refused to join the CFA. In just a few years, the CFA challenged the NCAA television plan under antitrust laws. Penn State and Notre Dame contributed the greatest financial support to the lawsuit initiated by the University of Oklahoma and University of Georgia, while several conferences also contributed to the legal challenge. In the end, the U.S. Supreme Court in 1984 ruled that the monopolistic NCAA television plan violated the Sherman Antitrust Act of 1890.[13] Conferences and individual institutions, such as Notre Dame, could then set up their own television contracts. Notre Dame eventually did just that in a national contract with NBC-TV. Penn State, despite the success of Joe Paterno's teams, did not have the national audience of a Notre Dame and had to work out television contracts as an independent. It made joining a conference more attractive than before.

Some minor inquiries of the Big Ten were made in the 1970s and 1980s. As long as Joe Paterno kept winning, it would get on national television and appreciate the large sums of money. But what if his teams were not as successful as before and Penn State lost the television revenue? Television was one of the reasons Penn State, with Joe Paterno in the lead, sought to form an all-sports eastern conference and then made inquiries about joining the Big Ten in the early 1980s. As early as 1970, Joe Paterno even suggested to Associate Dean of the College of Health, Physical Education and Recreation Karl Stoedefalke (a new faculty member from Wisconsin), on a football trip to Wisconsin, to raise a question whether people in the Big Ten might be interested in Penn State as a conference member.[14] John Oswald, a couple of years before retiring in the early 1980s, made an inquiry of the Big Ten commissioner, Wayne Duke, at the time Penn State defeated Ohio State in the Fiesta Bowl. Joining the Big Ten would help relieve some of the financial pressure on football money supporting the other 28 Penn State sports at the time. In addition, it might help the rather weak basketball program and apply pressure to build a new basketball arena to replace the outdated and insufficient seating in the 1929 Recreation Building.[15] A novice Penn

State undergraduate sportswriter, Tom Verducci, who would later gain visibility on the *Sports Illustrated* staff, made a prescient remark eight years before Penn State was voted into the Big Ten: "Picture this: Penn State and Nebraska will join the Big Ten Conference," Verducci wrote, "expanding the league to 12 schools playing in two six-team divisions." Sports Information Director Jim Tarman, who would become athletic director in another year, said that to his knowledge "there's been no official contact" with the Big Ten.[16] The Big Ten discussions did not go farther at the time, although just before Commissioner Wayne Duke of the Big Ten retired in spring 1989, Penn State's Jim Tarman asked about possible membership, and Duke said that Tarman should pursue it.[17]

Prior to this, however, discussions took place between Penn State's John Oswald and the leading football schools in the East in the early 1980s. Those schools included Syracuse, Rutgers, West Virginia, Boston College, and Temple, with Army, Navy, Virginia Tech, and South Carolina on the fringes of the discussion.[18] After Oswald's retirement, President Bryce Jordan wrote retired president Eric Walker that he was "not ready for it to be widely known yet, but I can tell you that I've been in quiet consultation for several months" with West Virginia's Gordon Gee and Rutgers's Edward Bloustein about an eastern conference to also include Boston College, Pittsburgh, Syracuse, and Temple.[19] As Pitt was content to remain an independent in football (and in the Big East for basketball) and go to bowl games regularly and not split the bowl income with conference members, Pitt was reluctant to join an all-sport eastern league at that time.[20]

With no success in creating an eastern all-sports league, Penn State, with two national championships, an expanded stadium, and general financial stability in the mid-1980s, entertained little discussion of joining a conference until President Bryce Jordan revisited his interest in the Big Ten as a natural fit for his institution academically first and athletically second. The key to further discussions with the Big Ten came when Jordan contacted University of Illinois president Stanley Ikenberry. Ikenberry had once been senior vice president for administration at Penn State before being hired as president of the University of Illinois. In fall 1989, Ikenberry was made chairman of the Big Ten's Council of Presidents, a group that met regularly to discuss many issues. Athletics were nearly always discussed, but this time expansion of the Big Ten was a major topic.

The fact that the Big Ten Conference had recently incorporated made a big difference in who would discuss bringing in new members of the conference. The 1987 Big Ten incorporation mandated that the Council of Presidents "have final authority over all Conference matters."[21] This superseded the faculty representatives, who had generally run the conference since its origins in 1895–96 as the Intercollegiate Conference of Faculty Representatives, a six- and then seven-state Midwestern conference composed of leading institutions, most of which had been founded before the Civil War. As had occurred historically at Penn State, there was often a cloudy picture of who had ultimate authority over athletics. In the

Big Ten there was conflict among faculty representatives, athletic directors, and the presidents. Before 1987, the so-called Joint Group of the Big Ten (presidents, faculty reps, and athletic directors) would discuss major issues, but the faculty representatives generally ran the conference. This was not the case in deciding whether Penn State would become the eleventh member.

The Council of Presidents discussions of Big Ten expansion in fall 1989 were secret and closed to faculty representatives and athletic directors. President Jordan made the initial contact with President Ikenberry of Illinois to see whether he would discuss the possibility of Penn State joining the Big Ten. As a former Penn State administrator, Ikenberry was very receptive to the idea. After discussing the possibility with Joe Paterno, Jordan sent Steve Garban, Ikenberry's former administrative colleague as vice president for finance and business, and Athletic Director Jim Tarman to meet secretly with Ikenberry.[22] With a better idea of Penn State's wishes, Ikenberry then brought up the matter at an October 25 Council of Presidents meeting in Chicago. The presidents weighed the value of expansion and decided yes, if it would involve "like-minded universities." Any new members would have to be a member of the Association of American Universities, a research consortium of the more elite American universities, and they emphasized that any new member would have to have a positive impact on athletic reform such as attempting to eliminate freshman eligibility and raising academic standards, both of which Penn State was in favor of.[23] There was a discussion of adding one or possibly two more Big Ten members. If it were 12, would Pittsburgh, Rutgers, or Syracuse logically be the eastern entry? The Big Ten presidents were "unanimous in their receptivity" toward Penn State according to Jordan's note taken in a phone conversation with Ikenberry. The Big Ten, Jordan believed, wanted to take action while Jordan was still president of Penn State. As Jordan was scheduled to retire in summer 1990, the action should take place as soon as possible and with "total confidentiality."[24] That was one good reason for not informing the Board of Trustees.

Penn State fit best into what the Big Ten presidents were looking for—membership in the research-dominated Association of American Universities (member since 1958), with solid undergraduate students, and a nearly impeccable athletic program—something the Big Ten was looking for during the major problems of athletic integrity rampant throughout U.S. colleges in the 1980s.[25] Paterno was seen as the essence of integrity by many, including President Hunter Rawlings of the University of Iowa, who Rawlings said "has won the respect of many of us in higher education."[26] Eliminating freshman eligibility was a major issue for the presidents in an effort to raise athletic integrity, something Joe Paterno had advocated for his entire career as head coach. Not making the minutes of the Big Ten presidents was the financial significance that Penn State could provide through an eastern expansion in the growing television market for football. Within two months, in early December 1989, and with no discussions with Big Ten faculty representatives or athletic directors, to say nothing of boards of trustees or the faculty of the various institutions, the Council of Presidents voted unanimously to bring Penn State into the Big Ten.[27]

Then all hell broke loose. There was dissent among Penn Staters but far more among opponents within the Big Ten. Both faculty representatives of the Big Ten schools and athletic directors felt the presidents had denied their voices in the decision. And they were right, for both groups had a tradition of involvement in major Big Ten decisions. The faculty at Ohio State University got to the point when the chair of the Athletic Council responded to all the presidents that the presidents had "violated the spirit of faculty governance on which the Conference was founded."[28] Indeed, the historical principle of governance had been violated. Yet only three years before, the presidents had consolidated power when they incorporated, giving the presidents ultimate power. With the outburst of indignation from all sides, the Council of Presidents almost immediately backed off its decision to bring Penn State into the conference. Because of the negative reaction to the presidents' action, the Council of Presidents quickly stated that Penn State was only "invited in principle," that it was not a done deal until answers to a number of questions were provided.[29]

Athletic directors and coaches, such as Michigan's Bo Schembechler, the man who was named football coach at Michigan when Joe Paterno turned down the job after his undefeated 1968 season, strongly opposed Penn State's entry into the Big Ten.[30] Two of the most visible power coaches in the Big Ten were Bo Schembechler and Bobby Knight, basketball coach at Indiana. Schembechler remarked, "this confirms the worst fear I have of presidents getting too much control in athletics" and volatile Bobby Knight shouted out, "Penn State's a camping trip" not an athletic destination. Both tried to convince their presidents to vote no on Penn State, and both were apparently successful, as Indiana's Thomas Ehrlich and Michigan's James Duderstadt eventually voted against the entry. Rick Bay, athletic director at Minnesota, also opposed the Council of Presidents action when it rejected input from the faculty representatives and athletic directors, saying what the presidents did was "bassackwards." Michigan State's athletic director, Doug Weaver, was less vitriolic but accurate when he said that "This decision is premature without more analysis."[31]

There was opposition at Penn State for several reasons, such as losing natural rivals, such as Pitt, West Virginia, and Syracuse, and the long-distance travel to Minnesota and Iowa, but a major complaint was that only a handful of administrators at Penn State were involved in the decision. Significant among them was one trustee, Joel Myers, who was angered that the trustees were not being consulted over the decision to join the Big Ten. (Ironically, Myers was still a trustee more than two decades later when he would be in a controversy over why he and all other trustees exited both President Graham Spanier and especially iconic Joe Paterno, as the Sandusky Scandal broke.) In December 1989, two weeks after the

Big Ten decision, Myers as a trustee felt slighted by President Jordan's actions taken without consulting the trustees. He must have felt like a character in Victor Hugo's *Les Misérables* who said, "not being heard is no reason for silence."[32] Myers complained to his fellow trustees, but evidently not publicly, questioning Penn State's legal counsel, who assured Jordan that it was his legal right to make the decision to join the Big Ten without trustee approval. "It is disappointing to be told," he wrote the Board of Trustees, "that my role as a trustee is to be 'advised' rather than 'consulted'" in making an important decision of joining the Big Ten.[33] Myers was ignored both by his fellow trustees and by President Jordan.

A further irony is that Pennsylvania state officials were notified of the Big Ten presidents' vote prior to any notification of the Board of Trustees. President Jordan held an early meeting with Helen Wise, secretary for legislative affairs under Governor Bob Casey; Michael Hershock, secretary of the Pennsylvania budget; and Frank Forni, Penn State lobbyist in Harrisburg. The group met almost immediately after the original Big Ten Council of Presidents in December 1989. In the meeting, Jordan told them of the likelihood of Rutgers, or possibly Pittsburgh, becoming the twelfth member. But the meeting was not about further expansion; rather, Jordan wanted the release of state money for the Convocation Center (basketball arena) of about $35 million that would be added to $10 million or so Penn State would raise.[34] Obviously coming into the Big Ten would put pressure on Penn State and the state government to fund the new basketball arena. Funding for the new facility arrived quickly, and the arena was given a euphemistic title, Academic and Athletic Convocation Center, and later the Bryce Jordan Center.

The Big Ten Council of Presidents backtracking to "invited in principle" put in jeopardy the whole question of joining the Big Ten. In the month after the presidents' initial vote on acceptance, a joint meeting of Big Ten presidents, faculty representatives, and athletic directors was called in an attempt to resolve the issue by opening debate over the value of Penn State's entry. The seventeen-member Transition and Expansion Committee of Faculty Representatives, Athletic Directors, and Women Athletic Administrators was formed with new Conference Commissioner Jim Delany as chair. For the next four months the committee gathered data that would be helpful when in late spring a vote by the presidents would again take place.[35]

Penn State needed to put its best foot forward, and a transition team was created to meet regularly with Big Ten officials, some of whom were less than friendly to Penn State's delegation. On the team were Jim Tarman, athletic director, John Coyle, faculty representative, Ellen Perry, Women's Athletics, and Herb Schmidt, associate athletic director. In addition, Budd Thalman, Sports Information, and Tim Curley, associate athletic director and NCAA compliance officer, were staff members. Steve Garban, vice president for finance and business, was the central administration representative to the group.[36] Problems were in search of solutions. Although Penn State graduated its athletes at a higher rate than most Big Ten schools, its standard for eligibility (grade point average relative to number of credits taken) was lower than the Big Ten standard. Several eligible Penn State athletes would be ineligible under Big Ten rules.[37] It is not surprising that after athletics were taken out of an academic unit in 1980 and given to a business unit, the Big Ten found that the Penn State faculty was less involved in athletic governance than faculty at other Big Ten schools had always been, something the conference required.[38] Another drawback was that the basketball arena at Penn State was far from meeting the standard of the Big Ten. All these concerns were met by Penn State officials, including a pledge that a new basketball arena would be built in the near future.[39] An aptly named Bryce Jordan Center with nearly 15,000 seats was soon constructed, but in the next two decades "filled to capacity" was a rarity, unlike the football stadium, which eventually reached sellouts of 107,000.

The question of the importance of the eastern television market was noted by Big Ten officials, but television exposure was not likely the most important factor to the presidents. Nevertheless, athletic administrators were often most interested in the business of athletics and how much additional television revenue might come from a Penn State eastern television market. Minnesota athletic director Rick Bay opposed Penn State's entry but admitted reluctantly, "I guess, ultimately, Penn State would help our television contract."[40] The additional millions of television homes were not inconsequential in any decision making. Penn State's athletic director, Jim Tarman, may have exaggerated when he replied to Rick Bay that the Penn State television market reached from Boston through New York, Baltimore, and Washington into Richmond, Atlanta, and into Florida—in other words nearly the entire East Coast.[41] Donna Shalala, chancellor of the University of Wisconsin, summed up the importance of Penn State and television expansion to the Big Ten by making "us more powerful as a conference, particularly as we are trying to add constituencies as we try to work within the NCAA." Shalala said, "in the long run it would be a financial gain, for our ability to attract more people to games." Besides, she believed, "Penn State has an aura around it."[42]

Although Penn State basketball, with consistently mediocre teams, would likely be a negative factor in Big Ten television revenue, its football would have a positive impact on income after Penn State's assigned football television rights with the CFA would cease in 1995.[43] The CFA had a multimillion dollar contract with about 60 major colleges, including Notre Dame and Penn State, beginning almost a decade before. The CFA television plan had been created after the CFA-backed lawsuit defeated the NCAA's monopoly television policy in the 1984 Supreme Court decision. Penn State's visibility as a football power and Joe Paterno's image would create a financial windfall from television revenues as soon as Penn State became a fulltime Big Ten member in the mid-1990s. Just as Penn State's possible entry into the Big Ten was being debated, the CFA was dealt a major blow. Notre

Dame, the prime national attraction for football telecasting, withdrew from the CFA football contract and created its own multiyear national television agreement with NBC for $38 million.[44] This left open the opportunity for conferences to withdraw from the CFA contract, adding more members to each conference and attracting larger television audiences and lucrative television deals. It was important for the Big Ten to expand and attempt to grab the large eastern television market.

Penn State was primed for the expansion, but there were many anxious moments for the administrators trying to get a majority of the Big Ten institutions to permanently vote Penn State in. President Jordan lived through nearly a half-year of uncertainty, as a power struggle developed in a number of institutions. He kept notes of each of his phone conversations with his ally at Illinois, Stanley Ikenberry. Michigan's president, "Duderstadt[,] a problem," he wrote on more than one occasion. "If we lose more than 4" votes, Jordan jotted down, "then a problem." He noted, "What's going on? We sort of hanging out there," for there is "dissension between athletics & presidents." Another time he wrote "Turning negative," and "Our people getting nervous." Of Indiana's basketball coach, he penned, "Bobby Knight is a problem." Of Notre Dame possibly becoming a twelfth member, he jotted down, "presidents not enthusiastic." Just a couple weeks before the June vote by the presidents, Jordan heard from Ikenberry that they were "counting noses now 'seems Okay.'" Three days before the vote, Jordan scribbled, "Mich—Hard no, Mich State—soft no, Northwestern—soft no."[45] Jordan's psyche was likely lifted somewhat by Illinois's president Ikenberry cheering him up in his numerous telephone conversations, but on the inside there is no question; he felt anguish.

The day before the Big Ten presidents met for the final vote, President Jordan sat down and wrote in preparation for a negative vote, "A statement by Dr. Bryce Jordan on Big Ten Vote Denying Penn State Admission." He wanted to be ready for the defeat of four possible votes against Penn State. "Venting his spleen," as Jordan's assistant wrote on a note of his diatribe against the Big Ten for voting "NO," the Penn State president wrote, "The vote handed down by the Council of Ten—in my personal view—is a vote against first-class intercollegiate athletics and first-class academics." He noted that Penn State ranked first in the nation in Fulbright Fellowships received and fifteenth in the nation in research expenditures. The football team, he wrote, has a 72.3 percent graduation rate in contrast with only 46.6 percent in the CFA. How could the Big Ten vote unanimously for Penn State in December and against Penn State in June? This was his feeling as he felt the vote might go against Penn State. His administrative assistant wrote on the statement that was, obviously, not delivered, "Last notes by BJ. We were working on this somewhat milder [version]."[46] The contingent statement was not needed.

The vote on June 4, 1990, was evidently seven to three to admit, though the exact vote may never be revealed. A three-hour discussion occurred in which "several members argued that the case for admitting Penn State had not been made." Most, however, disagreed and voted positively, admitting that Penn State might boost "the national reform effort by bringing another 'like-minded' institution into the Big Ten, . . . [and] Penn State's entry into the Conference would be a long-term financial plus for the Conference."[47] Of those who voted no, Michigan's James Duderstadt was negative during the entire period. He was likely joined by Indiana's Tom Ehrlich, who may have felt the pressure not to antagonize a power coach, Bobby Knight. There is the possibility that either Northwestern or Michigan State voted against Penn State. "In retrospect," President Jordan wrote his friend Stanley Ikenberry at Illinois, "the whole thing seems to have been more difficult than one would have thought." Jordan was right on target when he thanked Ikenberry for "making this happen." He told Ikenberry, "We are convinced that the long-term benefits to this institution will be extremely positive and we are very grateful for all you did in making the affiliation with the Big Ten happen—everything from sleepless nights to looking to good friends for support."[48]

It can be argued whether Penn State's entry into the Big Ten had a greater impact upon Penn State as an educational institution or on Penn State as an athletic power. But it is difficult to argue that anyone had a greater influence in the decision at Penn State than President Bryce Jordan. With the positive image of Joe Paterno nationally and within the Big Ten, and with the major help of a former Penn State vice president and then president of Illinois, Stanley Ikenberry, Penn State barely made it as an eleventh member of the conference. Twenty-one years later, the revelations of a former assistant coach's criminal behavior and how Penn State reacted to that behavior led the Big Ten to levy a tremendous penalty on the university. The Big Ten also put the mark of Cain on Joe Paterno's reputation by eradicating his name from the Stagg-Paterno Big Ten Championship Trophy while the NCAA removed his name from the Gerald R. Ford Award given in 2011 for leadership in college sport.[49]

CHAPTER 10

The Image of Joe Paterno's Grand Experiment

"I sing of arms and the man . . . to drive a man, noted for virtue, to endure such dangers, to face so many trials."
—Virgil, *Aeneid* (19 BCE)

"We will never sacrifice sound academic principles for athletic success."
—Joe Paterno (1972)

Well before Penn State's entry into the Big Ten and in the midst of World War II, a year before the last gasp Nazi Battle of the Bulge and the year the Allies invaded Italy below Rome, a Roman Catholic Jesuit priest and high school teacher at Brooklyn Preparatory High School asked a bright, seventeen-year-old Joe Paterno whether he would like to translate and study Virgil's *Aeneid*. The *Aeneid* was the Latin-Christian education classic, and Rev. Thomas Bermingham, a young Latin teacher, persuaded the youthful scholar and athlete to study it with him. The heroic epic *Aeneid* is about the preordained destiny of Aeneas, defeated Trojan warrior who escaped from the victorious Greeks in the Trojan War. Aeneas traveled the Mediterranean to found the city of Rome for the Trojans. This piece of essential reading for a well-educated Roman Catholic caught Joe Paterno's imagination, probably from the beginning lines that most young people would struggle to translate from the original Latin:

I sing of arms and the man, he who, exiled by fate first came from the coast of Troy to Italy . . . hurled about endlessly by land and sea, by the will of gods, by cruel Juno's remorseless anger, long suffering also in war, until he founded a city. . . . to drive a man, noted for virtue, to endure such dangers to face so many trials.[1]

Arma virumque cano, Troiae qui primus ab oris Italiam, fato profugus, Laviniaque venit litora, multum ille et terris iactatus et alto vi superum saevae memorem Iunonis ob iram; multa quoque et bello passus, dum conderet urbem, inferretque deos Latio, genus unde Latinum, Albanique patres, atque altae moenia Romae.[2]

To young Joe Paterno, this was not only an idealistic and romantic call to arms but also a call to duty from forces larger than oneself—a kind of preordained destiny for Aeneas and possibly for himself. Unfortunately, Paterno may never have translated the entire book of Virgil, for if he had, he would have discovered an Aeneas who abandons without warning his lover, Dido, the queen of Carthage, to pursue his fate, duty bound, and seek out the land of Italy as home for his beloved Trojans. Would Paterno ever have abandoned someone to pursue a personal goal in response to the strong influence of Virgil's Aeneas? Paterno later called the perseverance and suffering of Aeneas as the "us, we, team" of struggle rather than the "I, me" that people see in Homeric heroes, particularly Achilles of the *Iliad,* a warrior who refused to fight at one point for his team, the Greeks. The Roman hero, unlike the Greek hero, Paterno believed, was a "team player."[3] It was the team, the Penn State football team, that dominated Joe Paterno's entire life from age twenty-three, only a half-decade after working on translating Virgil's *Aeneid.*

Late in life, Paterno told a writer for *Forbes* that he "always admired the way Aeneas stood tall in the face of adversity knowing he had a destiny. I have tried to let that help guide me."[4] Paterno looked at the pious, courageous, and dedicated acts of Aeneas and overlooked the questionable moral acts that Aeneas performed such as abandoning his lover and slaying the unarmed Turnus, a rival for Latium, as the story progresses. Aeneas runs down a robed priest and, according to John Lessingham, a true scholar of Virgil, "grandstands like a real epic hero," not as Joe Paterno believed. The Aeneas Lessingham has depicted was in fact the grandstanding superstar.[5] Yet the heroic and selfless vision of Aeneas in Paterno's eyes, in his reading of an ancient Roman writer, is part of what morphed into Paterno's "Grand Experiment." Perceptions, it might be noted, throughout our lives are often more important than the revealed truth.

Was Joe Paterno unique? How many coaches had ever read Virgil or majored in English literature at an Ivy League institution? How many continued to read literature as they began their coaching careers? How many discussed literature with a spouse or a literature professor as Joe Paterno did while at Penn State? Joe Paterno was different, and he continued to quote from literature throughout his life as he put his imprint upon those he coached as well as the larger public. All of that became part of the Grand Experiment, a phrase coined early in his coaching career. The Grand Experiment was different from athletic programs at many schools, and Paterno used the phrase to advance the program at Penn State almost from the beginning.

The term "Grand Experiment" was given visibility by a writer for the *Philadelphia Daily News* in 1967. Bill Conlin, like Paterno, came from Brooklyn and attended Paterno's Brooklyn Prep, where he saw Paterno star in athletics. Ironically, six decades later, only a month after Paterno was fired as the Penn State coach, the controversial sportswriter for the *Philadelphia Daily News* was charged, as was Jerry Sandusky at the same time, with molesting children.[6] But in 1967, Conlin was attending one of Paterno's pregame Friday evening sessions with reporters. Paterno was "spouting off," as Paterno later said, about the Penn State program of football success in an educational setting, and Conlin called it "the Grand Experiment."[7] Coach Paterno used that appellation continually from the late 1960s until his death in 2012, raising his program to a loftier level, most have agreed, than other programs. The Grand Experiment was promoted, Paterno once said, particularly by Sports Information Director Jim Tarman. Paterno and Tarman "went around the state with a case of booze," Paterno told sportswriter Ron Bracken, "and had parties at hotels for the press" telling about the Penn State way. Why? Because, Paterno noted, "they wouldn't come here. We literally went on tour."[8] The Grand Experiment may have upset a number of rival administrators and coaches of big-time football programs as being both hypocritical and demeaning to them. On the other hand, the title would not likely have stuck in the imagination of the sports world if there were not a good deal of truth in it—at least in the early years of the Paterno era at Penn State.

Paterno admitted many times that his program was built on what Rip Engle and Ernie McCoy had created from the 1950s and early 1960s. So too was the Grand Experiment. The slogan was newly minted for Paterno when beginning an undefeated streak after the first several games in his second year of head coaching, a streak that ended more than thirty games later. In this regard, he matched the early success of Penn State's Hugo Bezdek in the early 1920s, but Paterno was not nearly as surly, at least early in his career, as was Bezdek, for Paterno was then very open and popular with the press. Early on, Paterno plugged the Grand Experiment in which he felt Penn State "could organize a program when a boy could do both . . . get a great education and play big-time football . . . and along with it have a good social life." Paterno, early in his head-coaching career, disagreed with those who "tell me that you have to let in a couple kids in the back door" academically.[9] Agreeing was Ridge Riley, head of the Penn State Alumni Association and a personal friend of Paterno. Riley wrote to an alum at the end of Paterno's first year as coach, "Penn State academically at present is not much below the Ivy League in its admission standards—and there are no double standards for athletes."[10] Later, however, when winning a national championship became a principal driving force for Paterno, he would change his position on admitting athletes who could not meet general academic requirements. But, in the first decade or so, he followed where Engle and McCoy led in creating the climate for the Grand Experiment.

In the late 1950s, while Paterno was still assisting Engle, an alumnus, Larry Foster, wrote to Joe Paterno about his recruiting in New Jersey and the impact that the Penn State climate had on high school athletes. One influenced athlete was Pete Liske, who would later star as a quarterback on successful teams in the early 1960s. Foster said that Liske and two other recruits picked Penn State because of the "caliber of men on the coaching staff," and that Liske had told him "Penn State coaches made you feel that football would be part of your college life rather than the crux of it." Foster told Paterno "it is a tribute to you, Rip and every member of the coaching staff that this attitude prevails."[11] Paterno was able to recruit in a similar way when he became head coach after his sixteen years under Rip Engle, and when the more formal Grand Experiment came into being.

The Grand Experiment was impressive because Paterno was not only winning regularly, but also the players he recruited from Pennsylvania and adjoining states were spread across a number of academic programs at Penn State and graduating with regularity. Not all his players were stellar students, but a number were. Despite football players having the next to lowest grade point average among athletes at Penn State in 1969 (only baseball was lower among the 14 men's sports), many were good students.[12] Despite the low 2.42 football grade point average, Paterno recruits who became academic all-Americans in the first half-dozen years included Dennis Onkotz, Charlie Pittman, Dave Joyner, Bruce Bannon, and Mark Markovich.[13] There were a number of others who placed a stamp of success on the Grand Experiment. These would include fine football players such as Mike Reid, a music major, who garnered Grammy Awards after playing pro football. One described Reid as a living prototype of Penn State's Grand Experiment, who could bisect a running back with "his forearm while on the playing field and quote Jean-Paul Sartre in the classroom."[14] Similarly, an intense linebacker in the early 1970s, Gary Gray, did very well academically in electrical engineering and became a highly successful investment banker. Like Paterno reading Virgil, Gray was fascinated enough by Ernest Hemingway's *The Sun Also Rises* to run with the bulls in Spain's Pamplona several times. There were plenty of other examples, but Gray's summation of the Grand Experiment may be as accurate as any. "We had good kids," Gray later wrote. He also stated Penn State had "kids who flunked out, kids who didn't go to class. We had kids who were here to play football, kids who were here to study, kids who looked at football as more of a sidelight." But, Gray said, "we had exceptional people who could go out there and do things better than our opponents."[15] That was part of the Grand Experiment.

The Grand Experiment was realized with an excellent 80 percent graduation rate and a similar winning percentage in the early years. Yet there was no acclaimed national championship either by the regular votes of sportswriters or by the infamous 1969 vote of President Richard Nixon after Penn State's second undefeated team. A decade later Penn State was undefeated going into the national championship game in 1979 against Bear Bryant's Alabama team—and lost. This, and pressures for a national championship, may have triggered a change in the Grand Experiment of Joe Paterno. At least, that is what Lou Prato believed. Prato, a longtime radio, television, and print journalist, also has written extensively on Penn State athletics and football and was a major figure in creating the Penn State All Sports Museum. Of the 1979 Alabama game loss, Prato has written, "That was the day 'The Grand Experiment' began to crumble."[16] A young sportswriter, John Clayton, agreed, but only after the next football season continued as a disaster for Paterno. "Mt. Nittany is casting dark shadows," Clayton wrote. "Beneath the shadows, Happy Valley, College football's Camelot, is crumbling."[17] The loss was devastating to Joe Paterno when Bear Bryant, according to Paterno himself, "outcoached me."[18] From then on, the drive to become Number One athletically appeared to dominate consideration of the academic side of the Grand Experiment athletic–academic theme. What Scott Etter observed of Penn State athletic history in the early decades of the twentieth century was becoming more evident a half-century later. "It was an uneven contest," Etter wrote about the period between the 1880s and the 1930s, "between the quest for intercollegiate success and the desire to maintain institutional integrity."[19]

Only a year after Joe Paterno's team lost a national championship bid to Alabama with two questionable calls on plays at the goal line and a disastrous twelfth-man-on-the-field penalty after confusion from the bench, Joe Paterno was chosen by President Oswald to become athletic director. As he took his new position in addition to coaching, *Sports Illustrated's* Douglas Looney asked him about the Grand Experiment. "After four undefeated regular seasons," Paterno retorted, "if the Grand experiment is not a success, I don't know what is." Then Paterno paused and added, "O.K., in the eyes of a lot of people we have to win a national championship or else Joe Paterno and the Grand Experiment are both failures."[20]

Penn State athletics, like other major football powers by then, already had an expensive athletic–academic counseling system in place. Previously, in the Engle era and the early years of the Paterno regime, there was one individual who tried to keep track of how well athletes, especially football players, were doing academically. That individual, for a quarter century, was an assistant football coach, Frank Patrick. But to prevent losing scholarship athletes to poor grades required a more elaborate administration. As a result, an athletic–academic counseling service was created, housed in a special building and financed by the athletic department. From its start as a position added to the duties of one assistant football coach, the importance of maintaining athletic eligibility as a major goal turned into a multimillion dollar adjunct to the athletic department. By the mid-1970s an outsider was recruited to replace coach Frank Patrick to head the counseling program.

Dr. Frank Downing had played quarterback at Brooklyn Technical High School at the same time that Joe Paterno competed at Brooklyn Prep. After football coaching and advanced degrees at the University of Miami and the University of Memphis, Downing moved into academic counseling at Memphis and then the University of Kentucky, where John Oswald had been president. He had helped form the National Association of Academic Advisors in the mid-1970s, just before being hired to head the counseling program at Penn State.[21] "All I do," stated Downing shortly after joining the Penn State athletic program, "is try to handle the little problems before they become big ones."[22] When interviewed, after Penn State hired him, he noted the quality big-time football team and its strong academics, and, he noted, "there's been nothing under the table."[23] He noted that Penn State athletes needed at least a 950 SAT score (mediocre at best, with general students at Penn State averaging higher than 1100) and a 2.5 high school GPA. But when asked about exceptions, Downing said that "there might be one or two exceptions made per year, . . . but Joe doesn't like exceptions."[24]

Yet early in Downing's career with Penn State, a full professor in the College of Business contacted the ombudsman, Ronald Smith, of the College of Health, Physical Education and Recreation, with a revelation about Frank Downing and academic–athletic counseling. The business professor said, "with some degree of rage that the athletic counseling office was placing great pressure to influence the grades of some of our athletes." The ombudsman then asked the dean of the College of Health, Physical Education and Recreation, Bob Scannell, in which the athletic department was housed, the following set of questions:

> What are the College guidelines regarding the athletic counseling program? Has the policy changed in the last two years? How is the athletic counseling program impacting upon the athletic program and upon our College? Is the increased visibility of the athletic counseling program worth the effort in relationship to the decreased good will of the rest of the University? What are the specific ethical problems which have been raised within and without our College?[25]

Out of this inquiry, the dean suggested to the ombudsman that he hold a meeting of several members of the athletic department and administrators of the college to try to resolve the questions that had been raised. At the meeting there was common agreement that pressure upon faculty for athlete's grades from Frank Downing's office must end. At almost the same time, a yearlong review of the office of Dean Bob Scannell concluded that "athletic counseling procedures must be above reproach academically."[26] In less than a year, Frank Downing left Penn State and with it his dream job heading up the athletic–academic counseling program. The athletic program continued to be viewed as exemplary in the outside world. Having the athletic department responsible to an academic unit and an academic dean appeared in this case to have some merit. Though this incident may have little to do with major athletic and academic changes soon to occur at Penn State, in a half-year Joe Paterno was chosen as athletic director and, possibly more important, athletics was removed from an academic dean and isolated in a business office.

While this internal question of academics and athletics was quietly being resolved, Joe Paterno was more determined than ever to have Penn State finally be crowned national champions. It is important to note that Paterno changed the football policy of rarely asking for presidential admits for those athletes who lacked academic credentials to be admitted into the university. There was a marked change from Athletic Director Ernie McCoy's statement just before

Joe Paterno became head coach. Then, McCoy told the Eastern College Athletic Conference, "our contention . . . [is,] to get into Pennsylvania State University you have to be a damned good student."[27] McCoy was backed by President Eric Walker, who confirmed that he "wanted no football players who had not been admitted by the University admissions officer as regular students."[28] Even Paterno admitted, "Back in the early days, we would never take an academic exemption. For a while we didn't, ever."[29] It certainly changed from what Paterno told Oswald only a few years earlier, when he assured Oswald "we will never sacrifice sound academic principles for athletic success."[30] Yet the policy changed quickly under President John Oswald when Joe Paterno became athletic director in addition to coaching.

By 1980, when Paterno took over as athletic director, one of his first actions was to ask President John Oswald for nine special football admits, about a third of Penn State football recruits, for special admission as athletes who failed to meet Penn State entrance requirements.[31] Of the nine special admits requested, President Oswald admitted all, evidently without even a question. Two years later, four of those presidential admits contributed to Penn State's first football national championship season: Kevin Baugh, Nick Haden, Terrence Nichols, and Jonathan Williams. Of the nine special admits, five of whom were minority athletes, only one graduated, Nick Haden, who was not a minority admit—an 11 percent graduation rate. Kevin Baugh, however, starred in the national championship game concluding the 1982 season by returning several punts for more than 100 yards against the University of Georgia, one for 65 yards in the 27–23 win over Georgia and its great back, Heisman Trophy winner Herschel Walker. From the perspective of a winning team, the decision by Oswald to admit inadmissible athletes to play football for Penn State helped lead to a national championship.

The change by Joe Paterno and John Oswald to circumvent the regular admissions policy led to what they considered a more important goal, being Number One in football. The Grand Experiment was successful on the athletic side but was tarnished academically. Integrity lost out to winning. Ironically, if not hypocritically, Coach Paterno was interviewed by the *Phi Delta Kappan*, a magazine dedicated to educational issues and policy. It occurred at almost the same time as Paterno was asking for multiple presidential admits. Responding to an article by John Underwood in *Sports Illustrated*, Paterno stated, "My feeling has been for many years that university presidents and the faculties have . . . evaded responsibility and they've compromised themselves." "Presidents and admission people," Paterno went on, "have to say no when they evaluate the application of an athlete who shouldn't be in school, because as a coach, if you can talk them into taking that youngster, it's very enticing."[32]

Although the number of Penn State football players graduating remained high relative to the numbers in most other big-time schools, the policy of using presidential admits to achieve athletic success detracted from the Grand Experiment. There appear to have been fewer special admits after the two national championships, but there was no question Penn State was moving in the direction of other big-time football powers in sanctioning presidential admits in the 1980s. More than a decade later, Paterno appeared to be above the special admit fray when he pronounced in his editorial piece in the *Wall Street Journal*, "we've been very selective academically. . . . Some schools will bring in athletes just to have a good team."[33] Nationally, more than 20 percent of all football and basketball players admitted into college did not meet academic requirement for admission. At the time, a national study showed more than half of all Division I black basketball players and more than one-third of all black football players were special admits. Less than 3 percent of the general student bodies were presidential admits, an indication of how important the two key sports were to most big-time institutions of higher education.[34]

Coach Paterno had good reason to ask for presidential admits for African American athletes, other than to just win a national championship. Penn State was, from the 1970s, attempting to recruit minority students to the main campus, and athletics was a major area that could be helpful in achieving greater African American representation. Interviewed by a Philadelphia sportswriter, Ray Didinger, in 1982, Paterno said he was "concerned we might not have enough black athletes, I could identify some kids who couldn't get in by our normal admissions procedures. . . . That started it and now we have a pretty good number of blacks on our squad."[35] At the time of the 1982 national championship, according to Didinger, the football team had seven blacks among the twenty-two starters and nineteen on the squad. It is surprising to note that Alabama, as an example, one of the last to desegregate athletics in the segregationist South, had ten black starters and thirty-five blacks overall.

Joe Paterno recognized that his football program, despite the Grand Experiment identity, could not be all that different from other programs that set less idealistic goals. Nearly everyone, both North and South, knew that in order to achieve national rankings, bowl invitations, and television engagements, African Americans had to be included in the winning athletic equation. This was especially true in the generation after President Harry Truman's order to desegregate the military in 1948, the 1954 Supreme Court decision opposing "separate but equal" segregation of the races, and more important, the civil-rights legislation of the 1960s. Paterno also could look north to Syracuse University, which from the mid-1950s and well into the 1960s had three great African American running backs, Jim Brown, Ernie Davis (the first black Heisman Trophy winner), and Floyd Little—all three all-Americans. Penn State generally lost to Syracuse and did so in Paterno's first year of head coaching when Floyd Little and Larry Csonka started for the Orangemen. It was not long before Paterno recruited a number of running backs nearly equal to the trio from Syracuse, beginning with Charlie Pittman, then Lydell Mitchell and Franco Harris (who ironically was as much Italian, like Paterno, as African American).

It is curious that blacks who were on dominant teams nationally in the 1960s and 1970s were mostly in the positions requiring speed and quick reactions, generally running backs, wide receivers, and defensive backs. This was true at Penn State and it was true across the nation among the big-time football schools. The positions in which blacks were little represented were quarterbacks, centers, guards, and inside linebackers, and not unimportantly, punters and placekickers and those who held the ball for placekickers. These were what were called central positions by sport sociologists studying racism in sport, positions that demanded a great deal of thinking. Though there is little evidence that Joe Paterno was a racist, the positions he recruited for and positions at which he played black athletes fit almost perfectly into a racist theory of centrality, where the more central, thinking positions went to whites and the outlying, reaction positions went to blacks. In a study of Joe Paterno's teams from his first to the early 1990s, Theresa Zechman found that in the first quarter century of Paterno's leadership there was an African American total of only one center, two quarterbacks, and eleven offensive guards. There were no placekickers, ball holders, or punters who were black. There were, however, in the peripheral, reaction positions 134 running backs, 129 defensive backs, and 113 ends and flankers. There were nearly twice as many African American defensive linemen as offensive linemen, which might say even more about reacting versus thinking positions.[36]

In 1970, the year after two undefeated seasons, Paterno was put in a difficult situation with Penn State's first black quarterback, senior Mike Cooper, and a white junior who had been recruited as star material, Bob Parsons. If Paterno picked Cooper to be the starter, people would say that he did so because he was black. If he picked Parsons, it was because Cooper was black. As it turned out, neither Cooper nor Parsons was successful in that important position, and after losing three games early in the season, both were rejected for sophomore John Hufnagel, who helped turn the rest of the season into another of Penn State's winning seasons.[37]

The question of blacks in important, decision-making positions would plague Paterno and Penn State in the future, just as it had in the past. Jesse Arnelle, a star African American football and basketball player in the 1950s, was invited back for the annual football banquet of the State College Quarterback Club in spring 1968. He was to be presented with the first annual alumni award, a Nittany Lion statue. Arnelle, a lawyer who would eventually be president of the Board of Trustees, asked for an extended time to speak at the award ceremony. Rather than accepting the award with grace, Arnelle felt compelled to criticize Penn State for a lack of concern for blacks. He said Penn State was only interested in the "Super Black," recruiting only the greatest of black athletic talent, and called it the "super black syndrome." This completely upset Coach Paterno, who was quoted as saying "I resent you not accepting the award because it comes from friends."[38] Paterno was, obviously, embarrassed about Arnelle and how his statements might influence the recruitment of blacks in the future.

Arnelle's attack upon the status of blacks at Penn State did not appear to have a great impact upon Penn State or the football team, for Paterno continued to be a super recruiter of both blacks and whites and have consistent winners. The reaction of African Americans to U.S. racism was at its height during the civil-rights movement and Vietnam conflict during the 1960s into the 1970s. Other institutions of higher education had far greater protests than that of Arnelle, as protests and strikes of black athletes spread across the nation. Probably the best known was the attempt by Harry Edwards to have black college athletes boycott the 1968 Olympics.[39] Paterno, like Aeneas in antiquity, stood firm, but he increasingly turned to greater recruitment of blacks and recruiting in a larger geographical area to keep competitive. Whereas Paterno had recruited 95 percent of football players in Pennsylvania and the four adjourning states of Maryland, New Jersey, New York, and Ohio in the early years of the Paterno era, he knew that he had to attract athletes from a larger geographical area in the future if he was to become national champion. By the 1980s, 20 percent of the recruits came from states other than those five states. As one researcher pointed out, Paterno recruited depth from Pennsylvania and the "real stars from outside Pennsylvania, often going to the South to recruit athletes with greater speed."[40] The quest for a national championship produced changes academically and athletically, detracting from the prominent Grand Experiment.

Even with all this stated, the program run by Joe Paterno, although not perfect, was probably the cleanest and most academically oriented of any big-time football program in the country. Paterno was given the opportunity to speak before the Board of Trustees and exclaimed, "We've been able to get to where we are our way. We haven't cheated. We've done it with people who legitimately belong in college."[41] It was an exaggerated boast after winning his first football championship, but mostly true. As sportswriter Ray Didinger wrote in 1982, "Happy Valley. The air is clean and so is the football program."[42] Not quite. The Penn State football team was nearly alone in the big-time realm in never having a major violation of the National Collegiate Athletic Association (NCAA) rules—and that continued until the Jerry Sandusky Scandal led to unrivaled and, in many people's minds, unjustified if not illegal sanctions by the national ruling body. It is not that the Penn State team led by Joe Paterno was perfectly clean. During his nearly half a century of head coaching, Paterno had, in fact, been sanctioned by the NCAA. Although the public perception was that the program was lily white, evidence points to several minor recruiting violations under Paterno. One incident that became public was the illegal recruiting of a star high school linebacker, Quintus McDonald, a "letter of intent" signing violation by Paterno in 1985.

Jim Tarman, the athletic director after Paterno, once said that Penn State had never had a football recruiting violation in his twenty-seven years at Penn State.[43] That statement, however, was not true either. Five years before, Penn State coaches contacted Mark LeBlanc illegally, and Jackie Shields had been given illegal workouts and a small gift in the Penn State training facility. Penn State president John Oswald received the private NCAA reprimand and censure, and Oswald told Paterno privately to "prevent any future violation of NCAA rules and regulations."[44] Until now, however, the LeBlanc incident was never made public. Instances such as these may seem insignificant, in light of the child sex abuse that first became known in the 1990s and that was not effectively dealt with to prevent future abuses, but the hypocrisy and denial behind them make any marks against the Grand Experiment appear more significant.

It must be admitted that violations by Paterno and the Penn State football program appear insignificant in comparison with those of other big-time institutions in the 1970s and 1980s. Serious cases of athletes admitted into college with inadequate educational backgrounds were not uncommon. Examples of Dexter Manley who attended Oklahoma State University and Kevin Ross at Creighton University were two cases of individuals who could not read upon entering college, but they participated throughout their collegiate careers and remained illiterate after completing their athletic eligibility. Then there was the case at the University of Georgia in which an academic counselor, whistleblower Jan Kemp, was fired for refusing to ask professors to change grades. Georgia's president was Fred Davison, and he was also the president of the College Football Association, which was dedicated to bringing in increased television revenues to its members, including Penn State. At about the same time, the University of Florida was guilty of 107 NCAA violations, including money paid to athletes. Probably the worst athletic scandal, after the point-shaving scandals of the post–World War II period, was that of Southern Methodist University in the 1980s. Southern Methodist received the NCAA "death penalty" after illegal recruitment and payment of players was uncovered, and the coaches, president, board of trustees, and a former governor of Texas were involved.[45] The death penalty of shutting down the football program came only after multiple violations over a number of years. The NCAA agreed that the death penalty or threat of the death penalty could not be given unless there were multiple violations. Penn State had none a quarter century later. Thus, the threat of the death penalty in the Penn State Sandusky Scandal following the Freeh report in 2012 was clearly in violation of the NCAA due-process rules in its constitution and bylaws.[46] Unfortunately for Penn State, its president, Rod Erickson, could well have known more about the NCAA and its history before agreeing to the NCAA's unreasonable, if not illegal, consent decree sanctions in 2012.

In the 1980s, however, while the number of national violations of NCAA policies was at all-time high, the Grand Experiment at Penn State appeared to most of the rest of big-time athletics across America to be the shining symbol of academic integrity and success on the field of play. There were no major violations of recruiting and subsidization, athletes graduated in superior numbers than at other institutions, and athletes were not placed in specific curricula in order to maintain satisfactory grade point averages for eligibility. The athletic program at Penn State was maintained within institutional control, if not educational control, while many others programs were still controlled by alumni and outside groups. But the transfer of athletics at Penn State from an academic unit to a business unit was suspect from an academic integrity standpoint. Just as important to the Grand Experiment, Penn State also continued its tradition of winning a substantial number of games and winning most of its many bowl games. It is significant that Joe Paterno was the first collegiate football coach to be honored as *Sports Illustrated*'s Sportsman of the Year in 1986, just before he won his second national championship. Author Rick Reilly commented in his hagiography: "Nobody has stayed truer to the game and at the same time truer to himself."[47] Reilly hadn't known of a Joe Paterno 1973 ploy in a home game against the University of Pittsburgh with its star running back, Tony Dorsett, probably the fastest back in the United States. Paterno let the grass grow an extra two inches and allowed a heavy rain to laden the tarpless field and slow Dorsett down. Later, when asked about the moral principles of the decisions in a Penn State sport ethics seminar, Paterno responded, "sometimes you hav'ta do what you hav'ta do."[48] A quarter century later, after his earlier glowing account of Paterno, Reilly came to another, negative, conclusion after the Sandusky Scandal erupted.[49] But Reilly, in his derogatory opinion of Paterno, almost certainly remained a minority among those at Penn State, in Happy Valley, and among the alumni. Many people remained true to the Grand Experiment and Joe Paterno throughout his career and after his death.

CHAPTER 11

Shaping Reality

Saving Joe Paterno's Legacy

"He is guilty of all the good he does not perform."
—Voltaire (1752)

"Joe Paterno was an icon, but not a saint, really just a man."
—Anonymous (2012)

With or without entry into the Big Ten, for many the legacy of Joe Paterno had been created by the 1970s and 1980s. Events in the 1990s and early twenty-first century would affect that legacy in Happy Valley and across the nation. Nevertheless, contradictions defined the character of the man who gave the face to Penn State and athletics. Paterno's many actions, both positive and negative, influenced how people would judge the Grand Experiment and his place in Penn State and sport history. A case can be made that Paterno was one of the most important individuals in the history of Penn State, possibly next to George Washington Atherton, president from 1882 to 1906, who in many ways helped to save a struggling institution. One might consider what an individual wrote shortly after Paterno's death in 2012: "Joe Paterno was an icon," the unidentified person wrote, "but not a saint, really just a man."[1] Those contributions and faults formed Paterno's legacy that came into play on a grand scale for Penn State and its athletics when the Sandusky Scandal broke in 2011.

With entry into the Big Ten, there was a marked rise in the academic status of Penn State and stiffer competition on the athletic field. It is hard to argue with the proposition that Big Ten membership was more valuable academically than athletically, including the two most important sports, football and men's basketball.[2] Esteem in sport follows winning in American society, and Penn State won less often in the two major men's sports after entry into the Big Ten. In the sixteen years prior to Big Ten admittance, Joe Paterno won nearly 80 percent of his games, but in the sixteen years of Big Ten competition his victory percentage was reduced to just over two-thirds. His image as a coach of winning teams and graduating players was established before the Big Ten entry, but the strong positive impression of Paterno as coach and as an individual remained nationally for the next two decades. Nevertheless, after joining the Big Ten, it was a struggle to try to approach the success he had previously achieved both academically and athletically. Of Paterno's nineteen Top Ten rankings by the Associated Press, thirteen came prior to the Big Ten entry, including both national championships. Success of the Joe Paterno Grand Experiment was due mostly to the period prior to competition in the Big Ten—the rest of his life was in the pursuit of maintaining the legacy achieved earlier in his career. Winning would continue, with major bumps in the road, but Paterno's legacy would be enhanced greatly by philanthropic work he and his wife, Suzanne, were involved in, particularly after Penn State's Big Ten entry and into the twenty-first century.

Other than the two national championships and 409 victories in football achieved by Joe Paterno, one of the greatest accomplishments was the number of postseason bowl wins that he achieved as head coach. He led the Nittany Lions to thirty-seven bowl games in his forty-six years as coach, and his record was a superior 24-12-1. Even more significant was winning three-quarters of twelve major bowl games. Paterno became the only coach to achieve victories in each of what were at one time the major bowl contests, Cotton, Orange, Rose, and Sugar Bowls. Only Frank Thomas of Alabama and William Alexander of Georgia Tech coached in the four major bowls, but both lost one of them. Being able to compete and be victorious in the Rose Bowl may have been a major goal of Paterno once Penn State entered the Big Ten and could then be invited to Pasadena. The 1995 Rose Bowl victory concluded the last of his five undefeated seasons.[3]

Paterno's record of five undefeated teams ranked far behind several coaches in the twentieth century, such as Gil Dobie's fourteen undefeated teams at the University of Washington and Cornell University and Fielding H. Yost's nine at Michigan. Paterno's record also was behind Frank Leahy's seven undefeated teams at Boston College and Notre Dame and Earl Blaik's at Dartmouth and Army. He also trailed by one the great Robert Neyland at Tennessee; Howard Jones at Yale, Iowa, and Southern California; Bernie Bierman at Tulane and Minnesota; and John Heisman at Clemson and Georgia Tech. But he tied Knute Rockne of Notre Dame, Pop Warner at Pittsburgh and Stanford, Percy Haughton at Harvard, Andy Smith at California, and Hugo Bezdek at Oregon, Arkansas, and Penn State. Paterno's accomplishment of undefeated seasons was one more than achieved by Bear Bryant at Texas A &M and Alabama, Amos Alonzo Stagg at Chicago, Bud Wilkinson at Oklahoma, and Woody Hayes at Ohio State in their gloried careers. But it was winning and the exploitation of the term Grand Experiment that set him apart from most big-time coaches.[4]

What further separated Paterno from many other coaches who had bronze statues planted on campuses across the nation was his plethora of philanthropic projects within Penn State University. The 2001 iconic bronze statue of Paterno, with the Number One finger raised and leading a quartet of Nittany Lion players, was nothing new to conquering sport figures.[5] In ancient Greece, a statue of a winning Olympian was often sculpted as a way for his city-state to honor him. Of course, there are the well-known ancient Greek statues of the Discobolus, Myron's discus thrower, and of Herakles or Hercules, the strongman. There have been numerous bronze statues of modern football and men's basketball coaches, such as Knute Rockne (Notre Dame), John Wooden (UCLA), Robert Neyland (Tennessee), Adolph Rupp (Kentucky), and Bear Bryant (Alabama) among others.[6] Yet only one has been removed—Paterno's. This was done in part to prevent the very popular Paterno bronze statue from being destroyed by angered individuals after the Louis Freeh report implicated Paterno as part of a cover-up in the Sandusky Scandal. It was also removed as a Penn State symbol because Paterno admitted doing too little to deter further child molestation on the Penn State campus.

Between Paterno's two national championships and the negativities resulting from the Sandusky Scandal, Paterno's national reputation was enhanced by major philanthropic endeavors, particularly in the last two decades of his life. Paterno took the initiative to get Penn State to raise private financial resources, for as he said, President "Oswald did not want to raise money."[7] Paterno, probably more than any other individual in the history of Penn State, would begin to raise money, not just for athletics but for the entire university. Few, if any, college coaches had given back to his university in a manner that Joe Paterno did later in his life. Paterno began his quest for giving and asking others to give to the university most emphatically after his first national championship season. After the 1982 season, the conquering hero was asked to speak to the Board of Trustees, and instead of giving a glowing account of his successful season, he told the trustees that this was a "let's grab the moment" in Penn State's history, a time to begin raising private money to make Penn State into a greater university. At the time, his ample income of $100,000 or so would not enable him to make huge donations on his own part, but his image as a national champion could be persuasive in reaching wealthy individuals to donate their riches to the betterment of the university. Shortly thereafter, incoming President Bryce Jordan announced a $200 million capital campaign goal that ended as a $352 million success. In future years, Paterno would be involved in a $1 billion campaign that would rise to $1.4 billion in 2003 and to $2.3 billion in a seven-year drive that ended in 2014 after his death.[8]

Although Paterno might have helped raise a billion or more dollars for Penn State over the years, he and his wife, Suzanne, gave millions of their own money to the university. If anything ensured his legacy, already achieved on the playing field, it was the donating of a significant amount of the Paterno financial worth to the university at which the coach had spent nearly a half century as its most visible employee. He took one action of symbolic significance in promoting his belief in a liberal arts education, when he almost singlehandedly saved the Classics Department from oblivion. The dean of the College of Liberal Arts, Susan Welch, was ready to drop classics from her college as poor administration and lack of students persuaded her to do in the early 1990s. Paterno pressured the dean to reconsider with a promise that money would follow.[9] Paterno's use of his institutional power was probably based on his own undergraduate liberal arts background at Brown University and of his earlier high school study of some ancient literature with a teacher, Father Bermingham. The result was the creation of a Department of Classics and Mediterranean Studies, and Joe Paterno and his wife created the Father Bermingham Scholarship Fund for Greek and Latin undergraduate students. When the Paterno family and others contributed a substantial endowment, possibly several hundred thousand dollars, the Classics Department was saved from extinction.[10]

Paterno and his wife Sue contributed to the liberal arts in a number of other ways. Both he and Sue served on the Liberal Arts Development Council in a Grand Destiny Capital Campaign. They endowed the Paterno Family Professor of Literature, held for a decade by Michael Bérubé, a distinguished professor in twentieth century literature. (Bérubé would later give up the professorship when Paterno was implicated by the 2012 Freeh report for covering up in the Sandusky Scandal.) The Florence and Angelo Paterno Graduate Fellowships in Liberal Arts were another contribution by the Paternos. So was the Paterno Fellows program, which brings liberal arts students into partnership with the Penn State Schreyer Honors College, as were fellowships in the School of Architecture and Landscape Architecture. The fact that the Paternos created the Paterno Family Fund in the Richards Civil War Era Center and that Sue founded the Liberal Arts Alumni Society Board contributed to their legacy. Being instrumental in donating a million dollars for the building of the Pasquerilla Spiritual Center on the University Park campus added to their honored place in Penn State history. That Joe Paterno was involved in the Grand Destiny Capital Campaign is a further indication of the Paterno influence on liberal education and Penn State in general.[11]

Nothing is of greater significance to Penn State and the Joe Paterno legacy than the building of a second major library on the University Park campus that is connected to the Fred Lewis Pattee Library. When Paterno spoke to the Board of Trustees, twenty-nine years to the day before he died, he told the trustees they should get moving to make Penn State great. He told the large board of thirty-two members that it was "in a lot of ways reactionary" and not forward looking. With all the attention Penn State received because of its first national football championship, Paterno said the board should not sit idle but should immediately elevate standards throughout the institution, raise millions of dollars, and among other things build a "better library."[12] To Paterno "without a great library, you can't have a great university."[13] First, Paterno decided to establish a Paterno Libraries Endowment for books. He contributed $20,000 to establish the fund, which was soon matched by both the Mellon Foundation of Pittsburgh and Philip Greenberg, whose university gift also helped build the Greenberg Indoor Sports Complex on campus.[14]

The dean of libraries, Stuart Forth, took Paterno at his word about libraries. Dean Forth went directly to Paterno to ask for help funding a Penn State library addition even though Forth was criticized for not first going directly to the Office of Gifts and Endowments for permission. Penn State could do little when someone with the status of Paterno accepted. "If it wasn't for you," Paterno wrote Forth, in the early 1990s, "I wouldn't be part of this critically important effort."[15] The Campaign for the Library was launched in 1992. Paterno was intensely involved in raising money for the library, quickly contributing a quarter million dollars and, probably more important, using both his name to bring donors and leading the one-on-one asking of individuals to contribute to what turned out to be a nearly $14 million contribution to a new structure. He even asked William Schreyer, president of the Penn State Board of Trustees and head of the firm emphasizing global investment banking, Merrill Lynch, to give $7 million for the library and have it named for Schreyer.[16] Schreyer did not contribute $7 million but did give something like a million dollars and had the Schreyer Business Library in the new facility named after him. A few years later, Schreyer and his wife Joan gave $55 million to endow the Schreyer Honors College. For those who feel that Joe Paterno was only self-serving and striving to have his name attached to the new library addition, there is little evidence for that view.[17] In any case, the new $34 million addition was completed in 2000 and named the Joe and Sue Paterno Library (the Paterno Library).

Just a year later, a greater celebration occurred when Joe Paterno's Penn State team beat Ohio State 29–27 for Paterno's 324th victory. That win made him the winningest Division 1-A football coach in National Collegiate Athletic Association (NCAA) history, one more than the coach he was never able to beat, Alabama's Bear Bryant. If the library would stand as a testament to Paterno's concern for learning, the victory to surpass Bryant was celebrated by far more people, indicating that the public's celebratory interest in football was far greater than its interest in the symbol of learning, the university library. As history would show a decade later with the Sandusky Scandal, the library with Paterno's name on it would remain while the statue, put in place less than a week after the 324th win, would be taken down and hidden away for future consideration. Surpassing Bryant's record and erecting a Paterno statue in his honor occurred a little later in the year that Paterno was informed by a graduate football coach, Mike McQueary, of a sexual incident involving a young boy and Jerry Sandusky in a Penn State football facility. "I backed away," Paterno later admitted.[18]

There is irony and tragedy in a coach at the height of his winning career saying "I backed away" from an incident occurring at nearly the same time. As Bill Schreyer, a friend of Joe Paterno and then Penn State's greatest financial contributor, said in his *Memoir*, "For those who have worked hard and earned the privilege and responsibility of leadership, there inevitably arrives a moment of truth." Schreyer believed that "most of the time it comes out of the blue, when you least expect it, . . . but it also can define your place in history." Schreyer undoubtedly was not thinking of Paterno two years before the Sandusky Scandal broke when he wrote those words, but it applies to the event that will almost surely have a lasting impact upon the Paterno legacy and the life of Penn State. Schreyer quoted an aphorism handwritten on the inside cover of his grandfather's Bible that might have some truth in it:

> Lose money and lose nothing.
> Lose health and lose something.
> Lose character and lose everything.[19]

Paterno may have seldom lost money, but he lost health quickly after the Sandusky revelations and died within weeks of his ouster as football coach. Only later did his character come under close scrutiny, when documents were uncovered suggesting, according to the Freeh report, that he might have been covering up the Sandusky sexual violations of a young boy in a campus football facility.

The image of "I backed away" should not be lost in determining the legacy of this idealized and iconic individual, nor can a discussion of the darker side of Joe Paterno's greatness be excluded when discussing his impact upon the athletic administration for a period of more than four decades. The isolation of athletics from the general public and the rest of the academic side of the university by placing the department within a business unit rather than an educational unit was not conducive to openness when problems arose. Like any aspect of society, such as a government-run post office, a business-run financial institution, a sectarian-run Roman Catholic Church, or a higher educational–run football team, problems, including criminal ones, must be dealt with. In the case of Joe Paterno, he wanted total control over his football program, including how "his" players would be dealt with when problems arose. Early on as head coach, if a player ran into trouble and the police were involved, the State College and University police would call up Paterno, and then Paterno would punish the miscreants in a manner he felt was appropriate to the misconduct. "The cops would call me," according to Paterno, "and I used to put [the football players] in bed in my house and run their rear ends off the next day. Nobody knew about it. That's the way we handled it."[20] And that is the way he wanted to handle it through his entire career.

It may be that there were fewer incidents of bad behavior by football players in the 1960s and 1970s than in the period that followed, or the vagaries in criminal enforcement changed in the latter years of the twentieth century. The number of criminal charges appears to jump at about the time Paterno's football teams were competing for his first national championship. Around the time of Paterno's traumatic loss to Alabama at the end of the 1970s, several events may have contributed to greater turmoil both athletically and in off-the-field delinquency. The type of player that fit well in to the Grand Experiment changed so that more presidential admits came to the program with poor academic backgrounds as Paterno expanded the 300-mile geographical area in which he was recruiting.

It was then that athletics were taken out of an academic unit upon Paterno's demands of President John Oswald when Paterno became athletic director, and athletics were placed de facto in a financial unit run by an ex-football captain, Steve Garban. Assistant coaches were released from any teaching obligations to devote full time to coaching, further eliminating academic responsibilities for those in the athletic department. The athletic facilities were upgraded to some of the best facilities in college athletics, helping to recruit more star players and possibly giving them a greater feeling of entitlement and, in football, the possibility of going pro being the principal reason for attending college rather than obtaining a meaningful education.

The Athletic Department set up a massive academic–athletic counseling program at that time, which may have helped keep the graduation level high among all universities across the nation, but at the same time athletes could more easily fall back on the help of athletic counselors to steer them to particular courses and their professors. This would take some of the responsibility the athlete had previously taken and place it upon the million-dollar program to keep athletes eligible. There is no question that academic counseling for athletes eliminated much of the counseling previously done by the academic professors and placed it upon nonacademics hired to do so by the Athletic Department. The question of what courses were best to take academically for the future might rather become what courses were best in order to remain eligible. Academic counseling definitely became more isolated just as the athletic administration became isolated in new athletic offices away from academia while being supervised under Steve Garban hidden away in a university business office.

What all these changes had to do with the apparent rise in delinquency among members of the football team is uncertain, but if helping to build character was an important part of the Grand Experiment, character is what appeared to have diminished among the football players as national championship aspirations rose. After the 1979 Alabama loss that, according to Paterno "hammered at my ego,"[21] both Paterno and the team fell apart. Not only were several key players declared academically ineligible, there were cases of fighting on campus, first-degree burglary charges with a player being shot at while at a bowl game, drunken driving as well as drinking on campus, and charges of rape.[22] Early in Paterno's career, he probably would not have recruited Pete Harris, who had an all-time record of interceptions in a season and who flunked out before the 1979 season. Why? Because as Paterno put it, Harris was "a goof-off in high school" and continued to be one in college. Paterno did not normally recruit "goof-offs" for his Grand Experiment.[23] A local sportswriter, Ron Bracken, may have summed up the football problem writ large at that time: "Fans who feed off the image of purity, who live vicariously through the athletes, who place them on a pedestal and grant them favored status," Bracken wrote, "help give those same athletes a feeling of diplomatic immunity." To Bracken, "when an 18- to 22-year-old athlete finds himself in that situation, it's tempting to take advantage of it."[24] Player entitlement does not score high on the Grand Experiment scale.

In the 1980s, some people began to make fun of the football situation even as Penn State won two national championships. Cynics for years after began referring to Penn State as "State Penn" as criminal charges and convictions of football players piled up. From 2002 through 2008, there were criminal charges against 46 players with a total of 163 various counts. More than half of the individuals charged were proven guilty.[25] When football exists outside the academic mission of a university, isolated and privileged, it is natural for a coach, rather than the university legal system, to want to do his own punishment of athlete wrongdoers. Paterno wanted this privilege to continue as before. Punishment by Paterno rather than university officials became manifest in the first decade of the twenty-first century as Paterno approached the age of 80. For years, much of the illegal activity of football players was treated as an insular activity, a privileged status without significant academic or administrative oversight. The insular oversight by Paterno came into conflict with a new vice president of student affairs when Vicky Triponey was chosen by President Graham Spanier to join his administration in the early 2000s.

Fifty years before Vicky Triponey was brought in to lead the Office of Student Affairs, Penn State data was presented to the Middle States Association accrediting agency for colleges in the Eastern United States. A statement was made in the early years of the Rip Engle coaching era: "There is no distinction for athletes made anywhere in the University's admission policies. All athletes must meet the same requirements for admission as any other applicant." It noted that only 86 of 201 athletes applying to Penn State met the high entrance requirements. Of significance here is the statement that "there is no distinction made between athletes and other students regarding probation and dismissal from the University."[26]

Fast-forward a half-century when Vicky Triponey was brought in to direct the Office of Student Affairs at a university with an entrenched power coach. Paterno had achieved not only a record number of football victories but had the power to tell a college dean to save its Classics Department from oblivion and to raise millions of dollars to build a new library. He was in position to dictate not only the functioning of the university but nearly everything about how the Athletic Department and his football program should operate. "Power coaches" across the nation have often dictated courses of actions, as evidenced by Adolph Rupp at Kentucky, Bear Bryant at Alabama, Bo Schembechler at Michigan, and Joe Paterno at Penn State. Only a few years before, Paterno admitted to a professor of organizational behavior in the College of Business Administration, Henry Sims, that he has "very positive ideas" on how to run athletics and has "a tendency to want COMPLETE control."[27] One can place that in context with a long-time policy, from the time of the Rip Engle era, of making no distinction between an athlete and any other student with regard to how they will be treated. With Joe Paterno's tradition of disciplining his athletes for crimes or campus violations, a conflict could easily arise between Paterno and a new female administrator.

There may be significance in a female being chosen administrator of student affairs. Paterno had always lived in a male-dominated world and had never experienced a strong-willed female administrator in his life and especially a woman who challenged his power to conduct anything dealing with his football program. Vicky Triponey was that person. During her interview for the position, President Spanier took her and her husband on a tour of the campus, including the dance marathon going on in Recreation Hall. "Penn State isn't just about athletics," Triponey responded to Spanier, "but also about fostering a sense of belonging in a very special learning community."[28] She probably should have added "but don't mess with athletics" in this new position. The insular athletic program was not used to having its traditions or place on campus disturbed. Paterno certainly was not in the habit of being challenged on or off the playing field and certainly not by a younger administrator, a woman, without athletic credentials.

Joe Paterno was raised and grew up in a nearly all-male sphere; though his mother had an influence on him, his sister, nine years younger, did not. He went to an all-boys high school in Brooklyn, was inspired by the male priests, in the male-controlled Roman Catholic religion. After serving in the all-male army at the end of World War II, he returned and entered the all-male Brown University, with his younger brother George, on an alumni athletic scholarship. He was single until his mid-thirties while coaching what many would call the most masculine sport at Penn State, where there were no women athletics for a decade and a half and no women administrators and no women physical educators in Recreation Building where he had an office. He lived for most of that time with an older assistant coach's family. His life was principally with the all-male coaching staff at Penn State until marrying a Penn State co-ed more than a decade younger than he. As coach, he dealt principally with male journalists and was evidently never interviewed by a national woman journalist until just before his death, when Sally Jenkins of the *Washington Post* conducted his last interview. Symbolically, he opposed having woman athletic trainers work with his team and opposed athletic scholarships for women.[29] It was not surprising that it would be difficult for Paterno to take orders relative to the conduct of his athletes from a female vice president whom he once described as "that old lady in Old Main."[30]

Just before Vicky Triponey came to Penn State from the University of Connecticut to head up the Office of Student Affairs, a major controversy erupted over a star defensive back, Anwar Phillips. He was allowed to play against Auburn University in a bowl game on January 1, 2003, after being expelled from school upon being charged with a felony sexual assault and aggravated indecent assault for an incident at a campus apartment during the regular season. He was expelled for the spring semester prior to the bowl game against Auburn University, but as the spring semester had not begun, Paterno allowed him to participate. After the Penn State loss, President Spanier admitted that Phillips should not have played. Shrugging off Spanier's remarks, Paterno responded, "I played him. It is nobody's business but mine."[31] Although Triponey did not have to deal with the Phillips case of student misconduct, she certainly heard about it when she joined the Penn State administration later that year. Soon, Triponey would have to deal with both Joe Paterno and Graham Spanier on similar disciplinary cases.

Before Triponey assumed the position of vice president of student affairs, the office had been held for a lengthy time by William Asbury, a strong friend of athletics. Asbury had been an all-American football player at Kent State University and played a few years as a running back with the Pittsburgh Steelers in the National Football League. There were evidently few conflicts between him as head of the Office of Student Affairs and Joe Paterno over disciplining football players. Triponey, on the other hand, had spent little time working in an institution with a big-time football program, her previous position having been at the University of Connecticut and before that Wichita State University. She did not accept Bill Asbury's appraisal that "We are Penn State and we are one. We are members of the same team, therefore we will do whatever it takes to protect the team, the culture around the team and university." That statement by Asbury, however, did not mean that he would protect the team and university by covering up criminal behavior.[32] The change in the vice presidency, however, probably indicated that athletes would be treated differently under a new Student Affairs administrator.

After dealing with several football player assault cases in 2004, Triponey e-mailed Athletic Director Tim Curley that she would treat the case of football player Maurice Humphrey, accused of accosting his ex-girlfriend and her friend, "like any other discipline matter and avoid any suggestion of undue influence in my decision making process."[33] She was learning that Joe Paterno was often involved in disciplinary cases in her office as head of student affairs and that he wanted Triponey to stay out of disciplining football players like Humphrey, one of Paterno's academically challenged presidential admits.[34] She also found out that even though athletes represented less than 2 percent of the Penn State student body, athletes were involved in about 20 percent of all cases of physical assault and sexual assault cases. Penn State, unfortunately, also ranked high for its number of disciplinary cases among Big Ten institutions.[35] So when Triponey met with athletic administrators, including Joe Paterno, in summer 2005 to discuss legal problems of the football team, she hoped for some cooperation from Paterno in legal matters. She was highly disappointed.

According to Triponey, Paterno dominated the summer meeting, emphasizing that he, not Penn State's Student Affairs office, knew best how to discipline football players. Further, he maintained, the off-campus violations should not be her concern but should be dealt with by State College police, not Student Affairs.

In addition, Paterno did not want to inform the public of athletes' acts of violence despite, as Triponey stated, "any moral or legal obligation to do so." After a testy meeting, she e-mailed athletic administrators Tim Curley and Fran Ganter that Paterno leveled "personal insults" at both Joe Puzycki, a Student Affairs assistant, and Triponey. Paterno said in the meeting that the Office of Student Affairs did not know what it was doing and that the office "knows nothing" about disciplining or working with college students. She told Curley and Ganter that "despite the coach's best efforts to provide discipline for their football players, they are STILL getting in trouble (at a disproportionate rate) and doing some pretty serious things." She told the two, "therefore, we simply can not support the above approach which appears to be Coach Paterno's agenda, . . . and if you agree with his assessment/agenda then it will be tough to succeed in a collaborative approach on these matters." Triponey did not want to "treat football players differently and with greater privilege" she wrote, and "it appears on our end to be a deliberate effort to use the power of the football program to sway our decisions in a way that is beneficial to the football program." She concluded by insisting athletics must "take steps to insure that the undue pressure on our decision making is eliminated."[36] The power struggle, of people with unequal power, was set.

Joe Paterno, however, for the first time in his head-coaching career, was under major criticism from administrators and fans. Going into the 2005 season, he had four losing years out of the past five, had gone to one bowl game and lost, and had no Top Ten finishes. In that period, the number of criminal charges the football players had far outnumbered the games they played. To complicate matters, at the end of the 2004 season, four Penn State administrators had gone to Paterno's home toward the end of the four win, seven-loss season to ask him to retire. In what must have been somewhat embarrassing to President Spanier, the foursome of Spanier, Vice President Gary Schultz, Athletic Director Tim Curley, and former Vice President and then member of the Board of Trustees Steve Garban met on Joe Paterno's home "turf" just off the campus, instead of asking him to come to the president's office. But then, in many ways Paterno was the "power coach" to whom less powerful individuals would come before, almost as one might get an audience with the Roman Catholic pope.

Paterno, as Joe Posnanski, his biographer, has convincingly explained, wrote a memo before the meeting indicating, "I am NOT going to resign, . . . I've raised millions of dollars, . . . I can rally the alumni, . . . [but] if I fail (7-4, 8-4 [record]) I retire" after 2005.[37] Paterno was ready for the meeting at which, he must have guessed, President Spanier and the others would ask him to conclude his career. According to Paterno, the quartet came with the idea "Maybe it's time to go, Joe. You ought to think about getting out of it." Paterno stated, "I had not intended to discuss that with them, because I felt I would know when to get out of it." When, during the Paterno kitchen meeting, Spanier said he was going to recommend to the Board of Trustees that 2005 would be the last year of Paterno's coaching,

Paterno, according to Posnanski, verbally jumped at Spanier, "You take care of your playground, and I'll take care of mine." For the public record, Paterno said he told his bosses, "Relax, get off my backside."[38] They soon left his home, away from a major power center of Penn State. Paterno directing higher administrators on what to do was not unusual, but in this case it seemed more significant. This power action was quite different from saving the Classics Department by force of his position as he had done the decade before.

The iconic coach had won another contest, and at about the same time he was not about to lose a challenge from a woman administrator of student conduct. Vicky Triponey was not likely to get much support from Athletic Director Tim Curley, whom she valued for his "typically collegial approach," but who was often considered a pawn to the dictates of Joe Paterno. Triponey was probably correct when she e-mailed Curley that she understood he was "caught in the middle of a very difficult situation" when it came to disciplining athletes under his administration.[39] Two weeks after her confrontation with Paterno, Triponey wrote Curley:

> In light of the Coach's disregard for our role and disrespect for the process, we will most certainly have to operate from a different perspective as additional cases unfold. I don't see how we can continue to trust those inside the football program with confidential information if we are indeed adversaries instead of valued colleagues, respected educators and trusted partners. And we cannot continue to consult with or even talk to those close to the football program as we try to make unbiased decisions about sanctions, appeals and other matters surrounding the code violations of football players.[40]

Soon Triponey complained to President Spanier about Paterno's attitude that he alone "knows best how to discipline his players . . . and their status as a student when they commit violations of our standards should NOT be our concern." Triponey charged Paterno with attempting to conceal from the public wrongful actions within the football program when she wrote, "Coach Paterno would rather we NOT inform the public when a football player is found responsible for committing a serious violation of the law and/or our student code, despite any moral or legal obligation to do so."[41]

Triponey even set up a meeting with coaches on the subject of student discipline. At the meeting, she described important federal and state laws that could come into play, legislation noted when the Sandusky Scandal erupted. These included information about the 1974 "Buckley Amendment" (FERPA) to protect student rights, the Clery Act of 1990 (Crime Awareness and Campus Security Act) to report and publish certain campus crimes, and Megan's Law of 1994 to register sex offenders.[42] Thus Triponey was attempting to make clear to those in athletics that laws demanded action from university officials, and athletes could not be isolated as Joe Paterno desired. Triponey, nevertheless, was going against not only "the Penn State way," as Graham Spanier would later say, but against the traditions of athletics generally in U.S. college athletics. For as Clifton R. Wharton Jr., head of TIAA-CREF (retirement and financial planning for nonprofits such as universities) tried to tell the Knight Foundation, which was working to reform athletics, "If you are a celebrity athlete, the rules and laws of society just don't apply to you."[43] In some ways, Wharton was reflecting the controversy between a Penn State power coach and his athletes and an administration officer.

By 2007, the relations between Paterno and Triponey were strained to the limit, and one of the two heads was cut off as if by a French Revolution guillotine without actual blood. In the early morning of April Fools' Day 2007, a street argument physically erupted between star football player Anthony Scirrotto, accompanied by his girlfriend, and Jack Britt and two friends. Britt and friends then went to a party while Scirrotto rounded up about 15 football teammates, who broke into the party, where another fight took place that helped to fill the local hospital emergency room.[44] According to Britt's father, a long-time police sergeant in Philadelphia, aggravated assault had occurred with blood everywhere. Enter District Attorney Michael Madeira, whose wife was the biological sister of one of Jerry Sandusky's adopted sons and would later send the Sandusky investigation to Attorney General Tom Corbett. When Madeira tried to prosecute Scirrotto and others involved, he found witnesses reluctant to speak against football players.[45] The result was a lack of evidence, and the nine felony counts and most of the lesser charges were dropped for the football players with two players pleading guilty to misdemeanors.[46]

The punishment from Penn State was even more controversial, as Paterno and Triponey disagreed on who should discipline the athletes. Before the Penn State judicial punishments were handed out, Paterno sent President Spanier an e-mail through his office assistant, Sandi Segursky, in which Paterno wanted to "make sure everyone understands that the discipline of the players involved will be handled by me." When Triponey received a copy of the e-mail, she replied to Spanier. "I assume he is talking about discipline relative to TEAM rules," though he did not state that. However, she stated "discipline relative to violations of the student code of conduct is the responsibility of Judicial Affairs." Triponey went on: "The challenge here is that the letter suggests that football should handle this and now Coach Paterno is also saying THEY will handle this and makes it look like the normal channels will be ignored for football players." Triponey asked Spanier, "Can you remind them of police and University responsibility?"[47]

Whether or not Paterno's dealing with Triponey might be called "bullying," there were enough instances of Paterno using his clout to get his way to put a blot on his nearly spotless image that he maintained on the national scene. A significant number of writers, some of whom created biographies of him, noted his bullying tactics throughout his coaching and administrative career, often unseen by the greater public. Gene Wojciechowski, a late biographer of Paterno, wrote

that Paterno "blustered. He intimidated. He ruled," a contradiction in the greatness that was in him.[48] Pete Thamel noted that Paterno was "a living icon on the
sidelines" but he "attempted to bully and manipulate administrators."[49] Biographer
Michael O'Brien, quoting local State College sportswriter Ron Bracken, believed
that "Paterno can be cranky, tyrannical, dictatorial, blunt, scathing," though he
can be "charming, beguiling, entertaining, and witty."[50] Even Joe Posnanski, who
wrote a book favorable to the coach, *Paterno*, after Paterno's death, commented
that Paterno "could be a bully."[51] Paterno's attorney son, Scott, while calling his
father's legacy as a "philanthropist, the saint" would agree several years before
Paterno was removed as coach that at times he was "the selfish autocrat."[52] Not
unlike many others who have been in positions of authority, Paterno could use
his power in a forceful and not always positive way.

His bullying was often directed at reporters, whom Paterno came to disdain
for what he considered uncalled for, inane, and stupid questions or comments.
One was a young Penn State *Daily Collegian* reporter who once asked Paterno
about any hypocrisy that might exist in his Grand Experiment, pointing out recent
arraignments of football players. When Paterno popped off with "You're a smart
ass and you can quote me on that," Denise Bachman, a journalism student and
sports editor of the school newspaper, reacted strongly. Not enjoying the bullying of the coach, she retorted in the newspaper, "Paterno is heading more in the
direction of becoming the jackass he thought his [unlawful] players were."[53] A
writer from the *Pittsburgh Press-Gazette* reinforced what happened to Bachman
when he said "Paterno was a bully with reporters, especially young ones."[54]

The successful bullying by Paterno soon ended the Penn State career of Vicky
Triponey. A Penn State study, commissioned by President Spanier and conducted
during the summer of 2007, supported Paterno's view that he, and not Vicky
Triponey, should be able to determine whether a disciplined athlete remaining in
school could be suspended from an extracurricular activity such as football. The
review and lengthy report was headed by Robert Secor, the vice provost emeritus
for academic affairs.[55] The Secor report provided support for President Spanier to
side with Paterno while putting pressure on Triponey to resign for "not fitting in
with the Penn State way." Triponey's husband, who was on the Penn State faculty,
would later state that the action of Spanier in support of Paterno's view showed
"the secretive, deceptive culture that prevails in the football program and at the
executive level of the university in acting as a shroud for the football program."[56]

It is not clear exactly how much pressure President Spanier put on Triponey to
resign, but the departed vice president indicated that Paterno wanted Triponey
out of her position or the iconic coach would raise no more funds for the university.[57] Spanier was caught in the middle between his choice of administrator
to punish student misconduct and a power coach who demanded that he, alone,
should control whether punished football players remaining in school would still
be able to compete. Coming to Spanier's aid was Robert Secor, whose academic

home was in the Liberal Arts Literature Department. Secor, a colleague of Sandy Spanier, the president's wife, announced that the committee decided in favor of Paterno.[58] Spanier sided not with Triponey but with Paterno. Paterno won. Triponey was gone.

Her departure was greeted positively by a number of students and some administrators, who considered her a controversial individual with a confrontational manner both inside and outside athletics. Students claimed she not only changed how student government operated but cut funding for the student radio station and altered the allocation of student fees.[59] One week before Triponey's resignation, one student wrote about the "four awful years of Triponey's tenure" with her "scatter shot managerial style and complete disinterest in genuinely promoting student welfare" and creating one "bureaucratic mess after another."[60] Triponey's "not fitting in with the Penn State way" cost her her position at Penn State.[61] And as in the firing of Hugo Bezdek as director of the School of Physical Education and Athletics six decades before, Triponey was given what amounted to a one-year sabbatical as she left quietly in disgrace for being one of the few who would stand up to the icon of Penn State.

Protecting the football program at Penn State through a modified justice system for athletes was not particularly unusual for a big-time athletic program, but it does alter the celebrated image of Joe Paterno. Paterno had been the positive image of Penn State for decades, but it became clear that—despite the many wins (409) he brought to Penn State in forty-six years of coaching and despite the fact that he helped bring Penn State to a position as one of the great universities in America—he had faults that likely contributed to the largest scandal in its history. When judging the number of positives of what has gone into Joe Paterno's Grand Experiment legacy, one might well consider what the philosopher Voltaire stated more than two centuries ago: "He is guilty of all the good he does not perform."[62] Protecting the football program that was so beneficial to Penn State was important to Penn State administrators, both inside and outside athletics for that was "the Penn State way." The Faustian bargain that athletic antagonist John Swinton predicted in 1978[63] seemed more manifest by the early 2000s. The selling out for a present gain without regard for future consequences, which Swinton noted just before Penn State's first attempt to become Number One in a national championship game, was about to become reality. The Faustian bargain was delayed several decades in the athletic administration of the Paterno era when a far more important issue arose than the eligibility of athletes who broke university rules. It came in the form of a child sexual abuse scandal.

Nittany (Happy) Valley, State College, and Mt. Nittany as seen in 1894 by Professor Fred Lewis Pattee and President George Atherton from Penn State's Old Main. This was the same year President Atherton allowed a failing student to continue playing football, remaining undefeated. Photo courtesy Penn State University Archives.

Hugo Bezdek, Penn State's first power coach, went thirty games without defeat in the early 1920s while earning a salary higher than that of the Penn State president. Photo courtesy Penn State University Archives.

Coach Bob Higgins and Dean Carl Schott were involved unsuccessfully in the "Great Experiment," winning big-time football without athletic scholarships. Photo courtesy Penn State University Archives.

Coach Rip Engle, without a losing season from 1950 to 1966, with President Eric Walker, who promoted Penn State's "Grand Experiment," but without the name, when Joe Paterno was an assistant coach. Photo courtesy Penn State University Archives.

Steve Garban, former football captain and in the Penn State business office, teamed up with Joe Paterno and President John Oswald to remove athletics from an academic unit, placing it in the business office in 1980. Photo courtesy Penn State University Archives.

Joe Paterno and President John Oswald helped isolate athletics from an academic unit by placing it in a business office, thus removing significant academic control over athletics. Photo courtesy Penn State University Archives.

Coach Rene Portland talks to Jen Harris, who sued Penn State in 2005 for violating sexual orientation and civil rights. Photo courtesy Penn State University Archives.

Joe Paterno, who hired Coach Rene Portland, congratulates Portland for twenty-five years of successful coaching shortly before Portland resigned under pressure for her illegal antilesbian violations of Penn State policy and federal legislation. Photo courtesy Penn State University Archives.

Vicky Triponey, vice president for student affairs, resigned under pressure for her conflict with Joe Paterno over punishing delinquent football players from 2004 to 2007. Photo courtesy Penn State University Archives.

Tim Curley, Joe Paterno's choice for athletic director, was centrally involved in the Vicky Triponey conflict in the early 2000s as well as the Sandusky Scandal. Photo courtesy Penn State University Archives.

Joe Paterno greets President Richard Nixon in 1970, maybe not sincerely, after Nixon snubbed his undefeated 1969 team while recognizing Texas as the national champion. Photo courtesy Penn State University Archives.

In 1973, Paterno chastised President Nixon at a commence address: "How could Nixon know so much about college football in 1969 and so little about Watergate in 1973?" Photo courtesy Penn State University Archives.

Jerry Sandusky was assistant coach at Penn State from 1969 to 1999, gaining iconic stature for helping bring two national championships to Penn State and for helping disadvantaged children. Photo courtesy Penn State University Archives.

Gary Schultz, vice president for finance and business, was Penn State administrator in charge of athletics when the Sandusky Scandal occurred. Photo courtesy Penn State University Archives.

Is this opening of pandora's box? Other children?

Gary Schultz's memo in 1998, "Is this opening of pandora's box?" was central to the question of Penn State's covering up of the actions of Jerry Sandusky. Photo courtesy the author.

Mike McQueary continued coaching with Joe Paterno after notifying Paterno of observing Jerry Sandusky in a shower with a young boy in 2001. Photo courtesy Penn State University Archives.

The Joe Paterno statue at the stadium, erected after Paterno's 324th victory, is held by a Korean War veteran. The icon was removed shortly after the Freeh report was released in 2012. Photo courtesy the author.

President Graham Spanier (1995–2011) had early knowledge of Jerry Sandusky's involvement with possible child molestation by Jerry Sandusky. Photo courtesy Penn State University Archives.

President Rod Erickson signed the controversial NCAA consent decree after the Freeh report investigation of Penn State administrators' involvement in the Jerry Sandusky Scandal, costing Penn State several hundred million dollars and institutional prestige. Photo courtesy Penn State University Archives.

CHAPTER 12

Insularity, The Second Mile, and Sandusky's On-Campus Incidents

"A man should be upright, not be kept upright."
—Marcus Aurelius (ca. 161–80 CE)

"Let us not be reluctant to tell our story, openly and honestly."
—President Graham Spanier (2011)

From the late 1970s, when Joe Paterno was picked to replace Ed Czekaj as athletic director and athletics were soon to be taken out of an academic unit of the university, athletics and especially football moved to isolate themselves further than previously from any academic control. Athletics were isolated both physically and psychologically at the university as two major buildings were constructed, the Bryce Jordan Center, where most administrative officers were housed, and the Mildred and Louis Lasch Football Building, where football reigned supreme. Former Dean of the College of Health, Physical Education and Recreation Bob Scannell, well before the Sandusky Scandal broke, feared that the administration of athletics after the Joe Paterno–Steve Garban–John Oswald coup (see chapter 8) was dangerous to the health of athletics. "The isolation that is created by this building, the Jordan Center, which is on the edge of campus and which in its office suites looks very different than a typical faculty office," Scannell said in his appraisal. "[I]t's a different environment, and that's something I sort of worry about as I look at the future."[1] Scannell was perceptive. At almost the same time that Scannell issued his forewarning, an incident was occurring in a remote building, the Lasch Building, where football dominated. The revelation of this and related incidents would eventually bring dishonor to those who had control of athletics and the entire university. Happy Valley and, indeed, the nation and beyond, was shocked with the grand jury revelations of November 4, 2011, that accused, with graphic details, former Penn State assistant coach Jerry Sandusky of molesting eight children.[2] Evidently most people did not have any idea of the veracity of the charges against Sandusky, who appeared to be highly respectable, even heroic, for founding in 1977 and developing The Second Mile program for disadvantaged and at-risk young children.

Rare were those who believed that the iconic ex-coach would be involved in child molestation. This was true even when the more public hint of a scandal arose in late March 2011. Then, a young reporter for the *Harrisburg Patriot-News*, Sarah Ganim, broke the news with headlines of a secret grand jury investigation of Sandusky by the Pennsylvania attorney general's office. At the time, few reacted, though a former 1970s football player under Paterno and Sandusky condemned Ganim's newspaper report. "I don't believe the allegations against Jerry . . . a person I have always admired," he wrote in rebuttal. The newspapers, he said, "are reporting vicious, hurtful rumors" about Jerry, whom he had never known "to take an alcoholic drink, never heard him utter a cuss word . . . or tell a lie."[3] He was reflecting what many people believed about the famous assistant coach, who helped bring two national championships to Penn State, helped numerous linebackers to have successful careers in professional football, and was President George W. H. Bush's 294th of 1,000 Points of Light for charity work in creating The Second Mile.

This was the Jerry Sandusky for whom Joe Paterno wrote probably the most outstanding letter of recommendation in Paterno's life a decade after The Second Mile came into being. A year after Paterno's second national championship, Sandusky applied for the head coaching position at Temple University in Philadelphia. Penn State's second national championship was won, 14–10 against the Number One–ranked University of Miami team in the most watched game in collegiate history. Then, the Sandusky-devised defense intercepted Heisman Trophy winner Vinnie Testavarde five times, the last one near the goal line with seconds remaining.[4] Sandusky had reached the height of his coaching career, when Paterno wrote the athletic director at Temple, Charles Theokas, to strongly urge Temple to hire Sandusky as its head football coach. Sandusky, Paterno stated, "has a marvelous character with an impeccable lifestyle, . . . is a role model, . . . [with] his commitment to human beings."[5]

This unusual letter is important, not because Sandusky was offered and then turned down the Temple University position, but because of the Paterno family rebuttal to the damaging conclusions about Joe Paterno in the 2012 Louis Freeh report on the Sandusky Scandal. The Paterno family, a year after Paterno's death, tried to help salvage his marred reputation with the lengthy "Paterno Report: Critique of the Freeh Report." In it, the Paterno family inaccurately stated, in a misguided assertion, "The two men [Paterno and Sandusky] despised each other from the start."[6] Although the two had quite different personalities—they seldom socialized, and their coaching styles contrasted as much as two late twentieth-century basketball hall of famers, mild-mannered John Wooden of UCLA and volatile Bobby Knight of Indiana—they did not despise each other from the start. If it were so, Paterno would never have kept Sandusky as an assistant coach for three decades or then told Sandusky after retirement that he could stay on as coach as long as Paterno remained coaching.

Joe Paterno must have been as surprised as anyone when a young graduate assistant coach, a couple months after the publication of Jerry Sandusky's autobiography, *Touched,* came to Paterno's house with a shocking account. There, in early 2001, twenty-eight-year-old Mike McQueary told Paterno that he had seen Jerry Sandusky in what appeared to be a sexual encounter with a young boy in the Mildred and Louis Lasch Football Building's shower room. McQueary could have physically challenged Sandusky at that moment, but he did not. What McQueary did first was call his father, and then he left the Lasch Building and drove to his parent's home. He then reported the incident to older individuals, including first his medical-administrator father and his father's friend, a nephrology doctor, Jonathan Dranov.

When advised to tell Joe Paterno of the incident, Mike McQueary visited Paterno the next day and told him that he had seen inappropriate sexual behavior by Sandusky.[7] Just to approach Paterno must have taken a certain amount of courage, because McQueary had a tenuous position as a graduate assistant, a low-paying and insecure position, even though McQueary had been a starting Penn State quarterback for one year a couple years before. There was, however, a conjecture that McQueary might have wanted to go to Paterno's house to see whether he could ingratiate himself to get the position as coach of the ends, a position just abandoned by Kenny Jackson, who had left Penn State for the Pittsburgh Steelers. There is no creditable evidence that the whistle-blower, McQueary, went to the Paterno house for any other reason than to report what he saw in the locker room.[8]

Joe Paterno, under oath ten years later, recounted the visit for the grand jury looking into the Sandusky investigation. He said that McQueary came over on a Saturday morning and told him that he saw Jerry Sandusky "fondling" a young boy, and that it was, Paterno stated, of "a sexual nature." Paterno said he "didn't push Mike to describe exactly what it was because he was very upset." At the end of his short audience with Paterno, the head coach thanked McQueary, saying "you did what was right" and that he would take care of the situation. Paterno waited a day to report this to his superiors because "I didn't want to interfere with their weekends." He then told his "de jure" superior, Tim Curley, "Hey, we got a problem," asking Curley to deal with the situation.[9]

The events of 2001 that followed took this form: The athletic director then informed his administrative boss, Vice President for Finance and Business Gary Schultz (who was in charge of Penn State police), of the late evening showering encounter of Jerry Sandusky with the youth in an isolated and nearly deserted building. Thus, very quickly, the central incident of the Sandusky Scandal was quickly known by four Penn State individuals—Mike McQueary, Joe Paterno, Tim Curley, and Gary Schultz—and two outsiders, Dr. Jonathan Dranov and John

McQueary. President Graham Spanier was soon informed. It was not the first Sandusky criminal incident, but what McQueary revealed became central to the saga of Penn State administrators dealing with the highly visible, but exceedingly insular, football program at Penn State. With the number of incidents with football players' on-campus and off-campus behavior becoming more newsworthy, there was certainly good reason to attempt to resolve this major problem within the athletic department and among several university administrators.

Jerry Sandusky in 2001 was no longer a Penn State employee, but he was much involved in Penn State and continued to be tied closely to the athletic department. His unusual retirement agreement included being given professor emeritus status (unusual for an assistant professor), an office on campus, a key to the training facility, a parking pass, four season tickets for football and two tickets to men's and women's basketball for life, and more important, a formal tie between Penn State and Sandusky's Second Mile corporation. The formal Sandusky Agreement with Tim Curley and Gary Schultz was to keep Penn State football closely linked with The Second Mile. "You and the University," the agreement read, "agree to work collaboratively with each other in the future in community outreach programs, such as The Second Mile, and other programs which provide positive visibility to the University's Intercollegiate Athletic Program."[10]

Obviously The Second Mile was beneficial to Penn State and athletics, just as the projection of Joe Paterno's Grand Experiment gave national publicity to both Paterno and the Penn State football program. For Jerry Sandusky, he was now tied to the athletic program for life. After Sandusky's retirement, Joe Paterno's football program would go the biblical second mile with Jerry Sandusky. The heavenly Sandusky–Penn State agreement was intended to bring recognition to The Second Mile at the same time it would build the Penn State brand by being associated with a do-good nonprofit organization, praised by the first president Bush and led by a widely recognized coach. Thus the Penn State Nittany Lion Mascot would wear The Second Mile T-shirt at fundraisers for Sandusky's creation. Rather than heaven, the Sandusky–Penn State compact ended in athletic purgatory if not hell for Penn State.

Ironically, the year before Penn State's out-of-the-ordinary 1999 retirement agreement with Sandusky, the first revealed transgression with young boys by Sandusky had already occurred, and with the knowledge of Penn State administrators. The first reported incident between fifty-four-year-old Sandusky and an eleven-year old boy took place on May 3, 1998, in the Lasch Football Building shower room. When The Second Mile boy (Victim 6 in the later criminal proceedings) returned home with wet hair, his mother inquired and the boy said he had showered with Sandusky after exercising on weight machines, playing a type of soccer with a ball made of wrapping tape, wrestling for several minutes, and then entering the shower, at which time Sandusky gave him a bear hug and made him feel "uncomfortable."[11]

Almost as soon as she could, the mother of so-called Victim 6 reported the incident to a credentialed psychologist, Alysia Chambers, who had previously worked with the boy. Chambers told her the incident should be, and was, reported to the Penn State police, who quickly interviewed the mother and her son that morning. The police then reported the incident to the Centre County Office of Children and Youth Services and soon reviewed the incident with Assistant District Attorney Karen Arnold. Within a day, Jerry Lauro of the Regional Office of the Department of Welfare in Harrisburg was contacted and an interview with Sandusky was scheduled. In the meantime a noncredentialed individual, John Seasock, who had a Children and Youth Service counseling contract, got involved in the case. Seasock concluded that "Sandusky didn't fit the profile of a pedophile." To the contrary, the credentialed Alysia Chambers believed that Sandusky did fit the profile of a pedophile.[12] Seasock was listened to and Chambers's observations were basically ignored.

Centre County District Attorney Ray Gricar was contacted because Sandusky kept calling the boy for 10 days after the showering incident. Sandusky's calls brought the State College Police Department to the boy's residence because Sandusky was expecting to pick up the eleven-year-old. In an unsuccessful "sting operation," detective Ralph Ralston and a reporting officer were hiding in two rooms of the apartment. When Sandusky arrived, the boy's mother told him that her son was acting differently, having nightmares, and she wondered if anything happened. Sandusky said, "I don't think so." When Sandusky asked whether he should "let him alone," the boy's mother said "yes." Sandusky left. Two weeks later, Jerry Lauro of the Office of Children, Youth, and Families in Harrisburg and a police officer interviewed Sandusky at the Lasch Building. Sandusky indicated that he had used "poor judgment" in showering with the boy. The Department of University Safety at Penn State then closed the case. "As a result of the investigation it could not be determined that a sexual assault occurred and SANDUSKY was advised of such," the report concluded, and "LAURO also advised that he agreed with Reporting Officer that no sexual assault occurred." When Sandusky stated that in the future he "wouldn't . . . shower with any child," the report unfortunately stated, "CASE CLOSED."[13]

What was not mentioned in the police report was whether Penn State administrators were notified of the Sandusky incident in a Penn State football building. More important, if notified, how did these administrators respond to the information they received about Sandusky and a young boy on university property? E-mails circulating among Vice President Gary Schultz, Athletic Director Tim Curley, and President Graham Spanier (Joe Paterno did not use e-mail) indicate that early on Penn State administrators knew about the showering incident. In confidential notes, Gary Schultz commented on a taped interview by police the day after the incident. According to Schultz, "Behavior—at best inappropriate @ worst sexual improprieties" and "at min.—poor judgment." Schultz wrote:

"Critical issue—contact with genitals?" The next day Schultz noted, "Is this opening of pandora's box? Other children?" After Curley was notified, he e-mailed both Schultz and President Spanier under the caption "Joe Paterno." Curley stated, "I touched base with coach. Keep us posted. Thanks."[14]

The incident was a high priority for the administrators. The day that Curley presumably touched base with Paterno, the coach was off to Nashville, Tennessee, for a Burger King franchise meeting. When Paterno returned, he almost imme-diately took off for a couple days with Rod Kirsch, the senior vice president for Development and Alumni Relations, and Diane Ryan, executive director of the Alumni Association, to the Seaport Hotel in Boston as part of Penn State's alumni relations and fund raising. Coming home, Paterno was soon off to Atlanta.[15] When he returned, Curley e-mailed Schultz about "Jerry," asking whether there was "anything new in this department? Coach is anxious to know where it stands."[16] With nothing forthcoming from Schultz, Paterno continued his whirlwind trav-els as he spent a couple days in Farmington, Pennsylvania.[17] By the end of the month, Curley had asked Schultz several more times for any information about the Sandusky affair but received none. The local district attorney, Ray Gricar, declined to prosecute the case, as the police investigating team concluded there was no criminal behavior, and the investigation was closed.[18]

With the case closed, there must have been a relieved feeling for not only Jerry Sandusky, but also the four Penn State administrators involved—President Spanier, Vice President Gary Schultz, Athletic Director Tim Curley, and Coach Joe Paterno. None of them asked Sandusky not to shower with children in the football locker room, nor did they have further discussions with Sandusky about bringing The Second Mile children onto campus. There evidently were no discus-sions with the administrators of The Second Mile, who worked closely, according to the Sandusky retirement agreement, with Penn State. They did not decide to monitor any future Sandusky activities with children or to question overnight programs with The Second Mile children on Penn State football facilities, nor did they suggest counseling for assistant coach Sandusky. Possibly more important, there was no evidence of any attempt to contact the child in question. They were obviously pleased that the investigation did not make front-page news bringing discredit to Penn State, the athletic program, or Paterno's Grand Experiment of winning football while maintaining academic integrity.[19] Although someone in retrospect could question why none of these activities was pursued, Jerry San-dusky was held in such high regard by so many people that most would believe it unthinkable for Sandusky to act as a pedophile.

Shortly before this first reported shower incident, Sandusky had already been told by Paterno that he would not be considered as the head coach to follow Paterno. Paterno's notes provided later by Paterno's lawyer to the Pennsylvania investigating team provides some insight. Paterno jotted down for Sandusky,

We know this isn't easy for you and it isn't easy for us or Penn State. Part of the reason it isn't easy is because I allowed and at times tried to help you with your development of 2nd Mile. If there were no 2nd Mile then I believe you . . . probably could be the next Penn State FB Coach. But you wanted the best of two worlds and I probably should have sat down with you six or seven years ago and said look Jerry if you want to be the Head Coach at Penn State, give up your association with the 2nd Mile and concentrate on nothing but your family and Penn State. Don't worry about the 2nd Mile—you don't have the luxury of doing both. One will always demand a decision of preference. You are too deeply involved in both.[20]

Because both Paterno and Tim Curley believed Paterno had the power to appoint the next coach indicates something about athletic administration at Penn State and the perceived or actual power of the coach. One might recall that in 1948, long-time coach Bob Higgins (1930–48) attempted to get his favored assistant coach, Earle Edwards, to follow him upon retirement, but Edwards was rejected in favor of Joe Bedenk, the year before Rip Engle and Joe Paterno came to Penn State. It is likely in 1998 that Paterno did have that kind of power. He had the clout to prevent the Liberal Arts College from abolishing the Classics Department only a couple years before and had pledged $3.5 million to the university only months before the first revealed Sandusky incident.[21] Paterno, along with his wife Sue, cochaired the library fund and were in the process of raising more than $14 million for the library project that was eventually to carry the Paterno name. Paterno was to be listened to even if officially he did not have the right to name his successor. Athletic directors, presidents, and boards of trustees generally appoint head football coaches, not a retiring coach. Yet Paterno knew he was special, and he was.

That was 1998, but in a little less than three years, the second Sandusky incident came to the attention of Schultz, Curley, Spanier, and Paterno. If the first incident in 1998 came as a complete surprise to the Penn State administrators, the second episode could only have raised red flags to those in charge. How the administrators would react would foretell the fate brought upon Penn State when the public knew of this incident and other similar cases a decade later. In the incident reported by Mike McQueary, Paterno and then Curley were the first administrators to know of a potential sexual violation committed by Sandusky in the football locker room. By 2001, Sandusky had fully retired, after rejecting an offer of an administrative position in athletics from Athletic Director Curley. By then, Sandusky had received a standing ovation at Beaver Stadium at the last home 1999 game, where he was embraced by two sons, Jon, a defensive back, and Matt, a Penn State football manager; given the Penn State Alumni Award; chosen national assistant coach of the year; provided a rousing retirement reception in the Bryce Jordan Center before an admiring public; and carried off the field following the 1999 Alamo Bowl victory.[22] Next to the more iconic Paterno, Sandusky was still a major face of Penn State athletics to many people, and to have him charged as a child molester on the Penn State campus would not only impugn Sandusky but would bring shame on the entire athletic program and on Penn State. Those involved in athletic administration at Penn State might have been served well had they followed the words of one of the few good ancient Roman emperors, Marcus Aurelius. He wrote in the second century of the Common Era, "A man should be upright, not be kept upright."[23] Penn State administrators kept Sandusky upright for a decade.

For most of the first decade of the twenty-first century, Jerry Sandusky was allowed to use Penn State facilities in company with young boys even though he had been questioned twice, with Penn State administrative knowledge, about improper relations with Second Mile children. What changed the climate was an interview by a Child and Youth Services caseworker who interviewed Aaron Fisher, a fifteen-year-old at Central Mountain High School. In spring 2008, Fisher broke his silence and charged that Sandusky was sexually abusing him while Sandusky was a volunteer football coach at the school. The star coach had been glorified by those associated with Central Mountain High School for volunteering to help coach in the new school about thirty miles from Sandusky's home. Fisher, one of The Second Mile children, was taken out of class with some regularity by Sandusky. Only after Fisher's mother called the school complaining of Aaron's missing classes did the boy tell the Central Mountain principal that Sandusky was abusing him. With some reluctance, school officials reported the alleged abuse, and the Clinton County district attorney investigated and then sent the case to the Centre County district attorney, Michael Madeira. Because Madeira's sister was married to one of Sandusky's adopted sons, Madeira withdrew from the case and sent it on to Pennsylvania attorney general Tom Corbett in March 2009.[24]

With the case in the attorney general's office, a grand jury investigation began, though much more slowly than some people believed should have taken place. Whether that is true or not, the investigation was prolonged long enough for Tom Corbett to get the Republican nomination for governor and win the governorship in fall 2010.[25] One year later, the grand jury charged Sandusky with violating eight children sexually. In graphic form, the grand jury indictment informed an unsuspecting public not only of Sandusky's sexual transgressions with young boys, but also of the fact that Penn State administrators, Paterno, Curley, Schultz, and Spanier had knowledge about the incidents. They knew about incidents of Sandusky on campus but only Paterno indicated they were sexual. Out of the legal presentment of the grand jury, Sandusky was soon arrested, and ironically had an unsecured bail set at $100,000 by a district judge, Leslie Dutchcot, who both volunteered at and donated to Jerry Sandusky's Second Mile.[26] Both Curley and Schultz were charged with lying under oath and failure to report the suspected child molestation to the police and child protection agencies. Paterno soon died, but President Spanier later was presented with charges similar to those against Curley and Schultz.

It is not surprising that all four Penn State administrators were reluctant to report the Sandusky incidents outside their immediate group, although Joe Paterno in 2001 followed protocol by informing Athletic Director Tim Curley in the chain of command. It is not surprising, because the insular nature of athletic administration at Penn State, as at other big-time institutions, provided cover over this issue and in other cases. Such an instance was a vice president for Student Affairs logically challenging the head coach's authority to discipline football players, a longtime practice of Paterno's. When Paterno confronted the official with the actual authority to discipline students at Penn State, Paterno won. Vice President Vicky Triponey was forced to resign the year before the Aaron Fisher disclosure.

Hiding the punishment of football players by isolating it from the eyes of someone officially empowered outside athletics was similar to how President Spanier limited information to the Board of Trustees. Spanier concealed a major problem in athletics by deciding to limit key information to the Board of Trustees gathered from the Pennsylvania attorney general's office in the months before the grand jury indictment. One could claim hypocrisy when, two months before the Sandusky indictment, Spanier told the trustees, "Let us not be reluctant to tell our story, openly and honestly."[27] At nearly the same time, Spanier came home from an athletic reform retreat of presidents from big-time athletic programs hosted by National Collegiate Athletic Association (NCAA) president Mark Emmert. Spanier, with a high degree of insincerity, stated that the presidents have "reached a point where we must pay more attention to these academic issues, to these integrity issues."[28] Yet he did not practice what he preached and was certainly not open in informing the Board of Trustees of his and the other three Penn State administrators' oath-bound testimony before the grand jury earlier that year that resulted in the Sandusky Scandal and eventually Spanier's own demise.

In this whole scenario, the organization that was tied to Penn State through Jerry Sandusky's retirement agreement, The Second Mile, escaped both an internal and an outside judicial accounting. Why this happened is not clear. The two-decade executive director of The Second Mile, Jack Raykovitz, was a licensed psychologist who was informed of the 2001 Sandusky–McQueary incident. It is not clear what the well-paid Raykovitz and his handsomely paid wife, Katherine Genovese, the two chief administrators of The Second Mile, did with their potential child abuse information. Were they protecting their own investment in The Second Mile, because their combined salaries were about 10 percent of the income of the organization?[29] As when President Spanier gave scant information to the Penn State Board of Trustees about Sandusky, most of the members of the board of The Second Mile knew nothing about the Sandusky situation. Bruce Heim, a force in The Second Mile and a leader in financial support, stated that the executive staff was well aware in 2001: "I stood up in that meeting," Heim explained, and "I advised Jack [Raykovitz] not to go to the Board with it."[30] And Raykovitz complied.

Much of the financial support for The Second Mile came from those like Bruce Heim who were involved in Penn State activities. Six individuals contributed $50,000 or more to Sandusky's organization in the year prior to the scandal, including long-time board members of The Second Mile Bruce Heim and his wife Susan, and a major contributor to Penn State and builder of Penn State facilities, Bob Poole and his wife Sandra.[31] Bruce Heim was a State College realtor and an instructor of insurance and real estate at Penn State. Heim, with an MBA degree from Penn State, contributed more than money, for he became a mentor at The Second Mile. Once he worked with a Penn State player who had been kicked off the football team for drinking and shooting arrows through the wall of his apartment before the fall football season of his senior year. E. Z. Smith, in Paterno's doghouse for this and other activities, was allowed back onto the team only after Heim supervised him at The Second Mile, where Smith mentored some of the at-risk children. After doing what Heim required of the star football player, Smith returned to the Penn State team and helped lead them to a victory in the 2005 Orange Bowl.[32]

Bob Poole was noteworthy for not only large donations to The Second Mile but for contributions to Penn State, including an endowed real estate professorship in the College of Business and scholarships for Schreyer Honors College students and athletic scholarships.[33] Poole also was directly involved with wealthy donors William Schreyer and Philip Sieg and Coach Joe Paterno in the $125 million construction of the Village at Penn State. The Village for retirees overlooking the stadium was an idea pushed by President Graham Spanier almost as soon as he headed the university in the mid-1990s. Builder Poole had a dozen Penn State building contracts in the first decade of the twenty-first century, and he received $25 million from Penn State in the two years before the Sandusky Scandal broke. Had the scandal not occurred, he was to be the construction manager for the $11.5 million Second Mile "Center for Excellence" to be built on Penn State land sold to The Second Mile. Poole's nearly $10,000 contribution to the Tom Corbett campaign for the governorship surely would not be a negative factor in Corbett's backing of The Second Mile's grant from the state to construct the multimillion dollar Center for Excellence.[34] Ironically, Bob Poole helped raise money for Leslie Dutchcot's political campaign for district judge. She was a volunteer for The Second Mile who, after her election, provided Jerry Sandusky with unsecured bail after his arrest.

It is not unexpected that not only were a number of The Second Mile contributors and board members tied to Penn State, but a majority of them graduated from the institution. They also were significant in Attorney General Tom Corbett's election to the governorship in 2010. Families and board members of The Second

Mile, most well connected to Penn State, gave more than $600,000 to Corbett political campaigns.[35] It is also not surprising that Governor Corbett agreed to release $3 million of state money to help build Jerry Sandusky's multimillion-dollar Center for Excellence for Second Mile children. The money was promised even after Corbett knew that a number of children claimed they were violated by Sandusky and were part of Corbett's grand jury investigation from 2009 until after he was elected governor. Revelations coming out of the Sandusky Scandal could only jeopardize The Second Mile, Penn State University, and the political ambitions of Tom Corbett.

The connectedness with Corbett and financial contributions to him may be a major reason that The Second Mile remained at arm's length from the Sandusky Scandal. Despite the fact that all the victims in the grand jury indictment were Second Mile children, no charges were levied against Second Mile officials for not reporting suspected child sexual violations stemming from Attorney General and then Governor Tom Corbett's grand jury investigation. This fact is especially curious because the administrator of The Second Mile and president of The Second Mile Board were informed of possible violations. Although it is clear that the three Penn State officials charged with crimes in the Sandusky Scandal were supportive of The Second Mile, no evidence has come to the fore that Tim Curley, Gary Schultz, or Graham Spanier contributed to The Second Mile after knowing of suspected child abuse by Jerry Sandusky. Joe Paterno, who was not charged, also apparently did not contribute to Sandusky's Second Mile, but he was severely criticized for not doing enough to stop child abuse. Meanwhile, Jack Raykovitz, executive director of The Second Mile, remained basically unscathed, as did others who contributed financially to The Second Mile and knew about potential violations by Jerry Sandusky.

The revelation that a high school freshman, Aaron Fisher, at Central Mountain High School was sexually molested by Sandusky in spring 2008 eventually led to the attorney general's grand jury investigation and the involvement of the same legal counsel for both Penn State and The Second Mile. Legal counsel Wendell Courtney and his wife Linette Courtney were both entwined with The Second Mile and Penn State. Ms. Courtney served on the state board of The Second Mile at the same time that she was a director of development for Penn State. More important, her husband, Wendell Courtney, attorney for a State College legal firm, McQuaide Blasco, was counsel to both The Second Mile and to Penn State.[36] A low-handicap golfer and former captain of the Penn State golf team, Courtney was aware of the questionable conduct of Sandusky at the same time that he competed in The Second Mile fundraisers at the Penn State golf course with Jack Raykovitz and Jerry Sandusky.

At the end of November 2009, Jerry Sandusky informed Jack Raykovitz that the founder of The Second Mile was being investigated after Aaron Fisher's accusation. When Sandusky left The Second Mile because of the investigation, it was called a retirement, not a resignation, by Katherine Genovese, second in command at The Second Mile, likely in an effort to save the image of the organization. The use of words to save the image was similar to Penn State's statement after football star Anwar Phillips was expelled for assaulting a female student on campus. Penn State's Sports Information told the public that Phillips was out of school for "personal reasons" rather than more correct word, "expulsion."[37] Meanwhile, at The Second Mile, Bonnie Marshall, who was hired to be The Second Mile development director, was completely kept in the dark by her superiors about Sandusky's behavior. She later claimed that the leaders of The Second Mile were conducting themselves like the Penn State administrators who managed charges against Sandusky—by remaining silent. "I'm seeing the same parallel track," Marshall was quoted. "[O]nly a few people need to know this. [They are] circling the wagons."[38]

Many people apparently had an incentive to do little or nothing for the two organizations that were tied together, including their conspicuous use of the exact same colors, blue and white. From a short-term perspective, remaining silent was successful as money kept pouring into The Second Mile and Penn State continued to be successful and fill its 107,000-seat stadium. In the long run, however, The Second Mile folded with the Sandusky revelations, while the image of Penn State was damaged and the football team was dealt a severe blow. There was a shared culture of silence at Penn State and at The Second Mile. One also could make the case of a culture of silence in the grand jury investigation at the state level under Attorney General Tom Corbett. When Corbett achieved the governorship, finally the sole investigator, a narcotics specialist, was augmented by a number of others and the investigation quickened.[39] But only after Corbett was elected governor.

The connection between The Second Mile and Penn State could also be seen in the legal counsel shared by the two organizations. It is not clear whether as legal adviser to Penn State and The Second Mile Courtney advised the leaders of the legal responsibilities for children that were demanded of them. From both sides, Courtney was well aware of potential problems for both organizations, but because of attorney–client privilege, it may never be known whether he advised them of legal accountabilities. Courtney removed himself as counsel of The Second Mile as the Sandusky Scandal broke publicly with the grand jury presentment on November 4, 2011. He had already been removed as Penn State counsel when, in early 2010, Penn State dropped Courtney's law firm, McQuaide Blasco, in favor of an internal counsel, Cynthia Baldwin, who had recently been president of the Board of Trustees.[40] While Courtney faded away from Penn State, the connections among Sandusky, The Second Mile, and Penn State remained until tragedy hit the next year.

The interconnectedness and shared culture of silence remained to the end of the Sandusky saga. At President Spanier's last Board of Trustees meeting, he not only brought two lawyers but also a public relations firm to the meeting. Before he could use the public relations firm, both he and the football coach were relieved of their positions by the Board of Trustees. The lack of transparency that had existed in the insular university and its athletic program continued as the Board of Trustees, rather than conducting a national search for an athletic director, chose one of its own board members and a former Penn State football player, Dave Joyner, to be the next athletic director to replace the fallen Tim Curley. The board also looked internally for its next president, Provost Rod Erickson, to replace a disgraced Graham Spanier. As two writers in *Sports Illustrated* commented shortly after the scandal broke, "Like Russian nesting dolls, there are levels of isolation within Penn State."[41]

Erickson, however, was highly respected as a long-time vice president and provost, though he was inexperienced in athletic affairs at Penn State and nationally. Further, he received flawed legal advice on potential sanctions that could be forthcoming. His almost complete lack of knowledge of the history of the National Collegiate Athletic Association, and that it would never legally give a "death penalty" to Penn State football, led to what has been termed the worst decision in his short tenure at Penn State. As a result of the lack of understanding and poor legal advice and extreme pressure from NCAA officials, President Erickson signed a consent decree rather than go through the NCAA's Committee on Investigations, the usual procedure. The draconian punishment by the NCAA was based on flawed conclusions in the $8 million Freeh report commissioned by Penn State.[42] The Freeh report condemned President Spanier, Vice President Schultz, Athletic Director Curley, and Football Coach Paterno along with the dominating and insular athletic culture of Penn State. Those in charge of Penn State's isolated athletic program had not, in the often-used words of Joe Paterno, taken "care of the little things" and thus the big things could not "take care of themselves." Jerry Sandusky, The Second Mile, and Penn State and its football program came to no good end, but not before the shared culture of silence was made manifest in the Penn State women's basketball program.

CHAPTER 13

Rene Portland and the Culture of Athletic Silence

"I think Rene has done a great job. . . . I hired her."
—Joe Paterno (2002)

"The ability to misuse another person and to find reasons to excuse it is a universal human trait."
—Scott Nolte (2006)

The culture of silence was no clearer in the athletic administration and at Penn State University than the case of the Penn State women's basketball coach Rene Portland from 1980 to 2007. Women's athletics seemingly had less need for a culture of silence, since women's athletics were not widely visible after being given varsity status beginning in 1964. Nevertheless, it occurred in the most important women's sport at Penn State—as basketball dominated women's sport across the nation. Basketball had been the leading women's sport in U.S. colleges since shortly after its invention by James Naismith. The sport for both men and women spread like a fire in an abandoned wooden shed once introduced by the Springfield YMCA School in 1891. A woman's physical educator, Senda Berenson, introduced the sport to the women of Smith College only months after its invention, and it grew rapidly across the country. No other sport, including field hockey, softball, and gymnastics, became the driving force that women's basketball did through the entire twentieth century.[1] Penn State had a women's basketball team by the first decade of the twentieth century, though not as a varsity sport. Once women had varsity athletics at Penn State, however, women's gymnastics was far more popular with Penn State fans than was basketball. For a few years, women's gymnastics filled the Recreation Building in the late 1970s and into the 1980s. One gymnastic meet with California State University at Fullerton in 1980 graced Penn State's Recreation Building with the largest crowd ever in the university's only arena. Far in excess of the seating capacity or fire regulations, there were fans three, four, or five deep on the track surrounding the seated crowd and spectators on the gymnasium floor almost up to the gymnastic equipment.[2] Yet basketball, once it had discarded the strange and restrictive game of six-player basketball in the 1970s, became more popular. Out went the rules where players were once forced to play only on one end of the court either on defense or on offense and later allowed one player to be a "rover" to play the entire court. It became a game that demanded greater athleticism that would attract more fans.

Intercollegiate athletics for women at Penn State were rather genteel and ladylike in their early years. Sport for women had existed since the end of the nineteenth century and a Women's Athletic Association was formed in 1918.[3] Penn State women, with little financial aid, played games, but with little interest outside of those who participated directly. Competition moved from Play Days (at which players from several schools divided up to play games and the home school sociably provided cookies and juice) to Sports Days (at which teams from a number of schools, with minimal coaching, played several shortened contests in one day), and finally, regular dual competition. Once athletic scholarships were offered, the level of competition jumped rapidly in the 1970s. This was especially true after Title IX of the Education Amendments Act of 1972 became law, banning sexual discrimination in educational institutions receiving federal aid.[4]

The Penn State intercollegiate teams that began officially in 1964 were given a small amount of financial assistance from the Athletic Department run by the dean and athletic director of the College of Health and Physical Education, Ernie McCoy. Two years before Joe Paterno became head football coach, Penn State had nine women's intercollegiate teams: basketball, fencing, field hockey, golf, gymnastics, lacrosse, softball, riflery, and tennis.[5] Much of the very limited competition was held on women's physical education fields or in the women's physical education facility, White Building. At the beginning, the varsity coaches were selected from the women's physical education faculty, whose full-time teaching schedules were then adjusted. A small number of spectators attended the contests, and, with the exception of gymnastics, competing at the national level was minimal. In gymnastics, a talented gymnast who was attending Penn State in the early 1970s, Karen Schuckman, won a national all-around title in gymnastics, the first Penn State woman who was a national champ. She was an anomaly. Not until Judy Avener became coach and Penn State first offered athletic scholarships in 1974 did gymnastics become the dominant women's sport. With the hiring of Rene Portland in 1980, however, basketball was soon to be the sport of choice of the Athletic Department, as it was in many institutions.

Within weeks of athletics being isolated from academic oversight by Joe Paterno, Steve Garban, and President John Oswald, Rene Portland became Paterno's major coaching hire in his two years as athletic director. Rene Portland may have shown her sense of self and poor sportsmanship in her first year at Penn State, when she commanded her team to score 100 points for her 100th victory as a college coach, accomplished by a full court press for the entire game against little Ursinus College.[6] Sheltered by coach Joe Paterno, Portland would soon use her insularity to carry out prejudicial actions on sexual orientation in which her being a Roman Catholic had significance.

Penn State had mostly physical educator-coaches when Rene Portland was hired in 1980 to singularly coach basketball. She gained some notoriety as a collegiate player whose team won several national Association for Intercollegiate Athletics for Women (AIAW) championships at a small Catholic college, Immaculata College, near Philadelphia in the early 1970s. Portland then began coaching at St. Josephs College and moved on as a successful coach at the University of Colorado a few years later. Penn State, striving to become national champions in several women's sports, including gymnastics, field hockey, and lacrosse, decided to hire the former Pennsylvanian with a 40-20 record at Colorado. The Roman Catholic Rene Portland came to Penn State under another Roman Catholic, Joe Paterno. Their being Catholic was important because of the stance of the Roman Catholic Church internationally, which strongly opposed homosexuality.

Strong opposition to a homosexual lifestyle was not particularly unusual in the 1970s and 1980s at Penn State nor with Catholics and many other Americans. Less than a decade before Portland arrived in Happy Valley, the Board of Trustees took up the case of the Homophiles of Penn State, who filed a suit against the institution for not allowing their group to be officially recognized as a student organization. Only after the U.S. Supreme Court in 1972 voted 9–0 in a similar discrimination suit in Connecticut did the trustees feel they would not win the case and must allow a homosexual group to be officially recognized on campus.[7] At Penn State the discrimination in sexual orientation, specifically lesbians in women's basketball, would eventually lead to a policy prohibiting that discrimination.

Rene Portland, like Joe Paterno among the men, would be the highest paid woman at Penn State, indicating the importance of the sport to the university's image. She would lead Penn State basketball to a highly successful level in the East and a 72 percent, 609-236, winning record in twenty-seven years with the Nittany Lions. She was never able to win a national championship, but she was the most successful basketball coach in the Big Ten and went to the final four national championships once in her lengthy career. She never attained an iconic image as did basketball coaches Pat Head Summitt at Tennessee and Geno Auriemma at Connecticut, or her esteemed coach at Immaculata, Cathy Rush, and she never approached receiving the accolades received by Paterno or even Jerry Sandusky. Still, she had a very strong following in Happy Valley that, with the powerful support of Joe Paterno, undoubtedly gave her a secure position that allowed her to defy an antidiscrimination policy at Penn State for much of her career. In addition, the Penn State athletic administration could find little fault in Portland for National Collegiate Athletic Association (NCAA) or AIAW violations, as it had with Portland's predecessor, Pat Meiser, under AIAW rules (1971–1982).[8] Meiser's illegal recruiting that violated a technicality in visiting a recruit's home was significant for being the first ever violation against a Penn State women's or men's team.[9] No known Portland violation for recruiting occurred until the early 1990s, when the NCAA cited her for being accompanied by an unauthorized recruiter of high schooler Mandy West.[10] Portland's record from this standpoint, if not perfect, was quite clean, just as was the record of Penn State nationally in all sports.

What was most disturbing to people who were looking out for the sexual orientation welfare of all women was Rene Portland's longstanding opposition to homosexuals in women's sport. To Portland, lesbianism, even outside a religious viewpoint, gave women's sport a bad name, during a time when many people recognized that a number of women's sports were dominated by homosexuals. The most visible players in several sports nationally were lesbians, including the most dominant woman athlete in the twentieth century, Mildred "Babe" Didrikson. Then, too, the same was true of two of the most visible professional athletes of the 1960s and 1970s, Billy Jean King and Martina Navratilova. What bothered Portland in addition to a number of lesbians playing basketball were a number of recognized lesbian coaches leading those players.[11]

For more than a quarter-century, Portland had a discriminatory policy that emanated from her team rules. "No drinking, no drugs, no lesbians" was quoted by a number of players as Portland's three team rules. No one in the athletic administration challenged her actions, which began early with a star high school player, Cindy Davies, almost immediately after Paterno hired Portland. Setting a state high school record of 2,322 points at Indiana, Pennsylvania, Davies contributed immediately to Portland's team. By Davies' sophomore year, Portland had suspicions of Davies dating the team's female student manager. Portland got rid of the student manager and confronted Davies in her office. About a quarter-century later, Davies finally told her side of the story. "It's seared in my mind," Davies revealed to a reporter only after basketball player Jennifer Harris began a lawsuit against discrimination by Portland in the first decade of the twenty-first century. Portland told Davies of the lesbian suspicions: "I don't know if it's true, but if I find out it's true, there's nothing that will stop me from going to your parents, the university, and the media." Davies recalled that it "felt like I was being blackmailed. . . . I was scared to death."[12] So scared that she kept it to herself, made the excuse that she wanted to devote time to her studies, left school, and returned home. She then attended Indiana University of Pennsylvania, starring on the team scoring 906 points in two years, averaging more than seventeen points a game, and setting records for field-goal and free-throw percentages. Along with a record-setting 38 points in a game against Clarion University and making the Kodak All-American team, she had a successful collegiate career in athletics away from the prying eyes of coach Portland.[13] She did not forget, however, her treatment by Portland and Penn State's lack of concern, when in her mid-forties she exclaimed, "they do not see how their coach is a bigot and discriminates against young ladies."[14]

At nearly the same time Davies arrived at Penn State, Portland exited the Gulas twins, recruited by Patty Meiser, the previous coach. Corinne and Chris Gulas were a year ahead of Cindy Davies at Indiana High School and came to Penn

State with high expectations. As a freshman, Corinne was the leading scorer for Penn State under Meiser the year before Portland's arrival. There were rumors that Portland had dropped them from the team for suspicions of being lesbians, though there were no formal complaints about discrimination. Those suspicions lingered for years, during which Portland eliminated those who might bring what she considered discredit upon her program for lesbian tendencies. Portland came out publicly with her anti-lesbian program when interviewed by the *Chicago Sun-Times* in 1986. As a recruiting device, Portland would initiate anti-lesbian discussions with the parents of recruits to reassure them that she would have no lesbians on her team. "I bring it up," she noted "and the kids are so relieved and the parents are so relieved." Portland emphasized her lesbian stance to the paper, "I will not have it in my program."[15] She kept up the theme for the next two decades despite Penn State creating a sexual orientation anti-discrimination policy in the early 1990s.

The *Philadelphia Inquirer*'s Jere Longman wrote a muckraking article about Rene Portland at the close of the 1991 basketball season, even quoting the best-known woman athlete at Penn State in the 1980s. Suzie McConnell, who made the 1988 U.S. Olympic gold medal basketball team after graduating from Penn State, was quoted as saying that Portland "does make it known when she's recruiting that she doesn't put up with homosexuality." According to Patti Longenecker, who played alongside McConnell, "She tells you, flat out, 'I don't have any apprecia-tion for the homosexual lifestyle. I won't have that on my team.'"[16] Fortunately for Portland, she did not make the same exceptions, as did the Ku Klux Klan earlier in the century, and attempt to eliminate other minorities, such as Negroes, Jews, or Catholics on her team. The Penn State Athletic Department apparently remained silent and did no investigation despite Portland's violations of federal law including Title IX.

There were major discussions at this time about sexual orientation at both the state and national levels. Pennsylvania's governor was slightly ahead of the federal legislature in addressing the issue. Despite being a Catholic and pro-life on the abortion issue, Democrat Governor Robert Casey (1987–1995), issued an executive order in 1988 stating that no government agency shall discriminate on the basis of sexual orientation or make other discriminations. Committees of the U.S. Congress were debating the category of "sexual orientation" in 1991 as the Portland situation developed at Penn State. These discussions led the new Penn State president, Joab Thomas, to find out the legal implications if Penn State did not have a sexual orientation clause in its policies. After discussions, Thomas suggested that a policy statement should be adopted by the Board of Trustees to help "protect all members of the University community against invidious dis-crimination, including members of the Penn State lesbian and gay community." His argument was supported by a survey of Penn State's gays and lesbians in which nearly three-quarters of those surveyed had been insulted because of their sexual orientation.[17]

The faculty advisor of the Lesbian, Gay, and Bisexual Student Alliance of Penn State, psychologist Anthony D'Augelli, decided to push for action after reading the newspaper account about Rene Portland's stance against lesbians on her team. Professor D'Augelli was an expert researching homosexuality and had recently published an article, "Homophobia in a University Community." Referring to the *Philadelphia Inquirer* article, D'Augelli wrote Athletic Director Jim Tarman, stating that Portland's actions were illegal and went against Penn State policies. He copied important individuals, including the head of Affirmative Action, Bonnie Ortiz, vice president for Underrepresented Groups, James Stewart; vice president for Student Services, William Asbury; and President Joab Thomas.[18] The university was now more clearly alerted to a problem that previously administrators knew existed.

It is surprising that Penn State's University Faculty Senate, an organization that often appeared to have only slightly more power than a high school student council, was already discussing the question of sexual orientation bias, when the *Philadelphia Inquirer* article came out. Almost immediately the Faculty Senate took decisive action on a proposed policy change when, on a 93–12 vote, it passed a recommendation to add a "Rene Portland" sexual orientation provision to the Penn State anti-discrimination policy in such areas as race, minority status, and religion.[19] Within two months, Penn State's conservative Board of Trustees took the advice of President Joab Thomas and added the "Rene Portland" provision to Penn State policy.[20] Rene Portland thereafter would defy university policy at her own peril.

Penn State and its athletic administration were alerted, and Jim Tarman sent a memo to all athletic personnel that sexual orientation was added to the anti-discrimination policy. He stated, however, that "anti-discrimination will be handled within the department, and . . . dealt with as matters of 'privileged information.'" There was no attempt by Tarman or any other athletic official to investigate sexual orientation discrimination in athletics or in the women's basketball program.[21] Tarman's boss, Steve Garban, as vice president of finance, concluded five months later that "the athletic department is still dragging its feet on a program for its staff" relative to sexual orientation training. A memo noted, "The Portland issue is far from dead."[22] It may not have been dead, but the discrimination was ignored for more than a decade, just as the first Sandusky incidents remained silently covered for more than ten years.

Rene Portland basically ignored the 1991 anti-discriminatory Penn State policy, though she said she was in compliance. Portland told sportswriter Robert Lipsyte that the 1991 action by Penn State "is a policy I have to work under as an employee of the University. That's all I'll say about it." Portland, Lipsyte stated, "is a

Queen Bee in Happy Valley, as the conservative, insulated campus is known."[23]
The discrimination remained until the first basketball player, from Portland's first
quarter-century at Penn State, condemned what Portland had done to her and
got outside support to take the charged violation to a federal court.[24] The soon to
be prominent Jennifer Harris case brought more headaches to Athletic Director
Tim Curley. It occurred at almost the same time that Vice President for Student
Affairs Vicky Triponey was placing Curley in a difficult position of following the
wishes either of Joe Paterno on student discipline of athletes or of the Penn State's
Office of Student Affairs in the handling of student discipline. Now Curley had
to deal with another difficult and power-laden question—allowing a successful
coach to continue to violate Penn State policy, a coach backed by Joe Paterno,
or take action to punish the most visible Penn State female coach. Instead of the
Athletic Department conducting an investigation of violations of the Penn State's
anti-discrimination policy, it was the Division of Affirmation Action that began
a study of Portland's discriminatory conduct.

Ken Lehrman, Vice Provost for Affirmative Action, began an investigation of
Rene Portland in October 2005, just prior to the Harris case, after the National
Center for Lesbian Rights reported Harris's allegations against Portland. This
was the first case filed in the Office of Affirmative Action since the 1991 sexual
orientation policy was passed by the Board of Trustees. After a half-year of study,
Lehrman reported to President Spanier that, indeed, Portland was guilty of discrimination by creating a "hostile, intimidating, and offensive environment"
relative to sexual orientation. President Spanier then decided to punish Portland,
not by removing her as coach, but with a $10,000 fine, possibly 1/50th of her sal-
ary, in addition to a written reprimand, mandatory involvement in a diversity
program, exit interviews of players upon graduation, and a statement about future
dismissal with cause.[25] Portland disagreed with the Lehrman findings but took
the penalty so she could continue coaching the next school year.

Meanwhile, Jen Harris proceeded with a civil case against Portland in fall
2005 after ousted Harris had transferred to James Madison University. The case
of Jen Harris remains disputed, for it never came to trial. What is known is that
tensions between Harris and Portland began during the previous season, but it
reached a breaking point after Penn State's loss to Liberty University in the first
game of the NCAA tourney, the seventh-straight NCAA invitation to the women's
tournament for Rene Portland. For a proud coach who had led her team to the
Final Four early in that decade, the Liberty defeat was difficult to rationalize.
Soon after the tournament loss to the little-regarded team, Portland dismissed
three players, Lisa Etienne, Amber Bland, and Jennifer Harris.

The first player to ever outwardly challenge Portland's actions involving charges
of lesbian activities, Jen Harris, went public a few months after Portland dismissed
her. Harris was not the average scholarship player, for she had been recruited by
colleges since sixth grade, had made McDonald's All-American, Women's Basketball Coaches Association All-American, *Parade Magazine* All-American, and

Nike All-American, scoring more than 2,000 points for Central Dauphin High School in the Pennsylvania capital, Harrisburg.[26] She did not, however, dominate at Penn State as many thought she would. Portland's attitude toward her might have had a negative impact. According to Harris, "Portland thought I was gay" and as a result Harris was "treated in a very demeaning manner. Whether I'm gay or not," she stated, "shouldn't matter." Similarly, Portland's call for Harris to do away with her African American hairstyle of non-feminine "cornrows and braids" was uncalled for, Harris believed.[27]

With the backing of the National Center for Lesbian Rights, the Harris lawsuit, combined with the Lehrman report, gave notice to the Athletic Department and Penn State that it might have a significant problem. Penn State spokesman Bill Mahon said that he was surprised that Harris would make a claim a half-year after dismissal, and like the Sandusky incidents, Mahon and Penn State officials were apparently wishing the charges would go away. They would not. Despite this being a high-profile federal case of discrimination, President Spanier never brought the Portland case of sexual discrimination before the Board of Trustees. This lack of action by the president occurred despite the fact that the Board of Trustees had ten pages of discussion about sexual discrimination before including it in Board of Trustee policy the previous decade.[28] Silence before the Board Trustees on any negative matter touching Penn State was a trait held by presidents before and after Spanier, but was noticeable in Spanier's sixteen years of heading Penn State.

The Harris versus Portland case included as defendants Athletic Director Tim Curley and Penn State in the federal civil action. It outlined the practices of Portland going back to 1980 and charged, "By their deliberate indifference, Penn State and Mr. Curley adopted a de facto policy and custom of permitting discrimination, harassment, intolerance and retaliation by Ms. Portland."[29] The "law of unintended consequences" generally is applied to actions whose results were not contemplated by those who took those actions, and Penn State's inaction on discrimination did have unplanned results.[30]

By early 2006 and the publication of the Harris lawsuit, Portland was in her first year that had a losing record, and it had been a decade and a half since the coach had threatened Cindy Davies to expose her as a lesbian. Harris was already playing on the James Madison University team. Of Portland, Harris stated, "I wouldn't wish it on my worst enemy, the horrible, humiliating, painful things she put me through." Harris was quoted as saying, "I don't want anybody else to ever experience it again."[31] The lawsuit contained twenty-two counts of civil-rights violations, both racial and sexual, under the Equal Protection clause of the Pennsylvania Constitution and the Fourteenth Amendment of the U.S. Constitution, freedom of speech under the Bill of Rights, and race and sex discrimination under Title VI of the Civil Rights Act of 1964 and Title IX of the Education Amendments Act of 1972. Harris asked for more than $50,000 in punitive damages. Portland, to the contrary, argued in the papers that Harris was dismissed for exhibiting "a work ethic and attitude that were detrimental to the success of our team."[32] Portland contended that "The sexual orientation or race of any player or person is irrelevant to me."[33] Both the Harris suit and the Ken Lehrman report disputed Portland's accounts.

Portland may have felt secure with a contract extension by Athletic Director Tim Curley good through 2009 and a Penn State administration that had never challenged either Joe Paterno's or Curley's support for her. Paterno had said more than once, "I think Rene has done a great job. That is one of the best things I have done for Penn State. I hired her." Curley was nearly as supportive when once questioned about Portland's handling of off-the-court issues such as lesbianism. "We are fully supportive of the actions taken by Rene Portland," Curley told a reporter. "We have the greatest confidence in Rene Portland as a coach."[34] One should remember that Portland received the 2005 Renaissance Person of the Year in Happy Valley after the Harris case was brought against Portland. She was honored for, among other virtues, being "a wonderful role model for young women."[35] To many, Portland was a beloved coach of a successful program.

The Harris versus Portland court case could have been settled in 2006 shortly after the President Spanier sanctions. A court-ordered mediation settlement, however, went awry. After a year of court maneuvering, the case was to be tried in a jury trial in June 2007, a year in which Portland coached under restrictions by President Spanier and, for the second straight year, had a losing record. These were the first two of her lengthy coaching career. Shortly before the trial, the two sides made a confidential settlement, and Harris withdrew the case as a condition of the settlement. The possibility that both sides gained financially from the settlement is highly likely. Harris had asked for punitive damages in the original case, and shortly after the settlement, Portland announced her retirement. As Penn State has had a history of settling disputes with monetary or other awards, it is likely that Portland received a considerable financial reward for leaving the university and then remaining silent. That is, unless Portland had committed some egregious act in the days before her resignation. Paying off high-profile coaches and administrators had happened previously. The first known was that of Hugo Bezdek being given a year's leave with pay for stepping down as dean of the School of Physical Education and Athletics (1936). Similarly, basketball coaches John Egli (1968), John Bach (1978), and Dick Harter (1982) were relieved of coaching responsibilities and either given another higher-paying position (Egli), a position with no responsibilities (Bach), or paid off with a significant sum (Harter). So too when Ed Czekaj was removed as athletic director (1980) and placed in a constructed position as assistant to a vice president in the university business office as his reward.

Within a month of Portland's resignation, an African American with a law degree, working in a successful basketball program at Notre Dame, was hired as the new women's basketball coach. Coquese Washington, who had played professional basketball for a short time, took over a program at its nadir. It took her three years to achieve a winning record and five years to win the Big Ten championship. There was not a great deal of discussion over lesbianism in Penn State basketball or in other sports. There was generally silence in Happy Valley relative to Rene Portland, from President Spanier as well, who told the trustees he was "thrilled to have Coquese" shortly after her hiring and again never mentioned Portland.[36] A documentary, though, brought to light the entire Portland situation, emphasizing her discriminatory actions against lesbians or perceived lesbians at Penn State. The documentary, *Training Rules: No Drinking, No Drugs, No Lesbians,* produced by Dee Mosbacher and Fawn Yacker, was released two years after Portland's resignation. Among those in the film was a Nittany Lion basketball player deposed in the early 1980s, Corinne Gulas. One of the ousted twins in the incident earlier in this chapter, Gulas indicated that one of the reasons that Penn State women's basketball lost regularly in the NCAA tournament was that they did not trust each other in close games. That Portland had played one player against another on the basis of their sexual orientation or perceived sexual orientation led, Gulas believed, to distrust among teammates when the game was on the line.[37] That certainly is a possibility, though it may have been that Rene Portland was so anxious to do well in the NCAA tournament that her anxiety was transferred to those on the floor. Neither her general lack of success in the NCAA tournament nor her longstanding bias against homosexuality were credits to Penn State and its athletic program into the twenty-first century. Maybe Scott Nolte was correct when he stated that "the ability to misuse another person and to find reasons to excuse it is a universal trait."[38]

How Penn State's administration and the Athletic Department responded to sexual bias for more than a quarter-century says something about the insular nature of Penn State athletics and high administrative officials. If the Portland reign at Penn State was a success for the most part on the basketball court, it did damage to the Penn State image in the long run. The Pandora's box at Penn State did not contain all the evils of the world, as did the Pandora's box of the ancient Hesiod's tale, but Penn State's box surely contained one of them, isolating evils that might mar the image of athletics. Athletic and university administrators were concerned about image, and as long as they could control the negatives by isolating them from the greater public, and as President Spanier did with his own Board of Trustees, they appeared satisfied to do just that rather than addressing the illegal and discriminatory actions head on. Just as in the Jerry Sandusky Scandal, both the president and his administrators and the athletic department remained silent about Portland when they could have taken action. In the long run, as in big-time athletics across the nation, the insular nature of Penn State athletics in hiding the negatives, rather than dealing with them, can have devastating results for the institution.

CHAPTER 14

The Board of Trustees, Insularity, and Athletic Administration

"There has been for many years a rubber-stamp culture on our college boards."
—Anne Neal (2011)

"Do not turn one blunder into two."
—Baltasar Gracián (1647)

Before Graham Spanier was chosen president of Penn State in the mid-1990s, a long-time president of George Washington University, Stephen Joel Trachtenberg, told a Penn State professor that he unfortunately could not pursue the Penn State presidency at that time because it was widely known, and to Trachtenberg positively, as the "Last of the Imperial University Presidencies."[1] If the Penn State administration was imperial, including athletic administration, and if it was insular and secretive about the athletic program, it was in part due to the policy and actions of the Board of Trustees that allowed it to be so. It was not always that way, but certainly the presidency of George Washington Atherton (1882–1906) was an example of a kingly presidency at Penn State and was similar to the presidencies at many American institutions of higher education in his day. That state of affairs, as will be seen, was also in evidence as result of Board of Trustee policy toward the upheaval at Penn State coming from the Vietnam War and civil-rights unrest around 1970.

University boards of trustees are generally organized to set policy for their institutions, but they often neither do that nor raise questions about how the administration is administering their polices. By tending to rubber-stamp the actions of a strong, imperial president, trustees could allow the president to conduct the university in a detrimental as well as a positive way. Penn State was confirming what has happened in many universities: "There has been for many years," President of the American Council of Trustees and Alumni Anne Neal has stated, "a rubber-stamp culture on our college boards."[2] From the 1890s until the 1960s, the full Penn State Board of Trustees had little influence on university policy. As

Penn State historian Michael Bezilla has shown, the entire board "merely ratified decisions that had already been made." It was, Bezilla emphasized, "neither democratic nor easily accessible to public scrutiny." Executive Committee secrecy, "conducting its own business in private," drove policy that was often beneficial to the growth of Penn State, but there could be negative outcomes as well.[3]

President Eric Walker (1956–1970) probably best described how the Board of Trustees Executive Committee and its president controlled the university in the 1960s, but he was careful to do so only after he retired. Board President Cappy Rowland, stated Walker, "was not democratic in any sense of the word." According to Walker, "things were decided not by the board of trustees but by the executive committee," often by only a few on the executive committee. Venting his spleen, Walker described the Executive Committee meetings: "The smoke-filled room of whiskey and beer, loud mouthed ignoramuses dispensing their ignorance on topics far beyond their ken." This, Walker wrote, led to "the unhappiness of the rest of the board at being steamrollered and denied the proper part in the trusteeship." Could Walker's background have influenced his terse description of the trustees and especially that of Cappy Rowland? To Walker, Rowland was a beer-drinking steamroller who "never read a book, never went to the theater, and never listened to music."[4] That Walker was born in England and received three degrees at Harvard in electrical engineering might have influenced how he felt about those he considered inferior and guilty of making unintelligent decisions in an alcohol-laden room.

If President Walker's description came even close to describing the leadership of the Board of Trustees as he was about to retire, it is little wonder that Walker supported a policy change giving the president more power. Yet it only came with turmoil created by the war in Vietnam and the civil-rights movement during the 1960s and into the early years of the 1970s.[5] Not only would the important turning point allow the president to administer the policies of the Board of Trustees, but the new president would be able to officially *set policy*. At Penn State, and elsewhere, not only were students vigorously protesting the Vietnam War, but also the civil-rights movement found African Americans making strong demands upon President Walker for greater black student, faculty, and administrative representation on campus. A greater racial balance was demanded. After several student protests and occupation of the administration building, Old Main, in spring 1970, the trustees met in a special emergency session specifically to deal with a "grave concern and even outrage" over the main campus student uprising.[6]

The pivotal event in administrative control occurred one month before John Oswald came from the University of California–Berkeley to head Penn State. Berkeley was a major scene of anti–Vietnam War rioting, on a much greater scale than at conservative Penn State. Nevertheless, members of the Penn State Board of Trustees, who felt the university was losing control to rebellious students and liberal faculty, decided to take more drastic action to curb unrest at Penn State and help President Walker, who felt he was under siege from student activists. Only the month before the Penn State Trustees met to change policy, the killing of four Kent State University students by the Ohio National Guard took place. This tragic event occurred only days after President Richard Nixon expanded the Vietnam War into Cambodia and triggered an increase in turmoil in a nation seemingly at war with itself. By this time, students at Penn State had already carried out protests such as taking over Walker's administration building, marching on the Ordinance Research Laboratory (a military research unit Walker had brought to Penn State decades before from Harvard University), and throwing rocks through the windows of the president's house, located in the middle of campus. When the Board of Trustees met in June 1970, they agreed to grant the president power to deal with the turmoil.

At that important meeting, which later had ramifications for athletic policy and Joe Paterno's place in it, the trustees voted to make the president "only be responsible to the Board of Trustees." The president would, however, have additional power to "establish policy," not just to administer policy. The trustees meant that the president could institute policy "concerning educational policy and planning, student affairs, admissions, graduation requirements, scholarships and honors, calendar requirements, business, planning, research and finance."[7] In other words, the president was boss of the university in both setting policy and administering it. The president was given nearly dictatorial powers, except that the Board of Trustees could fire him. No president was fired until the Sandusky Scandal, if Spanier's forced resignation could be called a firing.

The Board of Trustees also decided to create the University Council, which would, in many ways, bypass the University Faculty Senate that had been accustomed to legislating academic policy in the past. The University Council would, according to the Board of Trustees' mandate, "establish policy," but "under presidential revision and orders."[8] Faculty in the future could communicate with the trustees only through the president. Almost as soon as President Oswald came on campus, he spoke to the Faculty Senate about the new Board of Trustees policy. He opened by saying, "Don't think the turmoil reported [at Berkeley] drove me out to the valley in Pennsylvania which I erroneously assumed to be serene, tranquil and without problems." He told the senators that even though his new University Council would advise him and "shall establish policy," that it would "not replace the Faculty Senate."[9]

Soon, leaders of the faculty came to distrust the excessive power of the Penn State presidency. President Oswald on occasion reminded the faculty, as one faculty leader, Roy Buck, stated: Oswald "alone is accountable to the Board of Trustees." Robert Friedman, a well-known political scientist, was distrustful that "all activities seemed to be funneled through hierarchical channels." Mathematics professor Allan Krall believed "Oswald has so usurped power for himself" that his "arbitrary decisions" are made "to suit his whim of the moment." Friedman, who led a Faculty Senate committee to study university governance, made a perceptive comment that might have been said about future troubles at Penn State. "There is," Friedman wrote, "an excessive expectation that administrative personnel will conform."[10]

Relative to athletics, this usurpation and conformity happened in only a few years when athletics were taken out of an academic unit as President Oswald "usurped power for himself." He then placed athletics under another authority figure, Joe Paterno, and hid the department away in a business unit, with no discussion among others affected throughout the university. The major exception was Full Professor Joe Paterno. Much later, the same expectation to conform was eventually revealed when a small group of four administrators decided to keep the questionable child endangerment activities of Jerry Sandusky from the larger community to the absolute detriment of the university. Excessive presidential power and not having to report important matters to the Board of Trustees came to haunt several presidents other than Oswald.

The question could be raised how much information the Board of Trustees should be given relative to intercollegiate athletics, by far the largest and most important student activity dating back to the nineteenth century. For instance, just before John Oswald's presidency the Board of Trustees held a discussion on an important athletic policy. After Joe Paterno's first undefeated season, Penn State looked into formalizing an Eastern Big Four to determine eligibility questions with Pittsburgh, Syracuse, and West Virginia, teams Penn State often competed against in football and some other sports.[11] The trustees discussed the Big Four question, although it is not clear whether they achieved a consensus on a Big Four agreement. Though it was never entirely clear who made athletic policy, at least the trustees were informed. The familiarity of the trustees with the situation was quite different later when Oswald made a decision not to inform the Board of Trustees before removing athletics from an academic unit in 1980.[12]

In a similar athletic situation, the Board of Trustees was at least peripherally involved in the Penn State decision to withdraw from the Eastern College Athletic Conference (ECAC). The ECAC was created in the late 1930s to standardize eligibility rules and assign officials for numerous institution and athletic conferences in the East.[13] By the late 1960s, with nearly 150 institutions and a couple dozen conferences, the ECAC had become a bureaucracy to which Penn State contributed financially far more than any other institution because members were assessed on a percentage of football telecast and bowl revenues, not an equal membership fee.[14] Because the membership fee paid to the ECAC was considered unfair and membership was detracting from the national image Penn State wanted to achieve with the record Joe Paterno was achieving in football, Penn State withdrew from the ECAC in 1975. The policy change began with the athletic department and included discussions with the dean, the president, the trustee liaison to athletics, and the chair of the Board of Trustees.[15] Although many were involved in the decision, the entire Penn State Board of Trustees was only minimally involved in this important decision. One would have to go back no farther, however, than the 1970 Board of Trustees decision to allow the president to both make policy and administer it. That is, the Board of Trustees gave the president the authority to determine educational policy, student affairs, and business, among other activities; athletics was a part of all those activities.[16]

Though President Oswald informed the Board of Trustees about changes in policy toward athletics in the early years of his presidency, he covertly accomplished one dynamic change in policy at the end of 1979. That was Oswald's decision to move athletics into a prototypical business model from the educational one of the previous half-century. In doing so, the hypocrisy of President Oswald was apparent. Earlier in the year, Oswald reminded the Board of Trustees about the educational control of athletics at Penn State. "We are proud of the way in which this program is organized as part of one of the academic colleges," Oswald stressed, "and not a program that is set aside as a separate part of the university."[17] Only months later, after pressure from the iconic Joe Paterno, who arguably had more power than the president, Oswald took a diametrically opposite view to accede to the new athletic director's demands.[18] Without informing any of the trustees or discussing the change with them, as he had a few years before with the ECAC withdrawal, Oswald removed athletics from an academic college and academic dean, an important policy in place since 1930.

Athletics were to be administered under a business office in which a former football captain, Steve Garban, would be the principal liaison with new athletic director, Joe Paterno. Evidently no one from the Board of Trustees questioned the move after the fact even though it changed a half-century policy of the Board of Trustees and removed athletics from academic control. The trustees, unfortunately for Penn State's future, remained silent on this important issue, but did discuss a minor one. One could clearly see the irony of the trustees feeling the need to approve the establishment of an obscure community advisory board to its WPSX-TV station before President Oswald could act—this done in the same year that the president drastically changed athletic policy without Board of Trustees approval.[19] It was easy to question both the trustees' and President Oswald's priorities and how each decision might influence the future of Penn State. Nevertheless, there will likely always be questions about what actions the president may take acting alone, what the president needs to discuss with the trustees, and what issues the trustees alone can act upon.

At the end of the 1980s, another extremely important Penn State and athletic question arose. This time Oswald's successor, Bryce Jordan, was the center of the action, and he decided to act alone rather than inform the Board of Trustees. Again, like the withdrawal from the ECAC under Oswald, it dealt with a question of conference affiliation. The secretive Bryce Jordan was probably correct when he felt that discussing the matter with the Board of Trustees would be harmful, as the negotiations would likely become public if one of the thirty-two trustees was opposed to the move. Then, again, Jordan likely knew that none of the Big Ten presidents was informing their boards of trustees, or faculty, or athletic directors until after their first unanimous vote was taken to bring Penn State into the Big Ten.

Only Trustee Joel Myers, founder of AccuWeather, is known to have protested the secretive negotiations, favoring instead "discussion and debate." Myers believed the Board Trustees should not just be "advised" but should at the least be "consulted" on major policy actions taken by the president.[20] Two decades later, Myers finally got his wish to have the Board of Trustees take the reins of Penn State, but only after a scandal occurred.[21] Unlike the Big Ten decision in which there was no trustee discussion, Myers and the rest of the board voted unanimously, and in many people's eyes unjustly, to fire Joe Paterno as coach and on the same day the trustees removed the president, Graham Spanier, who had kept information from the board. Myers and a few other trustees may have rued the day in 1970 that the Board of Trustees gave the president the right to both make policy and execute it, without consulting the Board of Trustees.

Joel Myers was voted out as an alumni-elected trustee in 2014 after a third of a century of service on the board, principally because he was one of the trustees who voted to oust Joe Paterno three years before. It should be noted, however, that Myers tried to reform the Board of Trustees in the early 2000s by providing board members with more detailed information prior to meetings.[22] His attempt made common cause with previous complaints that the Board of Trustees was run, not by the entire board, but rather by the few, as when only members of the Executive Committee made decisions that were rubber-stamped by the other members.[23] In a memorandum exactly seven years before the day Paterno was fired, Myers asked for detailed information far enough before the meetings that all board members could make informed decisions. He called for outside legal counsel for better advice and for making the trustees, not the president, the ultimate authority in university governance. Board leaders turned a deaf ear toward Myers. Myers found out that the three most significant trustee players—President Spanier, president of the Board of Trustees and later University Counsel; Cynthia Baldwin; and Steve Garban—did not want additional scrutiny of Board of Trustees actions. The three powers of the trustees said "NO" to the proposal of Myers and several others.[24] Greater scrutiny was obviously lacking seven years later when the Sandusky Scandal broke, with only scant previous knowledge by any of the trustees or most others associated with Penn State.

How did the 1970 Board of Trustees decision to grant the president the power to make policy as well as administer it contribute four decades later to what became known as the Jerry Sandusky Scandal involving Joe Paterno, President Spanier, Vice President Gary Schultz, and Athletic Director Tim Curley? The four noted Penn State individuals were the most knowledgeable and were in position to handle the information about Sandusky's involvement with children on the campus. Not one of the individuals immediately showed concern for the children involved but were obviously apprehensive about the Penn State Pandora's box being opened to the detriment of the athletic program and the image of the greater Penn State. That there was potential child molestation surely came to their attention after a second noted incident was reported by graduate assistant coach who showed up early on a Saturday morning to tell Coach Paterno of what he saw in the locker room of Paterno's football building.

As to Joe Paterno specifically, he seemed to compartmentalize what he heard from Mike McQueary in the morning and kept it separate from a memorial service in which he participated in the afternoon. Paterno gave a heart-felt eulogy to Bernie Asbell, the principal author of Paterno's autobiography, *Paterno: By the Book,* on the afternoon of February 10, 2001. No one would have fathomed that only hours before, Paterno heard McQueary's revelation of Jerry Sandusky's sexual involvement with a young child.[25] The ability of important individuals to keep events segregated as they go through life was seldom more evident. Paterno was not alone. Even years later after a Pennsylvania grand jury questioned each of the four individuals, President Spanier kept most of the information about the grand jury from the Board of Trustees.

For sixteen years, the Board of Trustees had a good deal of faith in the leadership of Graham Spanier, with stellar annual reviews from surveys of board members and four contract renewals with hefty salary increases.[26] Spanier had led the way in a number of activities, such as creating a law school on the Penn State campus when the Dickinson School of Law merged with Penn State in 2000, and a proliferation of new buildings was added to the main campus. With the third-longest tenure as Penn State president (George Atherton, 1882–1906 was longer, as was Ralph Dorn Hetzel, 1927–1947), Spanier felt secure in reporting to the Board of Trustees almost entirely good news, while controversial or negative material was generally withheld. Spanier may have discussed problems with the several leaders of the trustees, but not with the full board.[27] One can almost count on one's fingers the number of negative situations discussed with the full Board of Trustees. The conformity to Spanier's policy setting by the trustees is striking.

It is remarkable that in May 2011, a half-year before the Pennsylvania attorney general released the Sandusky grand jury findings, no one from the Board of Trustees intensely questioned President Spanier about the release of "secret" grand jury information printed in the *Harrisburg Patriot-News* of March 31, 2011. The state capital's newspaper headlined "Sandusky Faces Grand Jury Probe." In the article, Sara Ganim, who would later win a Pulitzer Prize for her investigating, reported that a fifteen-year-old Central Mountain High School boy from nearby Clinton County said that he was molested by Sandusky a number of times over a four-year period. She also noted an earlier 1998 incident in the Penn State football locker room when Sandusky was showering with a young boy. Ganim even included the account of a Penn State police officer, Ron Schreffler, who hid in the youth's home to record the boy's mother talking with Sandusky about the incident. [28] All this was available to board members, but actions were heard at the level of pianissimo or pianississimo.

Evidently only one of the thirty-two trustees reacted to the article, but others must have known about it. No one drilled President Spanier at the next board meeting, though one trustee raised a question before the meeting. One day after the Ganim exposé, a trustee e-mailed Spanier thus: "What is the story on allegations against Jerry Sandusky that required testimony by Joe Paterno and Tim Curley, and I heard also [Gary] Schultz. Is this something the board should know [about,] be briefed on or what?" Getting no satisfactory answer from Spanier, two weeks later he again e-mailed the president. "I frankly think that, despite grand jury secrecy, when high ranking people at the university are appearing before a grand jury," the trustee emphasized, "the university should communicate something about this to its Board of Trustees." Upon which Spanier reported to University Counsel Cynthia Baldwin that one trustee member "desires near total transparency," something Spanier was strongly opposed to in his entire sixteen-year career of running the university.[29]

At the May 2011 Board of Trustees meeting, Spanier responded with obfuscating comments about the grand jury proceedings. (One should note the irony in the fact that, at the May meeting in which Spanier was mum about the Sandusky grand jury investigation, the president announced the naming of a football "Linebacker Coach's office" in Lasch Building with a $75,000 gift, while the greatest ex-linebacker coach, Jerry Sandusky, was under intense investigation.)[30] It is somewhat hard to believe even in the rubber-stamp group of trustees, no one, not even one of the seven lawyers on the Board of Trustees, was willing to do what lawyers do by questioning Spanier. Nor did anyone bring up the grand jury probe at the July or September 2011 Board of Trustees meetings.[31] Members of the Board of Trustees continued to do what Spanier had hoped they would do—nothing. After all, the 1970 Board of Trustees mandate that "the internal governance of the University shall be performed by the President" remained the law. And the board for decades followed the 1970 Standing Order IX, which directed trustees to "maintain confidentiality without exception" and required trustees to "advocate the University's interests, but shall speak for the Board only when authorized to do so by the Board or the Chair."[32]

Keeping quiet was demanded of board members, even if there was the possibility that trouble brewing was such that it might place Penn State in a perilous position. With board members enjoined to keep silence outside Board of Trustees meetings, with the faculty and staff as well as students being denied any access to the board except through the president, no independent sources of information were getting to the board except information given by the president.[33] It was a closed and insular institution not dissimilar to the closed and insular athletic department after it was taken out of an academic unit and placed in an isolated business office run first by a former football player and then his successor.

Once the grand jury report was made public, the Board of Trustees panicked. This might be expected of a group kept out of the information loop with respect to any negative Penn State activities. As the Board of Trustees had no general crisis plan of action, which any large organization should have, and a questionable crisis leader in Steve Garban as president of the Board of Trustees, it was not surprising that chaos resulted after the grand jury report. Garban, for instance, did not even read the grand jury report for several days after it was available in early November 2011.[34] It is no wonder that he did not take a leadership role for the next few days before the meeting that would exit both Joe Paterno and President Spanier from their principal roles at the university. When the tense Board of Trustees met on November 9, Garban, the football captain when Paterno was an assistant coach, a friend of Paterno, and an occasional drinking buddy of the coach, abandoned his leadership post, giving it to the Board of Trustees' second in command, John Surma. The next Board of Trustees president, Karen Peetz, remarked, "Part of being a leader at that level is to be a risk manager and think what might happen."[35] Garban did not. He and the board had no crisis plan in hand.

John Surma, a one-time club hockey player at Penn State, was taking over for the individual on the board, Garban, who arguably knew the most about Joe Paterno, who was involved in unsuccessfully persuading Paterno to retire from coaching in 2004, who understood athletics, and who was a prime mover to create the insular nature of the athletic program in 1980. Garban also was directly involved with all the individuals charged with covering up Sandusky's actions and Sandusky's involvement in the operation of The Second Mile, from which came all the victimized children. It is no wonder that Garban did not want to be directly involved in asking for a vote to fire Paterno. Instead he willingly gave that responsibility to Surma, the chief executive officer of U.S. Steel.

It is possible that John Surma may have been influenced in wanting to get rid of Paterno by his older brother, Victor Surma Sr., who had played for Paterno during Paterno's first two undefeated seasons toward the end of the 1960s. Surma evidently had a good experience as an undergraduate and with his football participation. But after his son, Victor Jr., decided in 2002 to "walk on" the Penn State football team rather than take a football scholarship at Kent State University, a dramatic change occurred. As an athletic strategy for the younger Surma, the choice to walk on could be considered an unwise move. When he had graduated from Penn State in 2006, Victor Jr. had played in only two games, having left the team during his senior year. Victor Sr. changed his mind about Paterno at about the time his son left the team without playing. Instead of joining a profession such as dentistry like his father, junior decided to become a model, which from a stereotypical standpoint might fit into his sexual orientation. Victor Sr. may have reacted to junior's lifestyle choices, which included drug problems. The father evidently felt that Paterno had destroyed his son's self-esteem and confidence. He began an e-mail diatribe against Paterno, calling the coach "the rat," as a number of players often did. In one reported e-mail that may have influenced Victor Sr.'s brother John as he came on the Board of Trustees as a business and industries representative in 2007, Victor Sr. stated, "The Rat has hurt so many young men; destroyed their self esteem, ruined their confidence." He went on, "I feel it is my obligation to expose his fraud to the national media before he checks out. . . . I hope you understand. I was a 3 year letterman—have no axe to grind."[36] But there was an ax, and it was sharp.

Was John Surma listening to his older brother's berating of Joe Paterno? Did John Surma feel the same way about the treatment of his nephew, Victor Jr., and how Paterno was thought by some to treat many players? Was Paterno treating players, law-breaking or not, differently in the early 2000s than he had in the past? For instance, in Victor Jr.'s years at Penn State, thirty-eight football players were charged with seventy-seven counts of criminal charges such as illegal drinking, assaults, and rapes.[37] Evidently Victor Jr. had been involved in one violation during a team drug test, but it was nothing like the case of Anwar Phillips, who was expelled for a sexual assault on the Penn State campus. Yet Phillips was allowed to participate in an important bowl game against Auburn at the conclusion of Victor Jr.'s freshman year, after which, when questioned, Paterno said, "I played him. It is nobody's business but mine."[38] It is difficult to judge what influence Joe Paterno's policies and the problems of Victor Surma's son had on both Victor and John Surma when John was brought onto the Penn State Board of Trustees the year after Victor Jr. left the football team.

It took John Surma three short years to be elected vice president of the Board of Trustees, and in another year he took over for Steve Garban as spokesman for the exiting of both Joe Paterno and Graham Spanier. It was a difficult situation for Surma and the rest of the board in the early days of November 2011, when operating without a crisis plan with a sudden change of leadership as Steve Garban left his board president post, and operating with a group of thirty-two trustees used to taking orders from President Spanier after Spanier had lost his creditability with the board. The trustees had an opportunity after the first public revelation of Sandusky's grand jury investigation more than a half-year before, when no one on the board took a leadership role, and those who rubber-stamped nearly everything failed to even raise questions about possible child abuse. Though the trustees could be charged previously for following the president blindly, there was in Graham Spanier an aura of confidence, some would call it arrogance, that suggested he, alone, could manage anything dealing with the grand jury investigation.

No member of the athletic administration should have been silent when there were reports of child rape on the Penn State campus in early 2001, and there should have been no silence from the rubber-stamp Board of Trustees almost exactly a decade later when an investigative reporter made headlines about a grand jury investigation of Jerry Sandusky. Unfortunately for Penn State, they did not follow the maxim of the seventeenth-century writer Baltasar Gracián, who wrote, "Do not turn one blunder into two."[39] Yet the Penn State president, athletic administrators, and trustees did just that. The entire Board of Trustees remained silent until the grand jury report was released. By then, it was too late for Penn State to endure unscathed and for Happy Valley to appear anything other than sad. Happy Valley's version of Pandora's box had been opened. Nearly everyone with knowledge failed in some way. Or as a key trustee, Ken Frazier, said, "We failed in our obligation to provide proper oversight."[40] Penn State's trustees wanted to move forward, past the Sandusky Scandal. Like any prisoner, however, Penn State's president and trustees had not learned that it is difficult to "MOVE FORWARD,"[41] as the trustees and new president Rod Erickson kept advocating, with a ball and chain tied around one's leg.

CHAPTER 15

Paterno, Spanier, Schultz, Curley, and the Penn State Pandora's Box

"We thought, because we had power, we had wisdom."
—Stephen Vincent Benét (1935)

"I backed away."
—Joe Paterno (2012)

Pandora's box in Happy Valley was indeed opened and with it a release of the evils of a child sexual predator laid upon the valley and far beyond. The original Pandora's box, the creation of the ancient Greek gods, specifically the supreme god Zeus, contained all the evils of the world. When Pandora turned the afflictions loose because of her curiosity, the happy and contented world was no longer. A multitude of curses was set free—from disease and devastation to hunger and hubris. *Hubris* is the Greek word for extreme pride and self-confidence—an overestimation of one's own competence. Was it extreme confidence within a group of four Penn State athletic administrators? Did they come to think, as Stephen Vincent Benét once wrote, "because we had power, we had wisdom"?[1] Did they feel they could keep the lid on the Happy Valley Pandora's box and protect the image of one of the great educational institutions in which the revelation of child violations was hidden away?

Who were these four individuals who isolated events related to Penn State athletics? Who were Tim Curley, Gary Schultz, Graham Spanier, and Joe Paterno? It may seem curious that Joe Paterno is often made the center of the Jerry Sandusky Scandal when he was never legally charged with obstruction of justice or covering up Sandusky's actions. A major reason is likely that Paterno is a much better story because of his iconic image as a winning coach of a squeaky-clean program with a high graduation rate and a coined phrase, the Grand Experiment; an educational philanthropist; and the most effective money raiser in Penn State's history. Who could say anything like that for Athletic Director Tim Curley, Business Vice President Gary Schultz, or the more visible President Graham Spanier? Although those three totaled a century of service to Penn State in administrative capacities, Joe Paterno alone served the university for sixty-one years, for nearly a half-century administering a football program and for a short two years, but extremely important ones, as athletic director.

Take Tim Curley, for instance. He was born and raised in State College across from Penn State's football field, called New Beaver Field, on the campus where his father was an administrator. He went to the local high school and attended the university, earning two degrees, one in physical education and another in counselor education. He was on the football team for four years but never played one minute.[2] He bled blue and white. As soon as he could, he joined the Athletic Department staff and rose to responsible positions, often doing the bidding of coach Paterno. Athletic Director Jim Tarman made him the coordinator of the effort to negotiate entrance into the Big Ten in 1990.[3]

When Tarman retired in 1993, Curley, not one of the other athletic administrators, Herb Schmidt, was the insider chosen along with the backing of Paterno, when an outsider, a woman, was strongly considered for the position. Curley was fortunate to have Paterno's support, but it may have cost him in the long run being so closely tied to the individual with power in athletics and in the entire university. A small but poignant example in the Curley–Paterno relationship comes to mind relative to the indoor football arena, Holuba Hall, constructed in 1986 as Penn State moved toward its second national championship. When Tim Curley became athletic director, he e-mailed a rule to all members of the athletic department because a new artificial carpet had just been installed. No foreign material, water bottles, chalk, cleats, could be brought into the facility. A few days later, Paterno held the football banquet in the facility, resulting in all kinds of materials ending up on the carpet. A friend of Curley's from middle school days jokingly e-mailed Curley, "Who's going to tell Joe to stop using the facility?" Curley e-mailed back, "Ha!"[4] Joe told the administrator over him, Curley, what to do, not the opposite, for Paterno was almost without exception the boss at Penn State.

Nevertheless, Curley's running of the athletic program for eighteen years was considered so clean that Mark Emmert, the National Collegiate Athletic Association (NCAA) president who tried to destroy Penn State's football program after the Sandusky Scandal and Freeh report, stated previously that Penn State's program sets the national standard for propriety. Behind the scenes, Curley could do little of importance that did not get the approval of Paterno.[5] He could not effectively deal with wayward athletes and with the Vice President for Student Affairs, Vicky Triponey, who dealt with such matters, because Paterno had the real power and bullied her out of the university. Triponey soon learned that Curley was, as she told Curley, "caught in the middle of a very difficult situation."[6] Later Triponey said that President Spanier told her that Paterno would no longer raise money for the university unless she was gone.[7] Curley could not work for an amicable solution to an athlete's punishment when he felt forced to take Paterno's position on the issue.

The likeable Tim Curley, to his high credit, worked very hard to make Penn State strong in all areas of athletics, both men's and women's. One of his goals, though never reached, was to bring the National Association of Collegiate Directors of Athletics Learfield Directors' Cup (formerly Sear's Cup) to the university by having the best NCAA winning record in a variety of sports. Yet being regularly in the Top Ten institutions in all sports, always behind the perennial winner, Stanford, was a credit to the Curley administration.

Less visible, but in a far more powerful position, was Gary Schultz, vice president for business and finance. He was Curley's boss, though it was Paterno's bidding that Curley did. Being an understudy for years to Steve Garban in running the business of Penn State, including athletics, Schultz took over after Garban retired in 1993. More than a decade before the Sandusky Scandal broke, Schultz kept a separate file on Sandusky at about the same time that he wondered in writing whether Sandusky's activity was the Pandora's box of Penn State.[8] Though Gary Schultz was considered a very successful administrator of the $4 billion yearly budget and an endowment of more than $1½ billion, he was in position to curtail activities of Second Mile children who were abused on campus. Gary Schultz apparently took no effective action for more than a decade to deal with potential problems of Sandusky and Second Mile children held in Penn State's Pandora's box.[9] It seems strange that Schultz's business deal to sell more than forty acres of Penn State land to Jerry Sandusky's Second Mile foundation went through well after the "Is this opening of pandora's box?" statement by Schultz in 1998.[10] This may have been just as injudicious as Pennsylvania attorney general Tom Corbett's slow investigation of Sandusky, by only one investigator, before Corbett's successful election as governor. Strangely, Governor Corbett agreed to the state giving $3 million to building a Second Mile facility, Center for Excellence, on the Penn State land when he knew Sandusky was being investigated by Corbett's own Attorney General's office. Gary Schultz silently worked with both The Second Mile and Tom Corbett.

Much more visible than either Tim Curley or Gary Schultz was President Graham Spanier. The Penn State president for sixteen years after his 1995 appointment, Spanier had spent the first decade of his career after achieving his Ph.D. at Northwestern University in 1973 as a professor at Penn State. He was in administrative positions at three institutions, including chancellor at the University of Nebraska, before returning to head Penn State. Former president Bryce Jordan even suggested Spanier as a possible Penn State presidential candidate shortly before Spanier was offered the position. Jordan, a consultant for the presidential search, called Spanier "active, alert, aggressive, people-oriented. A real 'comer' in the field of large-university administration."[11] Spanier's statement, while administrating the University of Nebraska campus, might be challenged later at Penn State. At Nebraska, Spanier told his governing board that in athletics there would be "no turning a deaf ear to improprieties in intercollegiate athletics."[12]

Spanier was a person who seemingly enjoyed administration and gained as much visibility as he could muster for both Penn State and himself. That is exactly what many successful presidents have done in the past. Whether it was staying in a dorm during the week new freshmen arrived on the University Park campus, playing washboard in a Dixieland band, wearing the Nittany Lion outfit and prancing around at events, or walking the football field with Joe Paterno with one hundred thousand or more spectators in attendance, Spanier was probably the most visible president in Penn State's history. Playing magic tricks before an assembled group of alumni and asking talented students in the fine Musical Theatre program to perform were part of his presidential gig. So too was his visible radio program, *To the Best of My Knowledge.* Most anything that would promote Penn State and a picture of his involvement was fair game. He would even create a television talk show inviting as his guests knowledgeable people to discuss programs that he felt Pennsylvania viewers would enjoy. He helped make Penn State more visible in the media than those who came before, and he was the force behind creating an information technology building that spans the busiest road running through State College and the university.

Sometimes his desire to get out front was hurried and harmful to the university. At times his actions were done in a rush or without gaining approval of his Board of Trustees.[13] An example of his poor judgment was his attempt to merge two divergent cultures into one. A disastrous case was the merging of the noted Geisinger Medical Center, a premier Pennsylvania medical health organization, with the Penn State Hershey Medical Corporation. This multimillion-dollar, two-year blunder beginning in 1997 did not work from the start. As researcher William Mallon has written, the merger was "like alchemists of old, they did not succeed in their attempt to slam two forms into one." The extreme hundred-million-dollar cost to separate the two unworkable units was a blot on his record.[14] In another mistake, before the Sandusky Scandal broke, he did not inform his Board of Trustees in the kind of depth needed so that the trustees could act responsibly. As Spanier told several members of the Board of Trustees a half-year before the scandal broke, "We deal with crisis every day at this university. We won't have a problem with this."[15] Shortly after the grand jury presentment was released, Spanier gave his unconditional support for both Tim Curley and Gary Schultz, and he changed press releases about the Sandusky revelations without board approval. His presidency was doomed.[16]

Yet it is Joe Paterno's involvement in the Sandusky Scandal, not that of Curley, Schultz, or Spanier, in which most people appear to be interested. Tim Curley, Gary Schultz, and Graham Spanier were not iconic representations of Penn State—Paterno was. So if his name was associated with the scandal in any way, it was almost a given that the Paterno story would override all others. The fact that the Paterno family and a number of insiders stated that Paterno and Jerry Sandusky never got along, an erroneous notion, added to the story. In addition, the known point that Sandusky resigned less than a year after the first noted Sandusky violation of a young boy in 1998 contributed to the speculation that Paterno got rid of his assistant coach because of Paterno's knowledge of the child molestation.

Sandusky's retirement needs further explanation. Nearly all those with inside knowledge agree that Sandusky's illegal actions with young boys were not related to his resignation. The Paterno family, after Paterno's death, wrote that the 1999 retirement of Sandusky was unrelated to the Sandusky child incidents.[17] Sandusky, in his autobiography *Touched*, agreed. Even though the Paterno family wrongfully has stated that "the two men despised each other from the start," the Paterno family was correct that Paterno's knowledge of the first revealed Sandusky act with a young boy in 1998 was not the reason Sandusky left his position at Penn State the next year.[18] Sandusky left because Joe Paterno told him that he would not become the next Penn State coach if he continued to be actively involved in The Second Mile, for a successful head coaching position would take far more time than Sandusky would devote solely to it.

Joe Paterno kept notes of his discussion with Jerry Sandusky on the possibility of Sandusky becoming head coach once Paterno retired. In early 1998, several months before the first allegations against Jerry Sandusky, Paterno sat down with Sandusky and told him why he would not follow Paterno as the next head coach. Although Paterno had given Sandusky great praise for the head coaching position at Temple a decade before, he had come to believe that Sandusky's considerable involvement with The Second Mile would be a hindrance to any head coaching position, especially the Penn State one, once Paterno decided to retire. "You wanted the best of two worlds," Paterno noted, "and I probably should have sat down with you six or seven years ago and said look Jerry if you want to be the Head Coach at Penn State, give up your association with the 2nd Mile and concentrate on nothing but your family and Penn State." He warned Sandusky, "Don't worry about the 2nd Mile, you don't have the luxury of doing both." If you were not "too deeply involved in both," he told Sandusky, "you probably could be the next Penn State FB coach."[19]

Paterno's belief that he would pick the next football coach went against Penn State tradition, for the athletic director, with the consent of the president, picked Paterno, and before him the Board of Athletic Control selected Rip Engle in 1950. Before Engle, the Board of Athletic Control chose Joe Bedenk, not Coach Bob Higgins, who advocated for Earle Edwards to succeed him. Bob Higgins, himself, was chosen by Board of Athletic Control in 1930, not by the previous coach, Hugo Bezdek. During World War I, the Graduate Advisory Committee chose Hugo Bezdek with the concurrence of the Board of Trustees.[20] Obviously, Sandusky believed Paterno had the power to select the next coach. If Paterno as coach had chosen his successor, he would have been the first coach in the century to do so. That both Sandusky and Athletic Director Tim Curley believed Paterno could pick his successor indicates that Paterno wielded great power and that his administrative superior Curley, as athletic director, did not. After the Sandusky Scandal broke, one trustee said of Paterno, "it's not his decision."[21] And it was not.

Because Joe Paterno was the central figure in the Penn State Pandora's box, it could be informative to consider how Paterno figured into the question of Jerry Sandusky and his involvement as a pedophile. As an individual into his eighth decade of life when the first Sandusky sexual encounter was known, a lifelong Roman Catholic with its well-publicized corruption through priestly homosexuality, and an informed reader of ancient Greek and Roman literature and its culture of homosexuality, is it realistic to believe that Joe Paterno did not know about homosexuality of a man and a boy or "rape and a man"? Evidence would indicate no. More than likely Paterno understood well this possibility. On the one hand, it is rather easy to believe that Paterno did not have a clue before 1998 that Sandusky was a pedophile. Hundreds of people who knew Sandusky through the years did not know, including coaches, players, administrators, ministers, and confidants. A detective, a police officer, a case worker and outside counselor for the Centre County Children and Youth Services, a psychologist who headed The Second Mile, a case worker for the Department of Public Welfare, and a district attorney were misled in rejecting the charges brought against Sandusky. Yet after the 1998 event and after learning in 2001 that Sandusky had been seen doing something sexual with a young boy in the Paterno-controlled locker room, being naïve about the possibility of "rape and a man" seems remote.

Paterno's background denies the naïve possibility. Having been in the all-male army in Korea at the end of World War II and returning to all-male Brown University to study literature, especially Greek literature, pretty much eliminates being naïve about human sexuality. Anyone who has read ancient Greek literature or seen ancient Greek art knows that homosexuality, man and boy, was rampant more than two thousand years ago. Even in Paterno's favorite book, *Aeneid,* that he said he translated from the original Latin with his high school teacher, two of Aeneas's soldiers, Nisus and Euryalus, were, by a common interpretation, most likely in a homosexual relationship:

> Nisus guarded a gate—a man-at-arms
>   With a fighting heart. . . .
> Euryalus was his comrade, handsomer
>   Than any other soldier of Aeneas. . . .
> One love united them.[22]

While at Brown University, if Paterno had traveled during his college years the fifty miles from Providence to Boston to visit the Museum of Fine Arts, he would have seen plenty of illustrations of pederasty in the abundant ancient Greek and Roman pottery. At the museum is one piece that in the twentieth century would be considered pedophilia—a man around 520 BCE is seen stimulating a boy's sexual organs.[23]

His literary interests after college continued in Happy Valley when, in the early 1960s, he met Suzanne Pohland, a freshman liberal arts major, who was dating an academically challenged football player. As assistant coach Paterno was trying to keep the player eligible; he talked with Pohland and found that they had a common interest in literature. As Paterno reveals in his autobiography, he and Suzanne later attended a lecture by Leslie Fiedler, a popular and controversial psychoanalytic literary critic who had just published *Love and Death in the American Novel*. In his lecture, Fiedler discussed whether Huckleberry Finn had a homosexual relationship with "Nigger" Jim. Fiedler believed there was homoerotic male bonding as part of males escaping from a domestic, female-dominated society. After the lecture, rather than discussing football, the two talked about the possibility of the homosexual association.[24] Yet in his last interview before his death, Paterno suggested that he was naïve about male–male sexual relationships. He told Sally Jenkins, after Mike McQueary's revelation that Sandusky was sexually involved with a boy in a shower, "I never heard of, of, rape and a man."[25]

In the intervening years between Paterno and Pohland discussing homosexuality and the 2001 account by Mike McQueary of the sexual incident in the football locker room, Paterno was indeed quite aware of homosexuality and man–boy relationships. That is true, if from nothing else than the nearly constant reports of priest–boy pedophilia in his Roman Catholic Church. He also could easily have picked up a copy of the recently published book by Penn State professor of history and religion Philip Jenkins, *Pedophiles and Priests: Anatomy of a Contemporary Crisis*.[26] Nevertheless, Paterno was much more familiar with the rapes and rape accusations from women against his football players on the Penn State campus than of his assistant coach and young boys.

Joe Paterno and the other Penn State athletic administrators must have been totally surprised when they were informed of the accusation against Jerry Sandusky in early May 1998. The inkling of a scandal began the day a mother of an eleven-year-old boy asked psychologist Alycia Chambers whether the mother was overreacting to Sandusky showering with her child in Paterno's locker room and after a Penn State detective, Ron Schreffler, interviewed the boy later that day. Vice President Gary Schultz, in charge of overseeing the police, soon learned of the investigation. Schultz jotted down a note: "Behavior—at best inappropriate @ worst sexual improprieties." The following day he wrote the most memorable "Is this opening of pandora's box? Other children?"[27] By then Athletic Director Tim Curley, President Graham Spanier, and Coach Joe Paterno also were informed of an investigation of one of the best-known assistant football coaches in America. In an e-mail with the subject line "Joe Paterno" to Schultz and President Spanier, Curley wrote, "I have touched base with the coach," meaning, almost assuredly, Paterno.[28]

The day Paterno was informed of the Sandusky allegations, he traveled to Nashville, Tennessee, to meet about a commercial venture with Burger King officials.[29] He was in and out of State College in the next few days to such places as Boston,

Atlanta, and Farmington, Pennsylvania. Yet the Sandusky allegations were not forgotten, as Tim Curley e-mailed both Gary Schultz and President Spanier that "coach wanted to know where Sandusky stands."[30] About a week later, Curley asked Schultz whether there was "anything new in this department. Coach is anxious to know where it stands." In another two weeks, after District Attorney Ray Gricar concluded that evidence indicated there was no criminal action by Sandusky, the investigation was closed. When Schultz was so informed, he wrote the athletic director and president, "I hope it is now behind us."[31] For more than a month beginning in May 1998, the Sandusky allegations were high on the list of concerns for Curley, Schultz, Spanier, and Paterno. It is not likely that the shower incident involving renowned assistant coach Sandusky would soon be forgotten. Nevertheless, the positive outcome for Sandusky might suggest to the quartet of administrative officials that Jerry Sandusky's involvement with children could be quietly disregarded.

Jerry Sandusky, however, did not put out of his mind Paterno's no-head-coaching edict handed to him earlier in the year. Sandusky said of his career position that he was "not pleased about the entire situation."[32] Sandusky eventually decided to take an early retirement but not before negotiating a retirement package early the next year, that few, if any, other assistant professors would ever be able to achieve. After Tim Curley asked Sandusky whether he was interested in an assistant athletic director's position (which he was not) and inquiring whether either Vice President Schultz or President Spanier was in need of an administrative assistant, a retirement package was agreed upon, highly favorable to the iconic assistant coach. First, he was given an unusual $168,000 lump sum, four free-choice football tickets for life, and two men's and women's basketball tickets for life. He was provided an office and phone for a decade and a locker and training room facilities for life. The university agreed to a five-year collaboration between the university and Sandusky in support of The Second Mile organization.[33]

President Spanier then agreed to give Sandusky an assistant professor emeritus of physical education/assistant coach status, something that had never before been provided, a provision the new Provost Rod Erickson was reluctant to offer but nevertheless agreed to. Then the administrators remembered that the emeritus status should be requested first by Barbara Shannon, the dean of Paterno and Sandusky's College of Health and Human Development, where Paterno was full professor. Could anyone believe that a less than powerful dean would question action already taken by the president and the provost? Not likely, and she dutifully agreed to originate the emeritus status, ex post facto, for her retiring assistant professor.[34] One could certainly criticize a popular administrator such as Rod Erickson, who very early in his positions as provost and thirteen years later early in his presidency, for acquiescing in two significant decisions, one giving emeritus rank to Sandusky and later signing a most damaging NCAA consent decree. The consent decree, offered by President Emmert of the NCAA, was prohibited by the NCAA's own due-process rules.

Though retired by summer 1999, Sandusky was hired back by Joe Paterno to coach the 1999 football season with the proviso agreed to by Paterno that Sandusky had "the option to continue to coach as long as [Paterno] was the coach."[35] Sandusky decided that 1999 would be his last season coaching at Penn State, and at the end of the season, he was feted and named the Assistant Coach of the Year by the American Football Coaches Association. In addition, he was honored by receiving the Alumni Award from the State College Quarterback Club at a retirement party at the Bryce Jordan Center before a thousand or so attendees. To conclude the regular season, Penn State played in the Alamo Bowl against Texas A & M, and Sandusky's defense shut out the Aggies 24–0, whereupon Sandusky was carried off the field by his players. Little noticed was Sandusky inviting one of The Second Mile youths to the Alamo Bowl. The first individual, victim number 4, to testify against Sandusky at the 2012 trial, stayed with Sandusky in a San Antonio hotel room.[36] This action, a violation of the 1910 Mann Act prohibiting sexual exploitation across a state border, was never pursued in the Sandusky case.

Just over a year later, Sandusky was reported to be seen by a graduate assistant coach, Mike McQueary, in a sexual encounter with a young boy showering in the Penn State football building. This time, Joe Paterno was notified within hours of the encounter after McQueary discussed it with his father and a medical doctor. McQueary told Paterno, according to Paterno's grand jury testimony under oath, "it was [of] a sexual nature."[37] In the fairly well known story, Paterno soon notified athletic director Tim Curley, who discussed it with Gary Schultz and Graham Spanier. Well aware of the 1998 incident, the administrators, specifically Gary Schultz, contacted Penn State legal counsel, Wendell Courtney, who billed Penn State with nearly three hours of time for consultation and research related to Sandusky. Vice President Schultz asked his chief of police, Tom Harmon, for the 1998 Sandusky report, which he evidently failed to ask for in 1998.[38]

Then the three administrators, with the knowledge of Joe Paterno, discussed the original action plan that included reporting the incident to the state Department of Welfare, informing The Second Mile, and telling Jerry Sandusky to bring no children to the Lasch football building. After discussing the action plan with Joe Paterno, however, Curley suggested a different course, to not inform the Department of Welfare if Sandusky cooperated with the administrators. Wrote Curley in an e-mail to Schultz and Spanier:

> After giving it more thought and talking it over with Joe yesterday—I am uncomfortable with what we agreed were the next steps. I am having trouble with going to everyone, but the person involved. . . . If [Sandusky] is cooperative we would work with him to handle informing the organization [The Second Mile]. If not, we do not have a choice and will inform the two groups [The Second Mile and Department of Public Welfare]. . . . What do you think of this approach?[39]

President Spanier responded affirmatively but, in an important side note, warned that Penn State is "vulnerable for not having reported it" to the Department of

Public Welfare. He told Curley, "the approach you outline is humane and a reasonable way to proceed."[40] Schultz agreed with Curley and Spanier. At this point and later, there is no indication that Paterno, Curley, Schultz, or Spanier had ever attempted to contact the boy involved or had a concern for possible future exploitation of the child. Joe Paterno later admitted, "I backed away."[41] The administrators were, though, according to Graham Spanier, attempting to protect the image of the football program and Penn State, for as he later explained, "I was concerned with what people will think, the visibility and the public relations aspect of it. I was not concerned with criminality."[42]

That President Spanier never mentioned the Sandusky-boy-McQueary incident to the Board of Trustees at its March 15–16, 2001, meeting was not unusual. Seldom did the president reveal bad news about anything, including putting Penn State at risk, at a full meeting of the Board of Trustees. More questionable was the decision by Spanier and Schultz to sell a piece of university property to Sandusky's Second Mile only months after the reported sexual assault by Sandusky on a juvenile from The Second Mile. Why, if Penn State administrators had decided to keep Second Mile children from showering with Sandusky, would they recommend to the Board of Trustees that university land could be sold to Sandusky's organization? While recommending not to inform the Department of Public Welfare of the 2001 Sandusky incident to protect the image of the university, President Spanier and Vice President Schultz were nevertheless willing to aid Sandusky in pursuing his plans for The Second Mile. While agreeing to the land sale, the president even praised Sandusky for his Second Mile work.[43]

When the two Sandusky incidents are considered together, it is difficult to give Penn State administrators passing grades even if what they were doing would later be considered lawful in the courts. The first 1998 incident was known by all four administrators—Spanier, Schultz, Paterno, and Curley—and the resulting action was a failure principally of law enforcement officials, justice officials, and child-protection authorities who lacked due diligence in pursuit of the case. The second, 2001, incident, however, was primarily a failure of university governance by the chief administrators who apparently gave greater consideration to the image of the university and its football program than to the welfare of children.[44] A writer, Michael Brand, had a similar but slightly different explanation: "While the Sandusky scandal is about the sexual abuse of young boys, the Penn State Scandal is about the collapse of principled leadership."[45]

The continual sins of Sandusky were hidden from university officials until 2008, when a teenager, Aaron Fisher,[46] at Keystone Central High School, thirty miles or so from the main campus of Penn State, accused the volunteer coach, Sandusky, of sexual misconduct that year and going back several years before. The ensuing case, reported to the proper legal authorities, got ratcheted up through the legal system to the state attorney general's office, held by future governor Tom Corbett. It was this case that brought about a grand jury investigation and eventual indictment of Jerry Sandusky and resulted in his conviction on forty-five counts of sexual misconduct and essentially a lifetime prison sentence.

Four Penn State administrators, Curley, Schultz, Spanier, and Paterno, were subpoenaed to testify before the grand jury in 2011, and all but Paterno were accused of lying to the grand jury and covering up the sexual abuses. A major legal problem arose when Penn State's legal counsel, Cynthia Baldwin, a former member of the Pennsylvania Supreme Court, attended the closed grand jury sessions in which three of the four, Spanier, Schultz, and Curley, believed she was representing them. Each told the judge that she was legal counsel, and Baldwin did not correct them. For instance, Curley's testimony began:

> CURLEY: "Good Morning. My name is Tim Curley."
> QUESTION: "You have counsel with you?"
> CURLEY: "Yes, I do."
> QUESTION: "Would you introduce her, please?"
> CURLEY: "My counsel is Cynthia Baldwin."[47]

If she was not representing the three, as she has claimed, then she should not have been allowed in the secret sessions. This could be considered enough cause for a judge to throw out the suits against the three Penn State administrators. In any event, a grand jury presentment by its nature is always a one-sided argument by the government that an illegal action has taken place and is thus subject to trial to prove an offense has been committed. The right of individuals to answer those charges and to appeal is part of due process in the United States.

One could argue that the isolation of athletics within a small inner circle of administrators was a contributing factor to the Sandusky Scandal and to other problems that came to exist over time. Even though the incidents of insularity in athletics at Penn State have been seen, the fact that athletics were separated from academic oversight in the latter years of the twentieth and into the twenty-first century is cause for concern at Penn State as it has been for big-time intercollegiate athletics nationally for much more than a century. The administration of athletics by individuals who lack significant academic credentials, as was the case for most of the administrators at Penn State after 1980, may have had a significant impact on the outcome of the Sandusky Scandal.

Of the four individuals involved in the Sandusky Scandal, only Graham Spanier had noteworthy academic credentials, but Spanier was far more of a promoter than an educator, doing what presidents do—promoting their universities. Like Graham Spanier, the presidents of Penn State were often at the center of events throughout its history, both positive and negative. The insular nature of Penn State, like that of many institutions, would lead to controversial actions if they became widely known. It would lead a president, George Atherton, in the 1890s to allow a failing student on the football team to compete toward the end of an undefeated season when the faculty rules said "no." The insular nature of athletics

would aid an alumnus, Casey Jones, in offering funding of athletes' educations
in the 1930s and 1940s, when the Board of Trustees policy specifically banned
athletic scholarships. The closed nature of Nittany Lion athletics allowed President
John Oswald to officially take athletics out of an academic unit, without Board
of Trustees approval, in 1980, and essentially placed it under a former football
captain, Steve Garban, in the university business office. The isolation of athletics
from the rest of the university allowed Joe Paterno as football coach–athletic
director to gain approval when he asked the president for a third of the incoming
freshman football players to enter the university without academic qualifications,
a group who then went on to help the university win its first national football
championship. The same insular athletic program and university administration
would later permit an expelled football star, Anwar Philips, to participate in a
bowl game because the expulsion date came after the bowl game by a few days.
In a similar vein, the university administration would later allow a basketball
coach, Rene Portland, to carry on a quarter-century of discrimination based on
sexual orientation among her players. Thus, it was not unexpected that athletics and university administration would keep the knowledge of a predatory or
potentially predatory child abuser in the Nittany Valley Pandora's box.

Most athletic administrators did not likely know ancient Greek mythology,
which might inform moderns, though the term Pandora's box was in the vocabu-
lary. Only one of the athletic leaders was likely knowledgeable about the ancient
Greek and Roman literature, an Ivy League–educated graduate in literature and
the winningest coach in big-time football history. As in ancient Greek literature,
Pandora's box had evils to be released; so too did the Happy Valley Pandora's box.
And a major evil was released in the form of a corruption of Happy Valley.

What is less well known is what was not released but contained in the bottom
of the original Pandora's box, and seemingly in the Nittany Lion Pandora's box
as well. It was, as the ancient myth revealed, an important positive virtue. The
remaining virtue left in the ancient Greek Pandora's box and presumably much
later in the one in (un)Happy Valley was—HOPE.

CHAPTER 16

From the Grand Jury to Beyond
the NCAA Consent Decree

"Power lodged as it must be in human hands, will ever be liable to abuse."
—James Madison (1829)

There did not appear to be hope in Happy Valley and beyond after November 4, 2011, when the grand jury presentment was officially released. There were multiple charges against Jerry Sandusky. Two Penn State administrators, Gary Schultz and Tim Curley, were charged with perjury and covering up Sandusky's acts. In addition, President Graham Spanier seemed to be in serious trouble with the law. What developed immediately were anger and panic among members of the Board of Trustees, who were kept nearly clueless by a president whom they had held in high esteem for more than a decade and a half. Penn State Counsel Cynthia Baldwin was little help during the crisis. Furthermore, the football coach, Joe Paterno, who achieved a record for longevity and who had more victories than any big-time football coach, was in deep trouble.

The coach, who was used to having his own way, told the board not to worry about him because he would retire when the season was completed. "Trustees," Paterno stated, "should not spend a single minute discussing my status."[1] Within hours, he was fired. The president, only a few hours before, was compelled to retire (or was fired), in part because he gave unconditional support for both indicted administrators. The president's departure drew much less concern than the firing of Joe Paterno. What drew immediate attention was the summary dismissal of an honored coach with sixty years at the university—and in a telephone call. His firing led to a riot by students and others who considered Joe Paterno, if not godlike, certainly iconic.

Stunned and panicking, the trustees, even before Paterno and Spanier were let go, felt compelled to quickly call for an independent study of the chaotic situation that led to the scandal. It was to be an investigation free of influence by the Board of Trustees or anyone else. A lawyer member of the trustees, Kenneth Frazier, who, along with other members of the board, raised no questions when President Spanier first informed the board of a grand jury investigation a half-year before, was chosen to lead in hiring an independent investigative team.[2] Louis Freeh's law firm was chosen in about two weeks in part because Freeh had great visibility as the former director of the Federal Bureau of Investigation (FBI).

The National Collegiate Athletic Association (NCAA) jumped into the scandal even before the Freeh firm was appointed. The NCAA, founded in 1905, had been the principal governing body of college sport since shortly after World War II. At the time of the scandal, it was led by a former college president at Louisiana State and the University of Washington, Mark Emmert. The NCAA presidential leaders and Emmert were under public condemnation for not being able to lead college athletics effectively. Emmert must have been embarrassed, despite his arrogant manner, for doing little to control violations of the NCAA constitution and bylaws, emphasized by recent major university scandals. These included player remuneration at the University of Miami, players at Ohio State University selling merchandise, payments to athletes at the University of Southern California (USC) and the forfeiting of the Heisman Trophy by USC's Reggie Bush, and attempts by Cam Newton's father, a minister, to receive $100,000 or so to have his son attend Mississippi State University.[3] Furthermore, numerous conference realignments to attract television dollars made it look like the commercial interests of college athletics were the only things that mattered to the universities.

Commercialism may have been the least of Emmert's and the NCAA's concerns, but it added to the fuel that fed the fire threatening the NCAA leadership and all of what was questionable about college athletics and increasingly about higher education in general.[4] Two retired Penn State professors in the early twenty-first century were discussing the increase of commercialism in higher education and at Penn State in the recent past, and not just in the athletic department. One ventured that "commercial ventures aren't necessarily evil, but secrecy is, especially in an academic environment." He said, "perhaps more openness is the answer." He suggested creating "a panel of students, faculty, and alumni that would assess all [commercial] deals before they're made." The other retorted that what was needed was "a board. A board of distrustees!"[5] Exactly. "Distrustees" may have been what was called for in place of the trustees at Penn State before the Sandusky Scandal broke, a group with less secrecy and more openness, one that questioned and did not follow blindly. A move toward less insularity and more clarity was needed by both the president and the Board of Trustees.

For Emmert and the NCAA leadership, however, the Penn State Scandal was a godsend in that they could use a lily-white institution with no previous major NCAA violations as the whipping boy, indicating that the NCAA was in charge and the presidents who ran the NCAA were doing something about the fetid side of college sports. To this end, Mark Emmert and his team of university presidents and legal staff composed a unique letter to Penn State that uncharacteristically threatened the institution. The intimidating NCAA letter, to a new and naïve president, might have led President Rod Erickson to believe that the NCAA would eventually punish Penn State with the banning of football for a year or more, if Penn State was shown to have complete lack of institutional control over athletics.

Less than two weeks after the scandal broke, Emmert's letter to new president Rod Erickson spoke of Penn State individuals "acting starkly contrary to the values of higher education," even though Penn State, while criminally liable under the 1989 federal Clery Act for not reporting sexual offenses, had not broken any specific NCAA rules. Emmert's letter indicated that the NCAA would use information gained from the criminal justice process in its review of the case. Still, it did not say that it would use non–criminal justice investigations, such as the Freeh study, rather than its own inquiry, which was required by the NCAA constitution and bylaws, an inquiry that was never carried out. This was a flagrant disregard of its own constitution and bylaws.[6] Emmert, and the other university presidents who followed him, could have learned from an early U. S. president, James Madison, who warned that "power lodged as it must be in human hands, will ever be liable to abuse."[7] So true—the NCAA abused its power.

For a half year, the Freeh investigators, a phalanx of mostly young lawyers, covered the university, searching computers and filing cabinets and sifting through hundreds of boxes of papers in the university archives. They also conducted more than 400 interviews, often using coercive methods, of individuals who were thought to have some knowledge of the administration of athletics and Sandusky. The investigation lacked subpoena power, used anonymous sources, and did not interview a number of key sources. After a half-year of investigation and collecting facts and opinions, the Freeh report, without questioning many of the most important individuals, issued its report. Many of the individuals closest to the scandal could not be interviewed or refused to be, including Vice President Gary Schultz, Athletic Director Tim Curley, University Counsel Wendell Courtney, Penn State chief of police Thomas Harmon, those in the district attorney's office, psychologists and those who worked with the Sandusky victims, Assistant Coach Mike McQueary, and Coach Joe Paterno—who died during the investigation. Though President Spanier was interviewed, it was only after the report was essentially completed. The Freeh report was handed to the Penn State Board of Trustees, the NCAA, and the public on July 12, 2012, after Penn State spent more than $8 million for the study.[8]

The shock of the Freeh report in July, and especially the showing of Joe Paterno's involvement in the scandal, was nearly as great as the disbelief about Jerry Sandusky in the grand jury presentment of the previous November. The four athletic administrators subpoenaed and questioned by the grand jury—Spanier, Schultz, Curley, and Paterno—were condemned in the report. Paterno, who had died from cancer a few months before, was condemned as much as the other three. "Mr. Paterno," the report noted of the coach, "was on notice for at least 13 years that Sandusky . . . was a probable serial pedophile." It went on to state that

"Mr. Paterno purposefully ignored this evidence."[9] The report read as if a lawyer were wrapping up a criminal trial of Paterno before a jury decided the case. Some would read and believe the report as a condemnation of Paterno for all time as a child-rapist enabler. Others would question the two major incidents, one in 1998 to be judged by child welfare employees, police, and a district attorney to not be creditable. The other in 2001 was more creditable in that Paterno was told of a sexual incident in a locker room—but was hardly a sign to Paterno or many others of a serial pedophile. This was one of several instances in the Freeh report in which questionable conclusions were drawn from the information at hand.

Another Freeh report conclusion was that the culture of football dominated *all* aspects of university, one of the elite public educational institutions in the nation. The report claimed that Penn State was infested with a "culture of reverence for the football program that is *ingrained at all levels* of the campus community." Furthermore, there was a transformation of "culture that permitted Sandusky's behavior" because the "Athletic Department was permitted to become a closed community," was "'an island' where staff members lived by their own rules" and allowed an "over-emphasis on 'The Penn State Way.'"[10] Although there was no question that with crowds of well over one hundred thousand attending football games, an athletic budget of close to $100 million, and an iconic coach at the helm, those affiliated with Penn State paid attention to the football program.

To state, however, that football at Penn State was "ingrained at all levels" was a conclusion that was a stretch of the imagination. One could easily conclude that the Office of Student Affairs was at one time unduly influenced by football and its football coach, but it was hard to say the culture of reverence for football was ingrained in the nationally recognized Department of Meteorology; the Applied Research Laboratory, the largest research component at Penn State since shortly after World War II; or in the notable Musical Theatre program of the School of Theatre that regularly turned out outstanding graduates. But with the prominence of a former FBI director heading the study, what was written in the Freeh report became gospel to many, including the National Collegiate Athletic Association (NCAA), which used the scandal at Penn State, rather than an NCAA investigation, for its own purposes.

Treated almost as severely as the four administrators of athletics and the athletic culture of Penn State was the Board of Trustees, who paid millions for the report. The Freeh report called the Board of Trustees a "rubber stamp" group of thirty-two members. It pointed out the Standing Order of the Trustees that "has a continuing obligation to require information or answers on any question on any university matter which it is concerned." Relative to the Sandusky Scandal and the grand jury investigation, the report said the board failed miserably. Trustees, who appeared to be reticent to ask pointed questions of President Spanier, tried to excuse themselves by indicating that Board of Trustees meetings were "scripted" by the president. One trustee told the Freeh investigators that Spanier showed the board "rainbows" continually but not the "rusty nails." True enough. Nevertheless, the report emphasized that the board failed in its "oversight responsibilities."[11]

The leaders of the NCAA, university presidents all, fully accepted the Freeh report as if they had done their own investigation of the situation. Even Ed Ray, president of the NCAA Executive Committee, questioned why the NCAA did not investigate on its own. "If Penn State could have Louis Freeh conduct an investigation over the last year," Ray, the president of Oregon State University, asked, "why haven't we done anything?"[12] With a costless-to-the-NCAA "investigation," led by the image of a former director of the FBI in Louis Freeh, the NCAA and Mark Emmert could feel free to use the conclusions of the Freeh report to issue numerous sanctions on Penn State and make it appear that the NCAA was finally in control of any future reprobate athletic program. According to one observer, "Emmert and the NCAA, in their zest to make themselves feel relevant, pounced within hours of the Freeh Report's release."[13] The NCAA could even take 111 victories away from Joe Paterno, even though the Sandusky Scandal had almost nothing to do with helping Penn State win any game. This action, hypocritically, was led by Emmert, who not long before the scandal called Joe Paterno "the definitive role model of what it means to be a college coach."[14] The harsher the sanctions, the better, was the conclusion of the NCAA leaders.

One poignant fact, seldom noticed, was that the NCAA removed from its website, by the time the Freeh report was released, a definition of the death penalty. Prior to the Penn State sanctions, one could find in the NCAA's "Glossary of Terms" this definition: "Death Penalty: The 'death penalty' is a phrase used by media to describe the most serious NCAA penalty possible. It is not a formal NCAA term. It applies only to *repeat violators*."[15] Because Penn State had never had a major violation, it was another reason that the NCAA could not by its own rules give Penn State the death penalty. One can only imagine that Mark Emmert ordered the website removal because if it were left in view he and the NCAA could only be embarrassed, or, as actually happened, the NCAA would be part of a lawsuit for violating its own due-process rules. Removing damning matter from the NCAA website added to the incriminatory e-mails subpoenaed a couple years later from the NCAA vice president of enforcement and the NCAA director of enforcement. Both Julie Roe and Kevin Lennon admitted that Penn State was "so embarrassed" that the administrators "will do anything" and the approach to Penn State is "a bluff," and acknowledged that the "NCAA has no jurisdiction over a strictly criminal case."[16]

That the NCAA violated its own rules and regulations was recognized by many knowledgeable individuals in the Penn State case. Tom Yeager, a long-time member of the NCAA Committee on Infractions, immediately called Emmert's letter "unprecedented" and said that the NCAA was, for the first time in its history, taking action outside its own rules.[17] Another well-known NCAA insider, Josephine Potuto, a lawyer from the University of Nebraska and former chair of the NCAA

Committee on Infractions, said that nothing in the NCAA constitution and bylaws gave it authority to hold institutions accountable for unethical behavior that was not related to athletic competition.[18] Two former presidents of the NCAA, Cedric Dempsey and Gene Corrigan, said that the NCAA broke its own rules when it did not carry out an investigation of Penn State and did not use the mandated Committee on Infractions when it sanctioned Penn State. In other words, the NCAA did not follow its own due-process procedures in issuing penalties against Penn State.[19] An immediate lawsuit and rejection of a forced consent decree could have been carried out by those in power at Penn State. Nevertheless, President Erickson and the Executive Committee of the Board of Trustees chose not to do so. Apparently no one on the thirty-two-member board read the NCAA constitution and bylaws to confirm the NCAA was following its rules. That included Governor Tom Corbett, who later brought a politically motivated lawsuit against the NCAA on the basis of unsupported monopolistic grounds. It was rejected by a federal judge, who called it an attempted "hail Mary" pass by the governor.[20]

Not carrying out due process was likely a far greater legal problem for the NCAA than Governor Corbett's claim of a violation of the Sherman Antitrust Act, though President Erickson probably was not aware of the fact. Furthermore due-process violations were not new at the NCAA. The ruling body had carried out questionable due process for a number of years but specifically in the Jerry Tarkanian case, involving a basketball coach at the University of Nevada–Las Vegas who had questionable recruiting practices. The NCAA used even more problematic harassment tactics in the case of Tarkanian and eventually paid him $2.5 million to keep his case of harassment away from a legal judgment. After investigative journalist Don Yeager wrote his condemnation of the NCAA in his *Undue Process: The NCAA's Injustice for All* in the early 1990s, the NCAA created a committee to suggest real due-process policies that would prevent hearsay evidence to convict universities, separate the enforcement staff from the NCAA Infractions Committee, and create a system of appeals, among other reforms.[21]

Unfortunately for Penn State, the NCAA under Mark Emmert reverted to some previous inadequate due-process policies when it used hearsay evidence in the Freeh report of 2012, neglected to conduct its own investigation of Penn State misconduct, and bypassed its own due process by illegitimately circumventing the Committee on Infractions. The 426-page NCAA Constitution, Operating Bylaws and Administrative Bylaws in 2012 clearly stated that the Committee on Infractions, not the NCAA presidents, was given the responsibility of enforcing the NCAA program and "imposing penalties" to "provide fairness." Furthermore, Article 19 of the NCAA's legal document unambiguously stated that ruling on violations of the NCAA policies "shall be solely that of the Committee on Infractions." That was, according to policies, the "fulfillment of NCAA policies and principles, and its resulting effect on any institutional penalty."[22] It could not be clearer than this. Even though the NCAA, by court rulings, does not have to follow the due process of the U.S. Constitution Fifth and Fourteenth Amendments or state constitutions (for Penn State lacks the status of a "state actor"), it was as if leaders of the NCAA deliberately bypassed the intent of due process found in the national and state constitutions for their own ends.[23]

A former NCAA faculty representative at Penn State, Scott Kretchmar, provided poignant comments about what he called the "draconian" NCAA sanctions that were based on the Freeh report. "If Penn State were going to be saddled with unprecedented levels of penalties," Kretchmar noted shortly after the NCAA sanctions, "one would expect commensurate levels of evidence." He summed up as well as anyone the case against the deleterious and unjust NCAA sanctions:

> Normal procedures were not followed by the NCAA. . . . We accepted a deal. . . . We had a choice between a death penalty with football or a death penalty without it. But were there no other choices? No time to defend ourselves? No opportunity to present evidence? . . . In short, what happened to due process?

Kretchmar caught the essence of the foul NCAA actions when he stated that the NCAA acted as "an organization that does not stay focused on its primary duties [and uses] sweeping accusations about a corrupt culture that are at odds with the facts."[24]

For Emmert to claim football at Penn State dominated the entire culture of the institution was the height of hypocrisy, for he had been chancellor of Louisiana State University when, in 1999, he fired the football coach, making the statement, "success in LSU football is essential for the success of Louisiana State University."[25] Thus, to Emmert, football at his institution was the culture needed to make the university successful. If football dominated the culture at Penn State, as Emmert proclaimed, what must it be at the other big-time institutions of higher education where it is even stronger and in need of "draconian" measures such as those he and the NCAA presidents forced upon Penn State?

Unfortunately for justice to reign, NCAA's president, Emmert, coerced new president Rod Erickson to sign the consent decree under the threat of a death penalty if Erickson did not do so—another kind of harassment originally found in the important Tarkanian case. What the NCAA did, according to a professor of law and director of the National Sports Law Institute at Marquette University, Andrew J. Mitten, was an unwarranted "rush to judgment," like vigilante justice, to demonstrate NCAA presidential control in a response to numerous other scandals. It would, Mitten pointed out, bypass the NCAA's own constitution and bylaws and its established system of due process. The chair of the Executive Committee of the NCAA, Edward J. Ray, inadvertently confirmed Mitten's observations, when the Oregon State University president stated, "We have to reassert our responsibilities and charge to oversee intercollegiate athletics. So the first question you asked is does this send a message. The message," emphasized Ray, "is the presidents and the chancellors are in charge."[26] But the NCAA Committee on Infractions, in the Penn State case, should have been in charge. By lacking due process, Penn State became the whipping boy for Mark Emmert's NCAA. Later, a former member of the Penn State Board of Trustees, Joel Myers, stated that the NCAA used "extortionate-like threats, . . . bullying, bluster, and bluffing" against his institution.[27] That was true, but Penn State's president did not comprehend this. In short, the NCAA threatened actions it had no right to take under its own constitution and bylaws.

The rookie president, Rod Erickson, however, did contact at least one supposedly knowledgeable lawyer who had been involved with NCAA violations in the past. Eugene Marsh, a lawyer from Birmingham, Alabama, and previously on the NCAA Committee on Infractions, was hired by Penn State to give advice and represent the university in discussions with Mark Emmert and the NCAA presidents about the proposed sanctions and a possible death penalty. Marsh later reported to the Penn State Board of Trustees that "the majority of the board of directors at the NCAA believed that the death penalty should be imposed." Marsh was told that the "NCAA board thought that it was the worst case of loss of institutional control they had ever seen" and that it was a Penn State University culture problem, a characterization borrowed from the Freeh report. Thus, the penalty that would be imposed by the NCAA would not only strongly penalize the university "but also to change the culture that allowed this activity to occur."[28] Marsh, who should have known better as a lawyer and former NCAA official, did not mention that the NCAA had broken its own constitution and bylaws and did not follow the due-process procedures created after the Tarkanian harassment fiasco.

Rod Erickson felt he had to make a judgment between punishments under a consent decree and a possible death penalty. Many people believed this was an unfortunate or ill-advised decision, when Erickson was threatened by the NCAA into agreeing to the toughest penalty ever issued by the national organization. In short, Erickson, without consulting his entire Board of Trustees, which had recently voted him into the presidency, agreed to the following seven penalties:

- $60 million fine
- Four-year football bowl ban
- Four-year athletic scholarship reduction in football from 85 to 65
- Five-year probation
- Vacating of 112 Penn State football victories, including 111 Paterno wins
- Athlete transfer rule waived for members of the football team
- Other penalties possible after the criminal trials[29]

In addition to the punitive component of the NCAA sanctions, a number of corrective or reform requirements were laid on Penn State, including the appointment of an Athletic Integrity Officer who would oversee whether the university was meeting all the demands of the NCAA. Almost immediately, the officer selected was the well-known ex-senator from Maine, George Mitchell.

President Erickson justified his decision to accept the consent decree as being preferable to the death penalty (as illegal as it was for the NCAA to levy one). Erickson later reasoned that because football at Penn State supported all the other twenty-six sports, all sports would be lost. In addition, the Big Ten might vote Penn State out of the conference, and, besides, new coach Bill O'Brien wanted to play and be on television. Furthermore, Erickson argued that any challenge to the consent decree would take years of litigation, and Penn State would probably lose to the NCAA. From an economic standpoint, Erickson believed an empty stadium would have a drastic impact on Happy Valley's economy. Erickson wanted to move on by making changes in how athletics was administered.[30] This time, unlike discussions with the Executive Committee relative to the consent decree, Erickson addressed the entire board. Nevertheless, as Erickson desired to "move forward," he made no recommendation to bring athletics under educators' control rather than having it in a business office of the university, arguably part of the problem of isolating athletics that likely contributed to the Sandusky Scandal.

A small minority of the trustees were hesitant to "move forward" without further consideration of the consent decree. One was Joel Myers, a long-time critic of how the Board of Trustees operated historically without full discussion by the entire board. Myers sent an e-mail to the full board recommending three steps before any Executive Committee acceptance of the consent decree. First, he wanted a review of the legal advice given to Erickson, likely questioning guidance given by attorney Gene Marsh. Second, he wanted the board to review the Freeh report, which it refused to do. Third, he wanted the full board to review the NCAA sanctions. Myers was unsuccessful. Soon, four trustees, led by Ryan McCombie, filed an abortive appeal to the NCAA not to strip the 112 victories.[31]

The 112 victories recorded as defeats may have been the most criticized of the NCAA sanctions, especially by the alumni.[32] Though a few on the board questioned the consent decree, the inaction of the trustees on the questionable conclusions, if not the facts, of the Freeh report and how the NCAA used the Freeh report as gospel truth for the consent decree angered many of the more than half-million Penn State alumni. None of the nine alumni members of the board, who voted to fire Joe Paterno in 2011, was reelected to the board in the next three years. All who ran were overwhelmingly defeated, including Joel Myers. Although hundreds of individuals criticized Paterno for ignoring the children who were molested by Sandusky, something that even Paterno admitted before he died of cancer, thousands protested how the trustees treated him after sixty-one years of successful coaching, his university leadership, and his philanthropy at Penn State. Paterno had carried out his legal responsibility by reporting the alleged child sexual misconduct, and only later did he admit "I backed away" from the child molestation issue. People could not understand the act of penalizing Penn State football and Paterno's victories when Paterno had acted legally and, according to the rational argument of informed attorney Andrew Mitten, no NCAA rules were violated in the Sandusky Scandal.[33]

After the inadmissible, if not illegal, actions of the NCAA, the family of Joe Paterno attempted to resurrect the positive image of Joe Paterno by denying the findings of the Freeh report and opposing the NCAA's use of the flawed document. First, the Paterno family offered a lengthy critique of the Freeh report, objecting to its lack of due process, lack of an independent investigation of the Sandusky case, and disregard for the NCAA's own fundamental policy on criminal versus athletic issues.[34] Then, in a more formal manner, the Paterno family used similar arguments and brought suit against the NCAA. Defendants in the suit included five members of the Board of Trustees, Al Clemens, Peter Khoury, Anthony Lubrano, Ryan McCombie, and Adam Taliaferro. Only one member, Clemens, had been a trustee when the 1998 and 2001 Sandusky locker room incidents had occurred. Clemens's membership on the Board of Trustees when the Sandusky incidents first occurred, however, was possibly important in getting the case to be heard. As a matter of justice, not only to Joe Paterno but also to Penn State, this case was potentially very valuable.[35]

The plethora of criminal and civil cases moved at a snail's pace after the swift jury trial and sentencing of Jerry Sandusky to at least thirty years in prison for conviction of forty-five counts of criminal acts of mostly pedophilia and sexual activities with prepubescent boys from the first known 1998 incident.[36] Confusing the future criminal trials of Graham Spanier, Gary Schultz, and Tim Curley was the activity of Penn State's counsel, Cynthia Baldwin. Because she failed to reveal that she was not counsel to the three Penn State administrators, when they indicated that she was their attorney at the grand jury investigation, there could well have been grounds to throw out the indictments of the three individuals. Baldwin, previously on the Pennsylvania State Supreme Court, should not have been at the hearings. It may never be known through a jury trial whether the three administrators were guilty of covering up the criminal activities of Jerry Sandusky.

Whatever the results of the criminal and civil suits, the future of Penn State athletics would come under a completely new athletic administration, headed by new president, Eric Barron, and a new athletic director, Sandy Barbour. Eric Barron had spent a good portion of his career previously at Penn State in the esteemed College of Earth and Mineral Sciences. Sandy Barbour was never affiliated with Penn State in her athletic administration career before coming from the University of California–Berkeley, where she was athletic director for ten years. Even the new football coach, James Franklin, was not previously affiliated with Penn State; he had success with an often downtrodden Vanderbilt University football program in the dominant Southeastern Conference. With a completely new top-level athletic administration and a majority of the Board of Trustees having been elected or chosen since the scandal began, many had renewed hope that athletics might be carried out in a more open manner, eliminating much of the insularity that had existed for years. There was less hope, however, that the new administration would reconsider the question of placing athletics away from the isolation in a business office and placing it under some academic unit where it might have a larger element of academic oversight. If that occurred, it would overturn the questionable decision in 1980 in which Joe Paterno, financial officer Steve Garban, and Vice President Robert Patterson advised President John Oswald to remove athletics from supervision by an academic dean and place it under a former football captain in a financial office far removed from anyone with academic credentials.

What about Happy Valley and the opening of its Pandora's box by the Jerry Sandusky Scandal? Does hope remain in the Pandora's box of Happy Valley, after evils were released as in ancient Greek mythology told by Hesiod? In contrast with the first woman created by Zeus, Pandora, who released evils and left hope in the box, would the first woman athletic director in Penn State's history build on what was left in Pandora's box, hope? It was difficult to determine the future direction of athletics from a study of the history of athletic administration at Penn State. David Gottlieb, a former sociologist at Penn State, may have offered something of worth when he once said, "Something happens to people who stay too long in a valley." Or as a former writer and editor at Penn State, Terry Denbow, wrote just before the Freeh report was released in 2012, "Maybe . . . Penn State is a victim of insularity. . . . Brigadoon wasn't real. Was the Grand Experiment . . . ? The valley," he stated, "resists easy exploration."[37] One might conclude that Penn State athletics in an isolated valley in Central Pennsylvania will probably never be as isolated in the future as it has been at times in its more than a century of existence. The evils, when attended to, may vanish, and Happy Valley will be left with hope.

TIMELINE

February 22, 1855	Penn State University is founded as Farmer's High School.
June 16, 1866	Baseball becomes Penn State's first intercollegiate contest.
Fall 1871	Six women are admitted into Penn State.
November 12, 1881	Football, rugby style, is first played against the University at Lewisburg (Bucknell).
1887	The Athletic Association is formed by Penn State students.
March 18, 1890	The Athletic Association adopts blue and white as school colors.
April 30, 1891	Students hire a physical educator and football and baseball trainer.
June 1891	A track surrounds a football and baseball field, soon named Beaver Field.
October 1891	A football training table is created with special lodging for athletes.
January 25, 1892	George Hoskins becomes physical director and football coach.
May 1892	Spring practice begins in football.
February 6, 1894	The Alumni Advisory Committee of the Athletic Association is formed to control athletic money.
November 21, 1894	President George W. Atherton allows a failing football player to continue playing.
June 17, 1896	Silvanus Newton replaces George Hoskins as physical director and coach.
Fall 1898	"Brute" Randolph becomes Penn State's first Walter Camp all-American.
July 31, 1900	W. N. "Pop" Golden is hired as physical director and coach. Athletic scholarships are offered by the Board of Trustees.
April 1901	Professor Fred Pattee's "Alma Mater" is published in the *Free Lance*.
November 22, 1902	Students pay for band expenses to Williamsport for a football game.
July 11, 1903	Trustees agree to build an athletic dormitory with a training table.
September 7, 1905	Trustees approved "Pop" Golden's request of twenty-five athletic scholarships.
September 29, 1905	"Pop" Golden is named head coach by the Athletic Association.
January 27, 1906	"Pop" Golden is officially named athletic director.
Fall 1906	William T. "Mother" Dunn is the first Penn State first-team all-American.
November 28, 1907	An Alumni Advisory Committee of the Athletic Association recommends a graduate manager after a Pitt loss.
January 1908	A graduate manager of athletics is created by the Alumni Association.

1908	The Faculty Senate votes that it has jurisdiction over athletic contests.
June 15, 1908	Trustees establish the Department of Physical Culture.
May 7, 1909	New Beaver Field for track, baseball, and football is dedicated.
Fall 1909	Bill Hollenback becomes football coach and produces winning teams.
July 14, 1910	The Alumni Advisory Committee advises physical education for all students.
May 1, 1911	The Alumni Advisory Committee proposes four years of eligibility.
June 1913	The Alumni Advisory Committee proposes eliminating the position of athletic director.
November 1913	A letterman's club, Varsity Club, is organized by alumni.
October 24, 1914	Tying Harvard in football is considered Penn State's greatest victory to date.
1918	The Penn State Women's Athletic Association is founded.
August 25, 1918	Hugo Bezdek is named football coach and director of physical education.
May 13, 1919	Hugo Bezdek's plan for mass athletics is presented to the Board of Trustees.
September 1, 1920	Winning produces a seven-year contract at $10,000 per year for Hugo Bezdek.
1921	An eastern conference of Ivy Schools, Penn State, Pitt, and Syracuse is suggested by Hugo Bezdek.
November 23, 1921	Hugo Bezdek's salary is raised to $14,000 after two undefeated seasons.
September 1, 1922	Hugo Bezdek is given a ten-year contract to remain at Penn State.
December 1922	Hugo Bezdek turns down an offer to manage the Philadelphia Phillies baseball team.
January 1, 1923	Proceeds from Penn State participation in the Rose Bowl game go to build a new athletic dorm.
March 13, 1923	The Alumni Advisory Committee of the Athletic Association donates twenty-three acres of land to Penn State.
June 10, 1923	President John Thomas gives athlete eligibility control to the Faculty Senate.
November 28, 1923	The Alumni Advisory Athletic Committee pledges $100,000 for an indoor arena.
September 15, 1924	Varsity Hall, now Irvin Hall, becomes the athletic dorm.
October 23, 1924	The Board of Trustees limits the number of athletic scholarships to seventy-five.
Fall 1925	Alumni in Pittsburgh are upset at Hugo Bezdek for losses to Pitt.
January 8, 1926	The Carnegie Foundation begins investigating intercollegiate athletics.
June 14, 1926	The Alumni's White Committee is appointed to study Penn State athletics.
September 8, 1926	Notre Dame's Knute Rockne okays broadcast of Penn State football game.
September 24, 1926	Ralph Hetzel is chosen president and leads the Great Experiment failure.

December 21, 1926	Joseph Vincent Paterno is born in Brooklyn, New York.
February 26, 1927	The J. Beaver White Committee asks for a reorganization of athletics, eliminating athletic scholarships and removing coach Hugo Bezdek.
May 1927	Penn State faculty and students approve the Beaver White Report.
July 28, 1927	Trustees create a Board of Athletic Control to govern athletics.
August 10, 1927	Board of Athletic Control ends athletic scholarships beginning in 1928.
October 1, 1927	The first home football Penn State radio broadcast (WPSC) is conducted.
January 10, 1929	The Pittsburgh Penn State Club forces issue on athletics under Bezdek.
January 19, 1929	Recreation Hall is opened, receiving a half million dollars from the state.
January 21, 1929	Trustees appoint the Warriner Committee to investigate athletics and coaching.
March 9, 1929	C. W. Heppenstall, an alumnus from Pittsburgh, calls for a coaching change.
June 15, 1929	Trustees accept the Warriner Report on athletics.
July 3, 1929	President Ralph Hetzel favors firing Bezdek, but not separating athletics from an academic department.
October 23, 1929	The Carnegie Foundation's *American College Athletics* condemns commercialism, professionalism, athletic scholarships, and alumni control.
January 9, 1930	The Board of Athletic Control recommends firing Bezdek.
January 20, 1930	The Board of Trustees votes to remove Hugo Bezdek as football coach and make him director of a new School of Physical Education and Athletics.
March 27, 1930	Bob Higgins, all-American in football, becomes head football coach.
September 1930	The Athletic Association Constitution states it controls athletics.
September 26, 1931	Alumnus B. C. "Casey" Jones begins recruiting and subsidizing in football.
1934	Ridge Riley is hired as the first sports information director.
January 1935	The National Collegiate Athletic Association (NCAA) code opposing all athlete subsidies is not supported nationally.
June 1935	The Alumni Association calls for investigation of losses in football.
February 14, 1936	Board of Trustees appoints the Special Trustees Committee on Athletics to investigate athletics.
June 6, 1936	The alumni ask to remove Bezdek from athletic administration.
September 29, 1936	The Athletic Trustees Report calls for the ouster of Hugo Bezdek.
October 3, 1936	Trustees change the title director to dean of physical education and athletics.
April 23, 1937	Carl Schott is chosen dean of physical education and athletics.
January 15, 1938	Athletes clustering in physical education is questioned by Board of Athletic Control.
September 26, 1938	Ridge Riley writes the first Penn State "Football Newsletter."
October 1, 1938	Penn State's radio network for football is established.

March 23, 1939	School of Physical Education and Athletics opposes women's intercollegiate athletics.
October 12, 1940	Fraternities are shown to be giving free room and board to athletes.
1941	The Quarterback Club is organized to raise funds for football.
June 7, 1941	Heinz Warneke is chosen to sculpt the "Lion Shrine" from 1940 class gift.
October 24, 1942	Warneke's Nittany Lion Statue sculptor is dedicated.
January 26, 1944	Gerald Arthur Sandusky is born in Washington, Pennsylvania.
1944	Joe Paterno translates Virgil's *Aeneid* with high school Latin teacher Father Thomas Bermingham, and it gives direction to his life.
November 17, 1945	Wally Triplett is first African American to start in Penn State football.
Summer 1946	Alumni purchase Theta Kappa Phi fraternity for a football dorm.
September 20, 1947	Instrumental "Casey" Jones's recruits begin an undefeated football season.
October 3, 1947	President Hetzel's death leads to liberalized views of athletic scholarships.
November 15, 1947	Penn State beats Navy, 20–7, in its first televised football game.
Fall 1947	Bob Higgins's first undefeated football team goes to Cotton Bowl.
December 1947	"We Are Penn State" tradition is begun by football captain Steve Shuey.
July 30, 1948	Trustees again allow athletic scholarships, about half going to football.
January 1949	Beaver Field is expanded, doubling capacity to 28,000.
March 9, 1949	Joe Bedenk is chosen over Earle Edwards as head football coach.
April 24, 1950	Charles "Rip" Engle is appointed football coach, bringing Joe Paterno as assistant.
March 30, 1951	Board of Trustees increases athletic scholarships to 200, 50 with room and board.
July 1952	Ernie McCoy becomes dean and athletic director of School of Physical Education and Athletics.
October 2, 1952	John D. Lawther becomes assistant dean under Ernie McCoy.
October 1952	The Levi Lamb Grant-in-Aid Fund is created.
March 27, 1953	Board of Trustees gives Dean McCoy full authority, reducing alumni athletic power.
November 13, 1953	The Penn State College becomes Pennsylvania State University.
December 4, 1953	School of Physical Education and Athletics becomes the College of Physical Education and Athletics.
October 20, 1954	Penn State's first national telecast game is at Franklin Field, Philadelphia.
January 11, 1955	Dean McCoy reports surplus athletic money goes to recreational facilities such as tennis courts, bowling alleys, rifle range, and ice skating rink.
July 15, 1955	Dean McCoy states that athletes' admissions are same as other students.
July 1, 1956	Eric A. Walker is named president with a strong interest in athletics.
December 5, 1958	Board of Trustees creates 175 athletic tuition scholarships, 75 with room and board.

April 1959	The Nittany Lion Club is established, bringing athletic financial support.
May 5, 1959	The Alumni Advisory Board recommends athletic "presidential admits."
November 14, 1959	The Beaver Field steel stands are moved, becoming Beaver Stadium.
May 13, 1960	The "obsolete" Alumni Athletic Association is abandoned.
ca. 1961	Joe Paterno and Suzanne Pohland discuss possible homosexual relations between Huckleberry Finn and "Nigger" Jim after literature lecture.
January 28, 1963	The School of Physical Education and Athletics opposes an academic–athletic division.
May 1963	Penn State enters eligibility agreement with Pitt, Syracuse, and West Virginia.
June 8, 1963	The College of Physical Education and Athletics becomes the College of Health and Physical Education.
Fall 1963	Jerry Sandusky begins three years of varsity football at Penn State.
June 16, 1964	Joe Paterno is named associate coach and likely successor to Rip Engle.
Fall 1964	Penn State's women's intercollegiate athletics begins officially.
October 7, 1964	Rip Engle asks to lower academic requirements for athletes.
January 28, 1965	Joe Paterno turns down the head football coaching position at Yale.
1965	Board of Trustees disbands the Alumni Advisory Committee of the Athletic Association.
February 18, 1966	Rip Engle announces his retirement as head football coach.
February 19, 1966	Joe Paterno is appointed head football coach at a $20,000 salary.
May 1966	Jerry Sandusky is Penn State student marshal as top college graduate.
October 18, 1966	Joe Paterno's first year as head coach ends in a 5-5 record.
October 19, 1967	Joe Paterno's "Grand Experiment" is coined by journalist Bill Conlin.
May 18, 1968	Jesse Arnelle, star athlete, class of 1955, criticizes "racial tokenism" at Penn State.
November 23, 1968	Joe Paterno is reportedly offered the Michigan head coaching position.
January 1969	Joe Paterno is voted the 1968 Coach of the Year.
July 1, 1969	Ed Czekaj becomes athletic director, succeeding retiring Ernie McCoy.
	Joe Paterno is granted full professorship with tenure.
Fall 1969	Jerry Sandusky is hired as assistant football coach.
December 6, 1969	President Richard Nixon presents national championship plaque to the University of Texas.
June 11, 1970	The Board of Trustees grants the university president power to not only administer Penn State but to set policy for the board to adopt.
July 1, 1970	John Oswald becomes president with new powers from Board of Trustees.

	Robert Scannell becomes dean of Health, Physical Education and Recreation upon Ernie McCoy's retirement.
January 1971	Joe Paterno goes to Green Bay, interviewing for Packer coaching position.
February 17, 1971	Robert Patterson becomes senior vice president for finance and operations, eventually in control of Penn State athletics.
November 19, 1971	Steve Garban is promoted to controller, a position that will lead to his importance in controlling Penn State athletics.
March 18, 1972	A student organization, Homophiles of Penn State, seeks recognition.
May 16, 1972	Joe Paterno speaks out against a Big 4 agreement with Pitt, Syracuse, and West Virginia favored by President John Oswald.
September 23, 1972	Penn State's stadium is expanded by 9,320 seats to total 55,279.
January 1, 1973	Joe Paterno signs football contract for $33,000—larger than Bear Bryant's.
January 5, 1973	Joe Paterno announces that he will stay at Penn State and not become head coach of the New England Patriots, rejecting a deal for more than a million dollars.
January 20, 1973	Trustee George H. Deike states the athletic program in an educational unit "could serve as an example for other major institutions."
February 12, 1973	Joe Paterno tells a gathering, "We want to be Number One."
March 31, 1973	Governor Milton Shapp declares "Joe Paterno Day."
June 16, 1973	Joe Paterno gives the commencement address, both chastising President Richard Nixon for slighting Penn State and challenging graduates that "when we are wrong, we must be mature enough to realize it and act accordingly."
November 19, 1973	Joe Paterno says he wants "to coach for another four or five years."
November 24, 1973	Coach Paterno allows grass to grow and rain to fall on the field without tarps to slow down Pitt and Tony Dorsett.
January 21, 1974	Joe Paterno donates honorarium from the Philadelphia Saints and Sinners Roast to the Children's Hospital in the name of Joey Cappelletti.
July 1, 1974	Penn State withdraws from the Eastern Collegiate Athletic Conference (ECAC).
March 15, 1975	After the ECAC withdrawal, Trustee Maurice Goddard asks "how the University makes athletic policies."
April 12, 1976	Dean Bob Scannell appoints an ad hoc committee on varsity athletics to recommend guidelines to deal with size and scope of athletics.
1977	The Second Mile is created by Jerry Sandusky to help at-risk children who have problems meeting societal expectations.
Fall 1977	Jerry Sandusky becomes defensive coordinator, replacing Jim O'Hora.
October 15, 1977	Joe Paterno misses his first game as head coach when son, David, fractures his skull in a trampoline accident.
January 1, 1979	Joe Paterno's team loses the National Championship to Bear Bryant's Alabama, 14–7, a several-year, devastating blow to Paterno.

February 8, 1979	Penn State university controller Steve Garban suggests that athletics be separated from the College of Health, Physical Education and Recreation.
May 2, 1979	A business professor charges athletic counseling with attempting to change grades of some athletes.
May 14, 1979	The University Thoele Committee Report recommends changes in athletics, but to retain the integration of athletics within an academic unit.
November 18, 1979	President John Oswald, Vice President Bob Patterson, Joe Paterno, and Dean Bob Scannell call for an athletic director change.
December 1979	Joe Paterno is asked to be athletic director, insisting that athletics be removed from any academic dean.
January 14, 1980	Joe Paterno becomes athletic director; athletics is removed from the dean's office in a silent coup d'état.
February 6, 1980	The NCAA informs President Oswald of Joe Paterno's illegal recruiting.
May 20, 1980	Rene Portland is chosen basketball coach by Joe Paterno.
Spring 1980	Joe Paterno asks for nine presidential admits for football. All are admitted. Four are vital in first national championship. Only one graduates.
July 30, 1980	Dean Bob Scannell becomes vice president for the Commonwealth Campus System.
November 28, 1980	Rene Portland pressures players to score 100 points for her 100th victory.
June 3, 1981	Penn State promotes an eastern intercollegiate athletic conference.
March 1, 1982	Joe Paterno gives up his two-year athletic director position to Jim Tarman.
January 1, 1983	Penn State wins its first football national championship, defeating Georgia.
January 27, 1983	Paterno speaks to the Board of Trustees, urging them to be Number One in more than football.
1983	Three additions to the stadium since 1972 increase seating to 83,770.
May 20, 1984	Paterno, at age fifty-seven, sees himself retiring in five or six years.
December 6, 1984	Joe Paterno's $20,000 gift establishes the Paterno Libraries Endowment.
February 28, 1985	Paterno breaks another NCAA rule in recruiting Quintus McDonald.
May 21, 1986	Penn State reports that Joe Paterno contributed $150,000 to Penn State's $200 million capital campaign.
June 16, 1986	Rene Portland opposes lesbianism: "I will not have it in my program."
December 22, 1986	Joe Paterno states that Jerry Sandusky's "character . . . is extraordinary."
1987	Joe Paterno declines consideration for head of the NCAA.
April 26, 1987	The football indoor practice facility, Holuba Hall, is dedicated.
December 6, 1988	Joe Paterno tells Temple University that Jerry Sandusky has "impeccable lifestyle."

October 1989   President Bryce Jordan is advised to move rapidly to get into the
                      Big Ten.

October 25, 1989   Illinois's President Stanley Ikenberry tells the Big Ten presidents
                      of Penn State's desire to join the Big Ten.

November 19, 1989   Congress passes the Clery Act, requiring the reporting of campus
                      crimes.

December 4, 1989   The Big Ten Council of Ten extends Penn State an invitation to
                      join the Big Ten.

December 7, 1989   President Bryce Jordan meets with state officials before informing
                      the Board of Trustees of the intent to join the Big Ten.

December 18, 1989   Trustee Joel Myers questions not being informed about the Big
                      Ten.

January 11, 1990   Board of Trustees is told that a 1970 Board of Trustees decision gave
                      presidents policymaking power, such as joining the Big Ten.

June 4, 1990   The Big Ten Council of Ten votes to confirm its December 1989
                      decision to accept Penn State into the Big Ten.

November 9, 1990   Jerry Sandusky's Second Mile receives the President George H. W.
                      Bush 294th Point of Light award for community service.

March 10, 1991   *Philadelphia Inquirer* charges Rene Portland with sexual discrimi-
                      nation.

March 19, 1991   Penn State Faculty Senate votes 93–12 to recommend adding a
                      sexual orientation provision to the school's antidiscrimination
                      policy.

May 16, 1991   Board of Trustees includes sexual orientation in its antidiscrimi-
                      nation rules.

September 1991   Penn State begins its first competition in a Big Ten championship.

November 29, 1991   Joe Paterno shows compassion writing to a twenty-year-old co-ed
                      who had a football-size malignant tumor removed, not an un-
                      common gesture for Paterno.

December 6, 1991   A fan suggests naming either the football field or Beaver Stadium
                      after Joe Paterno.

January 8, 1992   Joe Paterno announces at the NCAA that "I am winding down
                      my career."

April 2, 1993   Graham Spanier, at Nebraska, opposes any university "double
                      standard, turning a deaf ear to improprieties in intercollegiate
                      athletics."

December 8, 1993   Rene Portland receives an NCAA violation notice for illegal re-
                      cruiting.

December 30, 1993   Tim Curley is named Penn State athletic director, replacing Jim
                      Tarman.

July 14, 1994   A new Penn State library is named the Joe and Suzanne Paterno
                      Library.

January 1, 1995   Gary Schultz becomes senior vice president for finance and business
                      at Penn State and thus has control of athletics and the police.

January 6, 1996   The 15,000-seat Penn State Academic-Athletic Convocation Cen-
                      ter opens.

January 1998   Joe Paterno tells Jerry Sandusky he will not become head football
                      coach.

May 3, 1998	Jerry Sandusky sexually assaults an eleven-year-old boy in the original Penn State Lasch Building.
May 4, 1998	Alycia Chambers, a psychologist, calls Sandusky "a likely pedophile."
	Vice President Gary Schultz begins a confidential file on Sandusky, later concealed from the Special Investigative Counsel.
May 5, 1998	Schultz, upon notice of the Sandusky investigations, notes, "Is this opening of pandora's box? Other children?"
May 8, 1998	John Seasock, a Youth Services counselor, dismisses the Sandusky incident, stating "Sandusky didn't fit the profile of a pedophile."
May 13, 1998	Tim Curley asks for updates on the May 3 incident: "Anything new in this department? Coach is anxious to know where it stands."
May 15, 1998	Neither President Graham Spanier nor Vice President Gary Schultz notifies the Board of Trustees of the ongoing investigation of Jerry Sandusky.
May 27–June 1, 1998	District Attorney Ray Gricar declines to prosecute Sandusky. Case closed.
July 1, 1998	Steve Garban, former football captain, becomes a trustee.
January 19, 1999	Jerry Sandusky indicates that he wants to coach one more year.
March 1999	Penn State is informed of the illegal basketball recruiting by Coach Pat Meiser, resulting in probation by the Association for Intercollegiate Athletics for Women.
June 19, 1999	Jerry Sandusky reaches a retirement agreement, including use of athletic facilities, emeritus status, and Second Mile collaboration with Penn State.
June 30, 1999	Sandusky, after retirement, is rehired for the 1999 football season.
July 1, 1999	The new Mildred and Louis Lasch Football Building is opened.
November 1999	A $93 million renovation and expansion to Beaver Stadium is begun.
December 5, 1999	State College Quarterback. Club gives Jerry Sandusky its 1999 Alumni Award.
December 10, 1999	Jerry Sandusky is selected Assistant Coach of the Year.
December 28, 1999	Jerry Sandusky, in his last game, takes Victim 4 to the Outback Bowl.
January 1, 2000	Jerry Sandusky is a paid consultant to The Second Mile at $57,000 per year.
March 27, 2000	Rene Portland's women's basketball team advances to the Final Four.
April 14, 2000	Jerry Sandusky's testimonial and roast is held in the Bryce Jordan Center.
July 1, 2000	Scott Kretchmar follows long-time NCAA Faculty Representative John Coyle.
September 8, 2000	The Paterno Library is dedicated: The Paternos raised about $14 million for it.
November 2000	A custodian, James Calhoun, observes Sandusky molesting a young boy.
November 28, 2000	Jerry Sandusky's book is published, with its ironic title, *Touched*.
December 28, 2000	Jerry Sandusky has second interview for the Virginia head coach position.

February 9, 2001	Victim 2 is in shower room incident reported by Mike McQueary. Mike McQueary meets with his father, John, and Dr. Jonathon Dranov.
February 10, 2001	Mike McQueary reports the sexual attack to Joe Paterno, calling it "fondling" and of "a sexual nature." Joe Paterno memorializes Paterno book author Bernard Asbell hours after McQueary reported to him.
February 11, 2001	Joe Paterno reports the McQueary story to Vice President Gary Schultz and Athletic Director Tim Curley. Gary Schultz consults with University Counsel Wendell Courtney about the possibility of reporting "suspected child abuse."
February 12, 2001	Spanier, Schultz, and Curley discuss the Sandusky situation.
February 25, 2001	Schultz, Curley, and Spanier devise Sandusky game plan.
February 26, 2001	Curley and Schultz write coded e-mails, leaving out names and titles confirming the previous day's plan.
February 27, 2001	Curley, after talking with Joe Paterno, changes his mind about reporting Sandusky to officials. Spanier agrees with Curley in the "humane" approach but observes Penn State might become "vulnerable for not having reported it."
March 5, 2001	Curley meets with Sandusky, telling him not to bring children on campus.
March 16, 2001	President Spanier fails to report the Sandusky incident at the Board of Trustees meeting.
March 19, 2001	Curley informs The Second Mile's Jack Raykovitz of the Sandusky allegations. Raykovitz takes no Second Mile action.
April 30, 2001	Rene Portland and husband create two endowed basketball scholarships.
September 21, 2001	President Spanier and Gary Schultz ask for, and soon get, approval of Board of Trustees to sell 40.7 acres of land to The Second Mile.
October 27, 2001	Paterno achieves his 324th victory, surpassing legendary Bear Bryant.
November 2, 2001	The Joe Paterno bronze statue is unveiled outside Beaver Stadium.
2002–2008	Forty-six Penn State football players are charged with 163 criminal accounts, with 27 guilty in a seven-year period.
November 12, 2002	President Spanier and Tim Curley allow an athlete expelled for assaulting a female student to play in the Capital One Bowl.
November 9, 2004	Seven trustees ask for major changes in governance to provide for greater oversight, but the request is denied by Spanier and Cynthia Baldwin, the chair of the board.
November 21, 2004	Spanier, Curley, Garban, and Schultz visit Joe Paterno about retiring.
April 15, 2005	Ray Gricar, Centre County District Attorney, who closed the 1998 investigation of Jerry Sandusky, disappears and is presumed dead.
July 27, 2005	Rene Portland receives the local Renaissance Person of the Year Award.
August 11, 2005	Joe Paterno tells Vice President for Student Affairs Vicky Triponey to stay out of disciplining football players.

October 12, 2005	Ken Lehrman, director of Affirmative Action, begins an investigation of Jennifer Harris's charges of sexual discrimination against Rene Portland.
December 21, 2005	Jennifer Harris files a sexual discrimination lawsuit against Rene Portland, Tim Curley, and Penn State, finally settled out of court in February 2007.
April 18, 2006	Lehrman's affirmative action report says Portland discriminated and she is fined $10,000 and is required to participate in a diversity program.
May 12, 2006	President Spanier fails to inform the trustees of Portland's discrimination at a scheduled Board of Trustees meeting.
May 26, 2006	Joe Paterno is elected into the College Football Hall of Fame.
February 5, 2007	The Harris–Portland lawsuit is settled with no financial agreements noted.
March 21, 2007	Rene Portland resigns as women's basketball coach.
April 1, 2007	A group of football players enters an apartment in State College, after a street altercation, and attacks several students.
April 23, 2007	Coquese Washington is chosen to succeed Portland as basketball coach.
September 12, 2007	Vicky Triponey, vice president of student affairs, leaves her position at Penn State.
October 1, 2007	Player eligibility punishments are left to the coach by President Spanier.
November 18, 2008	Aaron Fisher's mother calls Central Mountain High School principal relative to her son's relationship with Jerry Sandusky.
November 25, 2008	The Second Mile votes to remain silent after Sandusky accusations.
February 22, 2009	Joe Paterno gives a memorable speech at the Dance Marathon (THON).
March 31, 2009	The Centre County district attorney, Michael Madeira, transfers Sandusky's case to the office of Pennsylvania attorney general Tom Corbett.
May 1, 2009	Tom Corbett initiates the Sandusky grand jury investigation.
November 2009	Jerry Sandusky resigns in the presence of dozens of The Second Mile volunteers.
December 14, 2010	McQueary is examined by the grand jury about Sandusky shower incident.
January 12, 2011	Tim Curley and Gary Schultz testify before the grand jury and indicate that Penn State counsel Cynthia Baldwin is representing them. Joe Paterno gives seven minutes of grand jury testimony.
January 2011	Joe Paterno negotiates a $5.5 million 2011 retirement package.
March 19, 2011	Board of Trustees meets, but Counsel Cynthia Baldwin is mute about the grand jury investigation.
March 22, 2011	Graham Spanier, accompanied by Cynthia Baldwin, meets with members of the Pennsylvania attorney general's office about Sandusky situation.
March 31, 2011	Sara Ganim, writing for the *Harrisburg Patriot-News*, reveals contents of the grand jury report, beginning the public part of the Sandusky Scandal.

April 1, 2011	Graham Spanier is asked by a trustee to brief the Board of Trustees about Sandusky.
April 13, 2011	Cynthia Baldwin tells the grand jury judge she was only representing Penn State, not Graham Spanier, who believed she was his counsel.
May 12, 2011	Graham Spanier reports to a closed Board of Trustees meeting, downplaying the allegation against Jerry Sandusky. Cynthia Baldwin says there are pending legal matters. No trustee raises a question, including seven lawyers on the board.
July 15, 2011	President Spanier and Counsel Baldwin fail to update the board on the Sandusky investigation at a scheduled meeting with the Board of Trustees, nor do board members raise any questions.
September 9, 2011	President Graham Spanier tells the Board of Trustees, "Let us not be reluctant to tell our story, openly and honestly."
October 28–29, 2011	Steve Garban discusses the grand jury situation with fellow board members John Surma and Jim Broadhurst.
October 29, 2011	Joe Paterno wins his 409th and last game as coach at Penn State, a 10–7 victory over Illinois.
November 4, 2011	Jerry Sandusky is indicted on forty sex-crime counts involving eight boys in a fifteen-year period. Perjury charges are brought against Gary Schultz and Tim Curley.
November 5, 2011	President Graham Spanier gives his public unconditional support to Tim Curley and Gary Schultz.
November 6, 2011	Gary Schultz and Tim Curley step down from their positions.
November 7, 2011	Athletic Director Tim Curley and Vice President Gary Schultz are arraigned on charges of perjury and failure to report sexual abuse.
November 8, 2011	Trustee President Steve Garban tells board Vice President John Surma, "You need to take this over," referring to the Sandusky Scandal. Penn State cancels Paterno's weekly press conference. Board of Trustees forms a committee to investigate Penn State failures. Joe Paterno leads a "We Are Penn State" cheer at his home.
November 9, 2011	The U.S. Department of Education announces it will investigate Clery Act violations. Joe Paterno states, "I wish I had done more." President Spanier resignation or firing is followed by Joe Paterno's firing. Sue Paterno returns a phone call to the Board of Trustees and states, "After 61 years, he deserved better" and hangs up. Provost Rod Erickson is appointed Penn State president. Tom Bradley is appointed football coach, replacing Paterno.
November 9–10, 2011	Penn State students and admirers of Joe Paterno riot upon notice of the firing.
November 11, 2011	A peaceful candlelight vigil for victims is held on campus.
November 13, 2011	Jack Raykovitz, twenty-seven-year president of The Second Mile, resigns.
November 14, 2011	Construction on The Second Mile Learning Center is halted.

	Paterno's name is removed from the Stagg–Paterno Big Ten Trophy.
November 15, 2011	Wendell Courtney, general counsel to The Second Mile, resigns.
November 16, 2011	Dave Joyner, a trustee, is appointed acting athletic director.
	Governor Tom Corbett freezes the $3 million Second Mile grant.
November 17, 2011	The NCAA announces it will investigate whether Penn State violated NCAA bylaws, with one possible result being given the "death penalty."
	Joe Paterno is reported to have curable lung cancer and is being treated.
November 21, 2011	Former director of the Federal Bureau of Investigation Louis Freeh is chosen to investigate the Sandusky Scandal.
January 14, 2012	Sally Jenkins interviews Paterno, who says, "I walked away."
January 22, 2012	Joe Paterno dies from lung cancer, a metastatic small cell carcinoma.
January 26, 2012	The Board of Trustees cancels issuing a Rod Erickson letter praising Joe Paterno.
	Nike president Phil Knight praises his hero Joe Paterno at a memorial.
May 4, 2012	Three new trustees, all opposing Paterno's firing, are elected.
May 8, 2012	Mike McQueary initiates lawsuit against Penn State in an employment dispute.
June 20, 2012	Matt Sandusky, Jerry's adopted son, reveals that his adopted father abused him.
June 22, 2012	Sandusky is found guilty on forty-five of forty-eight sexual abuse counts.
June 30, 2012	Cynthia Baldwin, Penn State chief counsel, resigns.
July 6, 2012	Former president Graham Spanier is interviewed by Louis Freeh and his law firm.
July 12, 2012	The Freeh report is released, condemning four Penn State administrators.
	NCAA has removed webpage definition of the death penalty, which stated it was only used against "repeat major offenses."
July 14, 2012	NCAA's Julie Roe states the NCAA was "bluffing" in threatening the death penalty.
July 22, 2012	The iconic Joe Paterno statue at Beaver Stadium is removed by President Rod Erickson.
July 23, 2012	Graham Spanier writes to the Board of Trustees of errors in the Freeh report.
	The NCAA levies penalties on Penn State: $60 million fine, four-year bowl ban, loss of forty football scholarships, and vacating all 1998–2011 wins.
	The Big Ten Conference votes to ban Penn State from the Big Ten championship game and bowl game revenue sharing.
	The NCAA removes Joe Paterno's name from the Gerald R. Ford Award.
July 25, 2012	The Board of Trustees issues a statement saying that it did not vote to accept the Freeh report—that a vote was not required.
August 6, 2012	Trustee Ryan McCombie wants to appeal the NCAA consent decree.

September 13, 2012   PS4RS, an alumni group, criticizes the Freeh report.

October 3, 2012   Former NCAA presidents Gene Corrigan and Cedric Dempsey question "due process" of the NCAA in the sanctions.

October 9, 2012   Jerry Sandusky is sentenced to thirty to sixty years in prison.

October 26, 2012   Cynthia Baldwin testifies before the grand jury that President Graham Spanier is "not a person of integrity."

November 1, 2012   Graham Spanier is indicted for perjury and obstruction of justice.

January 2, 2013   Governor Tom Corbett files suit against the NCAA for illegal sanctions.

January 4, 2013   State Senator Jake Corman sues the NCAA over the $60 million fine.

February 9, 2013   The Paterno family releases a lengthy report contradicting the Freeh report.

February 20, 2013   The Pennsylvania law is passed requiring the $60 million NCAA fine to remain within the state.

May 30, 2013   The Paterno family files a suit against the NCAA for lack of due process.

February 5, 2014   Jay Paterno and Bill Kenney file suit against Penn State.

August 11, 2014   Nine trustee alumni ask to vacate the NCAA consent decree.

August 13, 2014   The Board of Trustees votes 19–8 to support a Penn State–NCAA settlement.

September 8, 2014   The NCAA allows bowl eligibility and eighty-five full football scholarships.

November 5, 2014   NCAA's Julie Roe admission of "bluffing" Penn State into signing the consent decree becomes public knowledge.

November 9, 2014   President Eric Barron agrees to a "thorough review" of the Freeh report.

November 12, 2014   Documents show that the Freeh law firm communicated often with the NCAA.

November 14, 2014   The Board of Trustees opposes an internal discussion of the NCAA–Penn State consent decree.

December 15, 2014   A special Board of Trustees meeting, called by newly elected alumni trustees, is boycotted by other members of the board.

January 16, 2015   State Senator Jake Corman's lawsuit against the NCAA is dropped, and the NCAA restores 112 Penn State football victories.

January 28, 2015   New president Eric Barron states that the Freeh Report should not have been the basis of any decision facing Penn State.

February 10, 2015   State Senator Jake Corman calls on the NCAA Executive Committee to fire President Mark Emmert.

July 17, 2015   Old guard Board of Trustees member, Keith Masser, is re-elected board president over alumni dissident Anthony Lubrano.

October 6, 2015   Two former football coaches, Galen Hall and Dick Anderson, file a lawsuit against Penn State for back salaries not paid following the Sandusky scandal.

NOTES

Chapter 1. Life in Happy Valley

1. Many scholars trace the concept of American exceptionalism to the Frenchman Alexis de Tocqueville in *Democracy in America*, published in 1835 and 1840. Tocqueville wrote, "The position of the Americans is therefore quite exceptional." Alexis de Tocqueville, *Democracy in America*, trans. Henry Reeve (Project Gutenberg EBook, 2006), vol. 2, chapter 9. More recent of the many volumes on American exceptionalism include Godfrey Hodgson, *The Myth of American Exceptionalism* (New Haven, CT: Yale University Press, 2009); Seymour Martin Lipset, *American Exceptionalism: A Double-Edged Sword* (New York: W. W. Norton, 1997); Charles Murray, *American Exceptionalism: An Experiment in History*, 151170938-American-Exceptionalism-An-Experiment-in-History.pdf; and Donald E. Pease, *The New American Exceptionalism* (Minneapolis: University of Minnesota Press, 2009). A book on exceptionalism in U.S. soccer is Andrei S. Markovits and Steven L. Hellerman, *Offside: Soccer and Exceptionalism* (Princeton, NJ: Princeton University Press, 2001).

2. Steve Nicklas, Fernandina Beach, FL, "Letter to the Editor," *Centre Daily Times*, 12 November 2011, p. A7.

3. Samuel Johnson, *Rasselas, Prince of Abyssinia*, 1759, chapter 1; chapter 18, http://www.gutenberg.org/dirs./etext96/rslas1oh.htm, unpaged. I thank Sandy Stelts of Penn State Rare Books in Paterno Library for bringing this book to my attention.

4. George M. Graham, "A Tribute to Penn State College," *Penn State Alumni Quarterly*, vol. 2, no. 3 (April 1912), 11.

5. Ralph D. Hetzel to James R. Remick, Winchester, MA, 4 May 1927, and Hetzel to W. A. Jensen, Corvallis, OR, 22 March 1927, President Ralph Hetzel Papers, Box AU05–18, Folder "Correspondence: Penn State Period, 1927," Penn State University Archives.

6. When a Penn State songbook was published in 1906, President Atherton was opposed to having Pattee's song called the alma mater, for, as Atherton wrote Pattee, it was done "without my previous knowledge or authorization" even though "the literary credit belongs to you." George W. Atherton to F. L. Pattee, 16 May 1906, Fred Lewis Pattee Papers, Box 2, Folder 1, Penn State University Archives.

7. Fred Lewis Pattee, *The House of Black Ring: A Romance of the Seven Mountains* (New York: Henry Holt, 1905), 197.

8. Fred Lewis Pattee, *Penn State Yankee: The Autobiography of Fred Lewis Pattee* (State College: Pennsylvania State College, 1953), 146–47.

9. Fred Lewis Pattee, Coronado Beach, FL, to William L. Werner, Penn State, 5 January 1934, Fred Lewis Pattee Papers, Box 2, Folder 130, Penn State University Archives. Werner was named Pattee's literary executor and was most responsible for the publication of Pattee's autobiography after his death.

10. Pattee to Werner, 5 January 1934.

11. See discussions of the proposed airport project in the *Centre Daily Times*, 17 July 1936, p. 6; 20 July 1936, p. 1; 22 July 1936, p. 1; 24 July 1936, p. 1; 28 July 1936, p. 1; 18 August 1936, p. 1; and 5 September 1936, p. 1.

12. The Penn State Board of Athletic Control voted on 10 August 1927 to end athletic scholarships beginning in 1928. Thus the failed "Great Experiment" commenced with an attempt to win without athletic scholarships and by recruiting athletes out of the general student body. See Jack M. Infield, "The Development of the Physical Education and Athletic Policies at the Pennsylvania State University," PE 495 paper, Winter Term, 1973, Penn State University Archives.

13. Fred Lewis Pattee to W. L. Werner, 17 November 1929, Fred Lewis Pattee Papers, Box 2, Folder 128, Penn State University Archives.

14. Others who announced Penn State football games in the 1940s and 1950s include Tom Bender, Mickey Bergstein, Jack Barry, Claude Haring, Tom McMahon, Byron Saam, Ray Scott, Bill Suther, Chuck Thompson, Joe Tucker, and Woody Wolf. See Louis Prato, *The Penn State Football Encyclopedia* (Champaign, IL: Sports Publishing, 1998), 578.

15. Nadine Kofman, "The Origins of Happy Valley," *Town and Gown* (December 2004), 8–14.

16. Eric A. Walker to Charles A. "Rip" Engle, 28 December 1962, President Walker Papers, Box 04.14, Binder "Personal Reminiscences," Penn State University Archives.

17. Kofman, "Origins of Happy Valley," 12.

18. John Herbers, "Census Deems College Town a Metropolitan Area," *New York Times*, 22 July 1981, p. A14.

19. Ronald A. Smith, *Play-by-Play: Radio, Television, and Big-Time College Sport* (Baltimore, MD: Johns Hopkins University Press, 2001), 127–28.

20. Penn State Board of Trustees Executive Committee Minutes, 13 May 1949, Penn State University Archives. 100 athletic scholarships were prescribed worth $220 each. By 1951, 150 scholarships were offered.

21. Ronald A. Smith, *Pay for Play: A History of Big-Time College Athletic Reform* (Urbana: University of Illinois Press, 2011), 77–81.

22. *Philadelphia Bulletin*, 17 November 1978, p. A15.

23. Dave Zang, "American Brigadoon: Joe Paterno's Happy Valley," in Dan Nathan, ed., *Rooting for the Home Team: Sport, Community, and Identity* (Urbana: University of Illinois Press, 2013), 157–69.

24. Zang, "American Brigadoon."

25. Zang, "American Brigadoon," 159.

26. The *Gettysburg Times*, 22 December 1972, p. 13, reported that 20,000 Christmas cards were distributed free to people who wanted to send a personal message to Joe Paterno not to become a pro coach in the National Football League. Mimi Barash Coppersmith, a Penn State grad who would eventually become president of the Penn State Board of Trustees, and would later caution the trustees not to fire Paterno, put a picture of Joe Paterno on the cover of her *Town and Gown* magazine with the title "Joe Don't Go Pro."

27. Joe Paterno with Bernard Asbell, *Paterno: By the Book* (New York: Random House, 1989), 14.

28. "Penn State Commencement Speech by Head Football Coach Joe Paterno," 16 June 1973, http://pennstatemag.files.wordpress.com/2012/01/paterno1973commencement speech.

29. Paterno, *Paterno*, 215.

30. Donnie Collins, "'Hall Beckons Lions' JoePa," *Times Tribune*, 4 December 2007, Joe Paterno Vertical File, Penn State University Archives; and Ray Oarrukkim, "Paterno Simply Refuses to Act His Age," *Philadelphia Inquirer*, 1 January 1995, Joe Paterno Papers, Box 07594, Folder "Newspaper Clippings, Magazine Articles," Penn State University Archives.

31. Rick Reilly, "Guts, Brains and Glory," *Sports Illustrated*, 12 January 1987, http://sports.illustrated.cnn.com/vault/article/magazine/MAG1121846, unpaginated.

32. This important event in the 1979–80 year will be dealt with later.

33. Andrew Bergstein, "Penn State the Brand Name," *Town and Gown* (December 1999), 8–9.

34. "Quoting Joe: Paterno in His Own Words," *Town and Gown* (December 2000), 34.

35. "Quoting Joe," 34. In Joe Paterno's favorite book that he read with a priest in high school, Virgil's *Aeneid,* Aeneas endures both nature and man, and when "exposed to the fury of the winds and beaten against by the waves, endures all the violence and threats of heaven and sea, himself standing unmoved." That, I am convinced, was the kind of influence that reading the *Aeneid* had on Paterno. When, however, Aeneas abandons his lover Dido to set out to conquer Italy, the abandoned Dido cries out before she commits suicide, "Faithless one, did you really think you could hide such wickedness, and vanish from my land in silence?" Aeneas responds, "I do not take course for Italy of my own free will." In one, Aeneas stands alone unmoved, in the other, a larger force than himself is involved. See Virgil, *Aeneid* (19 B.C.E), x, 692, and A. S. Kline, translator, Book IV, p. 279, 331, Virgil, *The Aeneid,* 2002, http://www.poetryintranslation.com/PITBA/Latin?VirgilAeneid.htm. Paterno may have been most influenced by the first words of the *Aeneid*: "I sing of arms and the man . . . to drive a man, noted for virtue, to endure such dangers, to face so many trials."

36. Jerry Fisher, the son of a well-known radio broadcaster for Penn State football, Fran Fisher, worked for WBLF radio in State College, did play-by-play for Penn State's women's basketball, and worked for The Second Mile. *Centre Daily Times,* 1 July 2012, p. A8.

37. Zang, "American Brigadoon," p. 163.

38. Janice L. Korkos, Bonita Springs, FL, as quoted in Dan Good, "Penn State Officials Decided against Reporting Sandusky after Talking with Paterno: Report," *New York Post,* 2 July 2012, http://www.nypost.com/p/news/national/paterno_state_officials.

39. Mary Gage, letter to the editor, *Centre Daily Times,* 21 November 2011, p. A6.

Chapter 2. Penn State Presidents

1. Scott C. Etter, "From Atherton to Hetzel: A History of Intercollegiate Athletic Control at the Pennsylvania State College, 1887–1930," Ph.D. dissertation, Penn State University, 1991, iii.

2. Frank P. Graham to James R. Angell, 21 January 1936, President Graham Files, 1/1/4, Box 3, Folder "January 1936," University of North Carolina Archives.

3. Mary Partlow and John C. Pritchett, "John William Abercrombie, Thirteenth President of the University of Alabama, 1902–1911," unpublished manuscript, 1981, pp. 19, 21, University of Alabama Special Collection. Abercrombie is quoted in Suzanne Rau Wolf, *The University of Alabama: A Pictorial History* (University, AL: University of Alabama Press, 1983), 127.

4. President Rodney Erickson deferred to what he thought was necessary to preserve football at Penn State. He mistakenly agreed in 2012 to the NCAA sanctions after the

Jerry Sandusky Scandal and the Freeh report investigation under the threat that Penn State would receive the "death penalty" if Erickson challenged the sanctions. The NCAA, by its own rules, could not administer a death penalty without multiple major violations of NCAA rules of athletic competition. Penn State had no major violations.

5. Benjamin W. Dwight, "Intercollegiate Regattas, Hurdle-Races, and Prize Contests," *New Englander*, 25 (April 1876), 256; and Andrew W. White, "Diaries," vol. 14, July 14, 1875, Andrew D. White Papers, Cornell University Archives.

6. Morris Bishop, *A History of Cornell* (Ithaca, NY: Cornell University Press, 1962), 142; and Kent Sagendorph, *Michigan: The Story of the University* (New York: E. P. Dutton, 1948), 150.

7. For a deeper discussion, see Ronald A. Smith, "Presidents: Promoters or Reformers?" in his *Pay for Play: A History of Big-Time College Athletic Reform* (Urbana: University of Illinois Press, 2011), 34–41.

8. "Statement by Chancellor Graham Spanier," 26 June 1992, Chancellors' Central Files, Box 299, Folder 25, University of Nebraska Archives. In a long conversation with me in April 1995, Spanier said that without question the hiring of an athletic director at Nebraska was the most difficult problem he faced. See notes from a meeting with President Graham Spanier, 12 April 1995, Ronald Smith personal files.

9. Russ Rose, personal e-mail communication, 11 March 2015.

10. Ronald A. Smith, "Rutgers vs. Princeton: A Football First," in his *Sports and Freedom: The Rise of Big-Time College Athletics* (New York: Oxford University Press, 1988), 69–72; and H. P. Armsby, "Memorial to President George W. Atherton," *U. S. Department of Agriculture, Office of Experiment Stations* (Washington, DC: Government Printing Office, 1907), 31–36.

11. M. A. Kuntz, *Charlie Atherton: Son of Penn State* (n.p.: Xlibris Corporation, 2005), 11–15; and "James C. Mock '90," Notes of Ridge Riley, Ridge H. Riley Papers, Box 04.24, Folder 13, Penn State University Archives. According to Mock, President Atherton was not afraid of his son being hurt playing football, but he was concerned that he was too young and might be influenced by evil companions.

12. "Charles M. H. Atherton," The Pennsylvania State College Register of Grades, 1886–1904, GSTA02.01, Penn State University Archives.

13. Edwin W. Runkle, "The Pennsylvania State College, 1853–1932," manuscript, pp. 319–20, LD4481.P82/1933, Penn State University Archives.

14. Charles H. Brown, "Penn State Centennial Histories" (bound typescript, ca. 1953), LD4481.P82.B76, 1953, Penn State University Archives; Penn State Board of Trustees Executive Committee Minutes, 13 April 1888, 17 September 1891, 9 April 1894, Penn State University Archives; *Free Lance* [Penn State student newspaper], April 1891, p. 2, May 1891, p. 21, October 1891, p. 70, and June 1894, p. 40; J. E. Quigley, Football Manager, Penn State Athletic Association, to Penn State Faculty, 28 September 1893, President Atherton Papers, Box 9, Folder "Athletics," Penn State University Archives; and Lou Prato, *The Penn State Football Encyclopedia* (Champaign, IL: Sports Publishing, 1998), 36–37.

15. *Free Lance*, February 1894, p. 108.

16. Foot Ball Committee to President Atherton, 21 November 1894, President Atherton Papers, Box 9, Folder "PSC Athletics & Athletic Scholarships, 1888–1930," Penn State University Archives.

17. In the Oberlin game, playing a team that had recently beaten Ohio State University, Charlie Atherton, after a fair catch, kicked a field goal by placement rather than by a drop

kick. This game-winning field goal is generally claimed to be the first field goal by placement in history. Because the officials believed that the goal was kicked illegally, the teams agreed to allow Walter Camp, the "father of American football," to be the final arbiter. Camp wrote that it was legal and Penn State won 9–6. Nat Brandt, *When Oberlin Was King of the Gridiron: The Heisman Years* (Kent, OH: Kent State University Press, 2001), 144; and *Free Lance,* December 1894, p. 81.

18. Ronald A. Smith, "The Historical Monte Ward and Penn State University," Talk at the Centre County Historical Society, September 1993, Ronald Smith Collection.

19. Discussion of presidential admits from the Rip Engle and Joe Paterno eras will be addressed later.

20. Knowlton L. Ames to H. O. Stickney, 16 April 1889, in *Harvard Crimson,* 20 December 1889, p. 7. Stickney, however, went to Harvard and played on its football team—which later lost to Princeton 41–15 after Harvard unsuccessfully challenged the eligibility of 15 of the Princeton players.

21. J. Price Jackson to President Atherton, 12 January 1900, President Atherton Papers, Box 9, Folder "G Athletics," Penn State University Archives; and Penn State Board of Trustees Executive Committee Minutes, 31 July 1900 and 7 September 1905, Penn State University Archives. While the football team was gaining financial support from the trustees, the Penn State band was requesting money for band instruments and was turned down by the trustees, who indicated that "there were no College funds now available for such a purpose." Within two months, Andrew Carnegie donated $800 for the purchase of instruments for the College Cadet Band. See Penn State Board of Trustees Executive Committee Minutes, 30 October 1900 and 27 December 1900, Penn State University Archives.

22. Penn State Board of Trustees Executive Committee Minutes, 31 July 1900, 30 October 1900, 9 April 1902, and 9 June 1902. Golden's salary was raised to $3,000 in 1907, better than most salaries of professors at that time. A couple years before, Professors Pattee, Willard, and Foss were at $1,600, $1,800, and $2,000, respectively. Athletic Association Minutes Binder, 7 May 1907, Intercollegiate Athletics Records, Box AJ06, Penn State University Archives; and Penn State Board of Trustees Executive Committee Minutes, 15 June 1903, Penn State University Archives.

23. "Athletics at the Pennsylvania State College," 1903, President Atherton Papers, Box 9, Folder "PSC Athletics & Athletic Scholarships, 1888–1930," Penn State University Archives; and Penn State Board of Trustees Executive Committee Minutes, 15 June 1903, 11 July 1903, 29 July 1903, and 4 November 1903, Penn State University Archives.

24. In the 1920s, a more substantial building was constructed for athletes, Varsity Hall, and when athletic scholarships were done away with at the end of the 1920s, Varsity Hall was eventually turned into a dorm for students, Irvin Hall, which still exists near Recreation Building.

25. *Free Lance,* October 1893, p. 44, February 1894, p. 109, and April 1894, p. 10; and *State Collegian,* 6 February 1908, p. 3.

26. "Football Is Denounced," newspaper clipping, ca. 1905, in Sparks's scrapbook, Edwin E. Sparks Papers, Box 4, 03.04, Penn State University Archives.

27. *Penn State Collegian,* 13 October 1915, p. 3, and 24 November 1915, p. 24.

28. University Faculty Senate Minutes, Box AN05.12, Folder "1908," and "Alumni Advisory Committee to President of the Athletic Association," 8 June 1914, Athletic Association Alumni Advisory Committee Minutes Binder, 1913–1925, Intercollegiate Athletics Rec-

ords, Box AJo6.12, Penn State University Archives; and Michael Bezilla, *Penn State: An Illustrated History* (University Park: Penn State University Press, 1985), 78.

29. Athletic Association Alumni Athletic Advisory Committee Minutes Binder, 1913–1925, 16 July 1918, Intercollegiate Athletics Records, Box AJo6.12, and "Notes of Athletic Board Minutes," Ridge H. Riley Papers, Box 1, Folder 16, Penn State University Archives.

30. Penn State Board of Trustees Minutes, 25 January 1921, Penn State University Archives; Michael Bezilla, *Penn State: An Illustrated History* (University Park: Penn State University Press, 1985), 103–11; and "Brochure for Emergency Building Fund, 1922," Scott Etter Papers, Box 04961, Folder "1918–1924, Emergency Building Fund Inaugurated by Thomas," Penn State University Archives.

31. "State College Head Boosts Hugo Bezdek," newspaper clipping, 1921, HBMC Scrapbook 9, 1921 Season, Penn State University Archives.

32. At the end of the 1921 football season, Bezdek was paid $9,500 by the Athletic Association and $4,500 by Penn State College while Thomas a year later was paid $12,000. The mean salary of Penn State professors in 1925 was $3,600 with a maximum salary of a full professor being $4,600. It took until the late 1950s for any full professor to approach Bezdek's salary in 1921. See Athletic Association Alumni Advisory Committee Minutes, 23 November 1921, Intercollegiate Athletics Records, Box AJo6.12, Binder, 1913–1925, Penn State University Archives, Penn State Board of Trustees Executive Committee Minutes, 23 August 1923, and "The Pennsylvania State University Mean Salary by Academic Ranks," President Walker Papers, Box Ao5.12, Folder "Salary Information 1925–1956," Penn State University Archives. Bezdek was also given a $2,000 bonus following the undefeated 1921 season.

33. John M. Thomas, "Why I Believe in Football," *Third Corps Area Gazette,* vol. 1, no. 7 (October 19223), Ronald Smith Collection, Box 9310, Folder "Penn State Athletics," Penn State University Archives.

34. *Penn State Alumni News*, December 1922, p. 3.

35. Penn State Board of Trustees Executive Committee Minutes, 23 October 1924, Penn State University Archives. When the Carnegie Foundation for the Advancement of Teaching concluded its highly visible *American College Athletics* (New York: Carnegie Foundation for the Advancement of Teaching, 1929), Penn State topped the list of athletic-scholarship-granting institutions. By that time, however, Penn State had dropped all 75 of its scholarships under President Hetzel.

36. *Penn State Collegian*, 9 January 1923, p. 1.

37. "Notes on Athletic Board Minutes," Ridge H. Riley Papers, Box 1, Folder 16, Penn State University Archives and Michael Bezilla, *Penn State: An Illustrated History* (University Park: Penn State University Press, 1985), 118–19.

38. Penn State Board of Trustees Minutes, 24 September 1926, Penn State University Archives.

39. Howard J. Savage and others, *American College Athletics* (New York: Carnegie Foundation for the Advancement of Teaching, 1929), 256. Some other Pennsylvania colleges giving out athletic scholarships noted by the Carnegie Report were Geneva, Gettysburg, Lebanon Valley, Muhlenberg, and Ursinus. Penn State had the most.

40. Board of Athletic Control Minutes, 20 April 1937, Intercollegiate Athletics Records, Box AJo6.12, Binder, 1931–1950, Penn State University Archives.

41. As quoted by Bob Wilson, "Rambling Thru," *State College Times,* 19 November 1940, Ridge H. Riley Papers, Box 04.24, Folder 20, Penn State University Archives.

42. Higgins won 63 percent of his games (97 wins and 57 losses), but in his last decade of coaching his record was 62 wins and only 17 losses, or 78 percent. The strength of

schedule was not severe, with many games against such schools as Bucknell, Colgate, Lehigh, Muhlenberg, and New York University.

43. Ralph D. Hetzel, "Alumni Council Dinner," 2 November 1934, President Hetzel Papers, Box AU05.22, Folder "Speeches & Statements," Penn State University Archives.

44. From 1940 to 1945, Penn state won 9 and lost only 6 to the four named schools.

45. The alumni group James Beaver White Committee, which recommended abolishing athletic scholarships, reported its recommendations to James Milholland. James Beaver White to James Milholland, Penn State Alumni Association, 26 February 1927, John Oswald Papers, Box 10290, Folder "Athletics Relating to Academics, Admission, Policies, Etc 1979–1982," Penn State University Archives.

46. Penn State Board of Trustees Executive Committee Minutes, 30 July 1948 and 5 December 1958, Penn State University Archives. NCAA *Proceedings* (10 January 1948), 188–96; *New York Times*, 17 April 1948, p. 18. There were 100 athletic scholarships by 1949 and 250 by 1958.

47. "Lions' Eisenhower Favors Subsidies," Philadelphia newspaper clipping, 1 March 1951, President Eisenhower Papers, Box AR01.02, Folder "ME-Newspaper Articles-Penn State," 10 January 1951–10 November 1952, Penn State University Archives.

48. Milton Eisenhower, "Summary of the Report to Alumni on 'The State of the College,'" 14 June 1952, President Eisenhower Papers, Box AR01.02, Folder "ME Addresses, June 14, 1952–November 11, 1952," Penn State University Archives.

49. Ray H. Smith, "Evolution of Physical Education at the Pennsylvania State College Including Alumni Participation," 20 January 1932, College of Health, Physical Education and Recreation Papers, No. 04448, Box 1, Folder "College of H.P.E.R. Athletic Comm. of the Senate, 1922–1951," Penn State University Archives; Athletic Association Minutes Binder, 26 September 1907 and 14 December 1907, Intercollegiate Athletics Records, Box AJ06.12, Penn State University Archives; George R. Meek, "Graduate Manager's Statement of Football Account, Season of 1908," *State Collegian*, 1 April 1909; and *Free Lance*, 12 December 1907, p. 1. Neil Fleming was graduate manager for 33 years before Harold R. "Ike" Gilbert succeeded him in 1949. President Hetzel had recommended in 1947 that the graduate manager be provided with an office in Recreation Building for closer coordination between the graduate manager and the School of Physical Education and Athletics, one month before he died of a stroke. See Penn State Board of Trustees Executive Committee Minutes, 5 September 1947, Penn State University Archives.

50. Don Enders, "Ernest B. McCoy and Intercollegiate Athletics at the Pennsylvania State University, 1952–1969," M.S. thesis, Penn State University, 1973, p. 17.

51. Penn State Board of Trustees Executive Committee Minutes, 27 March 1953, Penn State University Archives.

52. Both Walker and Ernie McCoy supported women's athletics from an early time. Dean McCoy was chair of the NCAA advisory committee to cooperate with women "in efforts to expand such programs." College of Physical Education and Athletics Executive Committee Minutes, 22 January 1968, College of Health, Physical Education and Recreation Papers, 04448, Box 1, Folder "Col. of HPER Executive Comm, 1967–1968," Penn State University Archives.

53. Bezilla, *Penn State*, 263–65.

54. Eric A. Walker, memo to Chet Gnatt, 15 February 1970, President Walker Papers, Box 04.14, Binder "Personal Reminiscences," Penn State University Archives.

55. Eric A. Walker, "Penn State: Its Growth Under My Management," ca. 1971, President Walker Papers, Box 04.14, Binder "Personal Reminiscences," Penn State University Archives.

56. Eric A. Walker, "Presidency," ca. 1971, President Walker Papers, Box 04.14, Binder "Personal Reminiscences," Penn State University Archives.

57. Eric Walker believed that Ralph Hetzel "favored intramural games over intercollegiate sports." Under Walker's administration, "Our university was known for producing winning big-time football teams without compromising academic or ethical standards." Eric A. Walker, *Now It's My Turn: Engineering My Way* (Great Barrington, MA: Vantage Press, 1989), 177.

58. Athletic Advisory Board Minutes, 5 May 1959, College of Health, Physical Education and Recreation Papers, No. 04448, Box 1, Folder "Col. of HPER Athletic Comm. of Senate, 1957–1975," Penn State University Archives. Among the Athletic Advisory Board members were President Walker, Trustee B. C. "Casey" Jones, Ernie McCoy, and Ed Czekaj.

59. "Athletic Candidates Submitted to J. W. Oswald for 1980 Admission," President Oswald Papers, Box 10290, Folder "Athletics Relating to Academics, Admission, Policies, Etc. 1979–1982–1," Penn State University Archives. One presidential admit, Kevin Baugh, starred in the 1982 season and the Sugar Bowl victory over the University of Georgia for Paterno's first national championship team.

60. Douglas S. Looney, "A Lot of People Think I'm Phony," *Sports Illustrated*, 52 (17 March 1980), 45, Joe Paterno Vertical File, Folder "No Name," Penn State University Archives.

61. Penn State Alumni Records response to a telephone request, 20 September 2013.

62. Niccolò Machiavelli, chapter 18, "Concerning the Way in Which Princes Should Keep Faith," *The Prince,* http://www.constitution.org/mac/prince18.htm.

63. Walter Byers, *Unsportsmanlike Conduct: Exploiting College Athletes* (Ann Arbor: University of Michigan Press, 1995), 109.

64. Bryce Jordan, President Emeritus, "Paper on Athletics," ca. 1990, President Jordan Papers, Box 10400, Folder, "Presidential Control," Penn State University Archives.

65. *Intercollegiate Athletics: Choices for Reform* (Washington, DC: James Harvey, September 1990), p. 14, 19, 32. President Jordan Papers, Box 10400, Folder, "Presidential Control," Penn State University Archives.

66. Joe Paterno, "Score on the SAT to Score on the Field," *Wall Street Journal*, 16 March 1999, Joe Paterno Vertical File, Folder "2000s," Penn State University Archives.

67. Joseph V. Paterno to President John Oswald, 16 May 1972, Ridge H. Riley Papers, Box 03.01, Folder 24, Penn State University Archives.

Chapter 3. A Joe Paterno–Jerry Sandusky Connection

1. Joe Paterno to Charles Theokas, Temple University Athletic Director, 6 December 1988, Joe Paterno Papers, Box 07574, Folder "Recommendations 1970–1980," Penn State University Archives. Emphasis is mine.

2. Joe Paterno draft letter to Charles Theokas, Temple University Athletic Director, 6 December 1988, Joe Paterno Papers, Box 07574, Folder "Recommendations 1970–1980," Penn State University Archives.

3. Charlie Theokas, in an interview in 2011, admitted that Sandusky turned down the offer to coach Temple after meeting with Theokas and President Peter Liacouras in both State College and Philadelphia because of Temple's poor football facilities. Matt Breen, "Temple Wanted to Hire Sandusky in 1988," Philly.com, 11 November 2011, http://articles.philly.com/2011-11-11/sports/'30387537_1-second-mile-foundation-temple-athletic-director-jerry-sandusky.

4. Paterno had written a letter of high praise for Sandusky two weeks before his second national championship when Penn State beat Miami of Florida. In a letter to a local insurance agent supporting a humanitarian award for Sandusky, Paterno wrote, "His character and personal life-style is extraordinary." Further, in regard to The Second Mile, Paterno wrote, "Jerry is a humble man of great integrity and is only interested in what he can do for others, not what others can do for him." Paterno to John Walizer, State Farm Insurance Company, State College, 22 December 1986, Joe Paterno Papers, Box 07574, Folder "Recommendations 1970–1980," Penn State University Archives.

5. See, for example, "The Paterno Report: Critique of the Freeh Report," *Centre Daily Times*, 11 February 2013, which quotes the Paterno Report as stating, "The two men despised each other from the start. This was well-known among those who knew Joe Paterno and Jerry Sandusky." Joe Posnanski, in his book *Paterno* (New York: Simon and Schuster, 2012), 247–48, states that "the two were never close" and "clashed for many years."

6. See, for instance, Paterno to Andy Geiger, Stanford University Athletic Director, 14 December 1988, Joe Paterno Papers, Box 07574, "Recommendations 1970–1980," Penn State University Archives, in which he called assistant coach Ron Dickerson a "strong family man" with "marvelous personal habits."

7. The one exception might be George Welsh, an assistant coach under Paterno from 1973 to 1981, who had a 55-46-1 record at Navy before going to Virginia in the Atlantic Coast Conference, where in 19 years he compiled a 189-132-4 record.

8. I. P. McCreary, class of 1882, Erie, PA, to Mr. Sullivan, undated, ca. 1923, "Story of the 1881 and 1887 Teams," *Penn State Alumni News*, 10 (December 1923), 10–12. The White quote appears on p. 11.

9. The rule book used by the Penn State athletes in 1881 is found in the Penn State Archives: *Latest Revised Rules for Lacrosse, Foot Ball, Ten Pins, and Shuffleboard* (New York: Peck and Snyder, 1879), MSVF XXX-0056U, Penn State University Archives.

10. The 1936 Penn State Board of Athletic Control finally recognized the 1881 football team as having played Penn State's first football game. The board purchased a gold football and an "S" sweater for each member of the 1881 football team and presented them to the players during the 1936 Varsity Club dinner. See Board of Athletic Control Minutes, 13 March 1936 and 6 June 1936, Intercollegiate Athletics Records, Box AJ06.12, Binder "1931–1950," Penn State University Archives.

11. *Latest Revised Rules*.

12. McGill University in Montreal, Canada, first introduced rugby to Harvard in 1874. Harvard liked the game better than its own style of football, and within a year played Tufts College in the first U.S. intercollegiate rugby game. Ronald A. Smith, *Sports and Freedom: The Rise of Big-Time College Athletics* (New York: Oxford University Press, 1988), 74–76.

13. McCreary to Sullivan, 11.

14. McCreary to Sullivan, 10.

15. McCreary to Sullivan, 11. There was no statistical scoring for touchdowns, goals from the field, goals after touchdown, or safeties. That first occurred in 1883. See David M. Nelson, *The Anatomy of a Game: Football, the Rules, and the Men Who Made the Game* (Newark: University of Delaware Press, 1994), 443–44. See an early historical account of the game in Ken Rappoport, *The Nittany Lions: A Story of Penn State Football* (Huntsville, AL: Strode, 1973), 16–19.

16. *Free Lance*, April 1887, p. 3 and p. 5. For rugby football's transformation into American football in the 1880s, see Ronald A. Smith, "The Americanization of Rugby Football: Mass

Plays, Brutality, and Masculinity," in *Sports and Freedom: The Rise of Big-Time College Athletics* (New York: Oxford University Press, 1988), 83–98.

17. *Free Lance,* November 1887, p. 59, and December 1887, p. 70.

18. Louis Prato, *The Penn State Football Encyclopedia* (Champaign, IL: Sports Publishing, 1998), 28–29.

19. "Lewisburg, Centre & Spring Creek Railroad Minutes, 1879–1913," and "Bellefonte, Nittany and Lemont Railroad Minutes, 1879–1913," MG 286, Box 165, Pennsylvania Archives, Harrisburg; and *Democratic Watchman,* 24 July 1885, p. 8.

20. Prato, *Penn State Football Encyclopedia,* p. 29.

21. Nelson, *Anatomy of a Game,* p. 51.

22. Charles H. Brown, *Penn State Centennial Histories* (bound typescript, ca. 1953), LD4481.P82.B76, 1953, Penn State University Archives.

23. Louis E. Reber, "Recollections of the Pennsylvania State College, 1876–1907," Louis E. Reber Vertical File, Penn State University Archives; and Michael Bezilla, *Penn State: An Illustrated History* (University Park: Penn State University Press, 1985), 31–35.

24. Penn State Board of Trustees Executive Committee Minutes, 14 December 1888, Penn State University Archives.

25. Charles C. Hildebrand, Philadelphia, to Ridge Riley, Penn State Alumni Association, 30 October 1944, and *Free Lance,* December 1889, in Ridge H. Riley Papers, Box 04.24, Folders 12 and 13, Penn State University Archives; and James C. Mock to James H Coogan, University Park, 22 October 1951, Scott Etter Papers, Box 04961, Folder "Lavies," Penn State University Archives. Penn State had only nine players available and borrowed two from Lehigh's second team. Lehigh's Snake Ames, who later starred at Princeton "scored at will and often."

26. *Free Lance,* September 1890, April 1891, and June 1891.

27. Erwin W. Runkle, "The Pennsylvania State College, 1853–1932," unpublished manuscript, pp. 319–20, LD4481.P82/1933, Penn State University Archives.

28. Scott Etter, "From Atherton to Hetzel: A History of Intercollegiate Athletic Control at the Pennsylvania State College, 1887–1930," Ph.D. dissertation, Penn State University, 1991, pp. 54–56; *Free Lance,* October 1891, p. 70; and Prato, *Penn State Football Encyclopedia,* 36.

29. The trainer or coach participating in games was not particularly unusual in the 1890s at other institutions, since there were no systematized eligibility rules. For instance, the famous Amos Alonzo Stagg, a tenured faculty member and coach at the University of Chicago, played with the team in a game against Northwestern in 1892. Robin Lester, *Stagg's University: The Rise, Decline, and Fall of Big-Time Football at the University of Chicago* (Urbana: University of Illinois Press, 1995), 22.

30. Etter, "From Atherton to Hetzel," Ph. D. dissertation, Penn State University, 1991, pp. 56–58.

31. Etter, "From Atherton to Hetzel," p. 64; and Prato, *Penn State Football Encyclopedia,* 468.

32. *Free Lance,* October 1898, pp. 139 and 158, and November 1898, p. 190, as quoted in Etter, "From Atherton to Hetzel," p. 65.

33. Penn State Board of Trustees Executive Committee Minutes, 31 July 1900, Penn State University Archives.

34. Penn State Board of Trustees Executive Committee Minutes, 9 June 1902, Penn State University Archives.

35. Scott C. Etter, "The Golden Rule: Potential and Actual Control of Penn State College Athletics During the Atherton Era, 1882–1906," Exercise Science 444 paper, Spring 1990, Penn State University Archives.

36. Penn State Board of Trustees Executive Committee Minutes, 9 June 1902, Penn State University Archives; and Notes of the Athletic Association Minutes, 7 March 1905, Ridge H. Riley Papers, 04.24, Box 1, Folder 4, Penn State University Archives. The Faculty Committee on Athletics recommended that a scholarship be granted to Dunn "after careful investigation into the character of Mr. Dunn's work and his resources for pursuing a course here." John Paine Jackson, Chair of Faculty Committee on Athletics, to President G. W. Atherton, 21 March 1902, President Atherton Papers, Box 9, Folder "Athletics," Penn State University Archives.

37. Penn State Board of Trustees Executive Committee Minutes, 4 November 1903, Penn State University Archives. Some athletes were housed in the Armory before the Track House was built.

38. Joe Paterno with Bernard Asbell, *Paterno: By the Book* (New York: Random House, 1989), 62, 69, 71.

39. Penn State Board of Trustees Executive Committee Minutes, 15 June 1903 and "Athletics at the Pennsylvania State College," 1903, President Atherton Papers, Box 9, Folder "PSC Athletics & Athletic Scholarships, 1888–1930," Penn State University Archives.

40. Andrew Carnegie agreed to build a Penn State library if Penn State would pay for its upkeep, and to do so, the Board of Trustees charged a $3 per year library fee for each student. *Penn State Collegian*, 3 November 1910, p. 1.

41. Etter, "From Atherton to Hetzel," p. 72.

42. Etter, "From Atherton to Hetzel," pp. 72–73.

43. As quoted by Etter, "From Atherton to Hetzel," pp. 74, 75–76.

44. Prato, *Penn State Football Encyclopedia*, 73–74.

45. Joe Paterno's predecessor, Rip Engle, had a slightly better winning percentage in his 16 years at Penn State than did Paterno, with a 104-48-4 record, a 68 percent record. He never had a losing season.

46. *Penn State Collegian*, 1 April 1909, p. 9; and Alumni Advisory Committee to President of the Athletic Association, 14 July 1910, Athletic Association Alumni Athletic Advisory Committee Minutes Binder, "1913–1915," Intercollegiate Athletics Records, Box AJ06.12, Penn State University Archives.

47. *Penn State Alumni News*, 22, no. 10 (July 1925), 18–19.

48. Penn State Board of Trustees Executive Committee Minutes, 21 November 1912 and 9 June 1913, Penn State University Archives.

49. Murray Sperber, *Shake Down the Thunder: The Creation of Notre Dame Football* (New York: Henry Holt, 1993), 58.

50. William A. Maloney, Notre Dame Secretary, to Father Cavanaugh, 1 December 1915, President Burns Papers, UPBU, Box 43, Folder "Athletics," University of Notre Dame Archives.

51. Penn State Board of Trustees Executive Committee Minutes, 27 September 1918, Penn State University Archives.

52. "Quoting Joe: Paterno in His Own Words," *Town and Gown* (December 2000), 34.

Chapter 4. Alumni and Taking Control of Penn State Athletics

1. Eileen Morgan and Ray Blehar, "Join Our Peaceful March4Truth.com Today @ 3:30 PM, BOT Mtg, Outside the Penn Stater. Why? Because the Truth Matters," *Centre Daily Times*, 20 September 2013, p. B8.

2. "Penn State Alma Mater," http://en.wikipidia.org/wiki/penn_state_alma-mater; and George W. Atherton to F. L. Pattee, 16 May 1906, Fred Lewis Pattee Papers, Box 2, Folder 1, Penn State University Archives.

3. Morgan and Blehar, "Join Our Peaceful March4Truth.com," p. B8.

4. For example, when Penn State tied undefeated Harvard 13–13 in 1914, the *Penn State Alumni Quarterly* quickly reported that Penn State students greeted the returning heroes with a massive bonfire. Unfortunately, the five gallons of gasoline poured onto the wooden heap exploded, burning the Penn State captain, Elza "Yegg" Tobin, and blew out windows on the college buildings and a fraternity house. "The Harvard Game," *Penn State Alumni Quarterly*, 5 (October 1914), 28–32.

5. See the *Alumni Quarterly*, 3 (October 1912), and the *Penn Stater*, 100 (September–October, 2012).

6. *Centre Daily Times*, 5 May 2012, p. A1, A3; and *Penn State News*, 9 May 2014, http://news.psu.edu/story/315378.

7. *A Collection of College Words and Customs* (Cambridge, MA: J. Bartlett, 1851), 7. Columbia College formed an alumni society in 1829, Rutgers in 1837, Harvard in 1841, and Georgia in 1834. Yale started class reunions as early as 1824. Lyman Bagg, *Four Years at Yale* (New York: Henry Holt, 1871), 535. Daniel J. Boorstein, "Universities in the Republic of Letters," *Perspectives in American History*, 1 (1967), 369–79, called upon education historians to look at the influence of alumni on supporting and controlling universities. He suggested that the topic "the role of college 'amateur' athletics in enlisting support for institutions—is still to be chronicled." p. 376. Marilyn Tobias, *Old Dartmouth on Trial* (New York: New York University Press, 1982), p. 98, suggested "the alumni saw themselves as a group apart, a collegiate faction seeking status, influence, and power."

8. Guy M. Lewis, "America's First Intercollegiate Sport: The Regattas from 1852–1875," *Research Quarterly*, 38 (December 1967), 641.

9. *Boston Evening Transcript*, 28 September 1907, p. 2.

10. Athletic Association Minutes Binder, 14 December 1907, Intercollegiate Athletics Records, Box AJo6.12, Penn State University Archives.

11. *Report of the President of Harvard College, 1900–1901*, Harvard University Archives, p. 19; and Ronald A. Smith, "Far More Than Commercialism: Stadium Building from Harvard's Innovations to Stanford's 'Dirt Bowl,'" *International Journal of the History of Sport*, 25 (September 2008), 1453–74.

12. Charles W. Eliot, "Commencement—The Alumni Dinner," *Harvard Graduates' Magazine*, 12 (September 1903), 57–59.

13. Roger L. Geiger, educational historian, noted in his *To Advance Knowledge* (New York: Oxford University Press, 1986), p. 54, that "Athletic teams became the focus of alumni interests as was seen in alumni publications" and that fund raising for athletics predated organized university fund raising.

14. Michael Bezilla, *Penn State: An Illustrated History* (University Park: Penn State University Press, 1985), 20.

15. *Free Lance*, February 1894, p. 108.

16. Athletic Association Minutes, 12 May 1898, 7 June 1898, and 8 May 1899, Intercollegiate Athletics Records, Box AJo6.12, Binder 1896–1905, Penn State University Archives.

17. *Free Lance*, May 1897, p. 53, February 1899, p. 299, and June 1899, pp. 81–82.

18. J. Price Jackson to President George Atherton, 12 January 1900, President Atherton Papers, Box 9, Folder "G Athletics," Penn State University Archives.

19. J. Price Jackson to President George Atherton, 12 January 1900, President Atherton Papers, Box 9, Folder "G Athletics," Penn State University Archives; Penn State Board of Trustees Executive Committee Minutes, 31 July 1900; and Scott C. Etter, "The Golden Rule: Potential and Actual Control of Penn State College Athletics During the Atherton Era, 1882–1906," Exercise Science 444 Paper, Spring 1990, Penn State University Archives.

20. Montague Shearman, *Athletics and Football* (London, England: Longmans, Green, 1894), 241. At Harvard, William Hooper was appointed graduate treasurer in 1889. Harvard Athletic Committee Minutes, 12 December 1889, p. 246, Harvard University Archives; and John W. White, Chair of the Athletic Committee, Annual Report, 1889–1990, to President C. W. Eliot, ca. March 1891, UAI.5.150, Box 262, Folder "1891-Jan-May," Harvard University Archives. Harvard did not appoint an athletic director until 1926 when Bill Bingham was chosen. At Yale, Walter Camp became the graduate treasurer of the Financial Union, running Yale athletics. Eugene L. Richards, "Intercollegiate Athletics and Faculty Control," *Outing*, 26 (July 1895), 325–28. Princeton formed its Graduate Advisory Committee in 1885 to help give experience to undergraduates. Frank Presbrey and James Moffatt, *Athletics at Princeton* (New York: Frank Presbrey, 1901), 15.

21. "Athletics and Physical Education at The Pennsylvania State College," ca. 1930, Ridge H. Riley Papers, Box 04.24, Folder 18, Penn State University Archives.

22. *State Collegian*, 7 May 1908, p. 4.

23. Board of Trustees Executive Committee Minutes, 31 July 1900, Penn State University Archives.

24. Athletic Association Minutes Binder, undated, ca. 1913, Intercollegiate Athletics Records, Box AJ06.12, Penn State University Archives.

25. "George R. Meek '90," Ridge H. Riley Papers, Box 04.24, Folder 4, Penn State University Archives; and Jackie R. Esposito and Steven L. Herb, *The Nittany Lion* (University Park: Penn State University Press, 1997), 16.

26. Athletic Association Minutes Binder, 14 December 1907, Intercollegiate Athletics Records, Box AJ06.12, Penn State University Archives.

27. University Faculty Senate Minutes, Box AN05.12, Folder "1908," Penn State University Archives.

28. Bezilla, *Penn State*, 78.

29. George Meek, "Graduate Manager's Statement of Football Account, Season of 1908," *Penn State Collegian*, 1 April 1909, pp. 1–2.

30. Alumni Advisory Committee to President of the Athletic Association, 14 July 1910, Athletic Association Alumni Athletic Advisory Committee Minutes binder, 1913–1925, Intercollegiate Athletics Records, Box AJ06.12, Penn State University Archives.

31. Alumni Advisory Committee to President of the Athletic Association, 14 July 1910.

32. Action by the trustees was taken on 9 June 1913. "Athletics and Physical Education at the Pennsylvania State College," ca. 1932, Ridge H. Riley Papers, Box 04.24, Folder 18, Penn State University Archives.

33. "Athletics and Physical Education."

34. Alumni Advisory Committee to President of the Athletic Association, 8 June 1914, Athletic Association Alumni Advisory Committee Minutes binder, 1913–1925, Intercollegiate Athletic Records, Box AJ06.12, Penn State University Archives.

35. *Penn State Collegian*, 10 December 1913, p. 2.

36. Robert Patterson, former vice president for finance and business, interview with Jonathan B. Wanderstock, 1 April 1992, in Jonathan B. Wanderstock, "The 1980 Realign-

ment of the Penn State Athletic Program or the Quarterback Sneak: The Untold Story of Joe Paterno's Consolidation of Power," Exercise Science 444 paper, 18 April 1992, Penn State University Archives.

37. Alumni Advisory Committee Minutes, 15 June 1915 and 15 June 1916, Athletic Association Alumni Advisory Committee Minutes Binder, 1913–1925, Intercollegiate Athletics Records, Box AJ06.12, Penn State University Archives.

38. *Penn State Collegian*, 21 February 1917, p. 1, 4.

39. "BSD," "Penn State Legends: Dick Harlow," 24 June 2010, *Black Shoe Diaries,* http://www.blackshoediaries.com/2010/6/24/1529233.

40. Ray H. Smith to C. W. Heppenstall, Pittsburgh, 6 December 1917; George R. Meek to Ray H. Smith, 10 December 1917, Heppenstall to Smith, 10 December 1917, and Smith to Heppenstall, 18 December 1917, Athletic Association Alumni Advisory Committee Minutes binder, 1913–1925, Intercollegiate Athletics Records, Box AJ06.12, Penn State University Archives.

41. Gregory Kordic, *A Damn Good Yankee: Zen Scott and the Rise of the Crimson Tide* (Bloomington, IN: Author House, 2007), 66–73.

42. The Pittsburgh Penn State alumni wanted to establish athletic scholarships as memorials to both Levi Lamb and James "Red" Bebout shortly after the war. Athletic Association Alumni Athletic Advisory Committee Minutes binder, 1913–1925, 4 October 1919, Intercollegiate Athletics Records, Box AJ06.12, Penn State University Archives.

43. *Penn State Alumni News*, December 1918, p. 2.

44. Levi Lamb, France, to Ray Smith, editor of the *Penn State Alumni Quarterly*, May 1918, "Letter from the Front," *Penn State Alumni Quarterly*, 8 (April–July 1918), 167.

45. Don Enders, "Ernest B. McCoy and Intercollegiate Athletics at the Pennsylvania State University 1952–1969," M.S. thesis, Penn State University, 1973; and Athletic Advisory Board Minutes, 5 March 1954, Intercollegiate Athletics Records, Box AJ06.12, Binder 1951–1959, Penn State University Archives.

46. Athletic Association Alumni Advisory Committee Minutes, 16 July 1918 and 25 August 1918, Intercollegiate Athletics Records, Box AJ06.12, Binder 1913–1925, Penn State University Archives.

47. These events are detailed in chapter 5.

48. Earl of Chesterfield to his son Philip Stanhope, 22 February 1748, in Earl of Chesterfield, *Letters to His Son* (London: J. Dodaley, 1775), 321.

Chapter 5. Hugo Bezdek's Saga—Alumni, Trustees, and Presidents

1. "Pennsylvania State College Personnel Record, Hugo Bezdek," 17 May 1923, ABUF, Hugo Bezdek File, Penn State University Archives; Tim Cohane, "Hugo Bezdek: Hugo the Victor," in his *Great College Football Coaches of the Twenties and Thirties* (New Rochelle, NY: Arlington House, 1973), 20–25; David L. Porter, ed., *Biographical Dictionary of American Sports: Football* (Westport, CT: Greenwood Press, 1987), 45–46; and Lou Prato, *The Penn State Football Encyclopedia* (Champaign, IL: Sports Publishing, 1998), 102–5.

2. Board of Trustees Executive Committee Minutes, 27 September 1918, "Notes on Athletic Board Minutes," Ridge H. Riley Papers, Box 1, Folder 16; and Athletic Association Alumni Athletic Advisory Committee Minutes Binder, 1913–1925, 22 December 1918 minutes, Intercollegiate Athletics Records, Box AJ06.12, Penn State University Archives; and *Penn State Alumni News*, December 1918, p. 2.

3. Board of Trustees Executive Committee Minutes, 27 September 1918, "Notes on Athletic Board Minutes," Ridge H. Riley Papers, Box 1, Folder 16; and Alumni Advisory Committee Minutes, 16 July 1918 and 22 December 1918, Intercollegiate Athletics Records, Box AJ06.12, Penn State University Archives.

4. "Taped interview with Dutch Hermann, 1972," Ridge H. Riley Papers, Box 1, Folder 16, Penn State University Archives. Hermann was on the history faculty and head coach of basketball from the 1910s until the 1930s.

5. "Interview with J. S. 'Tiny' McMahon, 21 June 1973," Ridge H. Riley Papers, Box 04.24, Folder 7, Penn State University Archives.

6. "Notes on Athletic Board Minutes," Ridge H. Riley Papers, Box 1, Folder 16, Penn State University Archives.

7. Harvard Athletic Committee Minutes, 25 October 1920, Harvard University Archives; and Charles W. Kennedy, Chair, Princeton Athletic Association, to Henry Pennypacker, Chair, Harvard Athletic Committee, 9 January 1925, Committee on the Regulation of Athletic Sports, UA.I.10.175.12.1, Folder "January 1925," Harvard University Archives.

8. "Notes on Athletic Board Minutes," Ridge H. Riley Papers, Box 1, Folder 16, Penn State University Archives; and *Penn State Alumni News*, June 1920, p. 5.

9. Harvard Corporation Minutes, 25 September 1922, Harvard University Archives. The Law School's Roscoe Pound received $10,500 and Felix Frankfurter $7,500, and the famous historian Frederick Jackson Turner was at $8,000.

10. "Notes on Athletic Board Minutes."

11. John M. Thomas, "Why I Believe in Football," *Third Corps Area Gazette*, 1, no. 7 (October 1923), Ronald Smith Collection, Box 9310, Folder "Penn State Athletics," Penn State University Archives; *Penn State Alumni News*, 9 (December 1922), p. 3.

12. Michael Bezilla, *Penn State: An Illustrated History* (University Park: Penn State University Press, 1985), 103–19.

13. "State College Head Boosts Hugo Bezdek," newspaper clipping, 1921, HBMC Scrapbook 9, 1921 Season, Penn State University Archives.

14. "Hugo Will Stick with Penn State," *Penn State Alumni News*, 9 (December 1922), 5; "University Makes Offer to Bezdek to be Grid Coach," newspaper clipping, ca. December 1921, and "Bezdek Considered for 'U' Coach," *Minnesota Daily*, 13 January 1922, p. 1, Bezdek Papers, Box GSTA/A/02.33, Scrapbook Football Season 1922, Penn State University Archives; and Sara A. Hartman, Penn State Women's Student Government Association, to Hugo Bezdek, 3 December 1922, Bezdek Papers, Box GSTA/A/0233, Scrapbook Football Season 1922, Penn State University Archives.

15. Sol Metzger, "Everybody Playing at Penn State," *Outing*, 75 (October 1919), 17–20.

16. "Athletics and Physical Education at The Pennsylvania State College," 20 January 1932, Ridge H. Riley Papers, Box 04.24, Folder 18, Penn State University Archives; "Annual Report of Alumni Athletic Advisory Committee," Athletic Association Alumni Association Minutes, 10 June 1921, Intercollegiate Athletics Records, Box AJ06.12, Binder "1913–1925," Penn State University Archives; *Penn State Collegian*, 16 September 1921, p. 1; Penn State Board of Trustees Executive Committee Minutes, 23 January 1923, Penn State University Archives; "The Members of the Committee of Board of Trustees on the Department of Physical Education," Hugo Bezdek Report, 1919, Ridge H. Riley Papers, Box 1, Folder 18, Penn State University Archives; Jeff Byers, "Building a Foundation: Penn State Athletics in the Early 1920s," Exercise Science 444 paper, 30 April 1990, Penn State University Archives; and Athletic Association Alumni Advisory Committee Minutes, undated, ca. 1925,

Intercollegiate Athletics Records, Box AJo6.12, Binder "1913–1925," Penn State University Archives.

17. *Pittsburg[h] Dispatch* clipping, HBMC Scrapbook 9, 1921 Season, Penn State University Archives.

18. Glenn Killinger to Ridge Riley, 4 September 1973, Ridge H. Riley Papers, Box 1, Folder 16, Penn State University Archives.

19. Hinkey Haines, Penn Wynne, PA, to Ridge Riley, 29 May 1974, Ridge H. Riley Papers, Box 04.24, Folder 7, Penn State University Archives.

20. "Interview with Joe Bedenk," 8 August 1973, Ridge H. Riley Papers, Box 04.24, Folder 20, Penn State University Archives.

21. "Taped Interview with Dutch Hermann, 1972," Ridge H. Riley Papers, Box 1, Folder 16, Penn State University Archives. Stated Hermann, "Most of them were disgruntled because they hadn't gotten letters after the 1921 season when they thought they deserved them."

22. Tim Cohane, *Great College Football Coaches of the Twenties and Thirties* (New Rochelle, NY: Arlington House, 1973), 77–81; and David L. Porter, ed., *Biographical Dictionary of American Sports: Football* (Westport, CT: Greenwood Press, 1987), 242–43.

23. "Notes on Athletic Board Minutes"; and Athletic Association Alumni Advisory Committee Minutes, 21 October 1922 and 9 December 1922, Intercollegiate Athletics Records, Box AJo6.12, Binder "1913–1925," Penn State University Archives.

24. *Penn State Collegian*, 13 February 1923, p. 2; and Tom Verducci, "Penn State in the 1923 Rose Bowl: An Unlikely Finding to a Strange Season," Physical Education 441 paper, 2 November 1981, Penn State University Archives. Verducci eventually became a senior writer for *Sports Illustrated*.

25. "Athletic Relations at College," *Penn State Alumni News*, 13 (May 1927), 3–7; and Glenn Moore, "'We'll Get the Lion's Share': The Interrelationship of Football, Status, and Education at Penn State in the Late 1920's," Exercise Science 444 paper, 27 April 1990, Penn State University Archives.

26. Hugo Bezdek to President Abbott L. Lowell, 4 May 1926, and Lowell to Bezdek, 8 May 1926, President A. Lawrence Lowell Papers, Box U&AI5.160, 1925–28, Folder 72, Harvard University Archives. See also the Hugo Bezdek Vertical File, Penn State University Archives. Bill Bingham became Harvard Athletic Director on 4 January 1926 at $8,000 per year. He would chair the Athletic Committee and be a faculty member of Arts and Sciences at Harvard. Harvard Corporation Minutes, 4 January 1926, Harvard University Archives.

27. James Beaver White, Beaver White Committee, to James Milholland, President, Penn State Alumni Association, 26 February 1927, John Oswald Papers, Box 10290, Folder "Athletics Relating to Academics, Admission, Policies, Etc 1979–1982," Penn State University Archives. The committee was composed of White, class of 1894, George R. Meek, class of 1890, Boyd Musser, class of 1894, Arthur Mitchell, class of 1901, Emerson Davis, class of 1911, J. Orvis Keller, class of 1914, George Hesselbacher, class of 1916, and Alan Helffrich, class of 1925.

28. Ronald A. Smith, "More Than Commercialism: Stadium Building from Harvard's Innovations to Stanford's 'Dirt Bowl,'" *International Journal of the History of Sport*, 25 (September 2008), 1453–74.

29. Ronald A. Smith, "The 1920s and the Carnegie Report on College Athletics," in his *Pay for Play: A History of Big-Time College Athletic Reform* (Urbana: University of Illinois Press, 2011), 59–70.

30. The report was published in 1929 as *American College Athletics*, edited by Howard J. Savage, Harold W. Bentley, John T. McGovern, and Dean F. Smiley (New York: Carnegie Foundation for the Advancement of Teaching, 1929). It claimed, though not entirely correctly, "Penn State College . . . illustrates absolute alumni control," p. 82.

31. James Beaver White, Beaver White Committee, to James Milholland, President, Penn State Alumni Association, 26 February 1927, John Oswald Papers, Box 10290, Folder "Athletics Relating to Academics, Admission, Policies, Etc 1979–1982," Penn State University Archives.

32. Moore, "Lion's Share."

33. "Athletic Relations at College," *Penn State Alumni News*, 13 (May 1927), 5–7. Even more overwhelmingly, the alumni voted by more than 90 percent to create a new Board of Athletic Control and to separate physical education from athletics. Quite likely some alumni felt that the Board of Trustees should not provide the athletic scholarships as before, and that if athletes were to be financed, it should be done by alumni gifts, as at most institutions.

34. *Penn State Alumni Newsletter*, 13 (June 1927), 9.

35. Nancy C. Foley, "The Elimination of Athletic Subsidies at the University of Pittsburgh, 1936 to 1939," Exercise and Sport Science paper, 27 April 1987, Ronald Smith personal file.

36. Scott Etter, "From Atherton to Hetzel: A History of Intercollegiate Athletic Control at the Pennsylvania State College, 1887–1930," Ph.D. dissertation, Penn State University, 1991, p. 1.

37. G[eorge] A. Doyle and F. R. Clark, President and Secretary of Pittsburgh Penn State Club, to Penn State Board of Trustees, 10 January 1929, Ridge H. Riley Papers, Box 03.01, Folder 38, Penn State University Archives.

38. C[harles] W. Heppenstall, Chair Pittsburgh Alumni, to J. F. Warriner Committee of Board of Trustees, 9 March 1929, John Oswald Papers, Box 10290, Folder "Athletics Relating to Academics, Admission, Policies, Etc 1979–1982," Penn State University Archives.

39. "Analysis of Annual Reports of Penn State Athletic Association," 20 January 1930, Penn State Board of Trustees Executive Committee Minutes, 2 January 1930, Penn State University Archives.

40. Heppenstall to Warriner Committee.

41. J. B. Warriner, W. L. Affelder, and Furman H. Ginger, to Penn State Board of Trustees Executive Committee, 13 July 1929, College of Health, Physical Education and Recreation Papers, Box 1, 04448, Folder "Col. of HPER: Athletic Comm. of the Senate, 1922–1951," Penn State University Archives.

42. President R. D. Hetzel to J. B. Warriner, Lansford, PA, 3 July 1929, John Oswald Papers, Box 10290, Folder "Athletics Relating to Academics, Admission, Policies, Etc 1979–1982," Penn State University Archives.

43. J. B. Warriner to R. D. Hetzel, 6 July 1929, John Oswald Papers, Box 10290, Folder "Athletics Relating to Academics, Admission, Policies, Etc 1979–1982," Penn State University Archives.

44. "Notes of Downfall of Bezdek from Central Files," ca. 1937, Ridge H. Riley Papers, Box 04.24, Folder 18, Penn State University Archives.

45. Board of Trustees Executive Committee Minutes, 20 January 1930, Penn State University Archives.

46. Ridge Riley, "The Role of the Administration in the Development of Physical Education and Athletics at the Pennsylvania State University" paper, Ridge H. Riley Papers,

Box 04.24, Folder 18, Penn State University Archives; and Jack M. Infield, "The Development of the Physical Education and Athletic Policies at the Pennsylvania State University, 1926–1952," Physical Education 495 paper, Winter 1973, Penn State University Archives.

47. Board of Trustees Executive Committee Minutes, 20 January 1930, Penn State University Archives.

Chapter 6. *The Great Experiment That Failed*

1. For a fuller discussion of the background and influence of the Carnegie Report, see Ronald A. Smith, *Pay for Play: A History of Big-Time College Athletic Reform* (Urbana: University of Illinois Press, 2011), 59–70.

2. *New York Times*, 30 March 1925, p. 6.

3. *New York Times*, 24 May 1926, p. 10.

4. Howard J. Savage, Harold W. Bentley, John T. McGovern, and Dean F. Smiley, eds., *American College Athletics* (New York: Carnegie Foundation for the Advancement of Teaching, 1929), xv.

5. James Beaver White, Beaver White Committee, to James Milholland, Penn State Alumni Association, 26 February 1927, John Oswald Papers, Box 10290, Folder "Athletics Relating to Academics, Admission, Policies, Etc 1979–1982," Penn State University Archives; and "Athletic Relations at College," *Penn State Alumni News*, 13 (May 1927), 3–7.

6. Board of Trustees Executive Committee Minutes, 16 March 1928, 20 September 1929, and 27 March 1930, Penn State University Archives and "Bob Higgins New Coach," *Penn State Alumni News*, 16 (April 1930), 12.

7. Ronald A. Smith, *Play-by-Play: Radio, Television, and Big-Time College Sport* (Baltimore: Johns Hopkins University Press, 2001) 51.

8. Rea Read, Waynesburg College librarian, Waynesburg College, e-mail to Ron Smith, 21 October 2013. According to Read there were 38 seniors, 40 juniors, 73 sophomores, and 78 freshmen—a total of 229 men and women in 1930.

9. Casey Jones, Punta Gorda, FL, to Ridge Riley, 13 August 1973, Ridge H. Riley Papers, Box 04.24, Folder 20, Penn State University Archives.

10. "Alumni Nominees for the Board of Trustees, Biographical Sketches, 1969," Ridge H. Riley Papers, Box 04.24, Folder 20, Penn State University Archives.

11. Casey Jones to Ridge Riley, 18 August 1973, Ridge H. Riley Papers, Box 04.24, Folder 20, Penn State University Archives.

12. Nancy C. Foley, "The Elimination of Athletic Subsidies at the University of Pittsburgh 1936 to 1939," Exercise and Sport Science 444 paper, 27 April 1987, Penn State University Archives.

13. In eastern Pennsylvania, leading recruiters were J. R. Gilligan and the Scranton Club, who decided to recruit athletes to attend Penn State when athletic scholarships were abolished. By 1934, there were ten members of the varsity football team from the Scranton area. "Summary of J. R. Gilligan Statement to Alumni Council," 2 November 1934, President Hetzel Papers, Box AU05.22, Folder "Speeches & Statements," Penn State University Archives.

14. Casey Jones to Ridge Riley, 20 August 1973, Ridge H. Riley Papers, Box 04.24, Folder 20, Penn State University Archives.

15. "Interview with Sever Toretti," 27 May 1975, and "Alumni Nominees for the Board of Trustees, Biographical Sketches, 1969," Ridge H. Riley Papers, Box 04.24, Folder 20, Penn State University Archives.

16. Casey Jones to Ridge Riley, 20 August 1973.

17. Casey Jones to Ridge Riley, 20 August 1973. Earle Edwards nearly became head coach. When Bob Higgins retired, he recommended Edwards for the position. When Edwards was not chosen, he soon left Penn State and eventually had a reasonably successful career in coaching for seventeen years at North Carolina State University.

18. Casey Jones to Ridge Riley, 13 August 1973, Ridge H. Riley Papers, Box 04.24, Folder 20, Penn State University Archives.

19. Badger Board of the Junior Class, University of Wisconsin, *The Nineteen Hundred & Six Badger* (Madison, WI: n.p., 1905), 164, 275; and "Press Release, September 25, 1926," President Hetzel Papers, Box AU05.16, Folder "Newsclippings, 1917–1927," Penn State University Archives.

20. *Boston Transcript,* 16 March 1925, clipping, President Hetzel Papers, Box AU05.16, "Scrapbook," p. 73, Penn State University Archives.

21. Quoted in Scott Etter, "From Atherton to Hetzel: A History of Intercollegiate Athletic Control at the Pennsylvania State University, 1887–1930," Ph.D. dissertation, 1991, p. 239.

22. President R. D Hetzel to J. B Warriner, Lansford, PA, 3 July 1929, John Oswald Papers, Box 10290, Folder "Athletics Relating to Academics, Admission, Policies, Etc 1979–1982," Penn State University Archives.

23. See chapter 8 for details of the Paterno, Garban, Oswald coup d'état.

24. Ralph D. Hetzel, "Certain University Programs in the Commonwealth," *Penn State Alumni News,* 18 (January 1932), 4–8, 13, 21–23.

25. JoAnn Welsh, "The Development of Sports Information at Penn State," Exercise Science 444 paper, 28 April 1992; and Ralph D. Hetzel, "Alumni Council Dinner," 2 November 1934, President Hetzel Papers, Box AU04.22, Folder "Speeches & Statements," Penn State University Archives.

26. "Bezdek Favors Legalization of Scholarships for Athletes Here," *Penn State Collegian,* 4 January 1935, p. 1.

27. "Final Action on Athletics," *Penn State Alumni News* (October 1936), 5–8.

28. Board of Athletic Control Minutes, 19 October 1935, Intercollegiate Athletics Records, Box AJ06.12, Binder "1931–1950," Penn State University Archives.

29. "Hetzel Calendar, 1936," President Hetzel Papers, Box AU05.16, "Scrapbook," Penn State University Archives.

30. Ralph D. Hetzel, "Pittsburgh Testimonial Dinner," 16 April 1936, President Hetzel Papers, Box AU05.17, Folder "Address & Alumni Dinner," Penn State University Archives.

31. Ralph D. Hetzel to Ralph D. Hetzel Jr., London, 24 April 1936, President Hetzel Papers, Box AU05.18, Folder "Correspondence: Penn State Period, 1936," Penn State University Archives. Two months later, President Hetzel wrote his son that there were only two major clouds on the horizon, "alumni dissatisfaction with athletics" and how much money would come from the state for financing Penn State. Hetzel to Hetzel Jr., 24 June 1936, President Hetzel Papers, Box AU05.18, Folder "Correspondence: Penn State Period, 1936," Penn State University Archives.

32. "The N.C.A.A. Code of Recruiting and Subsidizing of Athletics," 1934, Board of Athletic Control Minutes, 13 March 1936, Intercollegiate Athletics Records, Box AJ06.12, Binder "1931–1950," Penn State University Archives.

33. "Final Action on Athletics," *Penn State Alumni News* (October 1936), 5–9, 23.

34. Vance McCormick Vertical File, Penn State University Archives.

35. James Milholland Vertical File, Penn State University Archives.

36. George H. Deike Vertical File, Penn State University Archives.

37. "Interview with Ralph R. 'Dutch' Ricker, '30," Ridge H. Riley Papers, Box 04.24, Folder 19, Penn State University Archives. Hetzel's meeting with Bezdek likely occurred on September 21 or 28, 1936. See "Hetzel Calendar, 1936," President Hetzel Papers, Box AU05.16, "Scrapbook," Penn State University Archives.

38. Board of Athletic Control Minutes, 20 April 1937, Intercollegiate Athletics Records, Box AJ06.12, Binder "1931–1950," Penn State University Archives.

39. Ron Smith, meeting with Graham Spanier, Chancellor, University of Nebraska, 12 April 1995, Chancellor's Office, University of Nebraska; and Graham Spanier to Nebraska Touchdown Club and Husker Beef Club, 23 July 1992, Chancellors' Central File, Box 299, Folder 25, University of Nebraska Archives.

40. Ralph D. Hetzel to Ruben J. Neckerman, Madison, WI, 20 March 1937, President Hetzel Papers, Box AU05.18, Folder "Correspondence: Penn State Period, 1937," and E. S. Bayard, Penn State, to L. L. Rummell, Ohio State University Trustee, 23 June 1939, Box AU05.18, Folder "Correspondence: Penn State Period, 1939," Penn State University Archives.

41. Ralph D. Hetzel to Walter M. Smith, University of Wisconsin librarian, Madison, 11 March 1937, President Hetzel Papers, Box AU05.18, Folder "Correspondence: Penn State Period, 1937," Penn State University Archives.

42. "Earle Opens 5-Million-Dollar Program in Recreation Hall as Thousands Listen," *Penn State Collegian*, 26 February 1938, p. 1, 4; Michael Bezilla, *Penn State: An Illustrated History* (University Park: Pennsylvania State University Press, 1985), 168–75; and "Penn State University Park Campus History Collection: History of Campus," Penn State Library Home Page/Departments/Special Collections/University Archives/Menu of Digitized Collections. http://www.libraries.psu.edu/psul/digital/upchc/history.html.

43. *Pittsburgh Sun-Telegraph*, 17 February 1940 newspaper clipping, President Hetzel Papers, Box AU05.16, Folder "Newsclippings, 1927–1947," Penn State University Archives.

44. Bob Wilson, "Rambling Thru," *State College Times*, 19 November 1940, Ridge H. Riley Papers, Box 04.24, Folder 20, Penn State University Archives.

45. "Interview with Joe Bedenk, 8 August 1973," and "Interview with Jim O'Hora, 28 May 1975," Ridge H. Riley Papers, Box 04.24, Folder 20, Penn State University Archives; and Lou Prato, *The Penn State Football Encyclopedia* (Champaign, IL: Sports Publishing, 1998), 145, 160, 168.

46. Ridge Riley, "It Was a Long Time between Bowl Games," *Centre Daily Times,* 26 December 1970, Ridge H. Riley Papers, Box 03.01, Folder 27, Penn State University Archives.

Chapter 7. *The Ernie McCoy–Rip Engle Era and the Beginning of the Grand Experiment in College Football*

1. Carl P. Schott to Milton Eisenhower, 23 March 1952, Ridge H. Riley Papers, Box 04.24, Folder 21, Penn State University Archives.

2. Casey Jones, Punta Gorda, FL, to Ridge Riley, 18 August 1973, Ridge H. Riley Papers, Box 04.24, Folder 20, Penn State University Archives.

3. Carl P. Schott to Milton Eisenhower, 23 March 1952, Ridge H. Riley Papers, Box 04.24, Folder 21, Penn State University Archives.

4. Carl P. Schott, memo to President Hetzel, 7 August 1947, College of Health, Physical Education and Recreation Papers, Box 3, Folder "Historical Information #2, 1945–1951,"

Penn State University Archives; and Susan Rayl, "Who Controlled Athletics at the Pennsylvania State University under the Presidency of Ralph Dorn Hetzel, 1930–1947," Exercise Science 444 paper, 2 May 1990, Penn State University Archives.

5. Athletic Advisory Board Minutes, ca. June 1951, Intercollegiate Athletics Records, Box AJo6.12, Binder "1951–1959," Penn State University Archives.

6. Robert K. Cochrane, Athletic Advisory Board chair, "Report of the Scholarship Policy Committee," Athletic Advisory Board Minutes, 7 June 1947, Intercollegiate Athletics Records, Binder "1931–1950," Penn State University Archives.

7. "The Eastern College Athletic Conference: Its Beginnings, Its Aims, Its Future," Folder "Robert M. Whitlaw Biography," Eastern Collegiate Athletic Conference Headquarters. A decade after the origin of the ECAC, its president, Ralph Furey of Cornell University, chastised the ECAC for still "just blundering here in the East" and having little influence over national NCAA policy as the ECAC was principally "interested in fighting each other." Eastern College Athletic Conference Minutes, 16 December 1947, ECAC Headquarters.

8. Penn State Board of Trustees Executive Committee Minutes, 30 July 1948 and 13 May 1949, and Athletic Advisory Board Minutes, 29 October 1949, Intercollegiate Athletics Records, Box AJo6.12, Binder "1931–1950," Penn State University Archives.

9. Athletic Advisory Board Minutes, 5 March 1954, Intercollegiate Athletics Records, Box AJo6.12, Binder "1951–1959," Penn State University Archives; *Penn State Alumni News* (March 1954), p. 15; and Don Enders, "Ernest B. McCoy and Intercollegiate Athletics at the Pennsylvania State University, 1952–1969," M.S. thesis, Penn State University, 1973, p. 22.

10. Earle Edwards to Ridge Riley, 23 January 1975, and Grover C. Washabaugh Jr. to Ridge Riley, 12 March 1975, Ridge H. Riley Papers, Box 03.01, Folder 31; and Interview of Joe Bedenk, 8 August 1973, Ridge H. Riley Papers, Box 04.24, Folder 20, Penn State University Archives. See also Ridge Riley, *Road to Number One: A Personal Chronicle of Penn State Football* (New York: Doubleday, 1977), 311.

11. "Milton S. Eisenhower New Penn State Head," newspaper clipping, 21 January 1950, Milton S. Eisenhower Papers, Box ARo1.02, Folder "ME Newspaper Articles—Penn State, January 21, 1950–December 11, 1950," Penn State University Archives.

12. Riley, *Road to Number One*, 319–20.

13. Athletic Advisory Board Minutes, 22 April 1950, Intercollegiate Athletics Records, Box AJo6.12, Binder "1931–1950," Penn State University Archives. In addition to Joe Paterno, Engle picked Penn State's Joe Bedenk as the second assistant coach.

14. "Summary of Personnel Changes: Period of June 1–30, 1950," Penn State Board of Trustees Executive Committee Minutes, 28 July 1950, Box ARo5.23, Folder "Executive Committee, 7/28/1950," Penn State University Archives.

15. Rip Engle Papers, Box 05.01, Folder "Engle Job Possibilities, 1943–1950," Penn State University Archives. An assistant professor of economics and commerce was salaried at $3,500. Paterno began as an instructor and assistant football coach. The mean salary of professors was $5,857. Engle achieved permanent tenure on 1 July 1952. A. O. Morse, Board of Trustees, to Charles A. Engle, 13 November 1952, Rip Engle Papers, Box 05.22, Folder "Penn State Correspondence, M-P, 1952–1973," Penn State University Archives.

16. Dennis Alan Booher, "Joseph Vincent Paterno, Football Coach: His Involvement with the Pennsylvania State University and American Intercollegiate Football," Ph.D. dissertation, Penn State University, 1985, pp.15–16, and Joe Paterno with Bernard Asbell, *Paterno by the Book* (New York: Random House, 1989), 55–56, 68.

17. Carl P. Schott, memo to President Milton Eisenhower, 23 March 1952, Ridge H. Riley Papers, Box 04.24, Folder 21, Penn State University Archives; and Rayl, "Who Controlled Athletics."

18. Milton Eisenhower, "Summary of the Report to Alumni on 'The State of the College,'" 14 June 1952, President Eisenhower Papers, Box AR01.02, Folder "ME Addresses, June 14, 1952–November 11, 1952," Penn State University Archives.

19. Eric A. Walker, "Penn State's Athletic Policy," President Walker Papers, Box 04.14, Binder "Unpublished Bits & Pieces," Penn State University Archives.

20. Ronald A. Smith, "The NCAA and the Sanity Code," and "Scandals and the ACE Reform Effort in the 1950s," in his *Pay for Play: A History of Big-Time College Athletic Reform* (Urbana: University of Illinois Press, 2011), 88–99, 109–20.

21. Gilbert, a long-time assistant to Graduate Manager Neil Fleming, took over the head position in 1947 after 33 years of the Fleming administration of athletics. Board of Athletic Control Minutes, 19 July 1947, Intercollegiate Athletics Records, Box AJ06.12, Binder "1931–1950," Penn State University Archives.

22. The chair of the Faculty Senate Committee on Research Policy, Robert Stone, told the School of Physical Education and Athletics that it should be doing more research. This led the School of Physical Education and Athletics to make a policy statement that "A high percentage of new personnel must be qualified for admission to the graduate faculty" while "the academic rank assigned coaches entails no academic obligation." The statement said, "It will require a sound employment and promotion policy, judiciously administered, to attract and hold many of the new staff we will require." School of Physical Education and Athletics Executive Committee Minutes, 1 December 1958, Physical Education and Recreation Papers, Box 04448, Folder "Col. HPER Executive Comm, 1957–1959," Penn State University Archives.

23. Michael Bezilla, *Penn State: An Illustrated History* (University Park: Penn State University Press, 1985), 263–77.

24. Eric A. Walker, "Presidency," ca. 1971, President Walker Papers, Box 04.14, Binder "Personal Reminiscences," Penn State University Archives.

25. "1958 Special Outside Assessment of PSU," President Walker Papers, Box 04.02, Folder "1958 Special Outside Assessment of PSU," Penn State University Archives.

26. John D. Lawther to Dean Carl P. Schott, 14 February 1949, College of Health, Physical Education and Recreation Records, Box 04455, Folder "College of HPER-Physical Education—John Lawther, 1936–1971," Penn State University Archives.

27. By 1958, all members of the prestigious Big Ten, except Michigan State, were in the Association of American Universities, including the universities of Michigan, Wisconsin, and a former Big Ten member, Chicago, all of which joined in 1900.

28. School of Physical Education and Athletics Executive Committee Minutes, 1 December 1958, Physical Education and Recreation Papers, Box 1, 04448, Folder "Col. of HPER Executive Comm, 1957–1959," Penn State University Archives.

29. School of Physical Education and Athletics Executive Committee Minutes, 25 March 1958, College of Health, Physical Education and Recreation Papers, Box 04448, Folder "Col. of HPER Executive Comm, 1957–1959," Penn State University Archives.

30. Noll Laboratory home page, http://www.noll.psu.edu.

31. "Attendance at School Faculty Meetings," College of Physical Education and Athletics, Faculty Meetings, ca. 1953, Box 04448, Folder "Col. of HPER Faculty Meetings, 1950–1953," Penn State University Archives. In the period from 1968 to 1996, during my tenure on the faculty, Joe Paterno attended only one faculty meeting, though he was a full professor in the physical education–kinesiology department. That meeting included a discussion of

how coaching salaries would be apportioned between the athletic budget and the physical education department in which a number of coaches taught various activities in the Basic Instruction Program, and a few taught in the Physical Education majors program.

32. "Alumni Nominees for the Board of Trustees, Biographical Sketches, 1969," Ridge H. Riley Papers, Box 04.24, Folder 20, Penn State University Archives.

33. "College of Health, Physical Education and Recreation," College of Health, Physical Education and Recreation Papers, Box 04448, Folder "Col. of HPER: Athletic Comm of the Senate, 1922–1951," Penn State University Archives; Ridge Riley, "The Role of the Administration in the Development of Physical Education and Athletics at the Pennsylvania State University," paper, Ridge H. Riley Papers, Box 04.24, Folder 18, Penn State University Archives; and Bezilla, *Penn State*, p. 279. The Board of Trustees Executive Committee determined that "as soon as possible, the Graduate Manager of Athletics will be provided with office facilities in the Recreation Building." Penn State Board of Trustees Executive Committee Minutes, 5 September 1947. In the seven years before Dean McCoy, Penn State played four new intersectional football teams, Michigan State, Nebraska, Purdue, and Washington State. In first seven years of McCoy's deanship, Penn State played thirteen intersectional teams. Joyce Gilbert Sipple, Ike Gilbert's daughter, could make a case that intersectional games became more prominent after the 1948 Cotton Bowl game against Southern Methodist when she says Gilbert "began to include intersectional teams to the football schedule—a pretty big step back in those days." Sipple, State College, letter to the editor, *Centre Daily Times*, 24 April 2013, p. A8.

34. Board of Trustees Executive Committee Minutes, 27 March 1953; and Enders, "Ernest B. McCoy," p. 17.

35. Carl B. Seeds, Washington, DC, to Ernest B. McCoy, 19 September 1959, and Athletic Advisory Board Minutes, 25 September 1959, Intercollegiate Athletics Records, Box AJ06.12, Binder "1952–1959," Penn State University Archives. By May 13, 1960, the Alumni Advisory Board reported that the Athletic Association was "obsolete" and superseded by rules of the NCAA, ECAC, and University Senate.

36. "College of Health, Physical Education and Recreation," College of Health, Physical Education and Recreation Papers, Box 04448, Folder "Col. of HPER: Athletic Comm. of the Senate, 1922–1951," Penn State University Archives.

37. Board of Trustees Committee on Educational Policy, Exhibit III, Policies Governing Intercollegiate Athletics, College of Health, Physical Education and Recreation Papers, Box 04448, Folder "Col. of HPER Athletic Comm. of Senate, 1957–1975," Penn State University Archives. Emphasis is mine.

38. Southeastern Conference Minutes, 10 December 1953, Records of the Office of the President, 1949–1966, Box 19, Folder "Southeastern Conference, 1951–53," Georgia Tech University Archives.

39. R. R. Neyland, memo to President C. E. Brehm, ca. 1948, President Brehm Papers, Box 2, Folder "Athletic Scholarships," University of Tennessee Archives.

40. Georg Burns, Latrobe, PA, to Ernest B. McCoy, 12 February 1962; and Athletic Advisory Board Minutes, 25 May 1962, College of Health, Physical Education and Recreation Paper, Box 04448, Folder "Col. of HPER Athletic Comm. of Senate, 1957–1975," Penn State University Archives.

41. Rip Engle, notes for a talk, December 1965, Rip Engle Papers, Box A01.21, Folder "Job Recommendations, 1953–1959," Penn State University Archives.

42. Rip Engle to Ernest B. McCoy, 7 October 1964, Rip Engle Papers, Box 05.22, Folder "Penn State Correspondence, 1952–1973," Penn State University Archives.

43. Athletic Advisory Board Minutes, 19 September 1952, Intercollegiate Athletics Records, Box AJo6.12, Binder "1951–1958," Penn State University Archives.

44. Eric A. Walker, "Presidency."

Chapter 8. *The Joe Paterno, Steve Garban, John Oswald Coup d'État*

1. Board of Trustees Executive Committee Minutes, 20 January 1930, Penn State University Archives.

2. Board of Trustees Executive Committee Minutes, 20 January 1930, Penn State University Archives.

3. "Athletic Relations at College," *Penn State Alumni News*, 13 (May 1927), 7.

4. Board of Trustees Committee on Educational Policy, 29 May 1957, Exhibit III, Policies Governing Intercollegiate Athletics, College of Health, Physical Education and Recreation Papers, Box 04448, Folder "Col. of HPER Athletic Comm. of Senate, 1957–1975," Penn State University Archives.

5. Board of Trustees Committee on Educational Policy, May 29, 1957, Exhibit III, Policies Governing Intercollegiate Athletics, College of Health, Physical Education and Recreation Papers, Box 04448, Folder "Col. of HPER Athletic Comm. of Senate, 1957–1975," Penn State University Archives.

6. About $500,000 of the cost of Recreation Building came from a $4 million appropriation from the state of Pennsylvania to Penn State. E. N. Sullivan, Penn State Alumni Association Secretary, to Ralph D. Hetzel, 10 May 1927, and Hetzel to Prof. E. T. Huddleston, University of New Hampshire, 14 December 1927, President Hetzel Papers, Box AU05.18, Folder "Correspondence: Penn State Period, 1927," Penn State University Archives.

7. "Draft of Press Release on Sports Research Institute," ca. February 1969, School of Physical Education and Athletics Executive Committee Minutes, 17 February 1969, College of Health Physical Education and Recreation Papers, Box 04448, Folder "Col. of HPER Executive Comm, 1967–1968," Penn State University Archives; and Chauncey A. Morehouse, "Sports Research Institute: A Workable Model at Pennsylvania State University," *Journal of Health, Physical Education, and Recreation* 42, no. 1 (1971), 31–35.

8. School of Physical Education and Athletics Executive Committee Minutes, 20 September 1963, College of Health, Physical Education and Recreation Papers, Box 04448, Folder "Col. of HPER Executive Comm, 1960–1964," Penn State University Archives.

9. In my first year at Penn State, I had long discussions with Massey about physical education and athletics and how he felt that athletics was a detriment to the development of physical education when it was in the same unit.

10. College of Health and Physical Education Executive Committee Minutes, 20 September 1963, College of Health, Physical Education and Recreation Papers, Box 04448, Folder "Col. of HPER Executive Comm, 1960–1964," Penn State University Archives. The College of Physical Education and Athletics had just been renamed the College of Health and Physical Education three months before. Women on the Executive Committee were Martha Adams and Lucile Magnusson. Others on the committee were Fred Coombs, Alan Gray, George Harvey, Ernie McCoy, Charles Stoddart, and Dutch Sykes.

11. Joe Paterno, memo to President John Oswald, ca. December 1979, John Oswald Papers, Box 10290, Folder "Athletics Relating to Academics, Admission, Policies, etc., 1979–1982," Penn State University Archives.

12. Jonathan B. Wanderstock, "The 1980 Realignment of the Penn State Athletic Program or the Quarterback Sneak: The Untold Story of Joe Paterno's Consolidation of Power,"

Exercise Science 444 paper, 28 April 1992, Penn State University Archives. This is a wonderfully researched paper by a graduate student.

13. Penn State Board of Trustees Minutes, 20 January 1979, Penn State University Archives.

14. Athletic Department Estimated Income and Expenses, 1979–1982, Box 10290, Folder "Athletics-Budget-1980–82," Penn State University Archives.

15. Joseph V. Paterno Contract, 19 December 1978, John Oswald Papers, Box 10290, Folder "Athletics Relating to Academics, Admission, Policies, Etc, 1979–82," Penn State University Archives.

16. Louis D. Brandeis, *Other People's Money—and How Bankers Use It* (New York: Frederick A. Stokes, 1914), p. 92.

17. See John S. Watterson, *College Football: History, Spectacle, Controversy* (Baltimore: Johns Hopkins University Press, 2000); Ronald A. Smith, *Pay for Play: A History of Big-Time College Athletic Reform* (Urbana: University of Illinois Press, 2011); John R. Thelin, *Games Colleges Play: Scandal and Reform in Intercollegiate Athletics* (Baltimore: Johns Hopkins University Press, 1994); and Murray Sperber, *Onward to Victory: The Crises That Shaped College Sports* (New York: Henry Holt, 1998). A number of other books that cite college sport scandals could be cited.

18. David Whitford, *A Payroll to Meet: A Story of Greed, Corruption and Football at SMU* (New York: Praeger, 2006), 113–35; John Watterson, "Sudden Death at SMU: Football Scandals in the 1980s," in his *College Football*, 353–78; and Walter Byers, *Unsportsmanlike Conduct: Exploiting College Athletes* (Ann Arbor: University of Michigan Press, 1995), 17–36.

19. "Penn State's Athletic Program," *Beaver Stadium Pictorial*, ca. 1972, Ridge H. Riley Papers, Box 04.24, Folder 4, Penn State University Archives. President Oswald reported in 1980 that the American Academy of Physical Education ranked the Penn State program Number One of the 60 national programs leading to the Ph.D. in physical education. Penn State Board of Trustees Minutes, 22 March 1980, Penn State University Archives.

20. Glenn "Nick" Thiel, Report to Board of Trustees Committee on Educational Policy, 29 May 1975, College of Health, Physical Education and Recreation Papers, Box 04448, Folder "College of H.P.E.R Athletic Comm. of the Senate, 1922–1951," Penn State University Archives.

21. Ridge Riley to Roger C. Witherell, Chatham, MA, 18 November 1975, Ridge H. Riley Papers, Box 03.02, Folder 53, Penn State University Archives. Actually, taxpayer money did help athletics, as in the construction of the McCoy Natatorium or the Recreation Building some years before.

22. Joseph S. M. Lau, C. T. Hsia, and Leo Ou-Fan (eds.), *Modern Chinese Stories and Novellas, 1919–1949* (New York: Columbia University Press, 1981), 68.

23. As quoted in Wanderstock, "1980 Realignment."

24. Robert J. Scannell memo to Chalmers G. Norris, Director of Planning and Budget Officer, 7 March 1977, College of Health, Physical Education and Recreation Papers, Box 44455, Folder "College of HPER: Correspondence with Chalmers G. Norris, 1973–1978," Penn State University Archives.

25. Wanderstock, "1980 Realignment."

26. Robert J. Scannell memo to Howard Thoele, Chair of the Dean Scannell Review Committee, 20 September 1978, Folder "Dean's Review," Ronald Smith personal file.

27. Joe Paterno with Bernard Asbell, *Paterno: By the Book* (New York: Random House, 1989), 215.

28. "Paterno: Progress," *Daily Collegian*, 21 September 1979, p. 5.

29. "Paterno: Progress," p. 5. The temporary ice skating facility was constructed at the time the Board of Trustees had approved constructing a $3 million Indoor Sports Complex for a variety of sports and student use and instructional facility. Board of Trustee Minutes, 10 November 1978, Penn State University Archives.

30. Ronald A. Smith, Chair, "Ad Hoc Committee on Varsity Athletics," 11 July 1978, Ronald Smith personal file. The committee consisted of coaches Judy Avener (gymnastics), Walter Bahr (soccer), Marilyn Eastridge (synchronized swimming), Max Garrett (fencing), Jim O'Hora (football), Ellen Perry (swimming), Gillian Rattray (field hockey and lacrosse). John Morris of Sports Information was ex-officio. The committee refused to rank-order the 31 teams of which they were a part.

31. Smith, "Ad Hoc Committee."

32. As quoted in an interview with Jonathan B. Wanderstock, 1 April 1992, in Wanderstock, "1980 Realignment."

33. Ron Smith notes from Dean Review Meeting, 14 November 1978, Ronald Smith personal file.

34. Howard W. Thoele, memo to Walter Bahr, Patricia Farrell, Steve Garban, Ben Niebel, and Ronald Smith, 14 May 1979, John Oswald Papers, Box 10290, Folder "Athletics Relating to Academics, Admission, Policies, Etc, 1979–92–1," Penn State University Archives. Quote emphasis is added.

35. Garban argued this point many times in meetings of the Committee to Review Dean Scannell's Office at which I was present.

36. R. J. Scannell and R. A. Patterson, memo to President John Oswald and J. V. Paterno, 23 November 1979, John Oswald Papers, Box 10290, Folder "Athletics Relating to Academics, Admission, Policies, Etc. 1979–1982–1," Penn State University Archives. The College Football Association (CFA) was formed in 1976 by most big-time football institutions, with the exception of the Big Ten and PAC-10 Conference schools. Penn State was part of the CFA, which was organized primarily to increase television revenue for its schools, and was an antagonist to NCAA television policies, leading to the 1984 Supreme Court case breaking up the NCAA television monopoly.

37. Adolph Rupp, "The Rupp" Tape (audiocassette), WHAS Productions, 1992, http://www.bigbluehistory.net/bb/rupp/html; and Harry Lancaster, *The Dark Side of Kentucky Basketball* (Lexington, KY: Lexington Productions, 1979), www.hopszone.net/Kentucky/dark%20side.htm. John Oswald had tried to force Adolph Rupp to desegregate the Kentucky basketball team by bring an African American onto his team, and Rupp resisted.

38. Rupp, "The Rupp Tape." Assistant Coach Harry Lancaster was told by Rupp that Oswald ordered "me to get some niggers in here. What am I going to do?"

39. Ron Smith discussion with Dave Colton, former Gifts and Endowments official at Penn State tennis facility, 7 August 2014.

40. Joseph V. Paterno to John Oswald, 16 May 1972, Ridge H. Riley Papers, Box 03.01, Folder 24, Penn State University Archives.

41. Joe Paterno to President Oswald, ca. fall 1979, President Oswald Papers, Box 10290, Folder "Athletics Relating to Admission, Policies, Etc. 1979–1982," Penn State University Archives.

42. Oswald quoted in "Statement of Coach Joe Paterno," 6 January 1973, Joe Paterno Papers, Box 07594, Folder "Sports Illustrated Issue," Penn State University Archives.

43. J. William Fulbright, *The Arrogance of Power* (New York: Random House, 1966), 3–4.

44. Paterno, *Paterno*, 87.

45. Jay Searcy, "The Kingdom and the Power of Joe Paterno," *Philadelphia Inquirer*, 30 August 1987, p. 17.

46. Tarman was quoted shortly after Penn State won its first football national championship. *Centre Daily Times*, 16 January 1983, D2.

47. Paterno, *Paterno*, 127.

48. "Coach Urges Trustees to Make Penn State No. 1 University," *Centre Daily Times*, 30 January 1983, Joe Paterno Vertical File, Folder "No Name," Penn State University Archives.

49. Scannell told me this news as I entered the faculty meeting, knowing that I had been involved in the review of the dean's office the previous year.

50. I, as ombudsman, proposed a series of questions raised of me about Oswald's decision, including the "possible recourses by those who feel that this decision has been most damaging to our College." Scannell responded, "Don't do it." Scannell at that time said that the separation of athletics from HPER is "not a major problem." Ron Smith memo to Bob Scannell, 23 January 1980, Ronald Smith personal file. This was confirmed by Scannell in an interview with the author, 16 January 2014, Boalsburg, Pennsylvania. Notes are in the author's possession.

51. As quoted in Wanderstock, "1980 Realignment."

52. As quoted in Wanderstock, "1980 Realignment."

53. François de La Rochefoucauld, *Reflections; or Sentences and Moral Maxims,* 1678 EBook no. 9105, http://www.gutenberg.org/files/9015/9105-h/9015-h-thm.

54. Robert Scannell, interview with the author, 16 January 2014, Boalsburg, Pennsylvania. Notes are in the author's possession.

55. John Egli discussion with Ron Smith, 30 April 1976, and 23 February 1980, Ronald Smith personal file. Egli had applied for the athletic director position when Ed Czekaj was chosen. President Walker, according to Egli, gave Egli a significant pay raise from $11,300 to $16,000 when he was placed in the Commonwealth System position.

Chapter 9. President Bryce Jordan and Penn State's Entry into the Big Ten

1. Penn State joined the Pennsylvania Intercollegiate Foot Ball Association in 1891. Lou Prato, *The Penn State Football Encyclopedia* (Champaign, IL: Sports Publishing, 1998), 32.

2. *Pittsburg[h] Dispatch*, clipping, HBMC Scrapbook 9, 1921 Season, Penn State University Archives.

3. Press release, May 1963, Ridge H. Riley Papers, Box 03.01. Folder 24, Penn State University Archives.

4. Board of Trustees Minutes, 20 May 1972 and 28 September 1973, Penn State University Archives.

5. For a discussion of the history of the freshman rule, see Ronald A. Smith, "The Freshman Rule: A Nearly Forgotten Reform," in his *Pay for Play: A History of Big-Time College Athletic Reform* (Urbana: University of Illinois Press, 2011), 197–206.

6. Joseph V. Paterno to John Oswald, 16 May 1972, Ridge H. Riley Papers, Box 03.01, Folder 24, Penn State University Archives.

7. Board of Trustees Minutes, 28 September 1973, Penn State University Archives; and Prato, *Penn State Football Encyclopedia*, 18.

8. Joseph V. Paterno, memo to Dean Scannell, 3 May 1972, Ridge H. Riley Papers, Box 03.01, Folder 24, Penn State University Archives.

9. *Washington Post*, 30 June 1973, clipping, Walter Byers Papers, Vol. CL, Folder "TV: Football, 1973," National Collegiate Athletic Association Headquarters.

10. Robert M. "Scotty" Whitelaw to John W. Oswald, 29 May 1973, Ridge H. Riley Papers, Box 03.01, Folder 1, Penn State University Archives.

11. Board of Trustees Minutes, 28 September 1973, Penn State University Archives. Withdrawal was effective 1 July 1974.

12. For a discussion of television and the College Football Association, see Ronald A. Smith, "TV Money, Robin Hood, and the Birth of the CFA," in his *Play-by-Play: Radio, Television, and Big-Time College Sport* (Baltimore: Johns Hopkins University Press, 2001), 143–52.

13. In NCAA v. Board of Regents of University of Oklahoma, the Supreme Court voted 7–2 to declare the NCAA television plan a monopoly, the first antitrust ruling against amateur sport.

14. Karl Stoedefalke, personal communication, 5 December 2013.

15. *Philadelphia Inquirer*, 16 December 1989, clipping, Office of the Senior Vice President for Finances Records, Box 03085, Folder "Intercollegiate Athletics-NCAA, 1990," Penn State University Archives.

16. Tom Verducci, "Penn State Move to Big Ten Just Rumor," *Daily Collegian*, 12 March 1981, p. 8.

17. Skip Myslenski and Ed Sherman, "Big 10 Asks Penn State to Join Conference," *Chicago Tribune*, 15 December 1989, pp. 1, 22.

18. Wesley W. Posvar, University of Pittsburgh Chancellor, to John W. Oswald, 3 June 1981, President Oswald Papers, Box 10290, Folder "Athletics Relating to Academics, Admission, Policies, Etc, 1979–1982," Penn State University Archives. Pitt was reluctant to join a league with its football team.

19. Bryce Jordan to Eric Walker, 30 November 1984, President Jordan Papers, Box 10405, Folder "Letters Signed & Sent—Nov. 1984," Penn State University Archives.

20. Provost Edward Eddy to Chancellor Wesley Posvar, University of Pittsburgh, 10 June 1981, President Oswald Papers, Box 10290, Folder "Athletics Relating to Academics, Admission, Policies, Etc, 1979–92," Penn State University Archives.

21. "Principles, Priorities and Guidelines Committee Survey" of the Big Ten, ca. 1990, President Thomas Papers, Box 10435, Folder "Big Ten Con.," Penn State University Archives.

22. Bryce Jordan, Austin, Texas, interview with Ronald A. Smith, 7 April 1994, University of Texas, Austin, in Ronald Smith personal file; and David Jones, "Welcome to the Big Ten: How Penn State Joined Storied Conference," *Penn Live*, originally 11 December 1994 http://www.pennlive.com/pennstatefootball/index.ssf/2013/07/welcome/big/ten/penn/state/20.html.

23. Council of Ten Retreat Minutes, 25 October 1989, President Thomas Papers, Box 10435, Folder "Big Ten Con.," Penn State University Archives.

24. Bryce Jordan, 26 October 1989, President Thomas Papers, Box 10435, Folder "Big Ten Con.," Penn State University Archives.

25. Council of Ten Retreat Minutes, 25 October 1989, President Thomas Papers, Box 10435, Folder "Big Ten Con.," Penn State University Archives. The scores on the Scholastic Aptitude Test of freshmen at Big Ten schools was as follows: Northwestern—1350; Michigan—1190; Illinois—1144; Penn State—1103; Wisconsin—1083; Minnesota—1025; Indiana—1014; Purdue—1005; Michigan State—990; Ohio State—981; Iowa—not available. Bryce Jordan, to ex-president Eric Walker, 31 August 1990, Bryce Jordan Papers, Box 10419, Folder "Correspondence 1987–1990," Penn State University Archives.

26. Hunter R. Rawlings III to Bryce Jordan, 8 June 1990, President Thomas Papers, Box 10435, Folder "Big Ten Con.," Penn State University Archives.

27. Big Ten Press Release, 19 December 1989, Office of the Senior Vice President for Finances Records, Box 03085, Folder "Intercollegiate Athletics—Big 10," Penn State University Archives.

28. David O. Frantz, Chair Athletic Council, and Judith Koroscik, Chair Steering Committee, Ohio State University, to University of Wisconsin University Senate, 20 March 1990, Chancellors Office Files, Box 2, Folder "Athletics-Big Ten-General '90," 94/43, University of Wisconsin Archives.

29. "Penn State Integration Facts," 30 July 1990, Budd Thalman Papers, Box A101.11, Folder "Big 10 Transition Committee, 1990–1991," Penn State University Archives.

30. Larry Lage, 'Penn State's JoePa Could've Been a Michigan Man," newspaper clipping, ca. 20 October 2009, Joe Paterno Vertical File, Penn State University Archives.

31. Robert Thomas Jr., "Surprise in Big 11," *New York Times,* 17 December 1989, p. S 1; and Austin Murphy, "Out of Their League?" *Sports Illustrated,* 7 May 1990, President Thomas Papers, Box 10435, Folder "Big 10 Con.," Penn State University Archives.

32. Victor Hugo, *Les Misérables,* 1862, http://www.gutenburg.org/files/135/135h/135h.htm.

33. Joel N. Myers to Board of Trustees, 18 December 1989, Office of Senior V-P for Finance Records, Box 03085, Folder "Big 10 Con.," Penn State University Archives.

34. Frank E. Forni memo to Steve Garban, Carol Herrman, Bryce Jordan, and William C. Richardson, 7 December 1989, President Thomas Papers, Box 10435, Folder "Big Ten Con.," Penn State University Archives.

35. "Penn State Integration Facts," 30 July 1990, Budd Thalman Papers, Box A101.11, Folder "Big 10 Transition Committee, 1990–1991," Penn State University Archives.

36. Jim Tarman memo to Intercollegiate Athletics Coaching and Administrative Staff, 13 April 1990, Budd Thalman Papers, Box A101.11, Folder "Big 10 Transition Committee, 1990–1991," Penn State University Archives.

37. Big Ten Conference Transition and Expansion Committee Minutes, 14 May 1990, Chancellors Office Files, Box 2, Folder "Athletics-Big-Ten-General '90," 94/43, University of Wisconsin Archives; and Combined Meeting of the Big Ten Governance/Academics Transition and Expansion Committee with Penn State Representatives, 21 March 1990, Budd Thalman Papers, Box A101.09, Folder "Notes, Agendas, 1990," Penn State University Archives.

38. Big Ten Conference Transition and Expansion Committee Minutes, 14 May 1990.

39. Combined Meeting of the Big Ten Governance/Academics Transition and Expansion Committee, 21 March 1990; and Big Ten Conference Transition and Expansion Committee, 14 May 1990.

40. *Philadelphia Inquirer,* 16 December 1989, clipping, Office of the Senior Vice President for Finances Records, Box 03085, Folder "I-C Ath. Big 10, 1990," Penn State University Archives.

41. James Tarman to Rick Bay, 16 May 1990, Office of the Senior V.P. for Finance Records, Box 03085, Folder "I-C Ath. Big 10, 1990," Penn State University Archives.

42. Brad Faldute, "Shalala Expects Council of Ten Will OK Addition of Penn State," *Wisconsin Capital Times,* 31 May 1990 clipping, President Thomas Papers, Box 10435, Folder "Big Ten Con.," Penn State University Archives.

43. Big Ten Conference Transition and Expansion Committee Minutes, 14 May 1990, Chancellors Office Files, Box 2, Folder "Athletics-Big-Ten-General '90," 94/43, University of Wisconsin Archives.

44. For a discussion of the CFA and television rights, see Smith, *Play-by-Play*, 143–76.

45. Bryce Jordan notes, 17 April 1990, 19 April 1990, 30 April 1990, 8 May 1990, ca. 28 May 1990, 30 May 1990, and ca. 2 June 1990, President Thomas Papers, Box 10435, Folder "Big Ten Con."; and Notes of Pres. Bryce Jordan, ca. June 1990, Office of the Senior V.P. for Finance Records, Box 03083, Folder "I-C Ath. Big 10, 1991," both in Penn State University Archives.

46. "Statement by Dr. Bryce Jordan on Big Ten Vote Denying Penn State Admission," ca. 1 June 1990, Office of the Senior V.P. for Finance Records, Box 03085, Folder "I-C Ath. Big 10, 1990," Penn State University Archives.

47. Big Ten Conference, Council of Presidents Executive Session, 4 June 1990, President Thomas Papers, Box 10435, Folder "Big Ten Con.," Penn State University Archives.

48. Bryce Jordan to Stanley Ikenberry, 11 June 1990, President Thomas Papers, Box 10435, Folder "Big Ten Con.," Penn State University Archives.

49. Adam Rittenberg, "Joe Paterno's Name off Big Ten Trophy," 15 November 2011, espn. go.com/college-football/story/_/id/7233492; and Guy Cipriano, "NCAA: Joe Paterno's Gerald R. Ford Award 'Taken Away,'" *Centre Daily Times*, 24 July 2012, p. B4.

Chapter 10. *The Image of Joe Paterno's Grand Experiment*

1. Virgil, "Invocation to the Muse," *The Aeneid Book I*, trans. A. S. Kline, 2002, http://www.poetryintranslation.com/PITBR/Latin/VirgilAeneidl.htm@Toc535054289; and *Aeneid,* Book I, 1–7, http://www.sacred-texts.com/cia/virgil/aen/aenlo1.htm.

2. Publius Vergilius Maro, *Aeneidos,* Liber Primvs (Virgil, *Aeneid,* book 1), http://www.thelatinlibrary.com/vergil/aen1.shtml.

3. Gary Moyer, "Penn State Stands for Something," *Philadelphia Inquirer,* 2 January 1995, p. A8; and Joe Paterno with Bernie Asbell, *Paterno: By the Book* (New York: Random House, 1989), 153.

4. Nicole Perlroth, "Joe Paterno on Power Ambition Glory," Forbes.com, 29 June 2009, Joe Paterno Vertical File, Penn State University Archives.

5. John Lessingham, "Joe Paterno's Aeneid," N&1, ca. March 2012, http://nplusonemag.com/joe-paterno-s-aeneid.

6. Tom Weir, "Columnist Bill Conlin Accused of Molesting 4 as Children," *USA Today,* 20 December 2011, http://content.usatoday.com/communities/gameon/post/2011/12/col; and *New York Times,* 21 December 2011, p. B17. Conlin died at 79 years of age on January 9, 2014. There were no lawsuits against Conlin because of New Jersey's statute of limitations.

7. Lou Prato and Scott Brown, *What It Means to Be a Nittany Lion: Joe Paterno and Penn State's Greatest Players* (Chicago: Triumph Books, 2006), p. ix.

8. "Penn State Profiles: Joe Paterno," in Ron Bracken, *Replays: A Collection of Veteran Ron Bracken's Award-Winning Articles and Personal Favorites* (State College, PA: Nittany, 2003), 10.

9. Ralph Bernstein, "'Grand Experiment' Paying Off for Joe Paterno and Unbeaten Penn State Team," *Gettysburg Times,* 20 November 1968, p. 11.

10. Ridge Riley to Frank E. Enstice, Belvidere, NJ, 14 December 1966, Ridge H. Riley Papers, Box 04.24, Folder 4, Penn State University Archives.

11. Larry Foster, President of the Penn State Northern New Jersey Alumni, to Joe Paterno, 11 September 1959, Rip Engle Papers, Box A01.20, Folder "Congratulatory Letters, 1955–1958," Penn State University Archives.

12. Penn State Board of Trustees Minutes, 13 June 1969, Penn State University Archives.

13. Louis Prato lists prominent Penn State football players through the years as well as academic all-Americans in his *Penn State Football Encyclopedia* (Champaign, IL: Sports Publishing, 1998), 447–546, 571.

14. Glenn Sheeley, "Reid: Grand Piano 'Grand Experiment,'" *Pennsylvania Mirror*, 13 April 1974, newspaper clipping, Ridge H. Riley Papers, Box 03.01, Folder 34, Penn State University Archives.

15. Bracken, *Replays*, 91–93.

16. Prato, *Penn State Football Encyclopedia*, 260.

17. John Clayton, "Dark Shadows Hovering over Happy Valley," *Pittsburgh Press*, 7 November 1979, newspaper clipping, Ron Smith Papers, Box 9360, Folder "Penn State Athletics," Penn State University Archives.

18. Paterno, *Paterno*, 215.

19. Scott C. Etter, "From Atherton to Hetzel: A History of Intercollegiate Athletic Control at the Pennsylvania State College, 1887–1930," Ph.D. dissertation, Penn State University, 1991, iii.

20. Douglas S. Looney, "A Lot of People Think I'm Phony," *Sports Illustrated*, 52 (17 March 1980), 45.

21. "Profile: Dr. Frank Downing," BocaBeacom.com, http://bocabeacom.com/news/featured-news-profile-dr-frank-downing; and Ken Rapport and Barry Wilner, *Football Feuds: The Greatest College Football Rivalries* (Guilford, CT: Lyons Press, 2007), 138.

22. *Miami News*, 9 November 1978, http://news.google.com/newspapers?nid=22068dat =19781109&id.

23. *Centre Daily Times*, 18 July 1977, p. 25.

24. Neil Rudel, "Holding Their Own: Penn State Student Athletes," *Roar! Inside Nittany Lion Sports*, 1, no. 1 (July 1979), 10–12.

25. Ronald A. Smith memo to Bob Scannell, 2 May 1979, Ronald Smith personal file.

26. Howard W. Thoele, Chair of the Dean Robert Scannell Review, memo to Walter Bahr, Patricia Farrell, Steve Garban, Ben Niebel, and Ronald Smith, 14 May 1979, President Oswald Papers, Box 10290, Folder "Athletics Relating to Academics, Admission, Policies, Etc, 1979–82," Penn State University Archives.

27. Eastern College Athletic Conference Minutes, 10 December 1965, ECAC Headquarters Archives.

28. Eric A. Walker, "Presidency," ca. 1971, President Walker Papers, Box 04.24, Binder "Personal Reminiscences," Penn State University Archives.

29. Bracken, "Penn State Profiles: Joe Paterno," in his *Replays*, 11.

30. Joseph V. Paterno to John W. Oswald, 16 May 1972, Ridge H. Riley Papers, Box 03.01, Folder 24, Penn State University Archives.

31. "Athletic Candidates Submitted to J. W. Oswald for 1980 Admissions," President Oswald Papers, Box 10290, Folder "Athletics Relating to Academics, Admission, Policies, Etc. 1979–1982–1," Penn State University Archives.

32. The article by John Underwood was "The Writing Is on the Wall," *Sports Illustrated*, 19 May 1980. The interview was in Bob Hammel, "Student-Athletes: Tackling the Problem," *Phi Delta Kappan*, 62 (September 1980), 7–13, http://www.jstor.org.ezaccess.libraries,psu .edu/stable/2038471=29?se.

33. Joe Paterno, "Score on the SAT to Score on the Field," *Wall Street Journal*, 16 March 1999, Joe Paterno Vertical File, Folder "2000s," Penn State University Archives.

34. *Intercollegiate Athletics: Choices for Reform* (Washington, DC: James Harvey, September 1990), 14, 19, 32, in President Jordan Papers, Box 10400, Folder "Presidential Control," Penn State University Archives; and "Intercollegiate Sports," Hearings before the Subcommittee on Commerce, Consumer Protection, and Competitiveness of the Committee on Energy and Commerce, House of Representatives, 102d Congress, 1st Session, 19 June 1991, p. 127.

35. Ray Didinger, "Paterno's Saintly Image Tarnished," Joe Paterno Vertical File, Folder "No Name," Penn State University Archives.

36. Theresa Zechman, "Race and the Theory of Centrality: Joe Paterno and the Penn State Football Team (1966–1991)," Exercise Science 444 paper, April 1992, Penn State University Archives.

37. Paterno, *Paterno,* pp. 154–55.

38. Rob Kolb, "The Return of Jesse Arnelle," *Daily Collegian*, 21 May 1968, p. 3.

39. See David K. Wiggins, "'The Future of College Athletics is at Stake': Black Athletes and Racial Turmoil on the Predominately White University Campuses, 1968–1972," *Journal of Sport History*, 15 (Winter 1988), 304–23.

40. Michael Boynton, "Expanding the Realm: The Change of Penn State Football Recruiting," Exercise Science 444 paper, 28 April 1992, Penn State University Archives.

41. "You Can't Cover Up 61 Years of Success with Honor," 21 September 2012, http://ps4rs.wordpress.com/category/uncategorized.

42. Didinger, "Paterno Saintly Image Tarnished."

43. *Daily Collegian*, 28 February 1985, p. 8.

44. S. David Berst, NCAA Director of Enforcement, to President John W. Oswald, 6 February 1980, and Oswald to Paterno and Robert Scannell, Dean, 14 February 1980, President Oswald Papers, Box 10338, Folder "Athletics-NCAA-CFA-TitleIX-2," Penn State University Archives.

45. Ronald A. Smith, *Pay for Play: A History of Big-Time College Athletic Reform* (Urbana: University of Illinois Press, 2011), 134–38, 170–72. A 13-page NCAA Florida Infraction Report is found in "University of Florida Infractions Report," 20 September 1989, Office of the Senior V.P. for Finance Records, Box 03086, Folder "Intercollegiate Athletics—NCAA, 1990," Penn State University Archives.

46. See Article 19, Enforcement, in the "Constitution, Operating Bylaws, Administrative Bylaws," 2011–2012 NCAA Division I Manual, effective 1 August 2011, http://2w22.ncaapublications.com/productdownloads/D112.pdf.

47. Rick Reilly, "Not an Ordinary Joe," *Sports Illustrated* (22 December 1986), http://si.com/vault/article/magazine/MAG1065673/index.htm.

48. James A. Peterson and Dennis Booher, *Joe Paterno: In Search of Excellence* (New York: Leisure Press, 1983), 252–58; and Ronald A. Smith, attending a 1970s Penn State sport panel on ethics. Penn State won 35–13 with Dorsett gaining less than four yards per carry.

49. Rick Reilly, "The Sins of the Father," 13 July 2012, http://espn.go.com/espn/story/_/id/8162972/joe-paterno-true-legacy.

Chapter 11. Shaping Reality

1. Reaction to Maxwell Edison, "Sara Ganim and Sally Jenkins at ASPE," 11 April 2012, http://www.blackshoediaries.com/2012/4/11/2940013/sara-ganim-and-sally-jenkins.

2. Some might argue that the rise in academic status came from the successful effort to raise funds in the Jordan administration at about the time of the Big Ten entry. Still, entry into the Big Ten may have given an additional philanthropy boost.

3. "Joe Paterno," www.sports-reference.com/crb/coaches/joe-paterno-1-html; "Joe Paterno," https://Wikipedia.org/wiki/joe_paterno; Patrick Clark, *Sports Firsts* (New York: Facts on File, 1981), p. 48; L. H. Baker, *Football: Facts and Figures* (New York: Farrar & Rinehart, 1945), p. 279; and Mike Poorman, "Penn State Coach Joe Paterno Dies (1926–2012)," *StateCollege.Com*, 22 January 2012, http://www.statecollege.com/news/local-news/penn-state-coach-joe-paterno-dies-1926/2012–986951.

4. "List of Undefeated Division I Football Teams," http://en.wikipedia.org/wiki/list_of_undefeated_ncaa_division_1_football_teams.

5. Lori Shontz, "Sculptor Knew His Creation Could Become Iconic," *Penn Stater* (27 January 2012), pennstatermag.com/2012/07/22/joe-paterno-statue-removed.

6. There are campus bronze statues of a host of individuals, both athletes and coaches: Vince Dooley (Georgia), Cam Newton (Auburn), Nick Saban (Alabama), and Tim Tebow (Florida). Professional sports have their own list that includes, among others, Muhammad Ali (boxing), Roberto Clemente (baseball), Babe Didrikson (golf, track), Joe DiMaggio (baseball), Althea Gibson (tennis), Josh Gibson (baseball), Magic Johnson (basketball), Bobby Jones (golf), Michael Jordan (basketball), Vince Lombardi (football), Joe Louis (boxing), Willie Mays (baseball), Bobby Orr (hockey), Jesse Owens (track), Arnold Palmer (golf), Babe Ruth (baseball), Willie Shoemaker (jockey), George Steinbrenner (baseball), Jim Thorpe (track), Bill Tilden (tennis), Jerry West (basketball), and Tiger Woods (golf).

7. Tape 12, Side 1 Transcript, Bernie Asbell Papers, 1950–2000, Box 07835, Folder "'82 Championship (inc. fight w/Oswald)," Penn State University Archives.

8. Jan Murphy, "Joe Paterno: A Life—A Fundraiser Supreme," *Penn Live*, 24 January 2012, http://www.pennlive.com/specialprojects/index.ssf/2012/01/joe_paterno_a_life.

9. Phone conversation with Paul Harvey, former Classics Department chair at Penn State University, 22 January 2014.

10. Pete Thamel, "For Paterno, Lover of Classics, Tragic Flaw to a Legacy," *New York Times*, 22 January 2012, http://www.nytimes.com/2012/01/23/sports/ncaafootball/joe-paterno-leaves-a-complicated-legacy.html. Sue Paterno told this writer that each of their children was required to take Latin in high school, part of the Paterno emphasis on liberal arts.

11. Susan Welch, "Farewell to Joe Paterno, a Legendary Liberal Arts Leader," February 2012, http://www.la.psu.edu/news/farewell-to-joe-paterno-a-legendary-liberal-arts-leader.

12. "Joe Paterno's Speech to the BOT Following His First National Championship," 22 January 1983, http://docs.google.com/document/d/1rm1/vpkrf7kmyctqjisepf8.

13. "University Libraries Mourn Coach Joe Paterno," *Penn State News*, 23 January 2012, http://news.psu.edu/story/152318/2012/01/23.

14. "Paterno Gift Launches Library Fund," *Centre Daily Times*, 6 December 1984, Joe Paterno Papers, Box 07594, Folder "Newspaper Clippings, 1980–1989," Penn State University Archives.

15. Joseph V. Paterno to Stuart Forth, 29 October 1992, Joe Paterno Papers, Box 07574, Folder "Library Project Correspondence, 1993–1998," Penn State University Archives.

16. Dave Gearhart, Vice President for Development, to Cheryl Norman, Secretary to Joe Paterno, 27 November 1992, Joe Paterno Papers, Box 07574, Folder "Library Project Correspondence, 1993–1998," Penn State University Archives.

17. "Solicitation Strategies for Joe Paterno Prospects," 1992, Joe Paterno Papers, Box 07574, Folder "Library Campaign Feasibility Study 1992–1995," Folder "Library Project Correspondence, 1993–1998," Penn State University Archives; and Gearhart memo to Norman, 27 November 1992.

18. "Joe Paterno Interview: Sally Jenkins Discusses Her Talk with Ex-Penn State Coach," 16 January 2012, http://live.washingtonpost.com/joe-paterno-speaks-to-sally-jenkins.html.

19. "Excerpts from 'Still Bullish on America: A Memoir' by William A. Schreyer" (2009), http://www.sch.psu.edu/about/schrayers/memoir.cfn.

20. As quoted in 2004 in the *Allentown Morning Call,* by Reed Albergotti, "A Discipline Problem: Paterno Fought Penn State Official over Punishment of Players," *Wall Street Journal,* 22 November 2011, http://online.wsj.com/news/articles/5B10001424052970204 443405770520736756640?mal=wsj.

21. As quoted in Joe Paterno with Bernard Asbell, *Paterno: By the Book* (New York: Random House, 1989), 215.

22. Douglas S. Looney, "A Lot of People Think I'm Phony," *Sports Illustrated,* 52 (17 March 1980), 35–36; Paterno, *Paterno,* 216–18; and Lou Prato, *The Penn State Football Encyclopedia* (Champaign, IL: Sports Publishing, 1998), 326–30.

23. Denise Bachman, "The Truth About Joe: A Saint He Certainly Ain't," *Daily Collegian,* 21 March 1980, Joe Paterno Papers, Box 07594, Folder "Newspaper Clippings, 1980–1989," Penn State University Archives.

24. Ron Bracken, "Nittany Lions Not Used to Off the Field Turbulence," *Centre Daily Times,* 28 August 1992, p. D1.

25. Paula Lavigne, "Has Penn State's On-Field Progress Led to Off-Field Problems?" *ESPN Outside the Lines,* http://sports.espn.go.com/espn/otl/news/story:id=3504915.

26. "Data Presented for Consideration of the Commission on Institutions of Higher Education, Middle States Association of Colleges and Secondary Schools," 15 July 1955, College of Health, Physical Education and Recreation Records, Box 04455, Folder "Intercollegiate Athletics," Penn State University Archives.

27. Henry P. Sims Jr., "Paterno on the Paradox of Leadership," manuscript, 26 November 1986, Joe Paterno Papers, Box 07594, Folder "Newspaper Clippings, 1980–1989," Penn State University Archives. Emphasis in the original. Paterno, in his autobiography with the help of writer Bernard Asbell, stated: "I was too sure of myself to listen to others . . . [and] something in me demands control of detail from top to bottom." *Paterno,* 87, 127.

28. Karen Trimbath, "Vicky L. Triponey: New Vice President for Student Affairs Committed to Penn State." *Uniting Student Affairs* (November 2003), http://www.sa.psu.edu/newletter/pdf/nov03.pdf.

29. In the year scholarships were first granted to Penn State women, Paterno was quoted as stating, "I am absolutely against scholarships in women's sports." See Dennis A. Booher, "Joseph Vincent Paterno, Football Coach: His Involvement with the Pennsylvania State University and American Intercollegiate Football," Ph.D. dissertation, Penn State University, 1985, p. 91.

30. Mike Jensen, "Vicky Triponey, the Woman Who Took on JoePa," *Philadelphia Inquirer,* 22 July 2012, http://www.philly.com/philly/sports/colleges/penn_state/Vicky _Triponey.

31. Kelly Whiteside, "Paterno Isn't All Smiles in Happy Valley," *USA Today,* 29 April 2003, Joe Paterno Papers, Box 07594, Folder "Newspaper Clippings, Magazine Articles," Penn State University Archives.

32. Kelly Whiteside, "Ex-Penn State Official Saw Paterno's 'Dark Side,'" *USA Today*, 22 November 2011, http://usatoday330.usatoday.com/sports/college/football/bigten/story/2011–11–22/paterno-discipline/51346682/1.

33. Vicky L. Triponey, e-mail to Tim Curley, Athletic Director, 12 July 2004, Office of the Vice President for Student Affairs Papers, Box 12016, Folder "Football," Penn State University Archives.

34. Humphrey petitioned to get back into Penn State, admitting that he could not qualify academically when first admitted and asked Triponey to allow him back in because he had changed from previously when "I partied too much and thought that since I was excelling football I could afford to slack off in my academics." Maurice Humphrey to Vicky Triponey, 14 June 2004, Office of the Vice President for Student Affairs Papers, Box 12016, Folder "Football," Penn State University Archives.

35. "Penn State Student Athlete Data Compared to Non-Student Athlete Data," 2005, and "Big Ten Discipline Data Comparisons," ca. 2004, Office of the Vice President for Student Affairs Papers, Box 12016, Folder "Football," Penn State University Archives.

36. Vicky Triponey, e-mail to Tim Curley and Fran Ganter, 12 August 2005, Office of the Vice President for Student Affairs Papers, Box 12016, Folder "Football," Penn State University Archives. Emphasis in the original.

37. Joe Posnanski, *Paterno* (New York: Simon and Schuster, 2012), 304.

38. Chico Harlan, "His Way," *Pittsburgh Post-Gazette*, 25 December 2005, Joe Paterno Papers, Box 07594, Folder "Newspaper Clippings, Magazine Articles, 2000–2007," Penn State University Archives; Posnanski, *Paterno*, 303–4; and David Jones, "Former Penn State President Graham Spanier Recalls Meeting with Coach Joe Paterno Following the 2004 Season," *Pennlive*, 23 November 2011, http://www.pennlive.com/midstate/index.ssf/2001/11/the_truth_behind_graham_spanier.html. Graham Spanier said the meeting was at the request of Joe Paterno. Maybe the administrators asked for a meeting, and Paterno asked them to come to his house.

39. Vicky Triponey, e-mail to Tim Curley, 18 August 2005, Office of the Vice President for Student Affairs, Box 12016, Folder "Football," Penn State University Archives.

40. Vicky Triponey, e-mail to Tim Curley, 19 August 2005, Office of Vice President for Student Affairs Papers, Box 12016, Folder "Pending Judicial Cases," Penn State University Archives.

41. Philadelphia Area Employment Lawyer, "Text of 2005 E-Mail from Vicky Triponey to Graham Spanier, 22 November 2011, http://employmentlaw101.blogspot.com/2011/11/text-of-2005-email. See also Albergotti, "Discipline Problem." Emphasis in the original.

42. "Vicky Triponey Calendars, 2005–2007," Office of the Vice President for Student Affairs Papers, Box 11716, Folder "Head Coaches Meeting," Penn State University Archives.

43. Clifton R. Wharton Jr. to President Creed Black, Knight Foundation, 11 November 1995, Bryce Jordan Papers, Box 10420, Folder "Black, Creed Correspondence 1994–1995," Penn State University Archives.

44. This writer went to the emergency room of the Mount Nittany Medical Center at 1:00 a.m. on April 1 and took the last bed, which was being saved for a heart patient, when I had my first attack of atrial fibrillation.

45. Lavigne, "Penn State's On-field Progress."

46. Jensen, "Vicky Triponey."

47. Brad Wolverton, "Paterno E-Mail Shows Coach's Influence on Disciplinary Matters," *Chronicle of Higher Education*, 5 July 2012, http://chronicle.com/article/paterno-e-mail-shows-coach/132773. Emphasis in the original.

48. Gene Wojciechowski, "Paterno a Study in Contradictions," http://espn.go.com/college-football/story/_/id/7488723/former-penn-state.

49. Thamel, "Paterno, Lover of Classics."

50. Michael O'Brien, *No Ordinary Joe: The Biography of Joe Paterno* (Nashville, TN: Rutledge Hill Press, 1998), ix.

51. "The Local Show: Publishing Predicament: Joe Posnanski and Paterno," YouTube, http://www.youtube.com/watch?v=kspic10127c.

52. Scott Paterno, "Scott Paterno on Joe Paterno the Teacher, the Father and the Man," *Penn Live*, 13 December 2009, http://blog.pennlive.com/patriotnewssports/2009/12/scott_paterno_on_joe_paterno_t.html.

53. Bachman, "Truth about Joe."

54. Milan Simonich, "Joe Paterno and the Fall of the Icon," *El Paso Times*, 10 November 2011, http://www.elpasotimes.com/ci_19304118. Simonich previously worked for the *Pittsburgh Post-Gazette*.

55. Robert Secor, Vice-Provost Emeritus for Academic Affairs, to President Graham Spanier, 22 September 2007 and Spanier to Secor, 1 October 2007, http://www.psu.edu/ur/pdf/judicialaffiars10-01-07.pdf. Spanier accepted the report.

56. Michael Meacham reply to "Who Is Vicky Triponey?" PS4EVER, 5 August 2012, http://ps44s.wordpres.com/29012/08/05/who-is-vicky-triponey/#comments.

57. Albergotti, "Discipline Problem"; and Scott Soshnick and Eben Novy-Williams, "Power Struggle," *Centre Daily Times*, 28 December 2011, pp. A1, A3.

58. *Centre Daily Times*, 2 September 2007, pp. A1, A3.

59. Jessica Bennett and Jacob Bernstein, "Meet Penn State's New Whistleblower, Vicky Triponey," *Daily Beast*, 23 November 2011, http://www.thedailybeast.com/articles/2011/11/23-meet-penn-state-s-new-whistleblower; and Lauren McCormack, "Student Groups Adjust to Leadership Change," *Collegianonline*, 14 September 2007, http://www.collegian.psu.edu/archive/2007/09/14/student_groups_adjust_to_lead.aspx.

60. Thomas A. Shakely, "Professionalism under Vicky: 'Extremely Difficult,'" *Safeguard Old State*, 5 September 2007, http://safeguardoldstate.org/sentinel/2007/09/05/professionalism.

61. Meacham reply to "Who Is Vicky Triponey?"

62. François-Marie Arouet (Voltaire), *Le Siècle de Louis XIV* (London: Fielding, Walker, Paternoster-Row, 1779), ch. 6, p. 89.

63. John Swinton, *Philadelphia Bulletin*, 17 November 1978, p. A15, Ronald Smith personal file.

Chapter 12. Insularity, The Second Mile, and Sandusky's On-Campus Incidents

1. Robert J. Scannell, "Interview with Scannell," 7 March 2002, ABBF, Penn State University Archives.

2. "Jerry Sandusky Grand Jury Investigation Report," 4 November 2011, http://www.attorneygeneral.gov/uploadedfiles/press/sandusky_grand_jury_presentment.pdf.

3. "Sensationalizing Sandusky," *Centre Daily Times,* 16 April 2011, http://pennlive.com/letters/index.ssf/2011/04/why_were_sandusky_allegations.html.

4. Rick Reilly, "Guts, Brains and Glory," *Sports Illustrated*, 12 January 1987, http://sportsillustrated.cnn.com/vault/article/magazine/MAG1126846.

5. Joe Paterno to Charles Theokas, 6 December 1988, Joe Paterno Papers, Box 07574, Folder "Recommendations 1970–1980," Penn State University Archives. Emphasis is mine.

Those who believe that Paterno gave Sandusky such praise to get rid of him should know that Paterno invited Sandusky to coach an additional year, 1999, after he had formally retired in spring 1999.

6. "The Paterno Report: Critique of the Freeh Report," 10 February 2013, *Centre Daily Times*, 11 February 2013.

7. "Jerry Sandusky Grand Jury Investigation Report."

8. "Searching for the Truth about the Sandusky Scandal," 16 August 2012, http://notpsu. blogspot.com/2012/08/20045-psu-messageboard-chat-gives.html.

9. *Commonwealth of Pennsylvania v. Timothy Marsh Curley*, Court of Common Pleas, Dauphin County, Pennsylvania, Nol. CP-MD-1374–2011, Transcript of Proceeding Hearing, 12 January 2011. The hearing took seven minutes.

10. *Centre Daily Times*, 16 July 2012, pp. A1, A3; Don Van Natta Jr., "Fight on State: In Wake of Scandal, Power Struggle Spread from Penn State Campus to State Capital," *ESPN the Magazine*, 4 April 2012, http://espn.go.com/espn/otl/story/_/id/7770996/in-wake-joe -paterno; and "Report of the Special Investigative Counsel Regarding the Actions of the Pennsylvania State University Related to the Child Sexual Abuse Committed by Gerald A. Sandusky," 12 July 2012, pp. 57–61.

11. Ronald L. Schreffler, "Penn State Department of University Safety Incident Report," 3 June 1998, http://notpsu.blogspot.com/2013/07/when-did-ray-gricar-close-his-sandusky. html.

12. Schreffler, "Incident Report."

13. Schreffler, "Incident Report."

14. "Report of the Special Investigative Counsel," pp. 47–48.

15. Joe Paterno Appointment Book (1998), Paterno Papers, Box 07574, Folder "Appointment Book," Penn State University Archives.

16. Tim Curley e-mail to Gary Schultz, 13 May 1998, "Report of the Special Investigative Counsel," p. 49.

17. Joe Paterno Appointment Book (1998).

18. "Report of the Special Investigative Counsel," p. 50.

19. "Report of the Special Investigative Counsel," pp. 51–52.

20. "Report of the Special Investigative Counsel," p. 57.

21. "Paternos Pledge $3.5 Million to Penn State," *Penn State News*, 15 January 1998, Joe Paterno Vertical File, Folder "2000s," Penn State University Archives.

22. Jack McCallum, "Last Call," *Sports Illustrated Vault*, 20 December 1999, http:// sportsillustrated.cnn.com/vault/article/magazine/MAG1017979/index.htm; and "Sandusky Awarded Assistant Coach of the Year," GoPSU Sports.com, http://www.gopsusports.com/ sports/m-footbl/spec-rel/121099aaf.html.

23. Marcus Aurelius, *Meditations*, Book 3, http://classics.mit.edu/antonius/ meditations.3.three.html.

24. Sara Ganim, "Sandusky Faces Grand Jury Probe," *Harrisburg Patriot-News*, 31 March 2011, http://www.pulitzer.org/files/2012/local.reporting/local01.pdf; Sara Ganim, "Jerry Sandusky Alleged Victim 1 Graduates after Being Bullied Out of School Is Ready to Testify," *Penn Live*, 10 June 2012, http://www.pennlive.com/midstate/index.ssf/2012/06/ Jerry_Sandusky; and L. Jon Wertheim and David Epstein, "This Is Penn State," *Sports Illustrated Vault*, 21 November 2011, http://sportsillustrated.cnn.com/vault/article/magazine/ MAG1192198/1/index.htm.

25. "A Report for a Democrat-Elected Attorney General about Republican Corbett Found That There Were No Undue Delays," H. Geoffrey Moulton Jr., "Report to the Attor-

ney General on the Investigation of Gerald A. Sandusky," 20 May 2014, http://filessource.abacast.com/commonwealthofpa/mp4_podcast/2014_06_23_report.

26. *Centre Daily Times*, 21 November 2011, p. A3.

27. Penn State University Board of Trustees Minutes, 9 September 2011, Penn State University Archives.

28. As quoted in Doug Lederman, "New Wave of the NCAA Reform?" *Inside Higher Education*, 11 August 2011, http://www.insidehighered.207elmp02.blackmesh.com/news/2011/08/11/new-wave.

29. Donald Gilliland, "Second Mile CEO Made More Than $132,000," 18 November 2011, http://www.pennlive.com/midstate/index.ssf/2011/11/second_mile.

30. Sara Ganim, "Jerry Sandusky's Crimes Put an End to Second Mile Charity: Special Report," 8 August 2012, *Pennlive.com*, http://www.pennlive.com/midstate/index.ssf/2012/08/second_mile.

31. "The Second Mile Annual Report 2010," http://hourofthetime.com/1-LF/sandusky2ndmile-annualreport2010.pdf.

32. Thomas L. Day, "My Second Mile: How I Grew Up with the Now-Doomed Organization," 30 November 2011, http://deadspin.com/e%27z%27-smith.

33. Justin Leto, "Penn State Attempts No-Bid Sale of Circleville Farm to S&A Homes," *Philadelphia Independent Media Center*, 22 April 2003, http://www.phillyimc.org/en/node/37745.

34. "Report: Joe Paterno, Leaders Had Ties," 6 December 2011, http://espn.go.com/college-football/story/_/id/7320780/penn-state; Luke O'Brien, "Paterno, Chairman of Jerry Sandusky's Charity Were Pursuing $125 M Real Estate Deal When Sandusky Was Caught Allegedly Sodomizing Boy," 5 December 2011, http://deadspin.com/robert-poole/.

35. Ganim, "Jerry Sandusky's Crimes"; and "Corbett and 'The Second Mile' Donors to His Campaign," 18 November 2011, http://broadandpennsylvania.blogspot.com/2011/11/Corbett-and-second-mile-donors.

36. *Centre Daily Times*, 21 November 2011, p. A3.

37. Ray Fittipaldo, *Pittsburgh Post-Gazette*, 6 April 2003, Bryce Jordan Papers, Box 10420, Folder, "Football Bowl Games and Players 2002–3," Penn State University Archives.

38. Ganim, "Jerry Sandusky's Crimes."

39. Bill Keisling IV, "'JoePa' Takes the Fall," 22 January 2012, http://www.yardbird.com/joe_paterno_takes_the_fall.htm.

40. "Special Report: Penn State Counsel Cynthia Baldwin's Role before the Grand Jury," *Harrisburg Patriot-News*, 2 February 2012, http://www.pennlive/com/midstate/index.ssf/2012/02.

41. L. Jon Wertheim and David Epstein, "This Is Penn State: Scandal, Shame, a Search for Answers," *Sports Illustrated*, 115 (21 November 2011), 46.

42. President Erickson was not informed about the NCAA Constitution and Bylaws that strictly outlawed a "death penalty" on an institution with no previous major violation. See *2011–2012 NCAA Division I Manual, Effective 1 August 2011*, "Constitution, Operating Bylaws, Administrative Bylaws," http://www.ncaapublications.com/productdownloads/d112.pdf, specifically, Article 19, 19.01.5, 19.5.2.1, 19.5.2.2, and 19.5.2(K). Erickson not once, in his e-mails to legal advisors prior to the consent decree, noted NCAA's Article 19.5.2.2 on enforcement, nor did he challenge the lack of due process provided in the Constitution and Bylaws. See "Legal Documents—Corman vs. NCAA," Erickson Exhibits, www

.senatorcorman.com/legal-documents-corman-vs-ncaa. Erickson rejected the request of Trustee Joel Myers to review the Freeh report, review the consent decree sanctions, or review the legal advice of Gene Marsh. See Rachel George, "Penn State Trustees Take No Action on Consent Decree," *USA Today*, 12 August 2012, http://usatoday30.usatoday.com/sports/college/football/bigten/story/2012-08-12/penn-state/57016128/1. Andrew Mitten, law professor and director of the National Sports Law Institute, pointed out all of the NCAA's illegal activities and unprecedented acts in the Penn State case in his "The Penn State 'Consent Decree': The NCAA's Coercive Means Don't Justify Its Laudable Ends, But Is There a Legal Remedy?" *Pepperdine Law Review*, 41 (2013), 321–48.

Chapter 13. Rene Portland and the Culture of Athletic Silence

1. Ronald A. Smith, "The Rise of Basketball for Women in American Colleges," *Canadian Journal of History of Sport and Physical Education*, 1 (December 1970), 18–36.

2. Penn State Sports Information says that the December 5, 1973, Penn State basketball game against Virginia with a State College star, Barry Parkhill, had the most fans, 8,600, but this writer was at both events, and the gymnastic meet was more crowded as fans sat on the basketball court next to the gymnastic equipment. Because men's basketball was the most important indoor sport, it was likely that this influenced Sports Information to decide what event was the largest.

3. Lois Stark, "Timetable of Administration Action and Student Activities Relevant to the Founding of the School of Physical Education and Athletics in 1930," May 1966, Ronald Smith personal collection.

4. For more detail on Title IX, see Ronald A. Smith, "Title IX and Governmental Reform in Women's Athletics," in *Pay for Play: A History of Big-Time College Athletic Reform* (Urbana: University of Illinois Press, 2011), 141–50.

5. Linda Wahowski, "Women's Athletics Looks Back in Time," *Daily Collegian*, 28 April 1989, http://m.collegian.psu.edu/archives/article.

6. Michael Weinreb, "On the Long and Illustrious History of Penn State Basketball," 15 March 2009, http://michaelweinreb.blogspot.com/2009/03/on-long. The game was won 101–68 on 28 November 1980. I wrote a memo to Portland soon afterward, indicating that her actions were not in line with Penn State tradition, and Portland came to my office to discuss my concern.

7. Penn State Board of Trustees Minutes, 18 March 1972, Penn State University Archives. The trustee minutes stated, "There is great concern . . . among the University's psychiatrists and psychologists and the Counseling Department, that this kind of organization could have a very serious and harmful effect on certain specified types of young people in the University community, especially those who for a variety of reasons may be suffering from some confusion with respect to their own sexual identity or orientation."

8. Terry E. Hess, "Penn State Athletics during the Oswald Administration (1970–1983)," Ex Sci 444 Paper, 2 May 1990, Penn State University Archives.

9. Meiser accepted an invitation to dinner in the home of a high school athlete after an unplanned introduction to the athlete's parents at a high school game. William Ulerich, Board of Trustee liaison to the Athletic Department, gave a report of the violation to the Board of Trustees. Board of Trustees Minutes, 25 May 1979, Penn State University Archives; and Denise Bachman and Joe Saraceno, "Meiser Wonders 'Why Penn State?'" *Daily Collegian* (9 April 1979) pp. 1, 10–11.

10. Cynthia J. Gabel, NCAA Enforcement Representative, to James Tarman, Athletic Director, 8 December 1993, Joab Thomas Papers, Box 10449, Folder "National Collegiate Athletic Association," Penn State University Archives.

11. Two researchers called Portland a "homophobic basketball coach." Whether she feared (phobic) homosexuals on her teams, or feared others would think she was a lesbian, can be questioned, for Portland appeared to fear few people in her career. That she discriminated is obvious. Phobia comes from the Greek "fear of," not "discrimination against." Homophobia is a morphed term to achieve an end. See Marie Hardin and Erin Whiteside, "The Rene Portland Case: New Homophobia and Heterosexism in Women's Sports Coverage," in *Examining Identity in Sports Media,* ed. Heather L. Hundley and Andrew C. Beltings (Thousand Oaks, CA: Sage Publications, 2010), 17–36.

12. Bob Hohler, "When the Fouls Get Very Personal: Player's Suit Claims Penn State Coach Was Biased against Lesbians," *Boston Globe,* 26 March 2006, http://www.clubs.psu.edu/up/psupride/articles/boston%20globe%2003262006A.pdf.

13. *Indiana Gazette,* 1 September 1992, p. 13.

14. "Former Lady Lion Cindy Davies Tells Her Story," 17 January 2006, http://boards.rebkell.net/viewpoint.php?p=1051378sid.

15. Bill Figel, "Lesbians in World of Athletics," *Chicago Sun-Times,* 16 June 1986, http://www.clubs.psu.edu/up/psupride/articles/chicago%20sun%times%200626986.pdf.

16. Jere Longman, "Lions Women's Basketball Coach Is Used to Fighting and Winning," *Philadelphia Inquirer,* 10 March 1991, http://articles.philly.com/1991–03–10/sports/25792217.

17. "Report of the Special University Faculty Committee to Review President Thomas's Proposed Amendment to the University's Non-Discrimination Policy," 19 March 1991, Board of Trustees Minutes, 16 May 1991, Penn State University Archives.

18. Faculty Advisor for the Lesbian, Gay, and Bisexual Student Alliance of Penn State [Anthony R. D'Augelli], memo to James Tarman, 15 March 1991, Office of the Senior V.P. for Finance Records, Box 03083, Folder "Intercollegiate Athletics, General," Penn State University Archives.

19. Penn State Faculty Senate Minutes, 19 March 1991, Penn State University Archives.

20. Penn State Board of Trustees Minutes, 16 May 1991, Appendix 1, Penn State University Archives.

21. Jim Tarman memo to Intercollegiate Athletic Personnel, 3 June 1991, Office of the Senior V.P. for Finance Records, Box 03083, Folder "Intercollegiate Athletics, General," Penn State University Archives.

22. Beth, memo to Carol, 9 October 1991, Office of the Senior V.P. for Finance Records, Box 03083, Folder "Intercollegiate Athletics, General," Penn State University Archives. No last names were included.

23. Robert Lipsyte, "Penn State Coach Will Abide by Lesbian Policy, But Won't Discuss It," *New York Times,* 20 December 1991, www.//www.nytimes.com/1991/12/20/sports/penn-state-coach-will-abide-by-lesbian-policy.

24. *Jennifer E. Harris v. Maureen T. Portland, et al.,* Civil Action No. 1:05-CV-2648, U.S. District Court, Harrisburg, PA, 3 January 2006.

25. Penn State Newswire, 21 October 2005, http://www.ivillage.com/forum/node/7152369; and Penn State Press Release, "University Concludes Investigation of Claims against Women's Basketball Coach," 18 April 2006, http://www.clubs/psu.edu/up/psupride/articles/press$20release%404182006.pdf.

26. *Harris v. Portland, et al.*

27. "Women's Hoops Blog," 14 October 2005, http://womenshoops.blogspot.com/2005/10/other-shoe-is-finally-dropped.html.

28. At the same meeting in which Spanier was congratulated on becoming chair of the National Security Higher Education Advisory Board, and after the Harris Case was reported, he remained silent until an unknown member of the board raised a question about the Portland allegations. There is no record of Spanier's reply. Penn State Board of Trustees Minutes, 4 November 2005, Penn State University Archives.

29. *Harris v. Portland, et al.*

30. Robert K. Merton," The Unanticipated Consequences in Purposive Social Action," *American Sociological Review,* 1, no. 6 (December 1936), 894–904, gave identity to the terms "law of unintended consequences."

31. Hohler, "When the Fouls Get Very Personal," http://www.clubs.psu.edu/up/psupride/articles/boston%20globe%2003262006.pdf.

32. *Harris v. Portland, et al.*

33. Rene Portland, "In Rebuttal: At Penn State Women's Basketball, Fairness Rules," *Pittsburgh Post-Dispatch,* 19 May 2006, Rene Portland Vertical File, Penn State University Archives.

34. "Coach Joe Paterno Press Conference," 15 October 2002, *GoPSUsports,* Joe Paterno Vertical File, Folder "2000s," Penn State University Archives; and *Daily Collegian,* 15 January 1998, p. 11.

35. "Rene Portland Named 2005 Renaissance Person of the Year," 23 July 2005, http://www.clubs.psu.edu/up/psupride/article/press%20release%20y232005.pdf.

36. Penn State Board of Trustees Minutes, 18 May 2007, Penn State University Archives.

37. *Training Rules: No Drinking, No Drugs, No Lesbians,* Wolfe Video and Woman Vision Film, 2009.

38. Scott L. Nolte, Artistic Director, Taproot Theatre Company, Seattle, WA, interview of the production *An Inspectator Calls* (2006) in Scott Nolte, e-mail to Ron Smith, 25 June 2013.

Chapter 14. *The Board of Trustees, Insularity, and Athletic Administration*

1. Penn State Professor John Swisher was at the French Embassy around 1994 at the time of the presidential opening at Penn State when he met President Trachtenberg, who mentioned the "imperial presidency." Discussion with John Swisher, 11 November 2014, Lemont, Pennsylvania.

2. As quoted by Jenna Johnson, "Penn State Scandal Lessons to University Presidents," *Washington Post,* 18 November 2011, http://articles.washingtonpost.com/2011-11-18/local/35281822_1_university.

3. Michael Bezilla, *Penn State: An Illustrated History* (University Park: Penn State University Press, 1985), 345.

4. Eric A. Walker, "Memories of Roger (Cappy) Rowland Penn State Class of '17," President Walker Papers, Box 04.01, Folder "Rowland, Roger 'Cappy' 4/82," Penn State University Archives.

5. Penn State Faculty Senate member Roy Buck discussed the history of Penn State governance stating that change occurred by trustee edict in 1970 during "a time when student unrest and distrust of the faculty were running very high." Buck, Chair, "Senate Ad Hoc Committee to Study the Implications of Collective Bargaining for Faculty Governance," University Faculty Senate Records, Box 06212, Folder "Implications of

Collective Bargaining for Faculty Governance Comte, 1973–74," Penn State University Archives.

6. Penn State Board of Trustees Minutes, 23 April 1970, Penn State University Archives.

7. Penn State Board of Trustees Minutes, 10 June 1970, Penn State University Archives.

8. Penn State Board of Trustees Minutes, 10 June 1970, Penn State University Archives.

9. Oswald's speech is found in the Penn State Board of Trustees Minutes, 7 July 1970, Penn State University Archives.

10. Robert S. Friedman, "Some Random Thoughts, Biases, and 'Subversive Ideas' for Committee on Governance Use Only," ca. Spring 1974, University Faculty Senate Records, Box 1, 05.14, Penn State University Archives; Roy C. Buck, "Statement on Governance," 5 March 1974, in "Friedman Committee-Governance," Notebook, ca. Spring 1974, University Senate Records, Box 1, 05.14, Penn State University Archives; and Allan M. Krall, memo to Robert S. Friedman, 19 February 1974, in "Friedman Committee-Governance," Notebook, ca. Spring 1974, University Faculty Senate Records, Box 1, 05.14, Penn State University Archives.

11. Frank Carver, Secretary of the University of Pittsburgh, to Asa S. Bushnell, ECAC Commissioner, 7 March 1969, College of Health, Physical Education and Recreation Records, 04455, Folder "College of HPER: Sports Teams Correspondence, 1969," Penn State University Archives.

12. Board of Trustees Minutes, 28 September 1973, President Oswald Papers, Box 10290, Folder "Pres. File-Letters Re: Athletic Teams-1980–81," Penn State University Archives.

13. "The Eastern College Athletic Conference: Its Beginnings, Its Aims, Its Future," Folder "Robert M. Whitlaw Biography," Eastern College Athletic Conference Headquarters; and Irving T. Marsh, "The E.C.A.C.—Its Accomplishments and Its Future Goals," *Harvard University Football Program vs. Brown*, 14 November 1964, p. 61, Eastern College Athletic Conference Headquarters.

14. Terry E. Hess, "Penn State Athletics During the Oswald Administration (1970–1983)," Ex Sci 444 Paper, 2 May 1990, Penn State University Archives.

15. Board of Trustees Committee on Educational Policy, 29 May 1975, Exhibit III, Policies Governing Intercollegiate Athletics, College of Health, Physical Education and Recreation Papers, Box 1 04448, Folder "Col. of HPER Athletic Comm. of Senate, 1957–1975," Penn State University Archives. The creation of the trustee liaison with athletics was created in 1965 when the trustees discontinued the Athletic Advisory Board. "Report of the Special Committee to Study the Place of the Athletic Advisory Board in the Organization of the University," 15 May 1965, Ridge H. Riley Papers, Box 04.24, Folder 8, Penn State University Archives.

16. Penn State Board of Trustees Minutes, 10 June 1970, Penn State University Archives. President Oswald gave an informational report on the history and development of policies governing intercollegiate athletics at the May 30, 1975, meeting. See the Penn State Board of Trustees Minutes, 30 May 1975, Penn State University Archives.

17. Board of Trustees Minutes, 20 January 1979, Penn State University Archives.

18. Joe Paterno to President John Oswald, ca. fall 1979, President Oswald Papers, Box 10290, Folder "Athletics Relating to Admission, Policies, Etc. 1979–1982," Penn State University Archives.

19. Board of Trustees Minutes, 23 March 1979, Penn State University Archives.

20. Joel N. Myers to Penn State Board of Trustees, 18 December 1989, Office of Senior V-P for Finance Records, Box 03085, Folder "The Big 10 Conference," Penn State University Archives.

21. Myers questioned the right of President Erickson to sign the Consent Decree to NCAA sanctions in 2012 without first going to the Board of Trustees. *Centre Daily Times,* 11 August 2012, p. A1.

22. Coincidentally, Myers's reform effort came the same month that four university administrators went to Joe Paterno's house to ask the coach to resign, November 2004.

23. Former member of the Penn State Board of Trustees Ben Novak explained how the trustees are divided into four groups, the power group, praetorian guard, emeritus trustees, and the majority, the "sheep," who are expected to rubber-stamp the power group's approval of the board president's actions. *Centre Daily Times,* 8 January 2012, p. A6.

24. Don Van Natta Jr., "Penn St. Leaders Passed on Reform," 18 July 2012, http://espn.go.com/espn.otl/story/_id/8175462/jerry-sandusky; and Dustin Hockensmith, "Graham Spanier, Cynthia Baldwin Put a Stop to 2004 Trustees Vote That Would Have Strengthened Oversight: Report," 17 July 2012, http://www.pennlive.com/midstate/inter.ssf/2012/07/graham-spanier.

25. The connection of the two events was brought to my attention by the wife of Bernie Asbell, Jean Brenchley. Paterno was funny, poignant, and lengthy as he eulogized the individual who had come to adore Paterno. The memorial was held at the Unitarian Universalist Fellowship of Centre County, 10 February 2001. Discussion with Jean Brenchley, 29 June 2014, and my own attendance at the memorial.

26. Spanier rationalized his virtues in a letter to the Board of Trustees, 23 July 2012, http://espn.lgo.com/pdf/2012/07/23/espn_otl_spanierletter.pdf.

27. A search of the Board of Trustees Minutes from 1995 until Spanier's dismissal in 2011 finds the president's message to the trustees filled with all the accomplishments of Penn State's administrators, faculty, students, alumni, and benefactors.

28. Sara Ganim, "Sandusky Faces Grand Jury Probe," *Harrisburg Patriot-News,* 31 March 2011, http://www.pulitzer.org/files/2012/local_reporting/local01pdf.

29. Dan Van Natta Jr., "Sources: PSU Trustees Left Furious," ESPN.com, 16 July 2012, http://espn.go.com/espn.tl/story/_/8169124.

30. Penn State University Board of Trustees Minutes, 13 May 2011, Penn State University Archives. The football office was named the Jay and Deanne May Linebacker Coach's Office and was in the Lasch Football Building in which Sandusky sexually violated a young boy.

31. In a well-written article ("In Wake of Scandal, Power Struggle Spread from Penn State Campus to State Capital," 13 June 2013, http://espn/go/com/espn/otl/tory/_/id/7770996/in-wake-joe-paterno), Dan Van Natta Jr. writes, "No trustee, sources say, asked a single question."

32. Penn State Board of Trustees Minutes, 10 June 1970 and 11 September 1970, Penn State University Archives; and Ben Novak, "How the Penn State Board of Trustees Really Works," www.bennovak.net.

33. Former trustee Ben Novak reinforced the statements in Standing Order IX that no independent sources of information may go to the trustees. *Centre Daily Times,* 9 January 2012, p. 4.

34. Pete Thamel and Mark Viera, "Penn State's Trustees Recount Painful Decision to Fire Paterno," *New York Times*, 19 January 2012, http://www.nytimes.com/2012/01/19/sports/ncaafootball/penn-state-trustees-recall-decision-to-fire-paterno.html?pagewanted-all.

35. Thamel and Viera, "Penn State's Trustees Recount."

36. Barry Bozeman, "The Surma Vendetta," *Voice of the FREEHdom Fighters*, 18 September 2012, http://notpsu.blogspot.com/2012/09/the-surma-vendetta.html.

37. Paula Lavigne, "Has Penn State's On-field Progress Led to Off-field Problems?" ESPN, 27 July 2008, http://sports/espn.go/com/espn/otl/news/story:id=3504925.

38. Kelly Whiteside, "Paterno Isn't All Smiles in Happy Valley," *USA Today*, 29 April 2003, Joe Paterno Papers, Box 07594, Folder "Newspaper Clippings, Magazine Articles," Penn State University Archives. In the first year and a half of Victor's career at Penn State there were thirty-six football players with disciplinary cases on file at Penn State, including some well-known players such as Andrew Guman, Michael Haynes, Maurice Humphrey, Tony Johnson, Jeremy Kapinos, Scott Paxson, E. Z. Smith, Yaacov Yisrael, and Alan Zemaitis. See "Football Players That Have a Discipline File from August 2002 to Present [ca. December 2003]," Vice-President for Student Affairs Papers, Box 12016, Folder "Pending-Judicial Cases," Penn State University Archives. A Big Ten study showed that Penn State had the greatest number of campus legal problems in 2005 and that athletes at Penn State, while being less than 2 percent of the campus population, had nearly 20 percent of all physical assault and sexual assaults on campus. See "Big Ten Discipline Date Comparisons," [ca. 2004] and "Penn State Student Athlete Data Compared to Non-Student Athlete Data," Office of the Vice President for Student Affairs Papers, Box 12016, Folder "Football," Penn State University Archives.

39. Baltasar Gracián, *The Art of Worldly Wisdom* (London, England: Macmillan, 1904), 129.

40. As quoted by Van Natta, "Sources."

41. Moving Forward was a mantra of Board of Trustees members and President Erickson after the signing of the damaging NCAA–Penn State consent decree in July 2012. "Penn State Issues Statement on Freeh Report," 12 July 2012, Legal Documents—Corman vs. NCAA," Erickson Exhibit 6, www.senatorcorman.com/legal-documents-corman-vs-ncaa.

Chapter 15. Paterno, Spanier, Schultz, Curley, and the Penn State Pandora's Box

1. Stephen Vincent Benét, "Litany for Dictatorships," http://www.swans.com/library/art6/zigo53.html.

2. Mark Brennan, "Overseeing It All [Tim Curley]," *Town and Gown* (September 2008), 40–41.

3. Athletic Director Jim Tarman appointed Curley to be the coordinator for the transition to the Big Ten. On the transition team was John Coyle, Steve Garban, Ellen Perry, Herb Schmidt, Jim Tarman, and Budd Thalman. Jim Tarman, AD memo, 13 April 1990, Budd Thalman Papers, Box A1001.11, Folder "Big 10 Transition Committee, 1990–1991," Penn State University Archives.

4. Robert Huber, "The Sins of Penn State: The Untold Story of Joe Paterno's Fall," *Philadelphia Magazine's Be Well Philly*, March 2012, http://www.phillymag.com/health/articles/the_sins_of_penn_state_the_untold_story_of_Joe_Paterno's_fall.

5. The Freeh report called Tim Curley the "errand boy" of Paterno. "Report of the Special Investigative Counsel Regarding the Actions of the Pennsylvania State University Related to the Child Sexual Abuse Committed by Gerald A. Sandusky, 12 July 2012, p. 75 [Freeh report], http://progress.psu.edu/assets/content/REPORT_FINAL_071212.pdf.

6. Vicky Triponey, e-mail to Tim Curley, 19 August 2005, Office of Vice President for Student Affairs Papers, Box 12016, Folder "Pending Judicial Cases," Penn State University Archives.

7. Scott Soshnick and Eben Novy-Williams, "Power Struggle," *Centre Daily Times*, 28 December 2011, p. A3.

8. Ryan Bagwell, "The Secret Story of Schultz's So-called 'Secret' File," http://www.bagwellforpennstate.com/blog/the-secret-story.

9. *Centre Daily Times,* 30 July 2013, p. A3.

10. Freeh report, p. 48.

11. Meeting with Trustee and Faculty-Student-Alumni Committees on Presidential Selection, ca. 1994, Bryce Jordan Papers, Box 10421, Folder "Consultant on Penn State Presidential Searches Information 1990, 1994," Penn State University Archives.

12. Chancellor Graham Spanier to University of Nebraska Board of Regents, 2 April 1993, Chancellors' Central Files, Box 299, Folder 26, University of Nebraska Archives.

13. One trustee, Keith Eckel, after the Sandusky Scandal broke, said that Spanier did not bring details to the board, stating, "I absolutely believe that we should have had earlier knowledge of this." Borys Krawczeniuk and Stephan J. Pytak, "2 Penn State Trustees Discuss Firing Paterno, Spanier," 18 November 2011, http://republicanherald.com/news/2-penn-state-trustees.

14. William T. Mallon, "The Alchemist: A Case Study of a Failed Merger in Academic Medicine," *Strategic Alliances in Academic Medicine* (2003), 26–37, http://journals.lww.com/academicmedicine/documents/mallon.pdf.

15. As quoted by the *New York Times*, 19 January 2012, http://www.nytimes.com/2012/01/19/sports/ncaafootball/penn-state-trustees.

16. "Report of the Board of Trustees Concerning Nov. 9 Decisions," 12 March 2012, http://live.psu.edu/strory/5834#rss49.

17. Joe Palazzolo, "Paterno Family: 'Everyone Shares the Responsibility,'" WSJBLOGS, 12 July 2012, http://blogs.wsj.com/law/2012/07/12/everyone-shares-the responsibility.

18. "The Paterno Report: Critique of the Freeh Report," 10 February 2013, *Centre Daily Times*, 11 February 2013, 14 pp.

19. Notes from Paterno's attorney to the special investigative counsel pertaining to the Sandusky retirement, Exhibit 3D, Freeh report, p. 199; and "Paterno Report."

20. Ray H. Smith, "Evolution of Physical Education at the Pennsylvania State College Including Alumni Participation," 20 January 1932, College of Health, Physical Education and Recreation Papers, Box 04448, Folder "College of H.P.E.R. Athletic Comm. of the Senate, 1922–1951," Penn State University Archives.

21. Dan Van Natta Jr., "In Wake of Scandal, Power Struggle Spread from Penn State Campus to State Capital," 13 June 2013, http://espn.go.com/espn/otl/story/_/id/7770996/in-wake-joe-paterno.

22. Louis Crompton, *Homosexuality and Civilization* (Cambridge, MA: Harvard University Press, 2003), 84–85.

23. See number 08.292 in the Museum of Fine Arts, Boston.

24. Joe Paterno with Bernard Asbell, *Paterno: By the Book* (New York: Random House, 1989), 77–78.

25. Sally Jenkins, "Joe Paterno's Last Interview," 14 January 2012, http://articles.washington post.com/2012–01–14/sports/35438962_1_paterno.

26. Philip Jenkins, *Pedophiles and Priests: Anatomy of a Contemporary Crisis* (New York: Oxford University Press, 1996).

27. Freeh report, p. 47.

28. Freeh report, p. 48.

29. Joe Paterno Appointment Book (1998), Paterno Papers, Box 07574, Folder "Appointment Book," Penn State University Archives.

30. Freeh report, p. 48. The Paterno family suggests that this quote may be referring to Jerry Sandusky, who was considering beginning a football program at the Penn State Altoona Campus. "Paterno Report."

31. Freeh report, pp. 49–50.

32. As quoted in Tim Curley, e-mail to Graham Spanier, 19 January 1999, Exhibit 3C, Freeh report, p. 197.

33. Tim Curley e-mail to Graham Spanier and Gary Schultz, 8 February 1999 and 10 February 1999, Exhibit 3A and 3B, Freeh report, pp. 193, 195.

34. Rodney A. Erickson, e-mail to Robert Secor, Vice Provost, 31 August 1999, Exhibit 3I, Freeh report, p. 211. This action was similar to one in my own experience when the provost gave immediate tenure and full professorship to a new dean of the School of Communications without required action by the Immediate Tenure Committee. I was on that committee with two others. All three opposed immediate tenure and a professorship, believing that the candidate would not likely be granted assistant professor status, to say anything of tenure, in any other university unit.

35. Tim Curley, e-mail to Graham Spanier and Gary Schultz, 13 June 1999, Exhibit 3G, Freeh report, p. 206.

36. Freeh report, p. 54; and Genaro C. Armas, "Jerry Sandusky Trial: 'Victim 4' Delivers Graphic Testimony," http://www.huffingtonpost.com/2012/06/11/jerry-sandusky-trial.

37. *Commonwealth of Pennsylvania v. Timothy Mark Curley*, Court of Common Pleas, Dauphin Co., PA, No. CP-MD-1374–2011, Transcript of Proceedings Hearings, 12 January 2011, p. 1 of testimony.

38. Freeh report, p. 69; and Charles Thompson, "Former Penn State Police Chief Testifies about Old Main Interest in Sandusky," 29 July 2013, www.pennlive.com/midstte/index.ssf/2013/07/former_penn_state_police_chief.html.

39. Tim Curley e-mail to Gary Schultz and Graham Spanier, 27 February 2001, Freeh report, p. 74.

40. Graham Spanier e-mail to Tim Curley and Gary Schultz, 27 February 2001, Freeh report, p. 75.

41. "Joe Paterno Interview: Sally Jenkins Discusses Her Talk with Ex-Penn State Coach," 16 January 2012, http://live.washingtonpost.com/joe-paterno-speaks-to-sally-jenkins.html.

42. Graham Spanier interview with the special investigative counsel, 6 July 2012, Freeh report, p. 73.

43. Freeh report, pp. 78–79.

44. Two types of institutional failure were suggested by Michael Bérubé, "Why I Resigned the Paterno Chair," *Chronicle of Higher Education*, 15 October 2012, http://chronicle.com/article/Why-I-Resigned-the-Paterno/134944.

45. Michael Brand, "The Unfinished Business in Happy Valley," *Voices of Central Pennsylvania*, October 2012, p. 23.

46. For Victim 1's account and that of his mother and a psychologist, see Aaron Fisher with Michael Gillum and Dawn Daniels, *Silent No More: Victim 1's Fight for Justice against Jerry Sandusky* (New York: Ballantine, 2012).

47. *Commonwealth of Pennsylvania v. Timothy Mark Curley*, grand jury transcript of Tim Curley, 16 December 2011, http://media.pennlive.com/midstate_impact/other/Curley-Schultz-Hearing-Transcript.pdf.

Chapter 16. From Grand Jury to Beyond the NCAA Consent Decree

1. "Joe Paterno to Retire; President Out?" ESPN.com, 9 November 2011, http://espn.go.com/college-football/story/_/id/7211281/penn-state.

2. Frazier was chief executive officer of Merck Drugs, and he led Merck out of the multibillion dollar Vioxx lawsuit in which the pain killer unfortunately led to heart attacks and strokes.

Fortunately for Merck, it settled nearly 50,000 cases for less than $5 billion when estimates were for more than $25 billion. Luke O'Brien, "Penn State Hired Merck CEO Kenneth Frazier to Investigate the Sandusky Scandal Because Penn State Is Dumb," *Deadspin.com*, 15 November 2011, http://deadspin.com/5859910.

3. Taylor Branch, "The Shame of College Sports," *Atlantic* (October 2011), http://www.theatlantic.com/magazine/archives/2011/10/the-shame-of-college-sports/308643/2.

4. A former Harvard president emphasized the increase of commercialism in universities in Derek Bok, *Universities in the Marketplace: The Commercialization of Higher Education* (Princeton, NJ: Princeton University Press, 2003).

5. Christopher McDougall, "They are . . . Penn State? Major Corporations Are Making a Lot of Good Things Possible at Penn State—and Making Some People Nervous," *Penn Stater* (March/April 2000), 31.

6. Mark A. Emmert to President Rodney Erickson, 17 November 2011, http://www.psu.edu/ur/2011/ncaa.pdf.

7. James Madison, Virginia Constitutional Convention, Richmond, Virginia, 2 December 1829.

8. "01–28–2015: PS4RS Applauds President Barron's Criticism of the Freeh Report," 28 January 2015., http:ps4rs.org/2015/01/28/ps4rs-penn-state-president. The Big Ten counsel, Jon Barrett, on July 7 asked the head of the Freeh investigation, Omar McNeill, "Did the Freeh Group interview Graham Spanier this week as contemplated? If so, can you share any information with us?" This was five days before the Freeh report was released. Jonathan A. Barrett, e-mail to Omar McNeill, cc: Donald Remy, 7 July 2012, McNeill Exhibit 11, "Legal documents—Corman vs. NCAA," www.senatorcorman.com/legal-documents-corman-vs-ncaa.

9. "Report of the Special Investigative Counsel Regarding the Actions of the Pennsylvania State University Related to the Child Sexual Abuse Committed by Gerald A. Sandusky" [Freeh report], 12 July 2012, p. 14, 16, 17, 71, 131.

10. Freeh report, 12 July 2012, pp. 17, 138–39, 18, and 129, respectively. Emphasis is added.

11. Freeh report, 12 July 2012, pp. 88, 100, 101, respectively.

12. Ed Ray e-mail to Julie Roe, Jim Isch, and Mark Emmert, NCAA officials, 12 July 2012, https://www.scribd.com/embeds/24569739/content_inner?escape=false&start_page=1.

13. "Heart of Dixie," response to "No Wonder the NCAA Is Fighting Discovery so Vehemently," 6 November 2014, http://csnbbs.com/thread-711030-page-2.html.

14. "Mark Emmert, NCAA Made Big Mistake with Penn State Sanctions," 26 July 2012, http://www.opposingviews.com/I/sports/ncaa-football/big-ten/mark-emmert.

15. NCAA "Glossary of Terms," http://web.archive.org/web/20101218213643/http:ncaa .org/wps/wem/ . . . /glossary+of+terms. Emphasis is added.

16. Kevin Lennon to Julie Roe and Roe to Lennon, 14 July 2012, https://www.scribd.com/ embeds/24569739/content_inner?escape=false&start_page-1.

17. Quoted in Peter Thamel, "N.C.A.A. Begins Penn State Inquiry," *New York Times*, 18 November 2011, http://www.nytimes.com/2011/11/19/sports/ncaafootball/ncaa-plans-inquiry.

18. Doug Letterman, "The NCAA Crosses a Line," *Inside Higher Ed*, 23 November 2011, http://www.insidehighered.com/news/2011/11/13/ncaa-inquiry-penn-state.

19. *Centre Daily Times*, 4 October 2012, p. A5.

20. Kevin Horne, "Judge Throws Out Corbett's Antitrust Lawsuit," 6 June 2013, http:// www.politics.com/judge-throws-out . . . 48501.

21. Don Yaeger, *Undue Process: The NCAA's Injustice for All* (Champaign, IL: Sagamore, 1991); Tom Farrey, "Tark Helped Take Bite Out of NCAA Investigations," ESPN.com, 29 November 2001, http://static.espn.go.com/ncf/s/2001/1126;1284943.html; and James Potter, "The NCAA as State Actor: Tarkanian, Brentwood, and Due Process," *University of Pennsylvania Law Review*, 155 (2007), 1269–1304.

22. 2011–2012 NCAA Division I Manual, Effective 1 August 2011, "Constitution, Operating Bylaws, Administrative Bylaws," http://www.ncaapublications.com/productdownloads/ d112.pdf (2 July 2014). See Article 19.5.2 (k) (2).

23. Rodney K. Smith, " A Brief History of the National Collegiate Athletic Association's Role in Regulating Intercollegiate Athletics," *Marquette Sports Law Review*, 11, no. 1 (Fall 2000), 9–22.

24. Scott Kretchmar, "The Future of the NCAA and Its Membership," 3 October 2012, at a panel on the NCAA at the State College Theatre, State College, Pennsylvania, Ronald Smith personal file.

25. Brent Schrotenboer, "Digging into the Past of NCAA President Mark Emmert," *USA Today*, 3 April 2013, http://www.usatoday.com/story/sports/ncaab/2013/04/02/ncaa.

26. Andrew J. Mitten, "The Penn State 'Consent Decree': The NCAA's Coercive Means Don't Justify Its Laudable Ends, But Is There a Legal Remedy?" *Pepperdine Law Review*, 41 (2013), 321–48.

27. Joel N. Myers, "PennLive Op-ed," 4 December 2014, http://www.pennlive.com/ opinion/2014/12/the_ncaa.

28. Penn State Board of Trustees Minutes, 12 August 2012, Penn State University Archives.

29. "Binding Consent Decree Imposed by the National Collegiate Athletic Association and Accepted by the Pennsylvania State University," 23 July 2012, http://www.washington post.com/up-srv/sports/ncaa-sanctions-penn-state.html.

30. Erickson stated his reasoning before the Board of Trustees. Penn State Board of Trustees Minutes, 12 August 2012, Penn State University Archives.

31. Rachel George, "Penn State Trustees Take No Action on Consent Decree," *USA Today*, 12 August 2012, http://usatoday30.usatoday.com/sports/college/football/bigten/ story/2012-08-12/penn-state . . . 57016128/1.

32. On January 16, 2015, the NCAA restored the 112 victories to Penn State football as part of a deal by which State Senator Jake Corman would drop a lawsuit coming up for trial in February 2015 against the NCAA that the NCAA likely felt it would lose.

33. Mitten, "Penn State 'Consent Decree,'" 334.

34. "The Paterno Report: Critique of the Freeh Report," *Centre Daily Times,* 10 February 2013.

35. *George Scott Paterno and Family of Joe Paterno, et al. v. NCAA,* Court of Common Pleas of Centre County, Pennsylvania, 30 May 2013.

36. Lawsuits surrounding the Sandusky Scandal include (1) *Pennsylvania v. Curley, Schultz, and Spanier,* (2) *The Paterno Family v. NCAA,* (3) *State Senator Corman v. NCAA,* (4) *Spanier v. Freeh,* (5) *NCAA v. McCord,* (6) *McQueary vs. Penn State,* (7) *Two Assistant Coaches v. Penn State,* (8) *Sandusky victims v. Penn State,* and (9) *Sandusky victims v. The Second Mile.* There are also possible violations of the Clery Act by the U.S. Department of Education, Title IX of the 1972 Educational Amendments Act of 1972, and judgments by the accrediting Middle States Association.

37. Terry Denbow, "Maybe, Just Maybe, Insularity Exists," *Centre Daily Times,* 12 July 2012, p. A8. Denbow wrote a beautiful comparison of Alabama and Penn State: "Football Fundamentalism and Penn State: They Got It Wrong in Happy Valley. Did Bryant Have It Right?" *Tuscaloosa News,* 5 August 2012, http://www.tuscaloosanews.com/article/20120805/NEWS/20809930?P-381tc=pq.

INDEX

Note: The Penn State division that includes its football program has had various titles. Cross references from each of these include: College of Health and Human Development; College of Health, Physical Education and Recreation; College of Physical Education and Athletics; Department of Physical Education; Physical Education Department; School of Physical Education and Athletics

Abercrombie, James, 12–13
academic integrity v. athletic success, 12–13, 15–16, 22–23, 73, 76, 201–2n4, 206n59. *See also* athletics realignment (1980); commercialism (and college athletic programs); Grand Experiment
academic-athletic model, 222–23n10. *See also* academic integrity v. athletic success; Grand Experiment
Ad Hoc Committee on Varsity Athletics (1972), 224n30
Aeneid (Virgil), 100–101, 166, 201n35
Affelder, William L., 50
Affirmative Action, 146–47
African Americans, 23, 57, 107–9, 147, 148, 151, 224n37
Alabama, University of, 8, 9–10, 12–13, 22, 41, 78. 81, 91, 103–4, 107, 113–19
Alamo Bowl, 134, 169
Alexander, William, 113
Alma Mater, 5, 35, 36, 199n6
Alumni Advisory Committee of the Athletic Association: athletic director relationship, 38–39; athletic eligibility code, 40; athletic scholarships, 16; Bezdek hiring, 43; coach selection function, 68; early authority over athletics, 38–40; Grand Experiment effect, 72–73; purpose and function, 31–32, 37, 76; replacement, 48
alumni and athletics, 16–21, 32, 35–42, 43–52, 54–63, 65–69, 72, 74–76, 80, 85, 102, 111, 120, 122, 181, 205n45, 205n49, 210n13, 212n42, 215n31, 215n33, 217n31, 221n35. *See also* alumni societies; Graduate Manager of Athletics; *specific alumni*
Alumni Quarterly, 41–42
alumni societies, 35–42, 210n7, 210n13, 211n20
American Council of Trustees and Alumni, 150
Ames, Knowlton "Snake," 16
Andrews, J.M.H., 61
Architecture and Landscape Architecture fellowships, 115
Arnelle, Jesse, 108–9
Arnold, Karen, 131
Asbell, Bernard, 9, 156, 241n25
Asbury, William, 121, 145
assistant coaches and promotion, 25–26, 32, 33, 34, 67
Association for Intercollegiate Athletics for Women (AIAW), 142
Association of American Universities, 70, 94, 220n27
Atherton, Charlie, 14–15, 30, 202–3n17
Atherton, George Washington, 5, 13, 14–17, 21, 29, 35, 38, 112, 150, 171–72, 199n6, 202n11
Athletic Advisory Board, 60, 65–66, 73
Athletic Association, 14–15, 37, 68. *See also* Alumni Advisory Committee of the Athletic Association
athletic control reform efforts, 47–52. *See also* academic integrity v. athletic success; Grand Experiment; Great Experiment
athletic department. *See also various other Penn State divisions which included its football program*
athletic field construction, 17
Athletic Integrity Office, 180
athletic power coup. *See* athletics realignment (1980)
athletic program academic scandals (1950s and 1960s), 79

athletic scholarships: Athletic Advisory Board recommendations (1947), 65–66; Board of Trustees, 16, 38, 203n21; Board of Trustees and Faculty Senate Committee of Scholarships (1948), 65–66; Carnegie Report, 19; early growth in numbers awarded, 38; elimination by Beaver White Committee (1927), 48–49; history, 7, 200n12, 200n20; Levi Lamb Grant-in-Aid Fund (1952), 66; National Collegiate Athletic Association code, 20; Thomas administration, 19, 204n35, 204n39
athletic-academic counseling, 104–5, 118–19
athletics conferences, 89–90. *See also specific conferences*
athletics policy control alternatives (mid-1920s), 47
athletics realignment (1980): criminal charges leveled against football players, 122–23; discussed and explained, 83–88; overviews, 10, 52, 58, 73, 75, 183; player character change with lowering athlete admission standards, 117–19; player disciplinary problem statistics, 242n38; player entitlement relationship, 117–19; presidential admit policy (for academically substandard athletes), 16, 22–23, 75, 105–7, 117–19, 121; Sandusky Scandal relationship, 88, 127, 171; "State Penn," 119; trustee approval lack, 76. *See also* academic integrity v. athletic success; business-financial model; commercialism (and college athletic programs)

Bach, John, 88, 148
Bachman, Denise, 125
Bahr, Walter, 82
Baldwin, Cynthia, 138, 155, 157, 171, 173, 182
Barbour, Sandy, 182
Barron, Eric, 182
Baugh, Kevin, 106
Bay, Rick, 97
Beaver, James A., 29, 35
Beaver Field, 17, 29, 44, 46, 162
Beaver Stadium, 24, 29, 36, 37, 46, 82, 133
Beaver White Committee (1927), 48–50
Bedenk, Joe, 7, 66, 162
Benét, Stephen Vincent, 161
Bentley, F.L., 61
Bergstein, Andrew, 10
Bermingham, Thomas, 100, 115
Berndt, Jerry, 25
Bérubé, Michael, 115, 244–45n44
Bezdek, Hugo: appointment as Director of the School of Physical Education and Athletics, 75; athletic scholarships elimination impact,

49–50; athletic scholarships recommendation, 58–59; background and experience, 42, 43–44, 113; coaching style and personality, 44–45, 46–47, 58–59; Director of Physical Education, 51, 58–59; firing as coach, 51, 75, 87; head of Physical Education Department v. coaching, 48–49; hiring by Penn State, 43; long-term coaching contract, 47–48; Paterno similarities, 43; Penn State tenure, 17–19, 21, 33, 34; resignation from Penn State, 61, 148; salaries, 51–52; as scapegoat for losses of 1930s, 59; sports facility and opportunity expansion, 46; undefeated streak, 19, 45, 89, 102
Bezilla, Michael, 151
Big Four Conference, 85, 90, 153
Big Ten Conference: academic status, 231n2; action against Paterno after Sandusky Scandal, 99; athlete eligibility standards, 97; coaches and athletic administrators from, 64, 70; College Football Association (CFA), 91; Council of Presidents, 93–96, 155; financial pressure for Penn State admission, 96–97; Hetzel connection, 57, 62; opposition to Penn State admission, 95–97; penalty on Penn State after Sandusky Scandal, 99; Penn State admission (1990), 23, 99; Penn State athletics administrative leaders transition team, 97–98; Penn State "invitation" by Council (1989), 94–95; Penn State membership, 89–99; Penn State Presidents' groundwork for admission, 92–94; prestige, 11, 18, 21, 23; study revealing Penn State players' physical and sexual assault incidents, 242n38; television revenue motivation, 98
blacks. *See* African Americans
Blaik, Earl, 113
Board of Athletic Control, 48, 49, 51, 60, 76, 215n33
Board of Trustees: academic-athletic model, 21, 67–69, 72–73; Athletic Association assistance, 15; athletic scholarships authorization, 6, 16–17, 20, 38, 66; athletics control, 76–78; athletics realignment (1980), 75, 79, 88, 89, 153, 154; authority to approve coach hirings, 165; Big Four Conference decisions, 153; Big Ten Conference admission groundwork, 91, 96, 154–55; as closed and insular, 157–58; Committee on Athletics, 59–61; concealment of football player discipline problems, 135; concealment of negative information, 149; discrimination based on sexual orientation, 142; early athletics decisions involvement history, 29–33; Eastern Collegiate Athletic Conference (ECAC), 91, 153–54; Executive Committee policy se-

crecy, 151; Grand Experiment, 67–69, 72–73; ignorance of Sandusky allegations, 243n13; intercollegiate athletics decision history, 38–43; 1960s turmoil reactions, 150, 151–52, 239–40n5; Paterno relationship, 79, 86, 109, 114, 115, 116; president's authority policy (1970), 152; Spanier firing, 155; Standing Order IX, 157–58, 241n33; University Council creation, 152; unofficial but actual power structure post athletics realignment (1980), 241n23; Warriner Committee (1929), 50–51. *See also* Board of Trustees and Sandusky Scandal; *specific trustees*

Board of Trustees and Sandusky Scandal, 241n33; alumni criticism, 35–36; appeal to NCAA regarding "death penalty," 181; failure to file suit against NCAA for consent decree and sanctions, 178; Freeh report allegations, 176–77; Garban leadership failure, 158; grand jury investigation and revelations, 135; ignorance of Sandusky allegations, 170; member comment regarding secrecy as Sandusky Scandal broke, 157; mishandling, 158–59; "move forward" advocacy post-Sandusky Scandal, 160, 181; Paterno firing, 10; Paterno relationship, 9, 79, 86, 109, 115, 116; power structure post-athletics realignment (1980), 241n3; Spanier firing, 139; Spanier obfuscation regarding grand jury proceedings, 157Standing Order IX, 157–58. *See also specific trustees*

Board of Trustees' Executive Committee. *See* Executive Committee (Board of Trustees)

Boston College, 79, 93, 113

Bracken, Ron, 102, 118–19, 125

Brand, Michael, 170

Brenchley, Jean, 241n25

Britt, Jack, 124

Bruce, Earl, 32

Bryant, Paul "Bear," 8, 9–10, 103–4, 114, 119

Bryce Jordan Center, 96, 97, 127, 133, 169

Bryne, Bill, 61

Buck, Roy, 152, 239–40n5

Bucknell, William, 26

Bush, Reggie, 174

Bush, Vannevar, 21, 68–69

business and athletics. *See* athletics realignment (1980)

business-financial model, 75, 77–78, 83–88. *See also* athletics realignment (1980)

Buskirk, Elsworth, 2, 71

Byers, Walter, 23

California-Berkeley, University of, 85, 151, 152, 182

Carnegie, Andrew, 31, 203n21, 209n40

Carnegie Foundation study of college athletics (1926–1929), 19, 49, 53–54

Center for Excellence (for Second Mile children), 136–37

Centre County Office of Children and Youth Services, 131

Centre Daily Times, 6

Chadman, George, 26

Chambers, Alycia, 131, 167

Chicago, University of, 17, 33, 42, 43, 70, 113, 220n27

Chicago Sun Times, 144

civil rights, 78, 107, 147, 150, 151

Civil Rights Act of 1964, 147

Classics Department, 115, 119, 123, 133

Clayton, John, 103–4

Cleaver, Clarence G., 28

Clemens, Al, 182

Cobbs, Duffy, 10

College Football Association (CFA), 84, 91–92, 97–98, 110, 224n36

College of Health and Human Development, 88, 168. *See also various other Penn State divisions which included its football program*

College of Health, Physical Education and Recreation, 82, 84–85, 88, 92, 105, 127. *See also various other Penn State divisions which included its football program*

College of Physical Education and Athletics, 2, 222–23n10. *See also various other Penn State divisions which included its football program*

commercialism (and college athletic programs), 3, 19, 49, 53, 56–58, 63, 91, 113, 174. *See also* academic integrity v. athletic success; business-financial model; salaries (sports directors and leaders); *specific coaches*

Committee to Review Dean Scannell's Office. *See* Dean Scannell Review Committee

compensation (athletic coaches v. faculty and administration), 54, 67. *See also specific coaches*

Conger, Ray, 77

Conlin, Bill, 101–2, 228n6

Cooper, Mike, 108

Coppersmith, Mimi Barash, 9, 200n26

Corbett, Tom: connections to Penn State, Sandusky and Second Mile, 124, 134, 136–37, 138, 163, 170–71; lawsuit against NCAA, 178; political ambitions connection conjecture, 134, 136–37, 138, 163, 178

Corman, Jake, 247n32

Cornell University, 7, 13

Corrigan, Gene, 178

Cotton Bowl and desegregation, 55, 57, 62, 63, 221n33

coup d'état. *See* athletics realignment (1980)

Courtney, Linette, 137

Courtney, Wendell, 137–38, 169, 175

cow college, 7, 10, 70

Coyle, John, 80

culture of silence, 96, 138–39, 140–49, 157–58. *See also* athletics realignment (1980)

Curley, Tim: athletics realignment (1980), 161–62; Big Ten Conference transition coordination, 242n3; Freeh report allegations and condemnation, 139, 175–76; Grand Experiment, 88; grand jury testimony, 171; Harris lawsuit of 2005, 147; lifelong Penn State connection, 242n3; lying under oath charge (2010), 134–35; Paterno relationship, 123, 162–63; professional life overview, 162–63; Sandusky allegations, 129–30, 131–32, 167, 169–70

Curtin, Max, 30

Czekaj, Ed, 71, 77, 82, 83, 84, 127, 148, 225n55

Daily Collegian, 41, 59, 125. See also *The Free Lance*

D'Augulli, Anthony, 145

Davies, Cindy, 143

Davis, Elwood C., 61

Dean Scannell Review Committee, 82–84, 224n35

death penalty, 79, 110, 139, 177, 179–81, 201–2n4, 236–37n42

Deike, George H., 61

Delany, Jim, 96

Dempsey, Cedric, 178

Denbow, Terry, 183

Department of Classics and Mediterranean Studies, 115

Department of Physical Education, 39–40, 51, 61, 69. *See also various other Penn State divisions which included its football program*

Devaney, Bob, 62

Didinger, Ray, 107, 109

Director of Physical Education, 51

Division of Affirmative Action, 146–47

Dobie, Gil, 113

Dorsett, Tony, 90, 111, 230n48

Dowler, Henry, 30

Downing, Frank, 104–5

Dunn, William "Mother," 31, 209n36

Dunsmore, J.A., 15

Dutchcot, Leslie, 134–35, 136

early football games, 27–30, 207n9, 207n10

early football management and administration, 31–32. *See also* Great Experiment; *specific coaches*; *specific presidents*

Eastern Collegiate Athletic Conference (ECAC), 65–66, 106, 153, 154, 219n7

Eckel, Keith, 243n13

Edwards, Earle, 56, 66, 133, 165, 217n17

Edwards, Harry, 109

Egli, John, 87, 148, 225n55

Eisenhower, Dwight D., 20, 21

Eisenhower, Milton, 20, 21, 61, 64, 65, 66

Eliot, Charles, 37

Emmert, Mark, 42, 135, 162, 168, 174–75, 177–80, 201–2n4

Engle, Rip, 20, 34, 43, 47, 63, 133, 209n45; academic-athletic model, 22; academic standards for athletes, 74, 119–20; athletic scholarships, 7–8; Grand Experiment role, 64–74, 102–3, 165, 219n13; Happy Valley ethos, 6–7; hiring by Penn State as coach (1950), 66; Paterno relationship, 20; professorship, 2, 219n15

Erickson, Rodney: accession to Penn State presidency, 139; athletic leaders' relationship, 13; legal advice failure, 180; "Move Forward" advocacy post-Sandusky scandal, 160, 242n41; NCAA consent decree acceptance, 178–81, 236–37n42, 241n21; NCAA intimidation early, 174–75, 201–2n4; NCAA sanctions (2012), 110–11, 168; Sandusky retirement, 168, 244n34

Etter, Scott, 12, 31, 104

Eugene Granley Special Athletic Committee (of the Alumni Association) (1935), 61

exceptionalism, 3, 199n1

Executive Committee (Board of Trustees), 60, 72–73, 151, 155, 181, 205n46, 221n23. *See also* Board of Trustees

Executive Committee of Athletic Department (under various Department names), 77, 151, 220n22

Faculty Committee on Athletics, 38

Faculty Senate, 145, 152. *See also* academic-athletic model; University Faculty Senate

Faculty Senate Committee of Scholarships, 65–66

Farrell, Patricia, 82

Father Bermingham Scholarship Fund for Greek and Latin, 115

Fennell, Tom, 32

Fiedler, Leslie, 167

finance and athletics. *See* athletics realignment (1980); business-financial model

Fisher, Aaron, 134, 135, 137, 170
Fisher, Fran, 7, 201n36
Fisher, Jerry, 11, 201n36
Fleming, Neil, 42, 61, 65
Florence and Angelo Paterno Graduate Fellowships in Liberal Arts, 115
football revenue: gate receipts, 32–33, 39, 47, 50, 77–78; subsidization of recreation and other facilities, 76–77, 78, 80–81, 224n29; television contracts, 91–92, 97–98, 110, 153, 224n35
Forth, Stuart, 116
Franklin, James, 182
Frazier, Kenneth, 160, 173, 245n2
Freeh report: contents, 175–77; impact, 175; NCAA first responses, 174; NCAA sanctions justification, 110, 139, 173–75; overviews, 162; Paterno family rebuttal, 128, 182; Paterno-related content, 117; Penn State leadership, 175–76
The Free Lance, 28, 29, 30, 32, 38
freshman ineligibility rule, 17–18
Friedman, Robert, 152–53

Gage, Mary, 11
Ganim, Sara, 128, 156–57
Garban, Steve: athletics realignment (1980), 10, 40, 58, 73, 75, 76, 80, 82, 84, 88, 118, 127, 141, 154, 163, 172, 183, 224n35; Big Ten Conference transition team, 94, 96–97; Board of Trustees leadership, 155, 158–59; Paterno relationship, 122, 158; Penn State policy forbidding sexual orientation discrimination, 145; Sandusky cover-up, 158; Scannell relationship, 82–84
Geisinger Medical Center, 164
Genovese, Katherine, 135–36
Georgia, University of, 9, 106
Gerald R. Ford Award, 99
Giftopoulos, Pete, 10
Gilbert, Ike, 68, 71, 72, 205n12, 220n21, 221n33
Gilligan, Jim, 63
Golden, William N. "Pop," 16, 30–32, 38–39
Gottlieb, David, 183
Graduate Manager of Athletics, 21, 36, 38–39, 40, 42, 44, 48, 51, 61, 65, 71, 72, 205n49, 221n33
Graham, Frank, 12
Graham, George M., 4
Grand Destiny Capital Campaign, 115
Grand Experiment: academic improvements in Department of Physical Education, 69–72; Alabama game loss (1979), 103–4; alumni control of athletics, 67–68; Athletic Advisory Board, 60, 65–66, 73;

athletic scholarships, 22; Board of Trustees statement (1965), 73; financial control of athletics, 71; intersectional football game introduction, 72; leader advocates, 64–65, 67; McCoy authority over athletics, 72–73; national championship quest impact, 103–4, 108; originators, 102; presidential athlete admissions, 22–23; promotion methods, 102; term origin, 102; Walker on, 69. *See also* academic-athletic model; Paterno's Grand Experiment
Granley, Eugene, 59
Gray Stone Manor, 56–57, 65
Great Depression, 2, 5–6, 20, 34, 50, 51, 56, 62
Great Experiment, 19, 49, 52, 53–63. *See also* academic integrity v. athletic success
Gricar, Ray, 131, 132, 168
Gross, Elmer, 77
Gulas, Corinne and Chris, 143–44, 149
Gyger, Furman H., 50

Haden, Nicholas, 22, 106
Haidt, Marie, 71
Happy Valley ethos, 2–3, 6–7, 8–9, 13, 109, 183. *See also* State College (town)
Harlow, Dick, 17, 26, 33–34, 40, 41, 42, 43, 46–47
Harmon, Tom, 169, 175
Harris, Dorothy, 2
Harris, Franco, 108
Harris, Jennifer, 143, 145–48
Harris, J.T., 61
Harris, Pete, 118
Harris v. Portland (2005), 143, 146–48
Harrisburg Patriot News, 128, 156–57
Hart, Albert B., 36
Harter, Dick, 148
Harvard tie celebratory bonfire, 35, 210n4
Harvard University, 13, 16, 21, 26, 28, 32, 33–37, 40, 45, 67, 73, 89, 113, 151, 152, 203n20, 207n12
Hayes, Woody, 113
Heim, Bruce, 135–36
Heim, Susan, 136
Heisman, John, 113
Heppenstall, C.W., 41, 50–52
Hetzel, Ralph Dorn, 150; academic integrity v. athletic success, 19, 57–58; achievements as Penn State president, 62; on Bezdek and School of Physical Education and Athletics, 51, 59–60; Bezdek firing, 75–76; building construction during administration, 62; on college football, 50; Great Experiment, 19–20, 53–63, 205n49; on Happy Valley ethos, 4–5

Higgins, Bob, 34; football game win record, 7, 20, 62; Great Experiment role, 53–63; hiring by Penn State, 54; Jones athlete recruiting relationship, 55; successor coach selection and preference, 66, 133; 217n17
Hildebrand, Charlie, 28
Hippodrome Field Day, 46
Hoggard, Dennis, 57
Hollenback, Bill, 32, 33
Homophiles of Penn State, 142
Horn, Stephen, 92
Hoskins, George W., 15, 29–30
Houghton, Percy, 113
Hufnagel, John, 108
Humphrey, Maurice, 121, 233n34

Ikenberry, Stanley, 93, 94, 98, 99
Illinois, University of, 93, 94
imperial university presidencies, 150, 239n1
intersectional football games, 72, 221n33
investigations of college athletics: Beaver White Committee (1927), 48–50; Carnegie Foundation study of college athletics (1926–1929), 192, 19, 48–50, 53–54; Eugene Granley Special Athletic Committee (of the Alumni Association, 1935), 59, 60, 61; National Collegiate Athletic Association investigation of college football (1920s), 49; Trustee Special Committee on Athletics (1936), 60; Warriner Committee research and recommendations (1929), 50–52. *See also* Freeh report
Irvin Hall, 46. *See also* Varsity Hall

Jackson, J. Price, 16, 38
Jackson, Keith, 7
James Beaver White Committee, 48–50, 205n45
Jenkins, Philip, 167
Jenkins, Sally, 167
"jock house" for athlete accommodation, 46. *See also* Gray Stone Manor; Varsity Hall
Joe and Sue Paterno Library, 115–16
"Joe Don't Go Pro" campaign, 9, 200n26
Joe Paterno Day, 9
Johnson, Samuel, 3–4
Jones, Ben C. "Casey," 55–57, 63, 64, 65, 72, 172
Jones, Howard, 113
Jordan, Bryce, 22, 23, 93–94, 98, 154–55
Joyner, Dave, 139

Kent State University, 121, 152, 158
Kentucky, University of, 22, 67, 68, 76, 79, 84, 85, 104, 114, 119, 224n37
Kirsch, Rod, 132

Knight, Bobby, 128
Kofman, Nadine, 6
Krall, Allan, 152
Kretchmar, Scott, 179

Lamb, Levi, 41–42, 66, 72, 212n42
Lasch Football Building. *See* Mildred and Louis Lasch Football Building
Lauro, Jerry, 131
La Vie, 38
Lawther, John, 2, 64, 67, 69–70, 71, 73, 77
Leahy, Frank, 113
LeBlanc, Mark, 110
Lehman, Katey, 6
Lehrman, Ken, 146, 147, 148
Lennon, Kevin, 177
Lesbian, Gay and Bisexual Student Alliance of Penn State, 145
lesbians, 142–49
Lessingham, John, 101
Levi Lamb Grant-in-Aid Fund, 42, 66, 72, 212n42
Liberal Arts Alumni Society Board, 115
Liberal Arts Development Council, 115
library fee, 31, 209n40
"Linebacker Coach's Office," 157, 241n30
Linsz, George, 27–28
Lipsyte, Robert, 145–46
Longman, Jere, 144
Looney, Douglas, 104
Love and Death in the American Novel (Fiedler), 167
Lowell, A. Lawrence, 45

Machiavelli, Niccolò, 22–23
Madeira, Michael, 124, 134
Mahon, Bill, 147
Mallon, William, 164
Marsh, Eugene, 180, 181, 236–37n42
Marshall, Bonnie, 138
Mason, H. D. "Joe," 61
Massey, Ben, 77, 222n9
Massey Report, 77
McCombie, Ryan, 181
McConnell, Suzie, 144
McCormick, Vance, 60–61
McCoy, Ernie: academic credentials, 70; academic standards for athletes, 74, 105–6; academic-athletic model, 2, 20–21, 76–77, 88; full authority over athletics granted by Board of Trustees, 72; Grand Experiment role, 64–74, 102; removal of athletic control from alumni, 67–68; women's athletics, 141, 205n52; big-time schedule, 221n33

McCreary, Irvin P., 26
McDonald, Quintus, 109
McIlveen, Henry Cooke "Irish," 32
McMullen, Joe, 32
McQueary, John, 129–30
McQueary, Mike, 116, 129–30, 133, 135, 156, 169, 170, 175
Meek, George, 38–39
Meiser, Pat, 142, 143, 144, 237n9
Miami, University of, 10, 104, 128, 174
Middlebury College, 18
Mildred and Louis Lasch Football Building, 127, 129, 130, 131, 157, 169, 241n30
Milholland, James, 20, 61, 205n45
Mitchell, George, 180
Mitchell, Lydell, 108
Mitten, Andrew J., 179, 181
Mosbacher, Dee, 149
"move forward" policy, 160,181
Musser, Boyd A., 61
Myers, Joel, 95–96, 155, 180, 181, 236–37n42, 241nn21–22

National Center for Lesbian rights, 147
National Collegiate Athletic Association (NCAA): athlete recruiting and subsidization standards, 65–66; Code of Ethics, 58–59; condemnations of Penn State athletic and senior university leadership and culture, 139; corruption and regulation violations of late 1940s and early 1950s, 68; "death penalty," 110, 177, 247n32; failure to conduct its own investigation of Penn State/Sandusky allegations, 177; first responses to Sandusky Scandal, 174; football revenue, 92; investigation of college football (1920s), 49; Penn State intimidation early in Sandusky scandal investigation, 174–75; power struggle of 1990, 98; sanctions against Penn State (2012), 109, 110, 139, 177, 179–81, 201–2n4, 241n21, 247n32; Sanity Code (athletic scholarships policy), 20; Supreme Court decision of 1984, 92, 97; threats against Penn State, 180; university scandals prior to Penn State's, 174; violations of its own rules and regulations, 177–79
national football championships, 8–10
National Football League (NFL), 9
National Sports Law Institute, 179
NCAA (National Collegiate Athletic Association). *See* National Collegiate Athletic Association (NCAA)
Neal, Anne, 150

Nebraska, University of, 13, 61–62, 72, 93, 163, 177
Nelson, Richard, 2
New Beaver Field, 17, 162
Newton, Cam, 174
Newton, Silvanus, 30
Neyland, Robert, 68, 73, 113, 114
NFL (National Football League), 9
Nichols, Terrence, 106
Nicklas, Steve, 3
Niebel, Ben, 82
Nittany Lions, 6, 8–10, 200n14. *See also* Nittany Valley; *specific athletics-related material; specific individuals*
Nittany Valley, 1, 4, 172. *See also* Happy Valley ethos; Nittany Lions; State College (town)
Nixon, Richard M., 9, 103, 152
Noll Laboratory, 71
Nolte, Scott, 149
North Carolina, University of, 12
Notre Dame, University of, 9, 33, 54, 60, 91, 92, 97, 98, 113, 114, 148
Novak, Ben, 241n23, 241n33

O'Brien, Bill, 181
O'Brien, Harold "Pat," 6
O'Brien, Michael, 125
Ohio State University, 33, 62, 72, 92, 95, 113, 116, 174, 202n17
O'Hora, Jim, 32, 77
ombudsman, 105, 225n50
Orange Bowl, 10, 59, 136
Oregon, University of, 61
Ortiz, Bonnie, 145
Oswald, John: 23, 76, 79, 85, 106, 114, 118, 240n16; on academic-athletic model, 154; academic credentials, 85; athletics realignment (1980), 10, 22, 23, 52, 58, 73, 75, 77, 83–84, 106, 127, 153, 154, 172, 183, 224n37; authority as Penn State president, 156–57; background and experience, 151–52; Big Ten Conference inquiries, 92–93; choosing athletic director, 85–86, 104, 106; NCAA reprimand and censure, 110; as president of Kentucky, 104; as promoter of athletics, 22
Outing Magazine, 46

Pac-8/Pac-10 Conference, 91, 92
Pandora's box, 8, 132, 149, 156, 160, 161, 163, 166, 167, 172, 183
Papic, Al, 62
Parsons, Bob, 108
Pasquerilla Spiritual Center, 115
Paterno (Posnanski), 125

Paterno, George, 67

Paterno, Joe: academic credentials, 85; all-male environment experience, 166; anti-Dorsett ploy (1973), 111, 230n48; arrogance and need for control, 232n27; as assistant coach, 20, 34, 66, 67; Athletic Director appointment, 79, 85–86; athletics realignment (1980), 77–79, 84–86, 111, 153, 161–62; "backed away," 116–17, 161, 170, 181; background, 4, 7; Bezdek similarities, 43; Big Four athletic conference, 90–91; bullying, 124–25; coaching record, 67; Commencement Address (1973), 9; compensation, 67, 77; dark side, 116–17, 119–26; death, 117, 134–35; disciplining errant players, 117, 124, 159; on ethics, 111; family efforts to protect legacy, 128, 182; favorite book, 201n35; Happy Valley ethos relationship, 1–11; hypocrisy, 106, 107; iconic status and alumni/student idolization, 112–13, 164–65, 173, 181; impact, 10–11; legacy, 24, 112–26; legend status, 112–13; literary/philosophical studies and quoting, 100–101, 166–67; male dominated environments, 120; national football championships, 8, 9–10; philanthropic projects, 113–16, 119–20, 133; Physical Education Department title, 2–3; player disciplinary problem statistics, 242n38; power, 119–26, 132–33, 159, 164–66, 233n38; presidential admissions for academically substandard athletes, 22, 106–8, 206n59; professorship, 2–3; on Sandusky, 128; Sandusky evaluation, 66, 128; Sandusky relationship, 24, 25, 34, 207n4; Sandusky retirement, 165, 168; Scannell relationship, 80–83; secrecy regarding football player criminal activity, 122–24; statue, 113–14, 231n6; success of Grand Experiment, 104; successor coach selection, 162; on tendency to force control, 119–20; Triponey power struggle, 119–26; undefeated seasons and national championships, 24; victories, national championships and postseason bowl wins, 113; *Wall Street Journal* editorial, 23; win percentage during first decade as coach, 7; win record compared with other coaches, 113; women's athletics, 120, 232–33n29. *See also* Paterno and Sandusky Scandal; Paterno's Grand Experiment

Paterno, Scott, 125

Paterno, Suzanne Pohland, 113, 115, 116, 133, 167, 231n10

Paterno and Sandusky Scandal: alleged ignorance of Sandusky pedophilia, 166–67; firing by Board of Trustees, 155; Freeh report, 139, 175–76; Garban relationship, 158; Sandusky allegations, 129–30. *See also* Paterno, Joe

Paterno: By the Book (Asbell), 156

Paterno family, 128

Paterno Family Fund in the Richards Civil War Era Center, 115

Paterno family lawsuit against NCAA, 182

Paterno Family Professor of Literature, 115

Paterno Libraries Endowment for books, 115

Paterno Library, 115–16

"Paterno Report: Critique of the Freeh Report," 128, 182

Paterno's Grand Experiment: academic integrity v. athletic success, 102–7; anti-Dorsett ploy (1973), 111; appearance, 110–11; athletic-academic counseling, 104–5; comparison with other NCAA member's practices, 109, 110; foundations, 102; minority player recruitment, 106, 107–9; national championship quest, 108, 109; NCAA sanctions for violations (unpublicized), 109–10; player recruitment violations, 109–10; players' academic performances in 1960s and 1970s, 103; presidential admissions (for academically substandard athletes), 22, 106–8, 206n59; pressure on faculty for athletes' grades, 105. *See also* Grand Experiment; Paterno, Joe

Patrick, Frank, 32, 67, 71, 104

Pattee, Fred Lewis, 5–6, 35, 62, 199n6, 203n22

Patterson, Robert, 82, 83, 84

paying athletes to attend Penn State, 16, 19. *See also* athletic scholarships

Pedophiles and Priests: Anatomy of a Contemporary Crisis (Jenkins), 167

Peetz, Karen, 158

Penn State Alumni Association, 35–37. *See also* alumni and athletics; alumni societies; Great Experiment; *specific alumni*

Penn State Alumni Newsletter, 50–52

Penn State Collegian, 38, 59, 125. See also *The Free Lance*

Penn State Hershey Medical Corporation, 164

Penn State Police: football player criminal behavior, 117, 121; Sandusky Scandal, 124, 131–32, 157, 166, 167, 169, 175

Penn State Scholarship Fund for aiding athletes, 42. *See also* Levi Lamb Grant-in-aid Fund

Penn State University. *See specific departments; specific events; specific individuals; specific policies*

Penn State University sexual orientation policy, 144–45

"the Penn State way," 69, 102, 124, 125, 126, 176

Pennsylvania, University of, 16, 26, 28, 30, 32, 33, 44, 59

Pennsylvania Intercollegiate Football Association, 225 n1

Perry, Ellen, 96

Phi Delta Kappan, 106, 229n13

Philadelphia Daily News, 101

Philadelphia Inquirer, 86, 144, 145

Phillips, Anwar, 120–21, 138, 159

Phillips, Bob, 32

Physical Education Department, 2–3, 48, 58, 79. *See also various other Penn State divisions which included its football program*

Pitt. *See* Pittsburgh, University of

Pittman, Charlie, 108

Pittsburgh, University of: assistant coaches, 32–33; Bezdek, 36, 42, 44, 46, 48, 49–51, 59; early football games, 7; Harlow, 41; Paterno and Conference membership considerations, 90, 94, 96; Paterno ethical violation (Dorsett), 90, 111, 230n48; Penn State alumni societies and activities, 38, 49–51, 55–58; training tables, 60. *See also* Big Four Conference; Big Ten Conference

Pittsburgh Alumni Club: 55. *See also* alumni and athletics; alumni societies; Penn State Alumni Association; *specific alumni*

Pittsburgh Press-Gazette, 125

Poole, Bob, 136

Poole, Sandra, 136

Portland, Harris v. (2005), 143, 145–48

Portland, Rene: background and experience, 142; Big Ten basketball coaching success and popularity, 142–43, 148, 236n2; Davies on, 143; discrimination based on sexual orientation, 143–49, 146–47; discrimination denials, 148; discrimination investigation, 238n11; McConnell on, 144; Paterno relationship, 141, 142; Penn State administration attitude, 149, 239n28; Penn State sexual orientation discrimination policy, 144–45; retirement, 148; sexual bias, 143–47, 149; trustee concern regarding homosexual students, 237–38n7; violations of federal law, 147–48

Posnanski, Joe, 125

Potuto, Josephine, 177–78

Prato, Louis, 103, 229n13

presidential admissions (for academically substandard athletes), 16, 22, 23, 73–74, 105–8, 121, 206n59

presidents (colleges and universities) and athletics, 12–23, 57, 150–54, 164, 171, 175, 177–79, 201–2n4, 238n1. *See also specific presidents*

Prince, Bob, 6

The Prince (Machiavelli), 12, 22–23

Princeton University, 14, 16, 26, 28, 45, 49, 73, 89, 203n20, 211n20

Pritchett, Henry S., 53–54

Psychology of Coaching (Lawther), 2

Public Works Administration (PWA), 5–6

publicity and intercollegiate athletics, 13–14, 22, 29, 49, 50, 130, 202n8

Radakovich, Dan, 32

Ralston, Ralph, 131

Randolph, Carlton "Brute," 32

Rasselas, Prince of Abyssinia (Johnson), 3–4

Rawlings, Hunter, 94

Ray, Edward J., 177, 179

Raykovitz, Jack, 135–36, 137

Rebout, James "Red," 41

Recreation Building, 76, 92, 222n6

recruitment of football players, 63. *See also* alumni and athletics; athletic scholarships; Jones, Ben C. "Casey"; presidential admissions (for academically substandard athletes)

"red shirting" athletes, 90

Reed, Dan, 32

Reid, Mike, 103

Reilly, Rick, 111

revenue and athletics. *See* athletics realignment (1980); business-financial model; commercialism; football revenue

Richards, Elton Jr., 9

Riley, Ridge, 58, 63, 80, 102

Rockne, Knute, 9, 33, 113, 114

Roe, Julie, 177

Roosevelt, Franklin D., 5–6

Rose Bowl games, 3, 19, 37, 44, 47, 91, 113

Rowland, Cappy, 151

rugby football, 26–27, 207n12

Rupp, Adolph, 84, 114, 119, 224n37

Rutgers University, 14, 29, 93, 94, 96

Ryan, Diane, 132

salaries (sports directors and leaders), 16, 18, 19, 32–33, 41, 44, 45, 47–48, 51, 59, 66, 75, 78, 86, 114, 148, 203n22, 204n32, 220–21n31

Sandusky, Jerry, 30, 33, 34, 66, 101, 153, 156; accolades, 133–34, 169; autobiography, 129; grand jury investigation and revelations, 127, 134–35; hiring by Penn State, 26; on his pedophile behavior, 131; indictment, 134–35; Mann Act violation, 169; national football championship (1987), 10; Paterno on, 34; Paterno relationship, 24, 25, 207n4; Penn State facilities, 134; post-retirement coaching, 234–35n5; prison sentence, 182; retirement, 130, 132–34, 135–36, 168, 244n34; sexual transgressions with young boys, 129–32; Temple coaching offer, 25, 206n3. *See also* Sandusky Scandal

Sandusky Agreement, 130
Sandusky Scandal: alumni connections, 136–37; arrest of Sandusky (2010), 134–35; athletic administration insularity connection, 135; athletics realignment (1980) relationship, 88, 127, 171; background, 127; Centre County Office of Children and Youth Services, 131; football isolation relationship, 127; grand jury investigation and revelations, 127, 134–35; interconnections of Second Mile, Penn State and business/government leaders, 134–39; law enforcement, attorney general and government office actions, 131; McQueary whistleblowing, 129–30; mishandling by Penn State leaders, 158–59; Paterno Report: Critique of the Freeh Report, 165; Penn State police, 130–31; regional and state political connections and implications, 136–39; Sandusky allegations, 167–68, 169–70, 241n25; Sandusky retirement agreement connection, 135–36. *See also* Board of Trustees and Sandusky Scandal; Paterno and Sandusky Scandal
Sanity Code of the National Collegiate Athletic Association (NCAA), 20
scandals, 68, 79, 110, 174, 179, 223n17–18
Scannell, Robert: academic-athletic model, 77; athletic-academic counseling, 105; athletics realignment (1980), 77–91, 127, 225n49, 225n50; career after Penn State, 87; Paterno relationship, 80–83; subsidization of recreation and other facilities, 77, 80–81
Schembechler, Bo, 95, 119
Schiano, Greg, 26
Schmidt, Herb, 96, 162
Scholl, Henry, 32
School of Physical Education and Athletics, 19, 21, 51–54, 58, 59–65, 67–72, 75–78, 87, 126, 148, 220n22. *See also various other Penn State divisions which included its football program*
Schott, Carl, 19, 20, 21, 61–62, 64–65, 67, 68, 72
Schreffler, Ron, 156–57, 167
Schreyer, William, 116
Schreyer Business Library, 116
Schreyer Honors College, 116
Schuckman, Karen, 141
Schultz, Gary: athletics realignment (1980), 161–62; Freeh report, 139, 175–76; grand jury testimony, 171; lying under oath charge (2010), 134–35; meets with Paterno, 122; professional life overview, 163; Sandusky allegations, 129–30, 131–32, 155, 157, 173–82; Second Mile program, 137, 163
Schwab, Charles M., 17

Scirrotto incident author location, 233n44
Scirrotto, Anthony, 124
Scott, Zen, 41
Seasock, John, 131
Second Mile program, 11, 24, 25, 66, 127–39. *See also* Sandusky Scandal
Secor, Robert, 125–26
Segurski, Sandy, 124
Shalala, Donna, 97
Shannon, Barbara, 168
Sherman Antitrust Act (of 1890), 92, 178, 226n13
Shields, Jackie, 110
Sims, Henry, 119
Smith, Andy, 113
Smith, E.Z., 136
Smith, Ray, 40–41, 42
Smith, Ronald A., 82, 224n30, 233n44
Southeastern Conference (SEC), 67, 73–74, 91, 182
Southerland, John Bain "Jock," 55
Southern Methodist University, 57, 79, 110, 221n33
Spanier, Graham: academic credentials and promotion skills, 13–14, 171–72; athletics realignment (1980), 161–62; background and experience, 61–62, 163–64, 202n8; Board of Trustees relationship, 135, 241n27, 243n13; firing by Board of Trustees, 155; Freeh report allegations, 175–76, 245n8; grand jury investigation and revelations, 159; grand jury testimony, 171; lying under oath charge (2010), 134–35; medical center merger failure, 164; obfuscation regarding grand jury proceedings, 157; personality, 164; Portland discrimination allegations, 149, 239n28; radio program, 164; replacement, 139; Sandusky allegations, 130, 167, 169–70; Triponey resignation role, 125–26; virtues, 241n26
Sparks, Edwin, 17–18, 40
Special Athletic Committee (of the Alumni Association) investigation (1935), 59, 60
Sports Illustrated, 93, 104, 106, 111, 139
Sports Research Institute, 76–77
Stagg, Amos Alonzo, 33, 42, 43, 99, 113, 208n29
Stagg-Paterno Big Ten Championship Trophy, 99
State College Quarterback Club, 108
State College (town), 1–2. *See also* Happy Valley ethos; Nittany Valley
"State Penn," 119
Stewart, James, 145
Stickney, Highland, 16, 203n20
Stoedefalke, Karl, 87, 92

Stone, Robert, 220n22
student fees to support athletics, 16, 31–33, 209n40
student management of early athletics, 27–30, 38
Surma, John, 158–59
Surma, Victor Jr., 158–59
Swinton, John, 8, 126
Swisher, John, 239n1
Syracuse University, 20, 46, 55, 59, 85, 89, 90, 93–95, 107–8, 153

Tait, Tom, 71
Tarkanian, Jerry, 178–79, 180
Tarman, Jim, 88, 162; Big Ten Conference admission, 93, 94, 96, 97; Curley hiring, 162; Grand Experiment role, 102; on Paterno, 86; on Penn State recruiting, 110; sexual orientation discrimination, 145
Temple University, 24–25, 90, 93, 128, 165, 206n3
Theokas, Charles, 24–25, 28, 128
theory of centrality, 108
Thiel, Nick, 77, 79
Thoele, Howard, 82
Thomas, Frank, 113
Thomas, Joab, 22, 144–45
Thomas, John, 18–19, 45
Thomas, P.E. "Pearl," 39
Title IX of Education Amendments (1972), 78, 141, 144, 147
To the Best of My Knowledge, 164
Touched (Sandusky), 129, 165
Trachtenberg, Joel, 150, 239n1
Track House, 17, 18, 19, 31, 46, 209n37
Training Rules: No Drinking, No Drugs, No Lesbians (documentary), 149
training tables for football players, 27, 29, 32, 39, 59, 60, 63, 82
Triplett, Wally, 57
Triponey, Vicky, 119–26, 135, 146, 162, 233n34
Trustee Special Committee on Athletics (1936), 60
trustees' financial support of football, 16, 20, 203n21
Turner, Frederick Jackson, 57

Underwood, John, 106, 229n32
University Council, 152
University Faculty Senate, 18, 39, 59, 61, 66, 69, 74, 145, 152, 153. *See also* academic-athletic model; Faculty Senate

Varsity Club, 40

Varsity Hall, 17, 19, 46, 47, 201n24. *See also* Irvin Hall
Verducci, Tom, 93
Vietnam War, 78, 86, 92, 109, 150, 151, 152
Virgil, 100–101, 103, 201n35. See also *Aeneid*
Voltaire, 112, 126

Walker, Eric, 6–7, 21–22, 64, 68, 69, 70, 73, 74, 93, 106, 151, 205n52, 206n57, 225n55
Walker, Herschel, 9, 106
Wall Street Journal, 23, 107
Ward, John Montgomery "Monte," 15–16
Warner, "Pop," 55, 113
Warriner, Jesse B., 50
Warriner Committee research and recommendations (1929), 50–52
Washington, Coquese, 148
Watergate Scandal, 9
Waynesburg College, 7, 55
Welch, Susan, 114
Welsh, George, 26, 32, 207n7
West Virginia University, 20, 47, 54, 85, 90–91, 93, 95, 153
White, Andrew D., 13
White, James G., 26, 27
White, John Beaver, 48, 49
White, J.T., 32
Whitelaw, Scotty, 91
Wilkinson, Bud, 113
Williams, Jonathan, 106
Wisconsin, University of, 62, 72, 92, 97
Wojciechowski, Gene, 124 -25
Woman's Athletic Association, 40
women's athletics, 21, 40, 70–72, 78, 80, 87, 96, 120, 130, 139–41, 201n36, 205n52, 232n29. *See also* athletics realignment (1980); Portland, Rene; Title IX of Education Amendments (1972)
Wooden, John, 114, 128
Works Progress Administration (WPA), 6
World War I, 17, 26, 33, 38, 40, 44, 46, 49, 55, 61, 66, 165
World War II, 5, 7, 34, 38, 42, 45, 47, 51, 55, 63, 64, 67, 76, 85, 90, 100, 110, 120, 166, 174, 176

Yacker, Fawn, 149
Yale University, 8, 12–14, 16, 26, 28, 32, 36, 49, 61, 67, 73, 89, 113, 211n20
Yeager, Tom, 177
Yost, Fielding H., 113

Zang, David, 8–9, 11
Zechman, Theresa, 108
Zilly, Ralph, 78

RONALD A. SMITH is a professor emeritus at Pennsylvania State University and author of *Pay for Play: A History of Big-Time College Athletic Reform*; *Play-by-Play: Radio, Television, and Big-Time College Sport*; *Sports and Freedom: The Rise of Big-Time College Athletics*; and *Big-Time Football at Harvard: The Diary of Coach Bill Reid*.

SPORT AND SOCIETY

A Sporting Time: New York City and the Rise of Modern Athletics, 1820–70
  Melvin L. Adelman
Sandlot Seasons: Sport in Black Pittsburgh   *Rob Ruck*
West Ham United: The Making of a Football Club   *Charles Korr*
Beyond the Ring: The Role of Boxing in American Society   *Jeffrey T. Sammons*
John L. Sullivan and His America   *Michael T. Isenberg*
Television and National Sport: The United States and Britain   *Joan M. Chandler*
The Creation of American Team Sports: Baseball and Cricket, 1838–72
  George B. Kirsch
City Games: The Evolution of American Urban Society and the Rise of Sports
  Steven A. Riess
The Brawn Drain: Foreign Student-Athletes in American Universities   *John Bale*
The Business of Professional Sports   *Edited by Paul D. Staudohar
  and James A. Mangan*
Fritz Pollard: Pioneer in Racial Advancement   *John M. Carroll*
A View from the Bench: The Story of an Ordinary Player on a Big-Time Football
  Team (*formerly* Go Big Red! The Story of a Nebraska Football Player)   *George Mills*
Sport and Exercise Science: Essays in the History of Sports Medicine   *Edited by Jack
  W. Berryman and Roberta J. Park*
Minor League Baseball and Local Economic Development   *Arthur T. Johnson*
Harry Hooper: An American Baseball Life   *Paul J. Zingg*
Cowgirls of the Rodeo: Pioneer Professional Athletes   *Mary Lou LeCompte*
Sandow the Magnificent: Eugen Sandow and the Beginnings of Bodybuilding
  David Chapman
Big-Time Football at Harvard, 1905: The Diary of Coach Bill Reid
  Edited by Ronald A. Smith
Leftist Theories of Sport: A Critique and Reconstruction   *William J. Morgan*
Babe: The Life and Legend of Babe Didrikson Zaharias   *Susan E. Cayleff*
Stagg's University: The Rise, Decline, and Fall of Big-Time Football at Chicago
  Robin Lester
Muhammad Ali, the People's Champ   *Edited by Elliott J. Gorn*
People of Prowess: Sport, Leisure, and Labor in Early Anglo-America
  Nancy L. Struna
The New American Sport History: Recent Approaches and Perspectives
  Edited by S. W. Pope
Making the Team: The Cultural Work of Baseball Fiction   *Timothy Morris*
Making the American Team: Sport, Culture, and the Olympic Experience
  Mark Dyreson
Viva Baseball! Latin Major Leaguers and Their Special Hunger   *Samuel O. Regalado*
Touching Base: Professional Baseball and American Culture in the
  Progressive Era (rev. ed.)   *Steven A. Riess*
Red Grange and the Rise of Modern Football   *John M. Carroll*
Golf and the American Country Club   *Richard J. Moss*
Extra Innings: Writing on Baseball   *Richard Peterson*
Global Games   *Maarten Van Bottenburg*

The Sporting World of the Modern South   *Edited by Patrick B. Miller*
The End of Baseball As We Knew It: The Players Union, 1960–81   *Charles P. Korr*
Rocky Marciano: The Rock of His Times   *Russell Sullivan*
Saying It's So: A Cultural History of the Black Sox Scandal   *Daniel A. Nathan*
The Nazi Olympics: Sport, Politics, and Appeasement in the 1930s
    Edited by Arnd Krüger and William Murray
The Unlevel Playing Field: A Documentary History of the African American
    Experience in Sport   *David K. Wiggins and Patrick B. Miller*
Sports in Zion: Mormon Recreation, 1890–1940   *Richard Ian Kimball*
Sweet William: The Life of Billy Conn   *Andrew O'Toole*
Sports in Chicago   *Edited by Elliot J. Gorn*
The Chicago Sports Reader   *Edited by Steven A. Riess and Gerald R. Gems*
College Football and American Culture in the Cold War Era   *Kurt Edward Kemper*
The End of Amateurism in American Track and Field   *Joseph M. Turrini*
Benching Jim Crow: The Rise and Fall of the Color Line in Southern College Sports,
    1890–1980   *Charles H. Martin*
Pay for Play: A History of Big-Time College Athletic Reform   *Ronald A. Smith*
Globetrotting: African American Athletes and Cold War Politics   *Damion L. Thomas*
Cheating the Spread: Gamblers, Point Shavers, and Game Fixers in College Football
    and Basketball   *Albert J. Figone*
The Sons of Westwood: John Wooden, UCLA, and the Dynasty That Changed
    College Basketball   *John Matthew Smith*
Qualifying Times: Points of Change in U.S. Women's Sport   *Jaime Schultz*
NFL Football: A History of America's New National Pastime   *Richard C. Crepeau*
Marvin Miller, Baseball Revolutionary   *Robert F. Burk*
I Wore Babe Ruth's Hat: Field Notes from a Life in Sports   *David W. Zang*
Changing the Playbook: How Power, Profit, and Politics Transformed
    College Sports   *Howard P. Chudacoff*
Team Chemistry: The History of Drugs and Alcohol in Major League
    Baseball   *Nathan Michael Corzine*
Wounded Lions: Joe Paterno, Jerry Sandusky, and the Crises
    in Penn State Athletics   *Ronald A. Smith*

REPRINT EDITIONS
The Nazi Olympics   *Richard D. Mandell*
Sports in the Western World (2d ed.)   *William J. Baker*
Jesse Owens: An American Life   *William J. Baker*

The University of Illinois Press
is a founding member of the
Association of American University Presses.

University of Illinois Press
1325 South Oak Street
Champaign, IL 61820-6903
www.press.uillinois.edu